A FUTURE FOR HOLINESS

PENTECOSTAL EXPLORATIONS

A Future for

Holiness

Pentecostal Explorations

EDITED BY

Lee Roy Martin

CPT

CPT Press
Cleveland, Tennessee

A Future for Holiness
Pentecostal Explorations

Published by CPT Press
900 Walker ST NE
Cleveland, TN 37311
USA
email: cptpress@pentecostaltheology.org
website: www.cptpress.com

Library of Congress Control Number: 2013903693

ISBN-10: 1935931350
ISBN-13: 9781935931355

Scripture taken from the NEW AMERICAN STANDARD BIBLE®, Copyright © 1960, 1962, 1963, 1968, 1971, 1972, 1973, 1975, 1977, 1995 by The Lockman Foundation. Used by permission.

The Graeca font used to print this work is available from Linguist's Software, Inc., PO Box 580, Edmonds, WA 98020-0580 USA tel (425) 775-1130 www.linguistsoftware.com.

BWHEBB, BWHEBL, BWTRANSH [Hebrew]; BWGRKL, BWGRKN, and BWGRKI [Greek] Postscript® Type 1 and TrueTypeT fonts Copyright © 1994-2009 BibleWorks, LLC. All rights reserved. These Biblical Greek and Hebrew fonts are used with permission and are from BibleWorks, software for Biblical exegesis and research.

CONTENTS

Introduction
Lee Roy Martin..1

PART ONE
BIBLICAL STUDIES

1. Wilderness: Holy Yahweh's Innate Habitat?
   Narelle Melton 9

2. The Acknowledgement of Holy Ground as Prerequisite
   to Israel's Advancement Under the Leadership of
   Joshua (Joshua 5.13-15)
   Robert C. Crosby...24

3. Beauty and Holiness in the Calling of Isaiah
   Jacqueline Grey..47

4. Holiness and the Path of Suffering: Lessons for
   Pentecostals from the Book of Hebrews
   Faith McGhee 57

5. Let the Holy Yet Be Holy: Holiness in the Apocalypse
   Dan Morrison..86

6. Have We Been Sanctified?: Renewing the Role of
   Experience in Interpreting the Biblical Text
   Scott A. Ellington...107

PART TWO
THEOLOGY

7. 'Not I, but Christ': Holiness, Conscience, & the
   (Im)Possibility of Community
   Chris E.W. Green..127

8. The Pentecostal Triple Way: An Ecumenical Model of the
   Pentecostal Via Salutis and Soteriological Experience
   Monte Lee Rice...145

9. Holiness and Economics: Towards Recovery of Eucharistic Being in a Market-shaped World
Daniela C. Augustine...171

10. Liberating Holiness for the Oppressed and the Oppressors
Patrick Oden...205

11. A Holy Reception Can Lead to a Holy Future
Daniel Castelo...225

PART THREE
PRACTICAL THEOLOGY

12. Twenty-First Century Holiness: Living at the Intersection of Wesleyan Theology & Contemporary Pentecostal Values
Johnathan E. Alvarado..237

13. Holiness, the Church, and Party Politics: Toward a Contemporary Practical Theology of Holiness
Antipas L. Harris..252

14. Holiness and Undocumented Immigration: A Dramatic Challenge to my Church
Wilfredo Estrada Adorno..272

15. The Practice of Holiness: Implications for a Pentecostal Moral Theology
Terry Johns...297

16. Holiness as Play: A Developmental Perspective on Christian Formation
Stephen Parker..312

17. From Fear-Based to Holiness-Based: Thoughts About the Work of the Holy Spirit in Youth Ministry
Joshua Ziefle..333

18. A Future for Holiness in Pentecostal Practice
Marcia Clarke...348

A Concluding Parable – The Fire and the Fence
Rickie D. Moore..358

Index of Biblical References..361
Index of Authors...367

ABBREVIATIONS

BECNT	Baker Exegetical Commentary on the New Testament
BibRes	*Biblical Research*
BZAW	Beihefte zur Zeitschrift für die alttestamentliche Wissenschaft
BZNW	Beihefte zur Zeitschrift für die neutestamentliche Wissenschaft
HTR	*Harvard Theological Review*
IBC	Interpreters Bible Commentary
IBS	*Irish Biblical Studies*
ICC	International Critical Commentary
JAAC	*Journal of Aesthetics and Art Criticism*
JITE	*Journal of Institutional and Theoretical Economics*
JPTSup	Journal of Pentecostal Theology Supplement Series
JSNT	*Journal of the Study of the New Testament*
JSNTSup	Journal for the Study of the New Testament Supplement Series
JSOTSup	Journal for the Study of the Old Testament Supplement Series
JTS	*Journal of Theological Studies*
NIBC	New International Biblical Commentary
NICNT	New International Commentary on the New Testament
NTC	New Testament Commentary
NTM	New Testament Monographs
OTL	Old Testament Library
Pneuma	*PNEUMA: The Journal of the Society for Pentecostal Studies*
SBL	Society of Biblical Literature
SNTS	Society for New Testament Studies
WBC	Word Biblical Commentary
WesTJ	*Wesleyan Theological Journal*
WTJ	*Westminster Theological Journal*

INTRODUCTION

LEE ROY MARTIN[*]

Early Pentecostalism emerged from the nineteenth-century holiness movement,[1] and holiness (both in theology and practice) has been a significant, if at times contentious, feature of the Pentecostal movement throughout its brief history. When I joined the Church of God in 1972, the ministers and members in Cumming, Georgia referred to their church as a 'holiness' church, and they expected every believer to seek after the experience of entire sanctification and to pursue a lifestyle of personal holiness. Key passages of Scripture relating to holiness were cited regularly and repeatedly. Those passages included the following:

> Pursue peace with everyone, and holiness, without which no one will see the Lord (Heb. 12.14).

> But as he who called you is holy, be holy yourselves in all your conduct; for it is written, 'You shall be holy, for I am holy' (1 Pet. 1.14-16).

> ... let us cleanse ourselves from every defilement of body and of spirit, perfecting holiness in the fear of God (2 Cor. 7.1).

> For this is the will of God, even your sanctification ... (1 Thess. 4.3).

> For God has not called us unto uncleanness, but unto holiness (1 Thess. 4.7).

---

[*] Lee Roy Martin (DTh, University of South Africa) is Professor of Old Testament and Biblical Languages at the Pentecostal Theological Seminary in Cleveland, TN, USA and Editor of the *Journal of Pentecostal Theology*.
[1] Donald W. Dayton, *Theological Roots of Pentecostalism* (Studies in Evangelicalism; Metuchen, NJ: Scarecrow Press, 1987), pp. 38-108. Cf. Steven Jack Land, *Pentecostal Spirituality: A Passion for the Kingdom* (Cleveland, TN: CPT Press, 2010), pp. 37-43.

Unfortunately, my generation was taught a form of holiness that was sometimes equivalent to legalism. Holiness was viewed as individualistic and outwardly observable. There was little concern for institutional holiness, communal holiness, or social holiness. Pentecostals were known for their external holiness teachings – no jewelry, no makeup, and no worldly amusements. Although the church was best known for what it stood against, paradoxically there was often a positive spirituality underneath the outward layer of prohibitions. The Pentecostal church advocated a holiness spirituality that exemplified what Steve Land has called 'a passion for the kingdom'.[2] The joyful singing, exuberant shouting, and unrestrained prayer were evidence of the manifest presence of God. In every worship service we prayed at the altar; we invited sinners to be saved; we prayed for the sick; and we prayed for people to be baptized in the Holy Ghost. New believers were expected to learn biblical teachings and follow Jesus wholeheartedly. For most of the members, church attendance was not just a religious duty to be added to their schedule of diverse activities. The church was more than a peripheral element in their otherwise secular lives. Instead, the church was central to their lives, the locus of their primary experience of community.

With the growth of the Charismatic movement and the spread of Pentecostalism into the mainstream, the legalistic and externally focused brand of holiness came under fierce attack. In reaction to perceived legalism, some Pentecostals began to border on libertinism, and the traditional holiness that had been taught with certainty and (unwarranted?) confidence was soon replaced by an uncertain and ambiguous doctrine. My discussions with pastors, laity, and seminary students suggests that the biblical demand for holiness is still widely recognized but is not widely understood or taught. For whatever reasons, our members cannot make sense of the biblical teaching on holiness; our pastors feel unprepared to address the doctrine of sanctification; and very few of our scholars have produced significant publications in the area of holiness theology.[3]

---

[2] E.g. the subtitle of Land, *Pentecostal Spirituality: A Passion for the Kingdom*, p. 2 and *passim*.

[3] However, in biblical studies, I would point to J. Ayodeji Adewuya, *Holiness and Community in 2 Cor. 6:14-7:1: Paul's View of Communal Holiness in the Corinthian Correspondence* (New York: Peter Lang, 2001); and *idem*, *Transformed by Grace: Paul's*

In light of current trends and needs in the Church, perhaps it is time for us to evaluate the continuing importance of holiness as a doctrine and sanctification as an experience. While we can look to the past for indications of crucial Pentecostal beliefs, we must consider present and future contexts as we formulate our theology. Holiness is emphasized in the biblical text, but what should be the shape of the doctrine in today's context, both locally and globally? Is sanctification an important experience? If so, how do we teach it and facilitate its continuation?

Pentecostal scholars are beginning to construct contemporary contextual theologies to meet the changing needs of this generation. I would suggest that a reconsideration of holiness should be a part of the constructive theological agenda. God is holy, and the Church is called to imitate God's holiness, but each generation must discover for itself how a commitment to holiness affects its theology and practice. It is time for us to take a fresh look at holiness in its individual, communal, institutional, and global expressions.

I would encourage Pentecostal scholars to identify both opportunities and challenges for the future of holiness in Pentecostalism from the perspectives of the various academic disciplines. We should explore the implications of holiness for Pentecostal theology, peacemaking, justice, global concerns, ethics, postmodernity, ecology, ecumenism, social responsibility, ecclesial structures, ministerial practices, Christian formation, missional practices, intercultural engagements, immigration, civil society, political systems, personal relationships, and more. These explorations should proceed from biblical, theological, historical, ecumenical, practical, cultural, aesthetic, and missional perspectives.

This book is an attempt to stimulate conversation regarding Pentecostal approaches to the theology of holiness. Most of the chapters are revisions of papers that were presented at the 2013 Annual Meeting of the Society for Pentecostal Studies, which met in conjunction with the Wesleyan Theological Society. I served as the

---

View of Holiness in Romans 6-8 (Eugene, OR: Cascade Books, 2004). In theology, I would mention Daniel Castelo (ed.), *Holiness as a Liberal Art* (Eugene, OR: Pickwick Publications, 2012); and *idem, Revisioning Pentecostal Ethics: The Epicletic Community* (Cleveland, TN: CPT Press, 2012); Dale M. Coulter, *Holiness: The Beauty of Perfection* (Cleveland, TN: Pathway Press, 2004); R.H. Gause, *Living in the Spirit: The Way of Salvation* (Cleveland, TN: CPT Press, Rev. and expanded edn, 2009); and Land, *Pentecostal Spirituality.*

Program Chair for the SPS, and worked with Jason Vickers of the WTS in the planning of the program. When we chose the topic of holiness for the conference theme, we were unsure of the response that we would receive. However, we were quite thrilled with the number and quality of papers that were presented at the conference. We were also pleasantly surprised by the level of interest and the depth of dialogue that emerged from the SPS and WTS membership.

Upon seeing the positive response to the conference theme of holiness, I decided to edit and publish a collection of papers from the conference. In the selection of chapters for the book, I was concerned to involve a group of Pentecostal scholars who were diverse in regard to academic discipline, gender, age, ethnic group, and nationality. The book includes three sections, based broadly upon the disciplines of biblical studies, theology, and practical theology. I deliberately excluded a section on history because, as the title of the book suggests, I wanted the studies to envision the future of holiness rather than reflect upon its past. Hopefully, this work will suggest fruitful avenues for the continued exploration of holiness and its place in the global Pentecostal movement.

This volume illustrates a number of specific ways that Pentecostal scholars can contribute to future discussions of holiness. In the field of biblical studies, I would propose both the revisiting of the classic texts on holiness and the exploration of other texts that can illuminate the Bible's teaching on holiness. The biblical texts should be viewed with fresh eyes, utilizing newer hermeneutical methods, and proceeding from a diversity of global contexts. It is time that a new generation of Pentecostal biblical scholars examine the biblical foundations of our teachings on holiness and sanctification.

In the field of theology, I would hope that the doctrine of holiness would find its place within the larger context of the developing Pentecostal Theologies of Frank Macchia, Steven Land, Amos Yong, Simon Chan, Kenneth Archer, and others. Perhaps our theologians can show how holiness impacts the formulation of soteriology, ecclesiology, pneumatology, and eschatology. The different streams of the Pentecostal-Charismatic movement should dialogue about holiness and explicate areas of commonality. Furthermore, we should dialogue with other Christian traditions in regard to holiness and spirituality, holiness and society, holiness and technology, holiness and global concerns of materialism, militarism, and nationalism.

From the perspective of practical theology several concerns come to mind, such as holiness and ministry, holiness and youth, holiness and ecclesial practices, social holiness, holiness codes, and personal, experiential holiness – i.e. sanctification – in the local church. We might address the future of sanctification as an experience. Is it an important experience? If so, how do we emphasis it and facilitate its continuation? Finally, I would argue that we have not wrestled sufficiently with the inherent Pentecostal tension between purity and power, and we have not constructed a theology that accounts for that tension in light of the Bible, church history, and our common experience.[4]

Although the essays in this volume do not address or solve all of the issues that I have mentioned above, they nevertheless represent the kind of work that I believe we should be doing. It is hoped that they will generate interest in and further discussion of our theology of holiness.

---

[4] The importance of this topic for Pentecostals is highlighted by Simon Chan, *Pentecostal Theology and the Christian Spiritual Tradition* (JPTSup 21; Sheffield: Sheffield Academic Press, 2000), pp. 86-96. See also Lee Roy Martin, 'Judging the Judges: Searching for Value in These Problematic Characters', *Verbum et Ecclesia* 29.1 (2008), pp. 110-29.

PART ONE

BIBLICAL STUDIES

1

WILDERNESS: HOLY YAHWEH'S INNATE HABITAT?

NARELLE MELTON[*]

Introduction:

In the Bible, the image of the wilderness is laden with ambiguity, fear, dread, and wonder. The wilderness is depicted as a ruthless, isolated, and arid environment. Yet, surprisingly this fearsome place – 'the vast and dreadful desert' (Deut. 8.15) – is a central backdrop within the Pentateuch for theophanic encounters. Where one would traditionally expect Yahweh's divine self-disclosure to occur within central memorialized places, established cultic centres, or even prominent cities, this is not the case. He becomes known in remote and wild places.[1]

In his *The Pastor: A Memoir*, Eugene Peterson commences his reflection by situating his personal narrative within a geographical landscape.[2] That is *place;* the place of Stanwood and New York City, Baltimore and Vancouver. He recognizes the role that 'soil and stone, latitude and longitude, lakes and mountains, towns and cities' had in his life of faith and this kept it 'rooted, in *place'.*[3] Specifically, he reflects,

---

[*] Narelle Melton (MDiv, Alphacrusis College) is a PhD candidate at the University of Birmingham. She serves as Program Director (Bachelor of Contemporary Ministry) and Associate Lecturer (Old Testament Studies) at Alphacrucis College, Sydney, Australia.
[1] Jon D. Levenson, *Sinai & Zion: An Entry into the Jewish Bible* (San Francisco: Harper & Row, 1987), p. 22.
[2] Eugene H. Peterson, *The Pastor: A Memoir* (New York: HarperOne, 2011).
[3] Peterson, *The Pastor*, p. 11.

this two acres of sacred landscape in the mountains of Montana has provided the material conditions for preserving a continuity of story ... it has provided a stable location in space and time to give prayerful, meditative, discerning attention to the ways in which my life is being written into the comprehensive salvation story.[4]

Peterson's framing of his memoir in this manner helps me to appreciate the significance of location for Israel's history, as the formative narrative of ancient Israel is situated in a place of dirt and rocks, isolation and barrenness, marginalisation and aridness, of wilderness. In this *place* – this wild yet holy ground – unique encounters with Yahweh God occurred and were written into their salvation story. But from our climate controlled armchair comfort, we tend to ignore and neglect the role that place or geography has in our formation, let alone the witness of Scripture.[5]

Hence, this realisation provokes a series of questions. Why do the biblical authors utilize the space and imagery of the wilderness? What does this lead us to discover about the nature of God? That is, why do key encounters that emphasize the holy nature of God predominantly occur in the wilderness in the narratives of Exodus? And how does the landscape of the wilderness foster and develop this revelation? A triggering assertion that has brought about this investigation is Walter Brueggemann's question; 'Is the wilderness a place that [Yahweh] prefers because of his peculiar character? Could it be that he is a God who most desires the interactions of the wilderness?'[6] These are the questions this study will pursue.

Wilderness Defined

First, we need to offer a definition. What is wilderness? Wilderness in its biblical usage encompasses a variety of terms, terrains, inhabitants and uses; hence a broad model for classifying wilderness is

---

[4] Peterson, *The Pastor*, p. 14.

[5] I like how Belden Lane states this, 'My fear is that much of what we call "spirituality" today is overly sanitized and sterile, far removed from the anguish of pain, the anchoredness of place' (Belden Lane, *The Solace of Fierce Landscapes: Exploring Desert and Mountain Spirituality* [New York: Oxford University Press, 1998], p. 20).

[6] Walter Brueggemann, *The Land: Place as Gift, Promise, and Challenge in Biblical Faith* (Minneapolis MN: Fortress Press, 2nd edn, 2002), p. 38.

required.[7] In developing a classification, we must also be cognisant of the human shaping that occurs to 'space', for 'land is never simply physical dirt but is always physical dirt freighted with social meanings derived from historical experience'.[8] In addition, as our source of information is an ancient text, our approach to unpacking the meaning of the geography and symbol of wilderness must also account for its literary nature. As Bar-Efrat nicely summarizes, 'Places in the narrative are not merely geographical facts, but are to be regarded as literary elements in which fundamental significance is embodied'.[9] Thus, when defining wilderness space one needs to be conversant with its physical geography, symbol-laden shaping as well as its literary portrayal,[10] hence a narrative-geographical method is utilized in this paper.[11] It is with these factors in mind that four

---

[7] The biblical dictionaries provide good definitions for the term מדבר (*midbar*) and its synonyms. The following is my conclusion as to the key aspects of how I will define wilderness within the biblical text.

[8] Brueggemann, *The Land*, p. 2.

[9] Shimeon Bar-Efrat, *Narrative Art in the Bible* (London: T & T Clark International, 2004), p. 194. Cf. Philip Sheldrake, *Spaces for the Sacred: Place, Memory, and Identity* (Baltimore: Johns Hopkins University Press, 2001), p. 15, who adds,

> It is appropriate to think of places as texts, layered with meaning. Every place has an excess of meaning, beyond what can be seen or understood at any one time. This excess permanently overflows any attempt at a final definition. A place can never be subordinated to a single valuation, one person's prejudices, or the assumptions of a single group. The hermeneutic of place progressively reveals new meanings in a kind of conversation between topography, memory and the presence of particular people at any given moment.

[10] See also Craig G. Bartholomew: 'Place is thus understood as a complex of factors, subjective, intersubjective, and objective. Examinations of place will attend to dimensions such as the natural landscape, patterns of weather and sky, human ordering of spaces and resources, and the individual and communal narratives in which the place is imbued' (Craig G. Bartholomew, *Where Mortals Dwell: A Christian View of Place for Today* [Grand Rapids: Baker Academic, 2011], p. 247).

[11] See John A. Beck, 'David and Goliath, A Story of Place: The Narrative-Geographical Shaping of 1 Samuel 17', *WTJ* 68.2 [2006], pp. 321-30 (322), who explains,

> Narrative-geographical inquiry is an interdisciplinary approach that seeks to blend the insights offered by both narrative criticism and the study of geography. It is related to the studies of physical, historical, and human geography but distinct from them. Physical geography investigates the land through the lens of topography, geology, hydrology, climate, forestation, land use, urbanization, and transportation. Historical and human geography examine the role such physical geography plays in the shaping of history and culture. By contrast to these more traditional forms of geography, narrative geography analyses the literary function of geographical references within a story. It

key aspects are utilized to provide an overarching model to define the nature of wilderness. Specifically, wilderness is designated as those spaces for ancient Israel that are isolated, arid, barren, and marginal.

First, wilderness is isolated. It is a remote, lonely and solitary place predominantly due to its ruthless landscape. It is difficult to survive in the harsh climate of the wilderness; and thus few people live there. The few people who do reside in the wilderness mostly live a nomadic/semi-nomadic lifestyle following the seasonal patterns of the desert to eke out their survival. As a result, the wilderness is removed and isolated from the norms and mores of civilisation.

Second, wilderness is arid. No matter what the terrain – Cenomanian limestone, Senonian chalk, sand dunes, or volcanic rock – little to no annual rain characterizes the desert landscape. Without the life-giving essence of water, wilderness is a place both physically and metaphorically, of death, curse, dryness, destruction, and ruin.

Third, the wilderness is barren. It is futile to use the ground for any persistent agricultural use, and it remains uncultivated. It may be used for seasonal grazing vegetation for flocks on the edges of wilderness boundaries. But again, wilderness is perceived as a place that is barren and of no value, due to its untameable and unusable nature by humans for agriculture. It is, accordingly, an uncivilized and unyielding land.

Wilderness is lastly, a marginal space. The wilderness acts both as a buffer zone, as well as a space outside the margins of civilized

---

acknowledges that the author may strategically use, reuse, and nuance geography in order to impact the reading experience'.

Beck utilises narrative-geographical methodology in *God as Storyteller: Seeking Meaning in Biblical Narrative* (St. Louis, Missouri: Chalice Press, 2008); 'Geography and the Narrative Shape of Numbers 13', *Bibliotheca Sacra* 157.627 (2000), pp. 271-80; 'Why did Moses Strike Out? The Narrative-Geographical Shaping of Moses' Disqualification in Numbers 20:1-13', *WTJ* 65.1 (2003), pp. 135-41; 'Geography as Irony: The Narrative-Geological Shaping of Elijah's Duel with the Prophets of Baal (1 Kings 18)', *Scandinavian Journal of the Old Testament* 17.2 (2003), pp. 291-302; 'Why do Joshua's Readers Keep Crossing the River? The Narrative-Geographical Shaping of Joshua 3-4', *Journal of the Evangelical Theological Society* 48.4 (2005), pp. 689-99; 'The Narrative-Geographical Shaping of 1 Samuel 7:5-13', *Bibliotheca Sacra* 162.647 (2005), pp. 299-309; and 'Gideon, Dew, and the Narrative-Geographical Shaping of Judges 6:33-40', *Bibliotheca Sacra* 165.657 (2008), pp. 28-38.

life. Israel is surrounded by wilderness regions, from the Sinai, Negeb, and Arabah in the south to the Judean deserts in the east and arguably the watery wilderness of the Mediterranean Sea to the west. Thereby the specific geography of Israel utilizes the wilderness as a natural buffer zone to any invading enemies as well as a marginal drift land or divide between the domestic agricultural lands and the true desert areas. Further, this conception of wilderness – at the margins – is unique and influential to the self-identity of Israel, for the fertile grounds are central and wilderness is the outer realm.[12] Therefore, this outside space is conceptualized for Israel as the place where danger, chaos, enemies, and cursedness prowl. Thus, those who inhabit the wilderness; usually criminals, prophets and refugees, are those who are seeking sanctuary as they are no longer welcomed by normal society.

Thus to reiterate, the wilderness is viewed as a place which is isolated, arid, barren and marginal, in geography as well as socially and metaphorically.

The Burning Bush and a Holy God in the Wilderness

In turning to the book of Exodus, it is clear that the landscape of the wilderness plays a pivotal role in the life of Moses and the ancient Israelites. Moses, originally the water-boy of civilized Egypt, lived in rural Midian among the family of Reuel, but is called out in the back of the desert by Yahweh in Exodus 3. In the space of two chapters (Exodus 2-3, although these cover approximately 40 years), Moses has gone from the populous civilized state of Egypt to seeking refuge in the pastoralist-nomadic camps of his priest father-in-law in Midian, to shepherding sheep at the utter back[13] of

---

[12] This is different from Australia, where the wild desert areas are internal and centrally located. Hence, Australians view wilderness, the red desert, as being a core element to their identity – the sacred centre. However, there are shifts presently within Australian spirituality to consider also the place of the seascape as significant. Cf. Nancy M. Victorin-Vangerud, 'The Sacred Edge: Seascape as Spiritual Resource for an Australian Eco-eschatology', *Ecotheology: Journal of Religion, Nature & the Environment* 6.1/2 (2001), pp. 167-85.

[13] See Exod. 3.1b 'and he led his flock to the far side (אחר) of the wilderness, and came to Horeb, the mountain of God' (TNIV). Other translations suggest that אחר could mean the *backside* of the wilderness (KJV), *beyond* the wilderness (NRSV) or even to the *west side* of the wilderness (ESV). As Durham expresses, 'He had driven the sheep well into the wilderness, perhaps even "beyond" or "behind" his customary routes. The whole impression is of a completely new and

the desert. And out of these three locations, it is in the remote and isolated place, at the dry and parched mountain[14] that the angel of the Lord appears to Moses in the burning bush (see Exodus 3). Moses, the child originally associated with water, encounters the presence of Yahweh God as a man 'in the dry desert and in flame', the very antithesis of his beginnings.[15] Why is this?

Furthermore, it is here at this marginal and desolate location that for the first time the noun *holy* (קדש, *qadash*) is used in the biblical canon.[16] Moses is informed that *this* place where he is standing is holy ground. This is not a normal dusty desert or an average mountain cleft; instead this *place*, this 'back of beyond' is different, distinctive, incomparable, and somehow holy. As the narrative continues, the visual imagery of the bush is subsequently superseded by God's speeches to Moses. Thus, this wild, rugged place becomes not only the place to *see* the curiosity of a flaming bush and to *feel* through the dust on one's unshod feet the holiness of God, but amongst the isolation and silent steadfast rocks to *hear* the reverberating revelation of Yahweh God which is to be remembered and re-enacted. The account of Exodus 3 is vivid and dramatic in its own right, as well as a pivotal moment within ancient Israel's salvific narrative. But I would argue that it is the *place* of wilderness, the desert backdrop, the very landscape of dust and dryness and desolation that highlights, paradoxically at times, the life-giving and salvific significance of this encounter.

To unpack this further, first, there is the bush. In the climate of the Near East any green vegetation is a sign of life, as such the theme of fruitfulness is linked to the imagery of trees, bushes and vines. How much more so a bush in the midst of the arid and dry

---

strange and distant place, one outside the familiar Midianite territory' (John I. Durham, *Exodus* [WBC 3; Waco, TX: Word Books, 1987], p. 30).

[14] The term חֹרֵב (Horeb) comes from a root that signifies dryness, drought, heat, and desolation (Edwin Yamauchi, 'חָרֵב', in R. Laird Harris, Gleason L. Archer, Jr. and Bruce K. Waltke [eds.], *Theological Wordbook of the Old Testament* [Chicago: Moody Press, electronic edn, 1999], I, pp. 318-20 [319]).

[15] Robert Alter, *The Five Books of Moses: A Translation with Commentary* (New York: W.W. Norton & Co., 2004), p. 318.

[16] R. Alan Cole, *Exodus: An Introduction and Commentary* (Downers Grove, IL: Inter-Varsity Press, 1973), p. 65. Previously the root is used in verbal form 'to sanctify' (Gen. 2.3).

wilderness terrain?[17] But yet this is a bush on fire. In this fiery image, the bush evocatively captures the presence of God, inviting and tangible yet otherworldly and untouchable. It equally can symbolize the people of Israel's experience of suffering and hardship but tenacity to survive despite their oppression. Hence, for Janzen, the burning bush is not just an arbitrary attention-getting device; instead as we shall explore later it is 'thematically integral to the narrative context'.[18] But the juxtaposition is apparent; in the arid, sterile, and barren landscape of the dark outer realm of the desert there is a fresh fruitful bush, alight with miraculous non-burning. It is against this backdrop of wild-ness that Yahweh discloses himself in fiery presence and even proclaims his identification with a non-people, a bush-like-people.[19]

Second, this place is isolated and removed from any human influence and civilisation. It is clear that Moses is outback (to use an Australian expression), although it needs to be noted not on a purposeful pilgrimage but just the routine occupation of shepherding. He is in a non-place, even a chaotic, ungodly, undomesticated place, doing a non-job with no agenda. But this is the place, in this wild-terrain, which the theophanic encounter occurs. Furthermore, this isolated wilderness in its silence and wordlessness becomes the territory in which the voice of God echoes. The combination of being isolated from human civilization and thereby removed from the clamour and expectations of societal norms, plus being in a rugged and ruthless environment where the senses are on high alert, cannot be ignored. For this creates a heightened environment to be profoundly impacted. For example, in Exodus 3, first God was seen and heard in this space in a new way: 'I AM who I AM'. Second, the wilderness became a place to hear a transforming word regarding

[17] Nicolas Wyatt, 'The Significance of the Burning Bush', *Vetus Testamentum* 36.3 (1986), pp. 361-65 (362-63).
[18] J. Gerald Janzen, '... And the Bush Was Not Consumed', *Encounter* 63.1-2 (2002), pp. 119-27 (120, 124).
[19] Cf. Fredrick C. Holmgren, 'Before the Temple, the Thornbush: An Exposition of Exodus 2:11-3:12', *Reformed Journal* 33.3 (1983), pp. 9-11, who writes,

Scrub people like scrub bushes count for little; few will care if they are abused or destroyed. But Yahweh cares. He discloses the depth of his caring in a symbolic action. By dwelling in and speaking from the lowly bush, Yahweh proclaims his identification with a no-account people. Israelites were 'bush' people (p. 9).

one's identity, for it is here that Moses realizes that he is not an Egyptian but a Hebrew.[20] And third, in the barren wilderness a promise of rescue and being delivered 'into a good and spacious land, a land flowing with milk and honey' (Exod. 3.8), was spoken and imagined to be possible for the ancient Israelites.[21] I would thus suggest that it is this being situated in a large and formless environment away from the requirements of others that one can dare to listen and perceive a new future as never before.

As a side note it is worthwhile to consider that although linguistically there is no link between מדבר (wilderness) and דבר (to speak), they both have the same root consonants דבר and this concurrence is intriguing.[22] Should God's speaking and wilderness be more weightily linked? Just as the chaos of the wild-waters of Genesis 1 are transformed by the word of God, does the barren landscape of nothingness underscore the nature of God's creative and transforming words?

Third, this place becomes designated as holy ground. This is seemingly absurd, for wilderness really represents 'the very antithesis of holiness, and even of reality. It was a "non-place"'.[23] This wilderness place was not anything special before the theophany of Yahweh (clearly displayed through Moses' actions and response).[24]

---

[20] Up until this point (Exod. 3.5), the reader and narrator have known who Moses is. But it is questionable as to what insight Moses had into his own identity. And it is assumed that he identified as an Egyptian, and not a Hebrew. It is only when God tells him that He is the God of his father, and his father's ancestors (3.6) that Moses would have begun to contemplate his ethnic identity. This is why it is so crucial that the singular form 'father' is used here, to place Moses within this ancestry lineage.

[21] 'The setting is the wilderness, and Moses' vocation is mundane ... it would not be the last time that God chose *a non-traditional, nonreligious setting for a hearing for the word*' (Terence E. Fretheim, *Exodus* [Interpretation: A Bible Commentary for Teaching and Preaching; Louisville: John Knox Press, 1991], pp. 53-54, emphasis original).

[22] Lynne Wall, 'Finding Identity in the Wilderness', in R.S. Sugirtharajah (ed.), *Wilderness: Essays in Honour of Frances Young* (London: T & T Clark International, 2005), pp. 66-77 (72).

[23] Wyatt, 'The Significance of the Burning Bush', p. 362.

[24] Young comments, 'to assume that the mountain was regarded as a sanctuary even before the revelation to Moses is unwarranted. The designation, "mountain of God", is merely used by anticipation, and there is no reason for supposing that Moses was expecting a revelation or that he came to seek such' (Edward J. Young, 'Call of Moses, Part II', *WTJ* 30.1 [1967], pp. 1-23 [1-2]). See also Jo Bailey Wells, *God's Holy People: A Theme in Biblical Theology* (JSOTSup 305; Sheffield: Sheffield Academic Press, 2000), pp. 28-29.

But with the presence of holy Yahweh, at this dusty, craggy desert mountain, this place and Moses became set apart. A new boundary was created.[25] This *place* is holy. The narrative highlights this further, as the notion of sacred space is explicitly referenced in this passage for the first time in the Hebrew Bible through the combined terms *holy* and the word for *place* (מָקוֹם, *maqom*), which is used as a technical Hebrew term for a sanctuary or holy place.[26] Further, it is in this *holy place* that Moses is brought to the end of his own limitations and ability, so much so he cannot approach and hides his face (Exod. 3.5-6). There are no secrets as he stands raw and exposed, before the wild and holy One. However, this God that is threatening in his holiness is equally sustaining in his comfort.

But for me the mystery remains – that of all the places, in all the towns, in all the world, God walks into this space – this back of beyond desert place, to impact history and make it holy by his presence. Yet, when I reflect on the space of wilderness, I cannot help but concur with Brueggemann that 'wilderness and Yahweh belong to each other ... wilderness suggest[s] the peculiar mode and parameters of Yahweh's presence'.[27] Wilderness provides an innate backdrop, where Yahweh God's untamed yet beautiful, stunning yet fearsome, holy and other-ness nature, finds an affinity of expression unlike any other geographical terrain. For he is wholly 'other', separate, uncontainable and undomesticated by humans, just like the vast and howling desert of ancient Israel's perception. And it is here in the wilderness before a wild-God that Moses is stripped back, to

---

[25] 'Moses is being asked to consider that now, with the speaking of the divine voice from the bush, a new category has entered the world: a boundary to mark those places and spaces in which God is so present and those that he is not so present' (Oliver Davies, 'Reading the Burning Bush: Voice, World and Holiness', *Modern Theology* 22.3 [July 2006], pp. 439-48 [441]).

[26] Carol Meyers, *Exodus* (Cambridge: Cambridge University Press, 2005), p. 53. Davies, 'Reading the Burning Bush', also notes,

> Here we must recognise the pregnancy of the root *qdš* at Exodus 3:5. It appears to stand within the Priestly tradition and thus to designate the cultic separation which we have already seen at Genesis 2:3. But its place in the history of Moses' calling to serve God through his mission to his people, appears also to anticipate the ethical and political characteristics of the later Holiness Code ... The speaking of the divine voice then has significance not only for setting Israel apart as the chosen people of God, but also for shaping the world as a place where Israel's destiny, and ultimately human destiny, before God may be fulfilled (p. 446).

[27] Brueggemann, *The Land*, p. 40.

the limits of his very self, so that he realizes his full essence and dependence on the presence of God to bring life, rescue and meaning.

Seneh to Sinai: The Landscape of Wilderness

To continue unpacking the theme of wilderness' significance to the narrative, the book of Exodus repeats and even expands upon the themes of holiness, presence, divine revelation plus many similar literary motifs.[28] The narrative draws Moses' inaugural experience of the bush (סנה, *seneh*) in Exodus 3, into ancient Israel's experience with Yahweh at Sinai (Exodus 19-40). What cannot be missed, but is sometimes neglected, is the prominence of the wilderness landscape within the narrative. The wilderness encounter was not just for Moses alone, but also becomes pertinent for the formation of Israel's identity as a holy people, and arguably remains central for the generations that live in the Promised Land itself.

In tracing the motifs through the narrative from *seneh* (the bush) to *Sinai* we note many parallels beyond the word alliteration.[29] That is, instead of a bush on fire, they are guided by a pillar of cloud and fire (which is also burning but never consumed). They are brought to Mt. Sinai where God is *in* the smoke and fire,[30] just like the angel of the Lord was *in* the flaming bush (Exod. 3.2; 19.18). The Lord guided the people to this isolated and wilderness place, and not the shorter way via the land of the Philistines (Exod. 13.17-18).[31] This would seem a precarious choice, for God is marching them into the open gates of death.[32] But as Lane makes clear;

---

[28] Wells, *God's Holy People*, p. 29.

[29] Bernard P. Robinson, 'Moses at the Burning Bush', *Journal for the Study of the Old Testament* 22.75 (1997), pp. 107-22 (112).

[30] 'Mount Sinai was covered with smoke, because the Lord descended on *it in fire.* The smoke billowed up from it like smoke from a furnace, and the whole mountain trembled violently' (Exod. 19.18).

[31] Interestingly, Lane comments,

> The argument of the rabbis hinged on how the Hebrew word *kî* should be understood in this passage. Usually the term is taken to mean that God chose not to lead the Israelites by the northern route 'although' (*kî*) it was the shorter, less-troublesome way. Yet *kî* can also be translated 'because', suggesting something far more provocative in the context of the passage (Lane, *The Solace of Fierce Landscapes*, p. 44).

[32] Ulrich Mauser, *Christ in the Wilderness: The Wilderness Theme in the Second Gospel and Its Basis in the Biblical Tradition* (London: SCM Press, 1963), p. 21.

God intentionally opted for the more difficult landscape, as if this were habitually the divine preference. God's people are deliberately forced into the desert – taking the harder, more onerous and hazardous route – as an exacting exercise in radical faith. … Perhaps others can go around the desert on the simpler route toward home, but the way of God's people is always through it.[33]

Thus God is purposefully using the wilderness here to create a people of faith and holiness. He separates them from war, society, and civilisation, to bring them to this marginal, liminal, and consecrated zone to encounter him, alone. In response the people of Israel recognize the holiness of this moment. They do not approach the fierce and fiery Sinai carelessly, but consecrate themselves before approaching, similar to the command for Moses to remove his shoes and not approach the bush any closer (Exod. 19.10-13; 3.5). In addition, like Moses at the bush, it is in the void of this wilderness space that the voice of Yahweh God proclaims a new dawning. '*And God spoke saying* …' (Exod. 20.1), and with this refrain the words of the Decalogue, law, and covenant are delivered in the desert of Sinai. The terror and untamed nature of this wild-God is no more apparent than in Israel's response of fear and trembling, and seeking of respite from the voice of God, in this encounter of God speaking in the fire and thunder from the rocky mountain of Sinai (Exod. 20.18-19). The wilderness undoubtedly sets the scene for a formidable Yahweh God. Further, it fosters ancient Israel's formation into a holy, set apart people, unlike any other. Primarily because they are stripped back to fearful awe and worship, as they encounter a holy-wild Yahweh God whose nature is aligned with the wild-wilderness.

Sinai to the Tabernacle: Wilderness in the Land?
Moreover, these very same motifs can be traced from the narrative of the bush to Sinai and finally to the tabernacle itself. The tabernacle is the exemplar of holy Yahweh dwelling with Israel. But in examining the tabernacle, its articles and construction through a wilderness lens, it is apparent that the peculiarity of God who re-

---

[33] Lane, *The Solace of Fierce Landscapes*, p. 44. Lane continues 'They are shoved down the difficult path so there will be no thought of ever turning back. They cover gruelling miles of terrain so tortuous they will never be tempted to recross it in quest of the leeks and onions they remembered in Egypt' (p. 44).

veals himself in the wilderness is kept at the forefront within its construction.

First, there is a shift of the cloud and smoke to the tabernacle. This 'symbolizes Yahweh's *movement* with his people through the wilderness, not his *residence* on Sinai'.[34] Thus the portable tabernacle is used to carry the people through the wild chaos of the desert environment, with the tabernacle being the 'means by which the people of God can move in a secure and ordered way through a world of disorder on their way to a new creation'.[35] Paradoxically though, it is because the one who is comfortable and attuned to the wilderness – their holy, undomesticated and wild Yahweh – is with them, they are able to safely navigate their way through the arid, threatening desert. To clarify, it is not the space of wilderness in itself that is holy, but the One in the wilderness who makes it so. And it is Yahweh's preference to reveal himself and his nature in this wilderness space, as well as his ease within it, that is significant to note.

Furthermore, the tabernacle inextricably links the environment of wilderness, the ark, and the experience of Yahweh.[36] For example, the menorah or lamp stand within the holy place of the tabernacle is reminiscent of the burning bush. The menorah burns but is not consumed, and is a symbol of life, light, and grace here in the tabernacle as it was for Moses amongst the sterile wilderness backdrop.[37] Equally, as the Lord's presence made the wilderness holy in Exodus 3, likewise he sanctifies the tabernacle with his holiness and glory (see Exod. 29.42-46). Simple at-hand wilderness items such as acacia wood, goat hair, and so forth are used to construct the taber-

---

[34] George Coats, 'An Exposition for the Wilderness Traditions', *Vetus Testamentum* 22.3 (1972), pp. 288-295 (291).

[35] Fretheim, *Exodus*, p. 269. Fretheim adds,

At this small, lonely place in the midst of the chaos of the wilderness, a new creation comes into being. In the midst of disorder, there is order. The tabernacle is the world order as God intended writ small in Israel. The priests of the sanctuary going about their appointed courses is like everything in creation performing its liturgical service – the sun, the trees, human beings. The people of Israel carefully encamped around the tabernacle in their midst constitutes the beginnings of God's bringing creation back to what it was originally intended to be. The tabernacle is a realisation of God's created order in history; both reflect the glory of God in their midst (*Exodus*, p. 271).

[36] Cameron S. McKenzie, 'Echoes of Time and Space: The Ark and the Exodus in 1 Samuel 4-6', *Didaskalia* 12.2 (2001), pp. 59-80 (69).

[37] Wyatt, 'The Significance of the Burning Bush', p. 364.

nacle. Further, the darkness, isolation, and silence of the marginal place is embodied in the holy of holies, especially with its being set apart as the most holy place, and its housing the ark and tablets of the testimony. From here the words of Yahweh continue to resound. Later in the Pentateuchal narrative other objects significant to the wilderness, an *omer* of manna and Aaron's staff for example, are kept within the tabernacle itself.

The wilderness portable sanctuary is then carried into the Promised Land and remains pivotal in the life of ancient Israel's worship. With this, I would argue that the wilderness experience is not dismissed nor does it become just a ritualized memory, instead wilderness is embedded into the national psyche of Israel. Particularly, via the role of the Levitical tribe who serve the tabernacle, *wildness* is still mediated. This is because the Levites were not allocated an inheritance of land; instead, Yahweh was their portion (see Deut. 10.1-9). As such they remain dependent on God and the sanctuary, just like Israel in the wilderness to sustain them.[38] They likewise served in the sanctuary to preserve and guard Yahweh's holiness-with-them. Further, in other passages that refer to the Levites (Deut. 12.11-12; 14.27-29; 18.1-8; 26.11-12), they are grouped with the disenfranchised people of society (for example, male and female slaves, aliens, widows, and orphans), the common element being their landless and 'outer' status. They are the isolated, marginal people of society. But God chooses these *landless* as objects of his particular care, and he uses the *wildness* of the Levites to mediate his character to others, even to the point of setting up Levitical refuge cities (Numbers 35) in which the normal expectations and laws of society are suspended for fleeing asylum seekers. So in ritual, social, and geographical actions, the Levites are used to indicate the significance of having borderland places and in-between people who mediate wildness amidst order and structure. Thus Yahweh, even in the Promised Land, is not reduced to religious posturing or traditional boundaries, but still displays his wild affinity for the non-traditional, non-places, and non-people.

---

[38] They were to live by the tithes of Israel (see Lev. 18.20-21). This brings to memory the utter dependence Israel had in the wilderness for God to provide their daily food, through the manna and quail.

Wilderness: The Habitat for a Wild-God?

All in all, the challenge of this study has been to see and hear and pay attention to the geography of wilderness within the Exodus narrative. As has been discussed, the fierce landscape of the wilderness evokes enormous energy within these formative biblical narratives as well as in our imaginations.[39] Hence as a point of application, especially for Pentecostals, I would recommend that we engage further with the energy and imagination, as well as the reality, of geographical landscapes. Pentecostals are ideally situated to take up this challenge, for their worldview holds an expectancy to encounter God in a concrete, though mysterious,[40] experiential manner.[41] Moreover, Pentecostals have a natural affinity to locate their personal story within the narrative of the biblical story, for Scripture serves 'as the template for reading the world'.[42] As such, I would propose that Pentecostals pay further attention to their own geographical landscapes and the significant role they play in their concrete interactions with God. Particularly I would encourage us to create space for *wild-ness* in all its fearsome ruggedness and beauty, and allow this to become a formative place to *see* and *hear,* in our spiritual journeying with God. Further, I would suggest that we contemplate how our own experiences can be interpreted through the template of the biblical narratives, especially the biblical images related to landscapes, terrains, and space. Thereby allowing the vivid landscapes of the biblical text to intersect with the inspired landscapes of our own story, so much so that one's story can find its *place* within the larger salvation story.

The biblical narrative suggests that God 'is one who thrives on fierce landscapes'.[43] He is not fearful or constrained by remote, iso-

---

[39] Lane, *The Solace of Fierce Landscapes*, p. 100.

[40] Tae Young So, 'Pentecostal Spirituality as Nurturing Vitality for Human Lives', *Journal of Pentecostal Theology* 18.2 (September 2009), pp. 246-62 (247).

[41] James K.A. Smith, 'Thinking in Tongues', *First Things: The Journal of Religion, Culture and Public Life* 182 (2008), pp. 27-31. Smith aptly summarises, stating that Pentecostals hold a worldview that 'emphasizes the goodness, necessity, and instrumentality of material elements: God's Spirit is active through concrete and material phenomena. It is a *gritty* spirituality – one that affirms all the messiness and awkwardness of embodiment, because it is in and through such embodiment that God's Spirit is at work' (p. 29).

[42] Jackie David Johns, 'Pentecostalism and the Postmodern Worldview', *Journal of Pentecostal Theology*, 1.7 (1995), pp. 73-96 (85).

[43] Lane, *The Solace of Fierce Landscapes*, p. 43.

lated, and formless landscapes. In fact they arguably become the innate landscape which best displays his creative and redemptive acts, as well as his other, holy, and fearsome, but sustaining nature. Further, this wild terrain becomes a place where one is deeply transformed in response to encountering God in his holy presence and identity-breathed words. Consequently, could we by creating 'wilderness landscapes' – whether physically or in our biblical imaginations – allow space for this wild-God to transform us? I would conclude affirmatively, yet with cautious nuance, for ultimately the terrain of the wilderness affirms that 'God cannot be *had* ... [whether] by concept, language or experience. God is a desert, ultimately beyond human comprehension'.[44] Therein he is truly a wild-God.

---

[44] Lane, *The Solace of Fierce Landscapes*, p. 12.

2

THE ACKNOWLEDGEMENT OF HOLY GROUND AS PREREQUISITE TO ISRAEL'S ADVANCEMENT UNDER THE LEADERSHIP OF JOSHUA (JOSHUA 5.13-15)

ROBERT C. CROSBY*

While Moses remains the foremost biblical model of a leader called by God to shepherd people out of bondage towards a promise, Joshua is the preeminent exemplar of leadership that actually brings them into the places of prophetic promise (i.e. across the Jordan River, into Canaan, etc.). Although Joshua served as a protégé of Moses, his entrée into the Promised Land was precipitated by a momentous and rather mysterious encounter with holiness in the form of a celestial being and a perspective-altering message. At the moment of the events described in Joshua 5, this leader had the task of moving the wandering tribes of Israel into Canaan. While his apparent need was to receive instructions on a necessary military advancement, he was instead first directed to do something unexpected, something seemingly more related to his soul than to his strategy, which would soon follow. The divine preparations of Joshua as a national leader of ancient Israel deserve the sincere reflection of those who would lead God's people today.

This study focuses on Joshua's encounter with the 'commander of the army of the Lord', as recorded in Josh. 5.13-15:

* Robert C. Crosby (DMin, Gordon-Conwell Theological Seminary) is Professor of Practical Theology at Southeastern University, Lakeland, FL USA.

Now when Joshua was near Jericho, he looked up and saw a man standing in front of him with a drawn sword in his hand. Joshua went up to him and asked, 'Are you for us or for our enemies?'

'Neither', he replied, 'but as commander of the army of the Lord I have now come'. Then Joshua fell facedown to the ground in reverence, and asked him, 'What message does my Lord have for his servant?'

The commander of the Lord's army replied, 'Take off your sandals, for the place where you are standing is holy'. And Joshua did so. (NIV)

The directive that came to Joshua from the 'messenger' (i.e. 'the commander of the army of the Lord') was twofold: One, to remove his shoes and, two, to be aware of holiness – 'take off your shoes for the ground where upon you stand is holy' (v. 15). This moment and others in the Old Testament embody apparent seasons of consecration in the lives of leaders that serve as precipitous preparations for divinely-appointed leadership roles and assignments. They imply a link between the role of holiness and the responsibility of godly leadership.

Background

In order to understand the preemptive appearance of the 'commander of the Lord' to Joshua en route to possession of the Promised Land, we must consider the surrounding circumstances of the hour and the particular placement of this encounter within the biblical metanarrative. For several reasons, this event represented a pivotal moment not only in the life of the patriarchal leader but also in the overall scheme of the Hebrew nation's development and journey. A few important acknowledgements include:

Moses Failed to Lead the Hebrew Nation into the Promised Land.

Although Moses was allowed by God to 'see' the Promised Land, it was because of his sin that he was not allowed to enter it (Num. 27.12). Although strict adherents to Reformed theology may be quick to point out that within Moses' original call from God at the burning bush, the leader was destined to bring the Hebrew people out of bondage and not necessarily to bring them *into* the Promised Land,[1] the text would, however, contend otherwise. The leader's failure to follow the directives of God at the waters of Meribah brought a pronouncement of punishment that would evidence that he might, in fact, have completed the journey had he fully obeyed the voice of God: 'But the Lord said to Moses and Aaron, "Because you did not trust in me enough to honor me as holy in the sight of the Israelites, you will not bring this community into the land I give them"' (Num. 20.12 NIV).

The sins of the people, as well as those of their leaders (Moses and Aaron), in the wilderness wanderings portray a period of confusion in those called to be God's chosen people. While the narrative in Numbers 20 portrays the efforts of God to establish Moses as a Spirit-led leader, the leader's anger clearly got the best of him on more than one occasion.[2] Not only did it represent an act of disobedience to God, it proved to be a slight to his practice of holiness and reverence, and, ultimately, to disqualify Moses for the completion of his God-given assignment.

The Death of Moses Brought about an Immediate Leadership Directive and an Agenda for a New Leader, Namely Joshua.
While Moses' failure at the waters of Meribah kept him out of his desired destination, it also opened an opportunity for Joshua to lead the people into the land of promise. Moses' shortcomings set an agenda of need for a new leader and, perhaps, a new *kind* of leader.

> Then the Lord said to Moses, 'Go up this mountain … and see the land I have given the Israelites. After you have seen it, you too will be gathered to your people, as your brother Aaron was,

---

[1] The Lord said,

I have indeed seen the misery of my people in Egypt. I have heard them crying out because of their slave drivers, and I am concerned about their suffering. So I have come down to rescue them from the hand of the Egyptians and to bring them up out of that land into a good and spacious land, a land flowing with milk and honey – the home of the Canaanites, Hittites, Amorites, Perizzites, Hivites and Jebusites. And now the cry of the Israelites has reached me, and I have seen the way the Egyptians are oppressing them. So now, go. I am sending you to Pharaoh *to bring my people the Israelites out* of Egypt (Exod. 3.7-10 NIV, emphasis added).

[2] The Pentateuch records at least four instances in which Moses' anger became a stumbling block to him in his life and leadership starting with his killing of the Egyptian (cf. Exod. 2.11-15; 11.8; 32.15-20; 34.27-28; Num. 20.1-13).

for when the community rebelled at the waters in the Desert of Zin, both of you disobeyed my command to honor me as holy before their eyes.' (These were the waters of Meribah Kadesh, in the Desert of Zin.)

Moses said to the Lord, 'May the Lord, the God who gives breath to all living things, *appoint someone over this community to go out and come in before them, one who will lead them out and bring them in,* so the Lord's people will not be like sheep without a shepherd'.

So the Lord said to Moses, 'Take Joshua son of Nun, a man in whom is the spirit of leadership, and lay your hand on him'. (Num. 27.12-18; emphasis added)

On the brink of Israel's seizing of Canaan, God would send not only the opportunity of advancement for Joshua, but a divine representative to ready or, at least, reaffirm him for the task of leadership. The requirements in this instance were immediate, as were the promises: 'Consecrate yourself today, for I will do amazing things among you tomorrow' (Josh. 3.5).

Joshua Would Be Called to Lead During a Period of Epochal Transition and National Revolution.

While Moses led the Hebrew children out of the place of their greatest bondage, Joshua would lead them *into* the place of their greatest blessing. Joshua had shadowed Moses as his protégé. He had experienced a unique and close view of Moses' leadership; however it was of one leading a people *out* of a place of great hardship and struggle. Joshua's responsibility would be quite different; it would be that of one who would lead a people *into* a place of opportunity and responsibility amidst a host of impending threats, enemies, and conflicts. In his leadership, Moses was effective at helping Israel to close an old chapter in her history; Joshua would help open a brand new one. While Moses helped the Hebrew nation shed a despised identity (i.e. 'slaves'); Joshua would help them embrace a desired one (i.e. a 'nation').

The process of his preparation for leadership included several key events, one of which involved a name change. Moses lent a specific meaning to Joshua with a change from his former name,

Hoshea which means 'he has delivered' (Num. 13.16; Deut. 32.44) to Joshua, 'the Lord has delivered'.[3]

Joshua's encounter with the 'commander of the army of the Lord' was precipitated by the reestablishment of covenantal rituals and events designed to renew Israel's God-given identity. The reinstitution of circumcision and Passover in Josh. 5.2-12 were the two key covenantal events. At this pivotal moment, 'Israel itself pauses in its travel and conquest activities to reinstitute circumcision, one of the important signs of the covenant. The new generation born in the wilderness had not been circumcised, but it was now time to rectify the situation'.[4] The time passed and the miles journeyed since leaving Egypt made it more of a distant memory in the peoples' minds and now 'one could say that the reproach of Egypt had [finally] been rolled away'.[5]

The events that occur in Joshua 5 are of such significance that even 'the places where the events take place are also renamed to commemorate what has happened (cf. Josh. 5.9)'.[6] After circumcision is reintroduced, the 'first Passover in the land is then celebrated. Manna ceases with the eating of the produce of the Promised Land, again to indicate and reflect that the time in the wilderness has passed.'[7] The foods of passage were fading; the 'milk and honey' meals of promise were at hand.

After carrying out the rituals of covenant renewal, finally 'Yahweh appears to Joshua through his messenger in preparation for the future battles'.[8] Thus, his encounter with this divinely-sent being is similar to Moses' meeting with Yahweh in the burning bush. The event draws 'a link with the exodus, and at the same time serves to present Joshua on par with Moses ... thus emphasizing Joshua's authority'.[9] Now that the people's identity was established, God would do the same with the leader's authority.

---

[3] Walter A. Elwell, 'Theology of Joshua', in *Baker's Evangelical Dictionary of Biblical Theology* (Grand Rapids, 1996), http://www.biblestudytools.com/dictionaries/bakers-evangelical-dictionary/joshua-theology-of.html.
[4] Pekka A. Pitkanen, *Joshua* (Apollos Old Testament Commentary, 6; Downers Grove, IL: InterVarsity Press, 2010), pp. 151-52.
[5] Pitkanen, *Joshua*, pp. 151-52.
[6] Pitkanen, *Joshua*, pp. 151-52.
[7] Pitkanen, *Joshua*, pp. 151-52.
[8] Pitkanen, *Joshua*, pp. 151-52.
[9] Pitkanen, *Joshua*, pp. 151-52.

Commander, Command, and Revelation – Holiness in the Preparation of Godly Leadership

Joshua's encounter with the 'commander of the army of the Lord' involved an unexpected confrontation with a divinely-placed being of some sort. A dialog ensues that serves as a prelude to the conquest of Jericho. The writer by virtue of the story's placement is setting a framework for understanding the divine interactions and implications of the soon-approaching battle, as well as the key role of the divinely-chosen leader amidst the campaign. This event includes the presence of a mysterious 'commander' who issues to the leader an order and an insight which combine to produce a revelation of paramount importance. He requires a specific act of the leader and, along with it he brings a specific awareness that places the act within its rightful context.

The Commander or the 'Third Force' Appears on the Battlefield and Joshua Responds.

This account implies that this 'commander' was, at the least, an angel but also quite possibly a physical form of God.[10] The term used here for 'man' is not the normal one, אדם, but rather איש which also can be used to refer to a spiritual being.[11] The image of an angel with drawn sword emerges in similar fashion in Num. 22.31 and 1 Chron. 21.16. Deuteronomy 1.30 similarly implies that YHWH will fight for his people.[12]

When faced with the warrior, there is no initial sign of fear on Joshua's part, rather that of boldness. He approaches the stranger straightforwardly and extends a common battlefield question. Joshua's question for the 'commander' reveals his two-dimensional interest: 'Are you for us or for our enemies?' (v. 13) The question does not appear to have a particular spiritual focus. 'The angel bears the word of the one who sends him, just as a messenger has the au-

---

[10] Walter Kaiser *et al.*, *Hard Sayings of the Old Testament* (Downers Grove: InterVarsity Press, 1988), pp. 191-92.

[11] F. Brown, S.R. Driver and C.A. Briggs, *A Hebrew and English Lexicon of the Old Testament* (London: Oxford Press, 1906), p. 35.

[12] 'Then I said to you, "Do not be terrified; do not be afraid of them. The Lord your God, who is going before you, will fight for you, as he did for you in Egypt, before your very eyes, and in the wilderness"' (Deut. 1.29-30).

thority of his sender; it is not a metaphysical question but a juridical one'.[13]

This appearance of a 'commander' before Joshua is unique in the Biblical narrative. 'There is no other mention in the Bible of Yahweh's army or host ... nor of its commander'.[14] Although the title 'the Lord of hosts' is used frequently for God in the Old Testament, among others evoking rank and authority,[15] 'the commander of the Lord's army is chief among these powerful beings. His appearance before Joshua at the start of the campaign [is] a potent, if terrifying, omen of success'.[16]

What Kind of 'Being'?

The Greek translators exhibit some hesitancy in the translation as they 'omitted the reference to Joshua's worship of the commander, undoubtedly because they thought it was blasphemous' to infer worship of an angel.[17] The intended initial readers 'of the story, however, would not have differentiated sharply between the commander and God who sent him, as indicated by similar Old Testament stories (cf. Gen. 16.7-14; Judg. 6.11-24; 13.2-23)'.[18] Some, however, would challenge this more lofty view of the 'commander', citing that

> The army of the Lord was an angelic host, and they assured victory to Israel if Israel was obedient (cf. Gen. 32:1-2; 2 Kings

---

[13] Robert G. Boling, *Joshua* (Anchor Bible; Garden City, NY: Doubleday, 1982), p. 199.

[14] A. Graeme Auld, *Joshua, Judges, and Ruth* (Philadelphia: Westminster Press, 1984), p. 35.

[15] Auld, *Joshua, Judges, and Ruth*, p. 35, writes,

> Of course 'the Lord of hosts' is a regular title for God in the Old Testament. Then Deuteronomy 4:19 describes sun, moon and stars collectively as 'all the host of heaven' and warns against according them worship. We shall see later in Joshua how Yahweh uses sun and moon to Israel's benefit. On the other hand the idea is clearly represented in the Old Testament that Yahweh presided over a divine court. The Song of Moses tells how the nations of the world were divided according to the number of these divine beings (Deut. 32:8-9); and the later chapters of the Book of Daniel talk of a 'Prince' (the Hebrew word is the same as commander here) who represents the interests of each people. (This is the origin of our own talk about 'guardian angels').

[16] Auld, *Joshua, Judges, and Ruth*, p. 35.

[17] Jerome F.D. Creach, *Joshua* (Interpretation; Louisville, Ky: John Knox Press, 2003), p. 60.

[18] Creach, *Joshua*, p. 60.

6:17). Though 'Joshua fell facedown', we cannot be sure that he realized he was in the presence of a supernatural being. In that culture persons would prostrate themselves before anyone in authority. Moreover, when Joshua said, 'Lord', he used the Hebrew word *adoni*, which was used to address human beings. He did not use the divine name 'Yahweh', which is translated 'LORD' in English, written with small capitals.[19]

The term used here for 'commander' or 'captain' can also mean 'prince'.[20] It remains that this is the sole place in the Old Testament in which we find this full title: 'commander of the army of the Lord'. In the *Aggadat Bereshit*, a homiletic Midrash on the Book of Genesis written in Hebrew (10th Century), Jewish scholars contend that this is Michael, the national angel (or 'prince'; Dan. 12.1) of Israel.[21] This conclusion, however, is often contended as unsubstantiated in the Biblical metanarrative.

Soggin argues that

the angel is not a being distinct from Yahweh, but in a sense is one of his hypostases, to the extent that the worship paid to him is directed to Yahweh himself (cf. Gen. 16:7; Judg. 6:12,14; 13:22; etc.). For in the LXX an angel is already a creature distinct from its creator, and consequently to accord it worship is a sin (cf. in the NT, Rev. 19:10; 22:9); here, too, the mention of Joshua's worship is suppressed.[22]

Joshua's Reaction

Joshua's response to the 'commander' in Joshua 5 reveals his leadership readiness. When confronted by this being, he 'instantly collapses in obeisance and asks what word the angel has for him'.[23] At this point,

Joshua now knows that, as when he was commissioned by Yahweh, he is to learn in advance the outcome of the battle through

---

[19] Donald Madvig, 'Joshua', in F.E. Gaebelein (ed.), *The Expositor's Bible Commentary* (Grand Rapids, MI: Zondervan, 1992), III, p. 275.

[20] Brown, *A Hebrew and English Lexicon of the Old Testament*, p. 978.

[21] Aggadat Bereshit 32.64.

[22] J. Alberto Soggin, *Joshua: A Commentary* (trans. R.A. Wilson; Philadelphia: Westminster Press, 1972), p. 78.

[23] R.B. Coote, 'The Book of Joshua', in L.E. Keck (ed.), *The New Interpreter's Bible* (Nashville, TN: Abingdon Press, 1998), p. 613.

the equivalent of divine war oracle being delivered directly from the source rather than through an intervening messenger or prophet. Joshua is not looking for a command (contrary to the NSRV), but that is the first thing he receives.[24]

The fact remains that the reaction of Joshua to the story is essential to the narrative. It conveys for the reader his 'faithful response' to the call. It proves again what God affirmed to Moses when he instructed him to appoint Joshua as the next leader of Israel. He said: 'Take Joshua son of Nun, a man in whom is the spirit of leadership' (Num. 27.18).[25] It also indicates that instead of prioritizing the receiving of a military strategy, he was placing himself in the hands of God, the 'divine warrior'.[26]

The argument that this event is a theophany or, perhaps, Christophany, is substantiated by the fact that the 'passage is more closely akin to the figure of the messenger of Yahweh who appears fifty-eight times in the OT, with eleven further occurrences of "messenger of God"'.[27] Butler argues,

Such a messenger commissions Gideon (Judg 6:11) and even appears briefly in the narrative of Moses' commissioning (Exod 3:2). Another brief appearance comes in the deliverance at the sea (Exod 14:19; cf. Num 20:16). Seeing the messenger can be equated with seeing God (Judg 13:22). As a military figure, the messenger destroys God's enemies (Num 22:23; 2 Sam 24:16-17; 2 Kgs 19:35). O. Keel argues on the basis of Near Eastern art that the scene here is one of commissioning in which the messenger hands the javelin in his hand to Joshua, noting the javelin in his hand in 8:18, 26, as well as the 'rod' of Moses in Exod

---

[24] Coote, 'The Book of Joshua', p. 613.
[25] Joshua's 'spirit' was further evidenced by his response, along with Caleb, to the potential conquest of Canaan after his expeditionary trip:

Joshua son of Nun and Caleb son of Jephunneh, who were among those who had explored the land, tore their clothes and said to the entire Israelite assembly, 'The land we passed through and explored is exceedingly good. If the Lord is pleased with us, he will lead us into that land, a land flowing with milk and honey, and will give it to us. Only do not rebel against the Lord. And do not be afraid of the people of the land, because we will devour them. Their protection is gone, but the Lord is with us. Do not be afraid of them' (Numbers 14.6-9 NIV).

[26] Creach, *Joshua*, p. 60.
[27] Trent C. Butler, *Joshua* (WBC, 7; Waco, TX: Word Books, 1983), p. 61.

4:17; 17:9. Whatever the scene imagined here, the present narrative has drastically altered it. The prince is never given opportunity to commission Joshua or hand over anything to him. Joshua continues talking and acting.[28]

Several of the early church fathers contended for the 'commander' as a divine appearance for several reasons. In his *Ecclesiastical History* (1.2), Eusebius of Caesarea writes that Joshua

> calls the leader of the heavenly angels and archangels and of the supernatural powers and as if he were, the power and wisdom of the Father, entrusted with the second rank of sovereignty and rule over all, … although he saw him only in the form and shape of a man … [This] is no other than he who also spoke to Moses.[29]

Additionally, Origen contends forcefully for a Christological appearance in the Joshua encounter:

> What is it that Jesus [Joshua] teaches us through this? That, doubtless, which the apostle says: 'Do not believe every spirit, but test if it is from God'. Therefore, Jesus [Joshua] recognized not only something from God but that which is God; for certainly he would not have worshiped unless he had recognized God. For who else is chief of the army of the powers of God except our Lord Jesus Christ? For every heavenly army, whether angels or archangels, whether powers or 'dominions or principalities or authorities', all these that were made through him, wage war under the chief himself, who is the chief of chiefs and who distributes sovereignty to the sovereigns. For he himself is the one who says in the gospel, 'Have power over ten cities', and, to another, 'Have power over five cities'. This is the one who has returned after accepting the kingdom (*Homilies on Joshua* – 6.2).[30]

Hess cites three points in support of this as 'a manifestation of the divine presence, and therefore more than an angelic visitation'. These include: (1) Joshua clearly worships this 'commander' and the

---

[28] Butler, *Joshua*, p. 61.
[29] John R. Franke (ed.), *Joshua, Judges, Ruth, 1-2 Samuel* (Ancient Christian Commentary on Scripture, 4; Downers Grove, IL: InterVarsity Press, 2005), pp. 30-31.
[30] Franke (ed.), *Joshua, Judges, Ruth, 1-2 Samuel*, p. 31.

worship is accepted. Mosaic law (Exodus 20 and Deuteronomy 5-8) prohibits anyone being worship except the 'Lord God'; (2) the revelation of holiness equates throughout the Bible as divine presence; and, (3) as the narrative continues in Joshua 6, the ongoing dialog continues with the 'commander' described as the 'Lord' ('Then the Lord said to Joshua, "See, I have delivered Jericho into your hand"' – v. 2).[31] In these instances, the 'distinctions between the messenger (angel) of the Lord and the Lord himself evaporate'. [32]

> Therefore, the events of 5:13-15 should not be seen as a separate narrative embedded between two others. Rather, they form the logical introduction to the instructions that follow. Just as God informed Moses of his mission after confronting him with the holiness of the place, so God charges Joshua with his special task after informing him of the sacred place where he is. Compare this with the commissioning scenes of the prophets Isaiah (ch. 6) and Ezekiel (ch. 1). In both cases, the demonstration of God's holiness precedes the charge given.

> In the New Testament, the same sequence occurs in the announcement to Mary (Lk. 1:26-38) and in the Transfiguration (Mt. 17:1-13; Mk. 9:2-13; Lk. 9:28-36). For the Christian, Christ's salvation, his saving presence, precedes his call to a life of discipleship (Rom. 5-6; Eph. 2:8-10; 4:1-16).[33]

While 'modernity insists that humankind is the moving force in history, which implies that God is removed from the process',[34] Joshua would discover, or re-discover, in this instance something quite the opposite. The writer of this book clearly 'believed that God was an effective power in history'.[35] In their estimation, 'humanity could do little to change or control it but was subject to its divinely initiated movements'.[36]

Joshua's initial question to him might be termed 'modern' in that it acknowledges only two forces in the approaching battle: 'Are

---

[31] Richard S. Hess, *Joshua – An Introduction and Commentary* (Downers Grove, IL: InterVarsity Press, 1996), pp. 126-27.
[32] Hess, *Joshua*, pp. 126-27.
[33] Hess, *Joshua*, pp. 126-27.
[34] Creach, *Joshua*, p. 60.
[35] Creach, *Joshua*, p. 60.
[36] Creach, *Joshua*, p. 60.

you one of us, or one of our adversaries?' (5:13). The commander's reply, 'Neither' (literally, 'No'), indicates that Joshua's question was wrong [or perhaps, incomplete]. A third force, a divine force that the commander represented, would determine the battle's outcome. When Joshua was jarred into that reality, he quickly did obeisance (5:14).[37]

The Command for the Removal of Sandals Is Significant to the Narrative and to Joshua's Preparation for Leadership.

Just prior to Joshua's encounter with the 'commander', the people had experienced a reaffirmation of their national and spiritual identities through covenant rituals, namely the practice of circumcision and the celebration of Passover. This came just prior to the conflict with Jericho. Now, there was a leader in place who needed preparation, affirmation, and confirmation prior to the battle.

Joshua's leadership advancement was initiated by an action and an acknowledgement. The action was to 'take off your sandals' (v. 15). The call for the removal of Joshua's shoes and its significance to the narrative and to the preparation for leadership requires further consideration.

First, the narrative shifts suddenly from communitarian covenantal events to an individual focus on Joshua, the leader, and his preparation. In fact, 'The narrative of 13-15 shifts subjects and locale in a startling fashion'.[38]

Second, whereas 'Joshua was not mentioned in the preceding notice about Passover, he alone is the subject here "in Jericho" (v 13)'.[39] Although the chronology of the passage is viewed as somewhat 'conspicuous through its absence' by some,[40] it is closely connected to Exodus 3, especially v. 5. While it has troubled many commentators since the narrative appears to be incomplete, a closer look at the literary components reveals the critical focus of the writer on the role of the leader and divine direction prior to the Jericho conflict. The faithful obedience of a leader to God is of paramount importance.

Israel's advancement into the Promised Land was prefaced with a command for leadership to acknowledge God and the holiness of

---

[37] Creach, *Joshua*, p. 60.
[38] Butler, *Joshua*, p. 57.
[39] Butler, *Joshua*, p. 57.
[40] Butler, *Joshua*, p. 57.

a specified place (Josh. 5.15). 'Holy ground' as used herein is an example of specified places set-apart for divine purpose. 'Holy ground' bears a relationship to personal and national holiness and to 'set-aparted-ness' within the lives of the godly. Of course, to this day, the general Judeo-Christian vocabulary assigns the term 'holy land' as a (if not, *the*) prominent descriptor for Palestine.

In the encounter, the 'commander' uses language with Joshua in this instance that 'duplicates God's command to Moses in Exodus 3:5'.[41] The reason Joshua is told to remove his sandals is specified; because the place is 'holy'. 'The Lord's first order to Joshua revealed to him that he was standing on holy ground'.[42]

It should also be noted that the practice of removing one's sandals was 'a sign of respect and humility in the ancient Near East'.[43] Muslims still practice this before entering a mosque.

Prior to this defining moment, it can be argued that Joshua was standing in what would better be described as 'heathen territory'; yet because God was with him, he was standing on holy ground. If we are obeying the will of God, no matter where He leads us, we are on holy ground; and we had better behave accordingly. There's no such thing as 'secular' and 'sacred', 'common', and 'consecrated', when you are in the Lord's service. ('Therefore, whether you eat or drink, or whatever you do, do all to the glory of God' – 1 Cor. 10.31, NKJV).

> The designation 'holy' uses the same word that describes the precious metal objects that are placed in the Lord's treasury (6:19). In the context of the final form of the story, Jericho is holy in that it is devoted to divine use and will be captured only through divine effort. In light of that fact, it makes sense that Joshua's commission would be to rely on the divine warrior. His primary 'task' in the conquest is the one he received at the opening of the book, namely, to trust that God would secure the land for Israel (Josh. 1:1-9).[44]

---

[41] Hess, *Joshua*, pp. 126-27.
[42] Warren W. Wiersbe, *The Bible Exposition Commentary: Old Testament* (etext, PC Study Bible, 2008, Biblesoft).
[43] W. Kaiser and D. Garrett (eds.), *Archaeological Study Bible* (Grand Rapids, MI: Zondervan, 2005), p. 309.
[44] Creach, *Joshua*, p. 60.

The call Joshua received from this heavenly being was to a higher and broader vision of the significance of the moment and of the presence of God at work within it. The commander, the call and the revelation represent a holiness (or sanctifying) process in the preparation of a leader. The 'commander' brought *a revelation of the holiness of God in a visible form*. The command called for an act of holiness of the part of the leader in the removal of sandals. Ultimately, this led to a renewed perspective for the leader, or *a vision of holiness*. The call of Joshua to lead Israel into possession of the land promised would bring with it deep challenges, even deep disappointments. Such a call would require deep preparations and such was Joshua's encounter with the commander.

Joshua was not the first to receive such a call. For one, there are striking similarities to the call of Moses:

> In both cases, Moses and Joshua are to take off their shoes, as the ground where they are standing is holy (v. 15; Exod. 3:5). Note that while Joshua asks for the message, the commander of Yahweh asks him to take off his shoes in reverence for the holiness of the place. The question then is, why is the place holy? Is it because of some inherent quality of the place or because Yahweh's messenger has now appeared?[45]

Consecration and commissioning events often accompany the preparations of godly leaders for their various calls to service in the Biblical narrative. In fact, patterns of such events can be noted. Jerome Creach cites a four-part pattern of such instances (i.e. Joshua, Gideon, and Moses): (1) A human meets God or an angel. (2) The human responds in fear or worship; (3) The deity or angel appoints the human to a specific task. (4) God or a heavenly representative gives a sign of assurance that the task will be successful.[46]

The Joshua encounter (5.13-15) employs at least the first two elements of this pattern of leadership commissioning and consecration, and possibly more. In fact the pattern creates an expectation that the 'commander' is poised to present special instructions concerning his strategy and role in the coming conflict. The expectation is intensified when Joshua asks, "What do you command your

---

[45] Pitkannen, *Joshua*, p. 150.
[46] Creach, *Joshua*, p. 59.

servant, my lord?" (v. 14)'.[47] The call to 'remove your sandals', so clearly reminiscent of Moses' call, adds to the anticipation. However, with the reader fully prepared to hear an assignment given to Joshua, 'the narrative [instead] ends with a barefoot Joshua – like Moses at the burning bush (Exod. 3.1-6) – who has been given nothing to do'.[48]

While the conscientious young leader, Joshua, approaches the 'commander of the army of the Lord' with an inquiry that reveals his battlefield orientation and preparations, instead of a call to arms he is issued a call to dis-sandal, to remove his protective footgear. Amidst all his understandable horizontal and combative posturing, God is at work to bring a new dimension to the leader's focus and preparation, to draw him to an awareness of divine commission and favor amidst his impending conflict. To lift his eyes 'to the hills from whence cometh [his] help ...'[49] God is at work to open his eyes as he later would for Elisha's servant on another battlefield.[50]

Overall, it seems the primary purpose of this 'commander' was not to place a sword in Joshua's hands but a clearer vision in his eyes. Donald Madvig writes,

> [The] purpose of the encounter was not to impart commands but to inspire Joshua with humility and reverence and to instill in him the confidence that God was with him and was in control (cf. 1:9) ... The command 'Take off your sandals' (15) does not indicate that this incident occurred in an ancient shrine. Rather, any place where God reveals himself is hallowed by that revelation (cf. Jacob at Bethel, Gen. 28:10-22).[51]

Vision and leadership are frequently cited as concurrent. Origen, in fact, wrote 'Maturity in spirituality is demonstrated by discerning between visions'.[52] The earlier commissioning of Joshua establishes this as God asserts to the emerging leader: 'Have I not commanded you? Be strong and courageous. Do not be afraid; do not be discouraged, for the Lord your God will be with you wherever you go' (1.9). Not only would he be called to 'go' as a leader, but also to

---

[47] Creach, *Joshua*, p. 59.
[48] Creach, *Joshua*, p. 59.
[49] Psalm 121.1.
[50] 2 Kings 6.15-17.
[51] Madvig, 'Joshua', p. 275.
[52] Cited by Franke (ed.), *Joshua, Judges, Ruth, 1-2 Samuel*, p. 30.

deeply acknowledge that 'the Lord [his] God' would be 'with [him] wherever' he would go.

Literary Considerations

The Leadership Journey Narratives of Moses and Joshua, among Others, Reveal Notable Comparisons.

The leader of Israel's exodus had not only been shadowed by a protégé in Joshua, their experiences of commissioning and call were extraordinarily alike. Madvig states that the 'similarity to Moses' experience at the burning bush is obvious (Exod. 3.1-6). These many parallels to the experiences of Moses confirm that Joshua is Moses' divinely chosen successor'.[53]

The words of the commander to Moses are reminiscent of Moses standing before the burning bush (Exod. 3.1-12). 'The commander's instruction confirms that the shrine at Gilgal is to be a sacred shrine like Horeb'.[54]

Joshua's experience is also similar to that of Jacob who wrestled with the angel at the Jabbok River (Gen. 32.22-32). In the cases of Moses, Jacob and Joshua, 'the human protagonist encounters a divine messenger before facing a life-and-death conflict',[55] yet Joshua's response is quite different than his predecessors. He does not contend nor wrestle with the messenger. Although he questions him, he responds willingly in obedience to the command. Some considerations of the unique response of Joshua as contrasted to Moses' and to Jacob's include: (1) Joshua is not personally corrected in the encounter as are the others. He also does not appear to have an interest in or desire for the coming conflict. Rather, he 'accepts it, perhaps looks forward to it'.[56] (2) The drawn sword garners Joshua's attention and respect. The symbol or action occurs in, at least, two other places in Scripture (Num. 22.23 and 1 Chron. 21.16). In each instance, the sword-wielding figure represents divine authority and the potential of divine judgment.[57] And (3), Joshua recognizes the rank of this figure as general and commander and, although he is himself as leader of Israel in a similar rank, he

---

[53] Madvig, 'Joshua', pp. 275-76.
[54] Coote, 'The Book of Joshua', p. 613.
[55] Hess, *Joshua*, pp. 126-27.
[56] Hess, *Joshua*, pp. 126-27.
[57] Hess, *Joshua*, pp. 126-27.

acknowledges 'the superior rank of the stranger. However, the concern is not which leader is more important but Joshua's willingness to accept the figure's authority and to respect this as a divine sign.'[58]

Mystical Appearances Precipitating Battles Appear in Ancient Literature.

Although there are aspects of Joshua's encounter with the heaven-sent messenger unique to it among similar biblical instances,

> such appearances, concomitant with the routine war oracle, are typical in traditional battle accounts is indicated by a remarkable Homeric parallel in which Athena, goddess of war and Odysseus' protector, appear to Odysseus prior to his battle with the suitors to assure him of victory.[59]

Interestingly, 'even in Athena's presence Odysseus wonders out loud how he is going to succeed; he seems no more aware than Joshua of the might that is standing before him'.[60]

While divine-like appearances are not unusual in their association with battles in ancient Near Eastern literature, 'Divine visitations on the eve of battle are'.[61]

> The divine word commanding the battle comes instead in the form of an oracle, while the divine presence is seen in the battle itself. In the Ugaritic Epic of Keret, however, the god El comes to King Keret in a dream with instructions for battle. Another closer parallel is when the Babylonian king Samsuiluna (eighteenth century B.C.) receives supernatural messengers from Enlil giving him instructions for a number of campaigns against Larsa and Eshnunna. Neither of these, however, are on the eve of battle – the armies have yet to be mustered.[62]

---

[58] Hess, *Joshua*, pp. 126-27.
[59] Coote, 'The Book of Joshua', p. 612.
[60] Coote, 'The Book of Joshua', p. 612.
[61] John H. Walton, Victor H. Matthews and Mark W. Chavalas, *IVP Bible Background Commentary: Old Testament* (Downers Grove, IL: InterVarsity Press 2000), etext, PC Study Bible, 2008, Biblesoft.
[62] Walton, Matthews, and Chavals, *IVP Bible Background Commentary*, etext.

Distinguishing Principles of Biblical Leadership and Holiness within Joshua's Experience

God is revealed throughout the course of Joshua's life as Holy and as the Deliverer of his people. God's character, and particularly his holiness, are 'evident throughout the book [of Joshua]'.[63]

> The divine holiness is found in the ceremonies that are commanded and observed. These include the memorial stones set up at Gilgal to commemorate the crossing of the Jordan River (4:19-24) with a special role for the priesthood and the ark of the covenant (chaps. 3-4); the Israelite circumcision (5:1-3); the Passover celebration (5:10); Joshua's confrontation with the commander of the Lord's army (5:13-15); the special instructions for crossing the Jordan with the ark (chaps. 3-4) and for marching around Jericho for seven days (chap. 6); the identification of the sin of Achan, his capital punishment, and the marking of the site of his burial (chap. 7); the erection of an altar east of the Jordan in order to remember the lordship of Israel's God (22:26-27); and the establishment of a memorial stone at Shechem after the ceremony of covenant renewal (24:26-27). These Acts and memorials point to God's special selection of his people. God's holiness could only be challenged at the peril of those who did so, whether in the case of Achan or of the many peoples who opposed the Israelites and thereby rejected God's will for his people. All faced death for their sins.[64]

The Seizing of Jericho was Precipitated by Steps of Dependency upon God.

In the Joshua 5-6 narrative, God is clearly seen as the One who establishes leaders. For example the placement of this story just before the conquest of Jericho serves as an affirmation of God's involvement in this leadership event. In fact, the 'theme of God's defeat of Jericho arises for the first time in Joshua 5.13-15'.[65] Creach describes it as

> a brief and somewhat cryptic story about Joshua's encounter with a mysterious heavenly figure who identifies himself as 'the

---

[63] Elwell, 'Theology of Joshua', online.
[64] Elwell, 'Theology of Joshua', online.
[65] Creach, *Joshua*, p. 59.

commander of the army of the Lord'. This account was likely placed before Joshua 6:1-27 to introduce the story of Jericho's fall with a word of assurance that the Lord would win the battle for Israel.[66]

The manifestations of divine presence for the purposes of affirming God's chosen leaders emerge in multiple instances Biblically.

God had promised to be with Joshua (Josh 1:5, 9), and the people had prayed that the Lord would be with him (vv. 16-17). The enemy knew that God was with Israel (2:8 ff), and Joshua had encouraged his people with this promise (3:9 ff). Joshua was now experiencing the reality of that promise! The Lord met him as Captain of the Lord's armies, whether in heaven or on earth. 'The Lord of hosts [armies] is with us; the God of Jacob is our refuge' (Ps 46:7, 11). Joshua would recall the song Israel had sung at the Red Sea: 'The Lord is a man of war: the Lord is His name' (Ex 15:3).[67]

The Role of Revisited Rituals and Renewal Play a Vital Part in Leading God's People.

Madvig identifies 5.1-9 as 'the covenant sign' God gives to his people, 5.10-12 as 'the covenant meal' (the last of the manna), and 5.13-15 as 'the true leader of the covenant people'.[68]

The events of this chapter are further evidence that the Conquest was to be accomplished by God's power, not man's. From a human point of view, it would have been wiser to fulfill the rituals of circumcision and the Passover on the other side of the Jordan where the Israelites were not exposed to their enemies. Celebrating them in the Promised Land, however, symbolized that the covenant relationship between God and Israel was a prerequisite for possessing the land. With this encounter the preparation for the Conquest was completed.[69]

---

[66] Creach, *Joshua*, p. 59.
[67] Wiersbe, *The Bible Exposition Commentary*, etext.
[68] Madvig, 'Joshua', p. 273-75.
[69] Madvig, 'Joshua', p. 276.

Prayer and Dependency upon God in the Life of the Leader and Amidst Life's Battles are Essentials.

('The Lord would speak to Moses face to face, as one speaks to a friend. Then Moses would return to the camp, but his young aide Joshua son of Nun did not leave the tent' [Exod. 33.11]). Apparently, it was prayer to which God returned this leader as he prepared to face the battle of his life. This was a characteristic implied by the literary technique of the author in Exod. 33.11.

The exegetical idea of this passage reveals '… a clear theological point',[70] one that resonates throughout the text in layers. It is this: 'Israel cannot fight without Yahweh's help, though Yahweh is able to do a great deal without Israel's help. The narrative highlights how Yahweh's might almost effortlessly makes up for Israel's weakness (6.16: "Yahweh has given you the town").'[71]

Joshua is revealed in this narrative as a fully obedient servant co-operating with the dictates and directives of the divine messenger. Apparently, he does not need any further commissioning. That was taken care of in Joshua 1. It seems, however, 'what he does need is a) personal confrontation with deity that confirms his commission and b) personal devotion to deity which confirms his readiness for the task ahead. These are provided here.'[72]

This passage implies that critical to the establishment of this leader over the nation is the establishment of God's sovereignty over his leadership. Thus, not only was the ground upon which Joshua stood 'holy', perhaps even more important was the *way* in which he would stand upon it (i.e. with sandals removed). Before the entrance into the land of promise, God would address the condition of a leader's feet. In the ministry of Christ, he would ultimately do the same. He would tend to, or 'wash', the feet of those who would lead people into the 'promised lands' of salvation (John 13).

The removal of Joshua's sandals was a reminder that every step he would take in battle would be overseen by God himself. It was vital for his leadership role that he recognize 'Yahweh has taken charge and is going to be responsible for their military success'.[73]

---

[70] Coote, 'The Book of Joshua', p. 613.
[71] Coote, 'The Book of Joshua', p. 613.
[72] Butler, *Joshua*, p. 61.
[73] Walton, Matthews, and Chavals, *IVP Bible Background Commentary*, etext.

Joshua would come to know that just as 'Moses had an encounter at the burning bush that communicated God's plan for the exodus, so Joshua's encounter is providing God's plan for the conquest'.[74]

The Development and Advancement of the People Emerges in Correspondence to the Development and Advancement of the Leader.

Leaders help and, at times, hinder, nations and their development. It is interesting to compare Joshua's encounter with a divine representative to that of David. While facing similar encounters, David fell down immediately in fear, Joshua, however, at first approaches the figure:

> *Joshua walked toward him.* An indication of Joshua's bravery facing, so he thought, a merely human warrior. David's reaction to the vision of a comparable warrior stationed 'between heaven and earth' was to collapse in sackcloth and make his confession (1 Chr. 21:16b-17). In this scene, however, Joshua's bravery is paired with a slowness of discernment. He must proceed to determine the loyalty of this person who seemed to be blocking the way.[75]

Some further considerations include:

The 'Mosaic Shadow' Reveals its Impact on Joshua's Leadership in the Similar Consecration Experiences of Moses and Joshua.

The process of sanctification and consecration within the lives of these two leaders were quite similar. Francis A. Schaeffer acknowledges the connection between Moses and Joshua citing 'a double continuity'.[76]

> Moses said to the people 'Don't be afraid. The same God who dealt with Sihon and Og will deal with the men across the river'. Then, turning to Joshua, he exclaimed, 'The same God who has been with me will go before you, Joshua. Don't be afraid!' Joshua had seen the leading of the Lord in the cloud and the fire. He had been in the tabernacle when God had spoken to Moses. So

---

[74] Walton, Matthews, and Chavals, *IVP Bible Background Commentary*, etext.

[75] Boling, *Joshua*, p. 97.

[76] Francis A. Shaeffer, *Joshua and the Flow of Biblical History* (Wheaton, IL: Crossway Books, 2nd US edn, 2004), p. 49.

he already knew this one who met him near Jericho. Joshua, looking back across Jordan, would have remembered all the wonders he had seen under the leadership of this same supernatural leader.

… Moses was dead, but the true leader would go on. Because this one said to Joshua, 'I have given into thine hand Jericho' (Josh. 6:2), and because he knew this one kept his promises, Joshua was able to turn to his people before the walls of Jericho and say without any fear, 'Shout; for the Lord hath given you the city' (Josh. 6:16).[77]

The narrative of Joshua's encounter with the 'commander' in Joshua 5 must have made for powerfully compelling story-telling in the Hebrew military encampments on the eves of battle. Clearly, the blessing of God on the battle and the battle's leader were of primary importance. In fact, 'the entire first quarter of the book of Joshua may be said to be dedicated to verifying that Joshua and his royal successor Josiah represent the authority of Yahweh'.[78]

So notable are the similarities between the commissioning encounters of Moses and Joshua that even the 'reply of the angel to Joshua's question is modeled exactly on that given by Yahweh to Moses in Exod. 3:5'.[79] The parallels are undeniable. 'Wherever he turns, Joshua cannot escape the Mosaic shadow'.[80]

Many leaders today are tempted to diminish, if not despise, the accomplishments of their predecessors, particularly their immediate ones. There is something about human pride that craves a favorable comparison. While there is a temptation to highlight the failures of preceding leaders, we are at one and the same time tempted to overlook their accomplishments no matter how grand. Such an approach to leadership, however, is undermining in that it robs communities, if not nations, of the empowering and enriching perspectives of posterity and communitarian identity.

God Is Seen as the One Who Fights on Behalf of His People.

The famed Negro spiritual lyric was 'Joshua fought the battle of Jericho'. However, Joshua's 'fighting' tactics were unconventional

---

[77] Shaeffer, *Joshua and the Flow of Biblical History*, p. 49.
[78] Coote, 'The Book of Joshua', p. 613.
[79] Soggin, *Joshua*, p. 78.
[80] Butler, *Joshua*, pp. 61-62.

and counterintuitive. They were not drawn from military expertise, rather from divine revelation and dependence. For, ultimately, 'Jericho is not fought for by force of arms. Arms are used only in the final slaughter of all those taken. At least it is not described as a battle which *Joshua* fought'.[81] Joshua's preparation by God in this instance is one of an eye-opening revelation and acknowledgment. He was not called upon at first to lift a sword, but to remove his sandals. Elizabeth Barrett Browning captured something of the lesson of Joshua as a leader in a stanza from her poem, *Aurora Leigh*:

> Earth's crammed with heaven,
> And every common bush afire with God;
> But only he who sees, takes off his shoes.
> The rest sit round it and pluck blackberries,
> And daub their natural faces unaware.[82]

The encounter with the 'commander' was not Joshua's first exposure to dependency upon God's presence. He had experienced a rich tutelage of observing and learning from a leader's decisions and walk with God. 'Joshua had read in the Book of the Law what Moses had said to the Lord after Israel had made the golden calf: "If Your Presence does not go with us, do not bring us up from here" (Exod. 33.15, NKJV)'.[83] Once again, 'like his predecessor, Joshua refused to move until he was sure the Lord's presence was with him'.[84] The Mosaic shadow was never far away from Joshua.

---

81 Auld, *Joshua, Judges, and Ruth*, p. 38.
82 Elizabeth Barret Browning, *Aurora Leigh*, section 86.
83 Wiersbe, *The Bible Exposition Commentary*, etext.
84 Wiersbe, *The Bible Exposition Commentary*, etext.

3

BEAUTY AND HOLINESS IN the CALLING OF ISAIAH

JACQUELINE GREY[*]

When the prophet Isaiah records his call to ministry in chapter six, it is a narrative of an overwhelming nature. The text locates this event in the year that King Uzziah died – a time of grief and vulnerability for the nation. In that year, Isaiah has a vision of the Lord seated high on a throne, with his robes and train overflowing and filling the Temple. It is a vision of both beauty and terror in which he beholds the holy and divine king. In this vision the prophet sees God as 'holy'. The seraphim – his attendants – encircle Yahweh, proclaiming 'holy, holy, holy'; describing the whole earth as full of Yahweh's glory. It is a picture of the transcendence of God – one that overwhelms the prophet and prompts him to volunteer to be a spokesperson to his nation.

This study explores the ideas of beauty and holiness in the calling of Isaiah. It considers the testimony of the prophet as an experience of the sublime in which, by beholding the glory of God, he opens himself to the wonder of self-transcendence. In particular, the link between beauty and holiness is explored. As noted by Elaine Scarry, beauty has the potential to de-center the beholder and to bring into greater perspective life, others – and in this case – the divine. Through this exploration of Isaiah 6, we will see that a comparable experience is described by the prophet. As he beholds the beauty of the Lord he experiences a similar unselfing in which

---

* Jacqueline Grey (PhD, Charles Sturt University) is Academic Dean and Lecturer in Old Testament Studies at Alphacrucis College, Sydney, Australia.

he is released from self-absorption and undergoes a de-centering. For Isaiah, the de-centering of his world is evident by his volunteering to act as a messenger in response to his vision.

The calling of Isaiah occurs at a time of high anxiety for the people of Judah. Their earthly king has died and they are vulnerable to the terror of attack by another kingdom; a very real and immediate threat. In this time of national insecurity, Isaiah has a vision of Yahweh. It is an overwhelming vision that enormously impacts his ministry thereafter. His vision is of the 'Holy one of Israel': God enthroned 'high and exalted'.

Of particular importance to this passage is the setting. The prophet describes seeing Yahweh, the God of Israel, enthroned in the inner sanctuary of the Temple in Jerusalem – an area restricted to priests. There is perhaps a little irony here as Uzziah is described in 2 Chronicles 26 as being struck with leprosy in the Temple when he tried (in his pride and arrogance) to burn incense in the altar; a role strictly allocated to the priests. So, in this passage of Isaiah 6, the king has died and the prophet is worshiping in the Temple – the Temple in Jerusalem (or Zion). While in this sacred space, he sees the Lord high and lifted up.

The image presented is that God is high above everything else. As Ps. 113.4 reminds us, 'The Lord is high above all nations, and his glory above the heavens!' The idea of the 'height' of God is one of the main emphases of Isaiah. In 40.22 Isaiah describes God: 'He sits enthroned above the circle of the earth, and its people are like grasshoppers. He stretches out the heavens like a canopy, and spreads them out like a tent to live in.' Isaiah is so caught up in the lofty vision of Yahweh that no earthly matter compares. It is a picture of transcendence and separate-ness. That is, God is set apart from the everyday concerns of Isaiah and separate from their humanity. As a characteristic of holiness may include the concept separation or being 'set apart', holiness is immediately linked with this vision of the transcendent God.

It is interesting that in the midst of seeing the grandeur of God in chapter six, Isaiah's vision is of an embodied figure. Despite being set apart from the everyday and human, God is personified and presented like a human; like a person sitting on a throne and wearing royal robes. Part of the reason for this is the inability of human language and cognition to conceptualize God – words cannot describe God, or perhaps even humanity understand God other than in human terms – but it also is part of the broader revelation of Isaiah throughout the book. Isaiah 57.15 highlights this dual character:

> For this is what the high and lofty One says –
> He who lives forever, whose name is holy:
> 'I live in a high and holy place,
> but also with him (or her) who is contrite and lowly in spirit,
> to revive the spirit of the lowly
> and to revive the heart of the contrite …'

While God is transcendent, he also dwells with the humble. While God dwells in a high and holy place, he does not dwell there alone. In Isaiah's vision he is surrounded by creatures of worship. He seeks worshipers with which to share this place. So Isaiah's God is specific, personal, and involved with his people, and yet absolutely distinct from them. This is essentially a description – in spatial terms – of the holiness of God. The prophet purports to experience an immediate and direct experience of God's holiness[1] through a vision of the throne room of the 'Lord of Hosts'. In this throne room, the King presides and rules, even though the earthly king (Uzziah) has died.

Yet the Temple is also a place of great splendor and beauty. As Ps. 96.6 notes, 'Splendor and majesty are before him; strength and beauty are in his sanctuary'. Psalm 84.1 begins 'How lovely is your dwelling place, O Lord of hosts!' The attendants in this Temple, serving this heavenly king, are the seraphs, literally 'burning ones'. This is the only passage in which they appear. Uhlig notes their connection to the dangerous desert snakes of Num. 21.6.[2] Brevard Childs also highlights the Ancient Near Eastern parallels – especially from Egyptian mythology. Egyptian mythology had ferocious serpent-like creatures as guardians of the sacred area. The seraphs add to this picture of the kingly court. The glory and holiness of God strike terror in the unholy and proud (Isa. 2.19), but in his at-

---

[1] Walter Brueggemann, *Isaiah 1-39* (WBC; Louisville: Westminster John Knox Press, 1998), p. 57.
[2] T. Uhlig, 'Too Hard to Understand? The Motif of Hardening in Isaiah', in D.G. Firth and H.G.M Williamson (eds.), *Interpreting Isaiah: Issues and Approaches* (Nottingham: Apollos/IVP, 2009), p. 65.

tendants they strike awe and reverence.[3] Their worship intensifies
the atmosphere as smoke (perhaps incense or smoke from offer-
ings? – again perhaps a deliberate ironic reference to Uzziah) fills
the Temple precinct. The picture of God created in this narrative is
one of both majesty and terror. The cry of the seraph ('holy holy
holy') continues to affirm that the whole earth is filled with his glory. Glory comes from the Hebrew root that means 'to be heavy';
the world is heavy with the presence of God. According to Goldingay, 'That glory is the outward manifestation of Yahweh's being
holy'.[4] However, glory is not only linked to holiness, but also to the
concept of beauty. This picture of a terrifying but majestic figure
reminds Isaiah (in the year that King Uzziah has died) that God, the
true king, was still on the throne; king over not just Jerusalem or
Judah, but the whole earth. This God whose glory fills the earth
humbles himself to meet with the prophet. The glorious, transcendent God reveals himself to humanity. He opens the heavens for
Isaiah to catch a glimpse of his true nature. Overwhelmed by God's
holiness, the prophet recognizes his own un-holiness. He recognizes not only his personal uncleanness, but the inadequacy of the Judean community he represents.

Here we have a problem: an unholy creature in the presence of a
holy God. The prophet reacts to this scene with an awareness of his
own uncleanness – perhaps preparing himself for punishment of a
leprous nature similar to Uzziah – and by recalling the uncleanness
of *his* people, the people of Judah. For Isaiah, this holiness of God
implies the exaltedness of God who is elevated above the created
world, and totally separate from the petty issues, political infighting,
and corruption of his world. In this picture, he gets a taste of the
abhorrence of the holy God for anything that is unholy, impure,
and anything that pollutes this essential nature of his character, such
as iniquity and corruption (sin). It is a picture of not only absolute
power, but also absolute purity. But Isaiah does not just recognize
his own guilt, but also the guilt of his people. This was not an individualistic society. The guilt of one was the guilt of all (and vice versa). He shares the selfsame sickness of all his people (*a la* Isaiah 1).
He associates with them in a new and vital way.

---

[3] Brevard Childs, *Isaiah* (OTL; Louisville: Westminster John Knox Press,
2002), p. 55.
[4] John Goldingay, *Isaiah* (NIBC; Peabody, MA: Hendrickson, 2001), p. 59.

What is Isaiah's response? Isaiah is terrified and pronounces his own guilt. The darkness of his own guilt is amplified in the light and presence of the holy God. When Isaiah recognizes his guilt and proclaims his own uncleanness, the seraph acts to provide forgiveness and cleansing. His sin has been 'covered' and purged as the seraph (one of the 'burning ones') must itself use tongs to pick up the burning coal. The transcendent God is also a personable God. God extends his will and person to touch an individual; to meet that person in their point of need. Rather than punish Isaiah for polluting the Temple precinct, Yahweh provides the remedy for him to join the worship. The prophet could not supply the remedy for his guilt from his own internal resources; it had to come from an exterior source. The coal touches his lips – the very vehicle of his role as a prophet and spokesperson. His sin has been 'covered'.[5] The imagery surrounding the commissioning is that of the heavenly court. Now the prophet is cleansed and 'set apart' (or made holy) from an entire nation of unclean lips. Now he is free to respond and volunteer when God calls.

The revelation of the holiness of God and the privilege of vision that Isaiah receives comes with some responsibility. Each writer of the Old Testament had a peculiar understanding of God. For Isaiah, it is a revelation of the holiness of God that encapsulates his message. As God is holy, so his creation is called to mirror the Creator. Isaiah's responsibility (as well as Israel's – and might I add our own responsibility) is to demonstrate the holiness of God in our world. Once impacted by this vision, the prophet Isaiah is not the same. The revelation of God as the 'holy one of Israel' becomes so imprinted on his understanding that he uses this term continually throughout the book to refer to God. It is used twenty-six times in the book: twelve times in chapters 1-39, and fourteen times in chapters 40-66. This phrase, 'the Holy One of Israel' becomes one of the standard ways in which God is identified in the book – for example: '… you have despised the Holy One of Israel' (Isa. 1.4)'; 'Thus says the Lord, your Redeemer, the Holy One of Israel' (43.14); 'thus says the Lord, the Holy One of Israel, and its Maker …' (45.11). In the rest of the Old Testament it is used only five times in total, demonstrating how unique this revelation was to Isai-

---

[5] Hebrew כפר, normally meaning 'to atone for'.

ah. This revelation was so real to Isaiah, that it characterized his knowledge of God and pervaded his message.

Because God is understood by Isaiah to be holy, it is expected then that this standard should be reflected in the lives of the followers of God. It represents a moral standard and purity of behavior. If God is holy then surely the followers of God should be holy also. As Isaiah, at the time of his call, encountered the holy God in the sanctuary, this encounter determined his whole preaching and the way he understood God. It also determined his expectation of how the people would respond to God and behave within their community. If Isaiah understood God as the 'Holy One of Israel', then God's followers should reflect this holiness in their social lives and politics and economics. Isaiah places before the people the standard of divine holiness – the standard by which the people should be living their lives in conformity with the holy character of God. Therefore, the judgment that Isaiah pronounces on Judah (particularly in Isa. 6.9-13) is a result of their inability to reflect the holiness of God. It is not a judgment on their attendance of worship service services (as Isaiah 1 is clear that they are praying), but their immorality and injustice in the social life of their nation. As Isa. 1.15 reminds us, they lift their hands in prayer but their hands are covered in blood. For Isaiah, worshipers are not just those who are located in the sacred set-apart spaces (such as the Temple), but are those who are reflecting the characteristics of the worshiped. If God is merciful and compassionate, then Isaiah's community (God's worshipers) should also be merciful and compassionate. If mercy and compassion are essential features of God's character, then the prophets believed that those who revered God – those who worshiped God – would have to exhibit that same mercy and compassion in their everyday actions. Isaiah's moral concern sprang from his personal experience of God in this vision of majesty and holiness. This concern for holiness and justice was partly the outcome of a profound religious experience and a privileged position of being able to discern the true character and nature of Yahweh. So having been purged, the prophet receives a message of justice and judgment for the community. But is this demand for justice only propelled by the vision of God's holiness? I would suggest that it is also driven by the vision of beauty.

According to Elaine Scarry, beauty presses us to a greater concern for justice.[6] She notes that beauty and justice are linked through the shared synonym: fair.[7] We can speak of being 'fair' in many different ways. A beautiful person has a fair face – not due to its color but because it is symmetrical and even. A fair sky is a sky without a dark cloud and without blemish. A fair vista is a scene of beauty and breathtaking panorama. But we also speak of 'fairness': when we speak of a 'fair playing field' we are talking of the demand for equity and justice. It is 'unfair' for someone to have more opportunities than someone disadvantaged. We desire fair arrangements in our business dealings, and object to something being 'unfair' if it is 'not right' or unjust. Scarry also notes that etymologically, fair comes from the idea of something having a loveliness of countenance or perfection of fit. This is not just about symmetry or form. True beauty is not trivial or superficial. Both beauty and justice point to something beyond ourselves and invites the search for something greater.

Beauty has the possibility to de-center us; it brings life into perspective. For example, in the presence of a sunset we lose self-absorption and undergo an unselfing. We realize how large the world is and how significantly insignificant we are. As Isaiah gazed upon the majesty of the Lord, there was process of de-centering. The prophet's concerns with his immediate situation – national politics and security – are suddenly put into the perspective of eternity. He is moved beyond himself and his self-absorption to a new place. Scarry calls this a state of 'opiated adjacency'; it is an acute pleasure (an opiate) combined with marginalization – a realization of being on the sidelines. Beauty gives us pleasure and bliss at the same moment that it places us on the margins. However because it is a blissful experience, we do not mind being on the sideline; we are happy to be in a secondary position as we recognize that we are not at the centre of the world. So an experience of beauty relieves us of the self-centered misconception that we are the focal point of the world and moves us to the margins, but also ironically makes us satisfied with being on the margins. This is similarly the result of Isaiah's vision. The vision causes him to realize that he, and his problems, are

---

[6] Elain Scarry, *On Beauty and Being Just* (Princeton, NJ: Princeton University Press, 1999), p. 109.

[7] Scarry, *On Beauty and Being Just*, p. 101.

not the centre of the world. When gazing upon the beauty of the Lord, all problems cease to exist and all that remains in the centre of his vision and world is Yahweh. He is no longer the hero of the story, but the supporting actor.[8] The result of Isaiah's vision is that he is moved from the centre of his world to the margins as he recognizes Yahweh as the centre.

Yet, it was not just a vision of 'fairness' (as in loveliness), but a vision also of terror that stirs this response from the prophet. His vision is of a majestic king so massive that his train fills the Temple; above him are the dangerous snake-like burning creatures, each with six wings, in continual worship round this figure. There is incense, smoke and noise; noise so loud that the doorposts were shaking. The brilliance and brightness of the vision would have been overwhelming. It is a vision worthy of science-fiction. The response of the prophet is to gape and suspend all thought.[9] He stutters: 'woe, lost, unclean'.[10] He is truly undone: not by a soft and pretty ruler but by a holy and terrifying autocrat of supreme power. Motyer notes the debated etymology of 'holiness' that includes both 'separateness' and 'brightness'.[11] This dual nature of God's holiness presented in the text is also highlighted by Brueggemann as being both majestic and terrifying. He writes, 'There is no coziness here, for God's presence is a source of deep jeopardy'.[12] Isaiah's encounter with the 'Lord of Hosts' is an experience of terror, 'heavy' with emotion. Even the application of the live coal to the lips of the prophet, thereby purging him of guilt, is a dangerous and painful experience.[13] So if the beauty and awesomeness of the Lord causes the prophet to be de-centered, why does the prophet volunteer to speak to the community? According to Scarry, beauty prompts replication and brings copies of itself into being.[14] When we see a beautiful face, vista, or sunset we take a photo, or draw it or paint it – sometimes multiple times. Beauty stimulates the impulse to reproduction and replication. As the prophet gazed upon the beauty of

---

[8] Scarry, *On Beauty and Being Just*, p. 113.

[9] Scarry, *On Beauty and Being Just*, p. 29.

[10] Brueggemann, p, 59.

[11] J. Alec Motyer, *The Prophecy of Isaiah: An Introduction and Commentary* (Downers Grove, IL: IVP, 1993), p. 77.

[12] Brueggemann, *Isaiah 1-39*, p. 59.

[13] Brueggemann, *Isaiah 1-39*, p. 59.

[14] Scarry, *On Beauty and Being Just*, p. 3.

the Lord, his preaching would become an act of replication. Just as he preaches throughout the rest of the book to call people to holiness, it may be suggested that this call for the people to mirror God is for them to replicate God. His preaching is a call for them to mirror the beauty and holiness of Yahweh.

In the church, we tend to focus on verses 1-8 and ignore verses 9-13, but it might be argued that the second section is more important as it is presented as the actual message given to Judah. Isaiah's name means 'Yahweh saves', the principle message of the book. Yahweh – God – is ready to save Israel, Judah, Jerusalem, and the exiled generations. But ironically, Isaiah does not save. His very ministry will be the means of the people not being saved but going into exile. But if salvation (and being saved) is a key theme of this passage and book, we can ask: being saved from what? Salvation assumes a need. Isaiah describes the situation of injustice – the religious and social decline of Judah – and puts the responsibility for it squarely on the shoulders of the people and their king. Beauty also intensifies our desire to repair the injuries of injustice.[15] As Isaiah has looked upon the awesome beauty of Yahweh, he is motivated not only to call them to holy living but also to repair the injustices he identifies in their community. They have sinned, and like the prophet before the throne of God, they also need cleansing. Justice is required. However as the reference to the exile suggests, they will themselves experience the justice of God in their separation from that which they have harmed – the land. Where they have perpetuated injustice they will be judged, but ultimately saved in restoration when their ashes will be turned to a crown of beauty (Isa. 61.3). Restoration is promised in which the 'holy seed' of 6.13 will remain and ultimately be renewed. The blackened and scarred stump is itself also a picture of beauty as the land is cleansed. From the ashes of judgment, as announced by the prophet, the reproduction and rebuilding of the community can continue afresh.

Isaiah's vision of the holiness and beauty of God not only de-centers the prophet, but can continue to de-centre contemporary readers as they also enter the experience of the sublime. As we read Isaiah's testimony, we can encounter God in a comparable vision of holiness and beauty. This kind of vision both de-centers us and in-

---

[15] Scarry, *On Beauty and Being Just*, p. 58.

spires replication. As we are moved by the beauty and majesty of Yahweh, in a state of 'opiated adjacency', we shift from being the centre of our world to the margins as we recognize Yahweh as the true axis. We discover that we are not the hero of our own story but instead are moved from self-centeredness to a place of being significantly insignificant. It also reminds us that our motivation can be stirred to imitate God – not out of a sense of religious morality, but in an attempt to replicate the awesome, wonder and holiness which we see in our Savior. As Isaiah understood God as the 'Holy One of Israel', we too are called to imitate and reflect this holiness in our social lives, politics, and economics. We can do this by a vision of the beauty of God. The beauty of God can propel us as prophets to volunteer to speak and call out for our communities to mirror the glory and fairness of God. In our attempt to mirror the holiness and beauty of God we can witness to the broader secular community that has so often only seen a superficial religiosity rather than the true beauty of God's grace demonstrated through the scars of the cross. By replication of the holiness and beauty of Christ, we promote justice and point to Christ as the rightful centre of our world.

4

HOLINESS AND THE PATH OF SUFFERING: LESSONS FOR PENTECOSTALS FROM THE BOOK OF HEBREWS[*]

FAITH MCGHEE[**]

Introduction

Pentecostals are among the heirs of the holiness movement, and the topic of holiness has enjoyed a prominent place in the Pentecostal pew since the inception of the earliest fellowships. Hundreds of years after the Methodist revival, we continue to deliberate on its meaning and relevance. As we appraise our current situation, we continue to strive for balance and integrity that will do justice to the biblical witness. Through the precious gift of hindsight, we can see the effects of inclining too far to one side of the path or the other – favoring the 'already' or the 'not-yet', the individual or the social, the human or the divine, the moral or the ethical, the material or the spiritual. We are still working to find our way past a holiness of abstention towards one that is theologically robust.

At the same time, Pentecostals are recognizing the need to elaborate a more functional theology of suffering. On the one hand, Pentecostalism has a certain affinity with the suffering, the persecuted, and those at the fringes of society. Its eschatological orienta-

[*] This paper was presented at the 42nd Annual Meeting of the Society for Pentecostal Studies (Seattle, WA, 2013). See the conference paper for appendices on the language of holiness and perfection in Hebrews and a biblical and cultural analysis of παιδεία.

[**] Faith McGhee (MDiv, Assemblies of God Theological Seminary) is a PhD student at the Assemblies of God Theological Seminary and a Missionary Associate for the Assemblies of God in Latin America.

tion and emphasis on empowerment offer hope, not only of a future free from suffering but of a bearable and changeable present. On the other hand, Pentecostals may emphasize faith and overcoming at the expense of biblical teachings on suffering and opposition. As Martin Mittelstadt observes, we 'have not adequately explored the biblical context of suffering and persecution in the life of Jesus, the disciples, and the early church'.[1]

This imbalance can lead to triumphalism or disillusionment. Moreover, believers will not have access to vital support and encouragement if they cannot acknowledge the reality of suffering and do not understand its redemptive value. Finnish scholar Veli-Matti Kärkkäinen aptly notes that we must enable people to address life's ultimate questions – suffering, death, the duality of human faith, and the mystery of God's hiddenness – as well as the *Anfechtung* (trial, temptation, assault, and perplexity) of the Christian life.[2] Yet, we must cultivate a theology that is more than a resigned acceptance of hardship or a completely eschatological expectation of respite. We need a theology that will provide hope and significance not just beyond, but also *through* our trials; one that can acknowledge, account for, and even embrace the reality of our sufferings; and one that can illuminate how hardships can be both 'divinely purposeful and personally beneficial'.[3]

This essay will explore how the author of Hebrews brings holiness and suffering into dialogue. Writing to believers facing trials and persecutions, the author insists that beyond a casual coincidence, there is a substantive link between Jesus' and the believers' own suffering and their holiness. Not only was Jesus himself perfected through suffering and obedience, but through his incarnation, identification with his brothers, obedient life, sacrificial death, victory over sin in resurrection and exaltation, and continuing role as high priest, he has also made and is making believers holy. In addition, the ongoing suffering of believers plays a role in their sancti-

---

[1] Martin William Mittelstadt, *Reading Luke–Acts in the Pentecostal Tradition* (Cleveland, TN: CPT Press, 2010), p. 128.

[2] Veli-Matti Kärkkäinen, *Toward a Pneumatological Theology: Pentecostal and Ecumenical Perspectives on Ecclesiology, Soteriology, and Theology of Mission* (ed. Amos Yong; Lanham, MD: University Press of America, 2002), pp. 168, 175.

[3] N. Clayton Croy, *Endurance in Suffering: Hebrews 12:1-13 in its Rhetorical, Religious, and Philosophical Context* (SNTS Monograph Series 98; Cambridge: Cambridge University Press, 1998), p. 2.

fication.[4] As they bear reproach, endure persecution, and receive discipline in their endeavors to be faithful and obedient children of God, their character is formed into the image of the suffering and exalted Christ.

I will proceed by briefly exploring the background of Hebrews, and then analyze specific passages in which the author relates holiness to the path of suffering. In the earlier chapters of the epistle, the author focuses on Jesus' own process of perfection and the benefits that he makes available to believers as a result of his faithful life and suffering death. The first part of the study will follow the author's train of thought through Heb. 2.9-18, a passage that comprises the major components of the author's arguments about Jesus' life and death (reiterated especially in chapters 4, 5, 7, and 9). The second part will mirror the author's shift in the latter portion of the book (chs. 10–13) to the specific circumstances of the readers and the concrete ways in which the author's instruction applies to their earthly trials. Finally, I will offer some reflections on the significance of these conclusions for the contemporary (North American) Pentecostal context.

Background

Hebrews is not a standard epistle. It does not begin with the author's name or with a formal greeting to the readers, but rather assumes the structure of a sermon.[5] This sermonic form is inextricably connected to the content, which alternates between indicative and imperative. The author is not engaging in speculative, abstract

---

[4] This essay will use the terms 'holiness' and 'sanctification' synonymously and incorporate the related concept of 'perfection' in Hebrews.

[5] Thomas G. Long, *Hebrews* (Interpretation; Louisville: Westminster John Knox Press, 1997), p. 2. With regard to organizing the epistle, the author wastes no time with perfunctory conventions, but proceeds to build the case for Christ's superiority. He demonstrates that Christ is a superior revealer and leader (1.1–4.13), high priest (4.4–7.28), and covenant mediator (8.1–10.18). In the last section of the book (10.19–13.25), the author gives further exhortations (10.19–39; 12.1–13.25) and holds up exemplars of the life of faith (11.1–40). Intertwined with arguments of Christ's superiority are warnings about problems that the readers face. The preacher warns his readers about neglect (2.1-4), unbelief (3.7-19), spiritual immaturity (5.11–6.3, 12, 20), falling away (6.4-20 or 19-25), not persevering to the end (10.26-31), and refusing to listen to God (12.14-29). Simon J. Kistemaker, *Exposition of the Epistle to the Hebrews* (NTC; Grand Rapids: Baker Book House, 1984), pp. 18-19.

theologizing – the indicative provides the foundation and credibility for his life-changing instruction.[6] He is not writing merely to inform his readers but to transform and motivate them. He wants them to *know, feel,* and *do.*[7] The intricate theology of Hebrews is thus a platform for action.[8] The author seeks to provide moral guidance for the audience's dilemmas and to exhort them to the way of life to which they have previously committed.[9] He writes to reinforce core teachings, challenge contrary worldviews, and impel the audience to actualize their new understanding in behavior.

The readers faced multiple challenges. Associating with the group and bearing the name 'Christian' materially damaged their honor and reputation, in both the political (Greco-Roman) and the religious (Jewish) spheres. Situated in a group oriented society, they faced intense pressure to conform to social expectations.[10] It seems that their greatest temptation was to revert to Judaism. Like the Is-

---

[6] The author is aware of arguments in favor of female authorship for Hebrews, but considering the masculine pronoun in 11.32 and for the sake of convenience, will use masculine pronouns throughout the essay.

[7] This is the language of *paraenesis* – advice or exhortation, persuasion or dissuasion. See Timothy R. Sensing, 'Towards a Definition of Paraenesis', *Restoration Quarterly* 38.3 (1996), p. 156. This exhortation is not unrelated to its literary context. See also David E. Aune, *The New Testament in Its Literary Environment* (Cambridge: James Clarke, 1987), p. 191; Abraham J. Malherbe, *Moral Exhortation: A Greco-Roman Sourcebook* (Library of Early Christianity; Philadelphia: Westminster John Knox Press, 1st edn, 1986), pp. 124-25.

[8] Various Greek verbs and constructions (such as triadic hortatory subjunctives at major discourse seams, the use of speaking and hearing oriented verbs, and the frequent use of οὖν) confirm this aspect of the author's purpose. Cf. Cynthia Long Westfall, *A Discourse Analysis of the Letter to the Hebrews: The Relationship between Form and Meaning* (Library of New Testament Studies 297; London: T & T Clark, 2006), p. 297. See esp. 4.11-16 and 10.19-25.

[9] Leo G. Perdue, 'The Social Character of Paraenesis and Paraenetic Literature', *Semeia* 50 (1990), pp. 6, 13. Perdue asserts that providing moral guidance (within a previously-shaped, comprehensive understanding of social reality) is the one overriding characteristic of all paraenetic speech. He categorizes the paraenesis of the early Christian movement as 'aphoristic' or subversive, since its content and function disassembled the prevailing social order in favor of a nontraditional social paradigm.

[10] deSilva discusses these at length in chapter four of David A. deSilva, *Bearing Christ's Reproach: The Challenge of Hebrews in an Honor Culture* (North Richland Hills: BIBAL, 1999). He notes that Christians were stigmatized because of Jesus' ignominious death, perceptions of 'superstitious' or barbaric religious activities, and alienation from society (e.g. withdrawing from social events to avoid idolatry). They were deprived of patron-client relationships and were set on the margins of society.

raelites in the wilderness, they were in danger of neglecting God's great salvation (2.1-4); hardening their hearts and turning away from God (3.7-19; 6.4-6); wavering, not persevering, forsaking the assembly, and throwing away their confidence (10.19-39); and refusing to listen to God (12.25). The message of the Preacher – the examples of faith that he offers, the promises that he uses to motivate his listeners, the warnings, the imperatives – point to a faith in crisis.[11] He exhorts the readers to imitate their forbearers in the face of trials and persecution. If they will only do this, they too will receive what was promised![12]

Context: Hebrews 1.1–2.8

In the first chapter of Hebrews, the author locates the readers within a redemptive-historical tradition and asserts that it has come to its intended eschatological climax in Christ – the heir of all things, through whom God made the universe, who sat down at the right hand of the Majesty on high.[13] In the remainder of chapter 1, the author continues to meditate on the person, work, and status of the Son. Through a catena of *ḥāraz* (chain quotations), including two key messianic Psalms, the author establishes the superiority of

---

[11] In chapter 11, for example, the Preacher reminds his audience that Noah endured mockery and stubborn indifference, but he persisted and became an heir of righteousness. Abraham and Jacob journeyed far from home with nothing but a promise, and God blessed them and made them heirs of his promise. Moses chose solidarity with God's people rather than pleasure and wealth, looking ahead to the reward, and he brought God's great deliverance to Israel. Others endured persecution and wandered the earth – homeless, friendless, powerless – and the world was not worthy of them!

[12] The author of Hebrews motivates the readers with promises of better things: better access to power, better promises, eternal honor, lasting possessions, a place in God's family, and an unshakable kingdom. These motivated them because they related to their felt needs and struggles.

[13] These are structured as three relative clauses, the last of which is modified by four subordinate clauses. George H. Guthrie, 'Hebrews' in G.K. Beale and D. A. Carson (eds.), *Commentary on the New Testament Use of the Old Testament* (Baker Academic, Kindle edn, 2007), loc. 33880. In this last honor, the author connects with Jesus' being the radiance of God's glory and exact representation of his nature, bearing up all things by the word of his power, making purification for sins, and having become as much better than the angels as he has inherited a more excellent name than they. Guthrie sees this as a possible allusion to Ps. 88.25, noting, 'The inherited "name," then, mentioned in 1.4, is, on this reading, not to be understood as an allusion to the title "Son," but rather as an honor conferred by God on the Messiah as the Davidic heir at the establishment of his throne and in association with God himself' (Guthrie, 'Hebrews', loc. 37049).

Christ vis-à-vis the angels – his superior name, his Sonship, his divine status, his Kingship, his agency in creation, his eternality, and his exalted position at God's right hand.[14] Furthermore, in appealing to these Psalms, both of which describe the triumph and dominion of the Lord's anointed within the context of intense opposition, the author cements in the reader's minds the relationship between Christ's obedient suffering and his exaltation.[15]

After warning the readers not to neglect the things they have heard (2.1-4), the author continues to juxtapose the supremacy of Christ and his suffering death. In verses 5-8, the author establishes that God 'did not subject the world to come to angels, but to man/the son of man'. He appeals to Psalm 8 for support, offering an implicitly Christological reading in continuity with his trajectory in chapter 1.[16] He acknowledges, however, that there is a period of intermediate tension between the pronouncement of absolute subjection and its visible fulfillment: 'He left nothing that is not subject to him. But we do not yet see all things subject to him'. In this interim, what we do see should fill us with hope and wonder: we see 'him who was made for a little while lower than the angels, Jesus, crowned with glory and honor'. Here the author braids together the earlier quotation from the Psalms with three concrete applications and explanations from the life of Jesus that lead into his discourse in 2.9-18:

---

[14] Milligan contends, 'it is only the essential Deity of the Son which can justify the expressions which are used regarding Him, or give its true meaning and power to His appointment by God to the office of "the apostle and High-priest of our confession"' (George Milligan, *The Theology of the Epistle to the Hebrews* [1899; repr., Minneapolis: James Family Publishing Co., 1978], pp. 74-88).

[15] The author's allusions and quotations would have evoked in the minds of the Hebrew readers the underlying narratives of the Psalms, which respectively attest to the triumph of God's plan for his anointed one over the vain scheming of earthly rulers and witness that God has appointed David's son to rule in the midst of his enemies, establishing him with an irrevocable oath as an eternal priest.

[16] He employs βραχύς temporally ('for a little while') to bracket Jesus' time on earth and infuses οἰκουμένη ('inhabited earth') with an expansive tone to include humans, angelic beings, and the rest of the created order through the eschaton. In this way, the author makes space to read this Psalm not merely as a celebration 'of the place of humankind over creation but of the place of the Son over 'the coming world'. In doing so, the author does not disfigure the original sense of the passage, but rather joins other New Testament voices in proclaiming that, through Jesus Christ, the Last Adam, Adam's appointment as ruler over creation has been fulfilled proleptically and perfectly.

1. He places *Jesus* in apposition to the one described in Psalm 8, making his Christological interpretation explicit. This draws attention to the historical setting of Jesus' suffering and death and reminds the readers of Jesus' vocation as the *Savior* of his people.[17]

2. He inserts the surprising words, διὰ τὸ πάθημα τοῦ θανάτου ('because of the suffering of death'), deeming this the basis of Jesus' being 'crowned with glory and honor'.[18]

3. He identifies Jesus' 'tasting death for everyone' as the purpose for which Jesus was made temporarily lower than the angels. The author will build upon this concept of vicarious death and atonement.

Holiness Through Christ's Faithful Life and Sufferings: Hebrews 2.9-18

Verse 9 forms the bridge to the author's commentary on what David deSilva calls 'the strange path of this pioneer (through suffering to glory)'.[19] In verses 10-18, the author probes the necessity and outcome of Jesus' incarnation and death to help the readers grasp the mystery of God's salvation. The logic of the passage is this:

In order to help   be sanctified (v. 11)
      his brothers (vv. 11, 12, 17),   reach glory (v. 10),
      children (v. 13),   be free from slavery to death
      those subject to slavery (v. 15),
      the offspring of Abraham (v. 16)

      by rendering the devil powerless through his death (v. 14),
      becoming a merciful and faithful high priest in things pertaining
      to God (v. 17),
      making propitiation for the sins of the people (v. 17), and
      coming to their aid in temptation (v. 18),
it was fitting (v. 10)   to be perfected through sufferings (v. 10),
      for the author of salvation

and necessary (v. 17)   to become part of the same family (v. 11),

---

[17] Kistemaker, *Exposition of the Epistle to the Hebrews*, p. 67.

[18] See Phil. 2.8-9. Delitzsch observes that 'throughout our epistle the Lord's exaltation to the right hand of God is represented as the reward for His obedience to the suffering of His atoning death'. Franz Julius Delitzsch, *Commentary on the Epistle to the Hebrews* (Edinburgh: T. & T. Clark, 1872), p. 305. Compare esp. 1.3; 2.9; 2.4-10.

[19] David A. deSilva, *Perseverance in Gratitude: A Socio-Rhetorical Commentary on the Epistle 'To the Hebrews'* (Grand Rapids: Eerdmans, 2000), p. 113.

for him	share in flesh and blood (v. 14),
	be made like his brothers in all (v. 17), and
	suffer temptation (v. 18).

The author restates and explains his argument four times (in verses 10-11, 14-15, 16-17, and 18), navigating the questions of *why* Jesus came, *what* this fittingly and necessarily involved, and *how* Jesus achieved the intended purpose. While there is some overlap, pausing to consider each of these elements will advance an understanding of Jesus' perfection and the holiness that believers receive through him.

Jesus Came to Sanctify His Brothers and Sisters and Bring Them to Glory

First, the author notes that the ultimate purpose of Jesus' life and death was to free his brothers and sisters from slavery to the fear of death, sanctify them, and bring them to glory.[20] Jesus, in total solidarity with humanity, tasted death on behalf of everyone (v. 10). Yet because of his sinlessness, he rendered powerless the one who had the power of death (v. 14) and freed believers from the fear of death. There is nothing now that is not subject to the vindicated and exalted Christ.

Taking *Jesus* as the One who completes all of these actions provides the basis for the quotations that assume him as the antecedent: the *he who sanctifies* is the same *he* who calls believers brothers and sisters and children (vv. 11-13) and partakes of flesh and blood (v. 14). Moreover, this interpretation preserves the force of the argument in verses 11-18, which elucidates Jesus' actions for humanity and persistently reiterates that Jesus was made like his brothers and sisters/children (vv. 10, 11, 12, 13, 14, 17, and 18).[21]

---

[20] Thompson and others (Attridge, Laub, Lane) identify God as both the one who leads many sons to glory and the one who sanctifies (James W. Thompson, *Hebrews* [Paideia Commentaries on the New Testament; Grand Rapids: Baker Academic, 2008], p. 74.) However, as deSilva notes, it is quite possible grammatically to take ἀγαγόντα ('leading') as an adverbial participle that is dependent on ἀρχηγὸν ('pioneer'), 'with which it agrees in gender, number, and case and with which it is linked by predicate position' (deSilva, *Perseverance in Gratitude*, p. 113).

[21] Jesus is undoubtedly the luminary in this passage. It is Jesus who rules over all things (vv. 7-8), tasted death for everyone, was crowned with glory and honor (v. 9), is the author of salvation (v. 10), sanctifies his brothers (v. 10), rendered powerless the devil (v. 14), freed believers from slavery (v. 15), helps descendents of Abraham (v. 15), became a merciful and faithful high priest (v. 17), made propitiation for sins (v. 17), and comes to the aid of those who are tempted (v. 18).

It is also noteworthy that the author continues to develop his storyline in exodus language and imagery. These three actions – freeing from slavery by a sacrifice, sanctifying, and bringing to glory – evoke the outcomes of the historical exodus (Exod. 6.6-7). The author is extending the contrast that he began in chapter 1.[22] Again, he taps into the authoritative tradition of the readers to proclaim that the same God who acted for Israel's salvation with mighty deeds in the first exodus rescues his people from their oppression and brings them to Zion (cf. Isa. 43.18-21).[23] This stresses the continuity of God's work from Genesis to Revelation. The *why* of Jesus' work – bringing many sons to glory – is the *why* of God's plan from the beginning. Hebrews shares the hope expressed in Exod. 6.6-8 and consummated in Revelation: 'Behold, the tabernacle of God is among men, and he will dwell among them, and they shall be his people, and God himself will be among them' (Rev. 21.1).[24]

Jesus was Perfected Through Sufferings

Second, the author remarks that it was fitting and necessary for Jesus to be perfected through sufferings, partake of flesh and blood, to be made like his brothers and sisters in all things, and be tempted. Two questions surface, the second of which will require more examination: *What kind of sufferings? In what way was Jesus perfected through them?*

Regarding the first question, the author describes various types of sufferings that Jesus endured, including physical, emotional, and spiritual experiences. He expressly identifies temptation (2.18; 4.15); weakness (4.15; 5.2); shame and reproach (11.26; 12.2; 13.3); hostile

---

[22] To reinforce how this deliverance was patterned after the exodus, the author includes the following exodus references and parallels in Hebrews: Jesus as God's firstborn (1.6); 11 mentions of Moses; provocation in the wilderness (3.8); those whom Moses led out of Egypt (3.16); a new covenant that is not like the one when God led the people out of Egypt (8.9-12); Jesus' redemptive death (9.15); Moses' bearing Christ's reproach (11.26); the Passover (11.28); passing through the Red Sea (11.29); coming to Mount Zion and the church of the firstborn (12.22); and receiving a kingdom and inheritance (12.28).

[23] Enns notes that biblical authors in both testaments recognized the typological nature of the exodus account and used it as a paradigmatic teaching and generative model for articulating God's subsequent redemptive acts (Peter Enns, 'Exodus/New Exodus', in Kevin J. Vanhoozer (ed.), *Dictionary for Theological Interpretation of the Bible* [Grand Rapids: Baker Academic, 2005], pp. 216-18).

[24] Robert H. Mounce, *The Book of Revelation* (NICNT; Grand Rapids: Eerdmans, 1998), pp. 288. He notes that this fulfills the basic theme of the Old Testament (cf. Lev. 26.11, 12; Jer. 31.33; Ezek. 37.27; Zech. 8.8).

opposition (12.3); ritual defilement (13.12); bearing sin and its curse (9.28); and ultimately, torturous death on a cross (5.7; 12.2-3) as part of Jesus' sufferings.[25] Hebrews 5.7 is a vivid representation of this vulnerable humanity of Jesus: 'In the days of his flesh, he offered up both prayers and supplications with loud crying and tears to the one able to save him from death'.[26]

There are three passages that explicitly address the second question. In 2.10, 5.8-9, and 7.28, we find the remarkable statement that Christ was perfected. Since no other New Testament writer frames Jesus' incarnational experience in these terms, this demands careful consideration.[27] In addition, the author of Hebrews occasionally uses the terms 'holiness' and 'perfection' in overlapping ways, which could lead some to conflate the two and conclude that Jesus was lacking in a *moral* respect.[28]

The author of Hebrews has in mind a very specific way in which Jesus was perfected, and he assures the reader of this by weaving several parallel components into each of the three passages that speak of Jesus' perfection. While none of the passages is exactly alike, they bear striking resemblance to one another, both in their underlying structural arrangement and in their thematic assembly. Considering the author's carefully articulated and elegant argumentation throughout the epistle, this could hardly be coincidental. Rather, this masterful communicator has provided signposts that, when followed, guide readers to the appropriate destination.

The first clue is that all the passages leading up to the statements about perfection quote from or allude to two key Psalms. Hebrews

---

[25] Other biblical writers mention additional sufferings, such as false accusations, mockery, physical exhaustion, homelessness, implicit poverty, betrayal by a close friend, and God-forsakenness on the cross.

[26] The author reveals other aspects of Jesus' inner life, such as exercising faith and trust in God (2.13) and being moved sympathetically towards his brothers and sisters of account of his likeness to them (2.17).

[27] This is part of the unique contribution of this author, together with the high priesthood of Jesus. Perhaps Luke comes the closest to the first with his statement 'Jesus kept increasing in wisdom and stature, and in favor with God and men' (Lk. 2.52). Regarding the second, Paul depicts Jesus as a mediator and one who intercedes for believers (1 Tim. 2.5; Rom. 8.34), which are priestly functions.

[28] For example, compare Heb. 10.10, 'By this will we have been sanctified through the offering of the body of Jesus Christ once for all', and Heb. 10.14, 'For by one offering he has perfected for all time those who are sanctified'. The author also repeatedly emphasis Jesus' sinlessness.

1.13 quotes from Ps. 110.1; and Heb. 1.13; 5.6; 6.20; and 7.17, 21, 24 all quote or allude to Ps. 110.4, 'You are a priest forever according to the order of Melchizedek'.[29] Also, two of the passages (1.5; 5.5) quote from Ps. 2.7, 'You are my son; today I have begotten you,' and the third alludes to the Psalm ('For the Law appoints men as high priests who are weak, but the word of the oath, which came after the Law, appoints a son, made perfect forever' (7.28). These quotations function in context to reinforce how Jesus, as divine son, is supremely qualified as high priest.[30]

The second clue is that each contains a reference to Jesus as the source of salvation. The author asserts in 2.10 that it was fitting 'to perfect the author of their salvation through suffering'; in 5.9, he notes that 'Having been made perfect, he [viz., Jesus] became to all those who obey him the source of eternal salvation'; and in 7.25, he concludes that Jesus 'is able also to save forever those who draw near to God through him'.[31] These show that the *result* of Jesus' having been perfected is that he is able to save completely those who draw near to God through him. Thus, it is in his capacity as savior and high priest that Jesus was made perfect.

The third clue is that each of the passages supports the conclusion that Jesus was perfected *by means of* suffering. We find in 2.10, 'It was fitting for him to be perfected through sufferings'. In 5.8, the author offers a slightly different perspective – 'He learned obedience from the things which he suffered. And having been made perfect'. Learning obedience was part of being perfected, and the

---

[29] 'You are a priest forever according to the order of Melchizedek' (Heb. 5.6); 'Jesus has entered as a forerunner for us, having become a high priest forever according to the order of Melchizedek' (Heb. 6.20); 'You are a priest forever according to the order of Melchizedek' (Heb. 7.17); 'The Lord has sworn and will not change his mind, "You are a priest forever"' (Heb. 7.21); and 'Jesus, on the other hand, because he continues forever, holds his priesthood permanently' (Heb. 7.24).

[30] In 4.14, the author asserts that Jesus is a great high priest because he is the son of God. In 5.15, he argues that Jesus is a better high priest because he did not appoint himself; rather, God said, 'You are My Son'. Finally, in 7.28, the author contrasts the son with men who are weak.

[31] Vos notes that ἀρχηγός is compound from ἀρχή and ἄγω, and signifies 'one who leads at the beginning or the head'. It also means 'author' as the one who finishes first; Jesus is the first to share in the life that others will later be made to share in. Here, 'Christ draws us after himself to salvation. He led the way to glory' (Geerhardus Vos, *The Teaching of the Epistle to the Hebrews* [ed. Johannes G. Vos; Nutley: The Presbyterian & Reformed Publishing Company, 1976], p. 96).

obedience to which the author refers is a willingness to suffer (Mt. 26.39). Finally, in 7.27, the author places the emphasis not on the process of perfection, but on the fact that Jesus is a better high priest – a son made perfect forever – who was appointed by an oath and did not need to offer sacrifices for his own sins.

The convergence of these themes and assertions in the three passages about Jesus' being perfected leads to the conclusion that it was specifically *in his capacity as high priest* that Jesus was perfected.[32] His sufferings were the bridge between his humanity and his high priestly office as the son of God. It was fitting and necessary for him both to relate fully to his brothers and sisters in their weakness and trials and to overcome his temptations and disinclination to suffer that he might pave the way for his family to follow him to glory. While this necessarily implies that the perfection of believers is qualitatively different from that of Jesus (we are not sinless and are not perfected to function as high priests), the author focuses throughout the epistle on the continuity between Jesus' experiences and those of his followers.[33] As believers encounter these types of temptation and suffering, they are enabled through Jesus' faithfulness to follow his example.

---

[32] In his signal study on perfection in Hebrews, Petersen also identifies this *fitness for office* as the implication of perfection in Hebrews remarking, 'The Son of God is the ideal priest, realizing all the requirements and possessing all the virtues of priesthood' (David Peterson, *Hebrews and Perfection: An Examination of the Concept of Perfection in the 'Epistle to the Hebrews'* [Cambridge: Cambridge University Press, 1982], p. 12). See also Vos, *The Teaching of the Epistle to the Hebrews*, p. 104.

[33] While the author refers to both Jesus and believers as holy, it is critical to note that he makes careful verbal distinctions. He never speaks of Jesus using the ἅγιος word group except as the one who effects holiness for others; Jesus is never made holy. Furthermore, the author employs two words within the same semantic domain as ἅγιος exclusively in regard to Jesus: ὅσιος (holy, devout, pious, dedicated, or sanctioned by God's law), used in 7.26, and ἄμωμος (without fault; morally blameless, or irreproachable), used in 9.14 (see Johannes E. Louw and Eugene A. Nida, *Greek-English Lexicon of the New Testament: Based on Semantic Domains* [New York: United Bible Societies, 2nd edn, 1989. BibleWorks, v.8], §88.24-35). In this way, the author highlights the discontinuity between the sinless innocence of Jesus and the inherent human condition of defilement and sin. Together, these two descriptions highlight Jesus' unique and absolute qualification as a holy high priest and a spotless sacrifice. Just as with ἅγιος, the author of Hebrews carefully nuances his use of the τέλειος word group when he speaks of Jesus and of believers. Jesus is made perfect through sufferings and obedience, and always in connection with his high priestly office; believers are made perfect through Jesus' sacrifice (Heb. 10.14).

Jesus Accomplished and Fulfills His Work Through His Role as High Priest

Third, Jesus both accomplished and continues to fulfill his work through his role as high priest.[34] He is able to do this because he is both essentially *similar* to his brothers and sisters and qualitatively *different* from them. At the end of the discourse, the author distills Jesus' qualifications as high priest into two words: *merciful* and *faithful*. These bring together Jesus' perfect solidarity with humanity and his absolute sinlessness, and they point to both his qualification and his ongoing function as high priest.[35] On the one hand, if Jesus *himself* (2.18) were not tempted and did not suffer, he would not be able to sympathize with ('suffer with') the weakness of those he was appointed to represent or to appropriately come to their aid.[36] Through his perfect identification, he is able to extend *mercy* and grace to believers in their time of need.[37] On the other hand, if Jesus were not sinless and did not obediently pass through suffering and temptation, he could not be considered a *faithful* high priest to make propitiation for the people's sins. Jesus became a priest on the basis of the power of an indestructible life (7.16).

The author describes Jesus' death with the overlapping metaphors of propitiation, atonement, and cleansing. Jesus became like his brothers and sisters *so that* he could become a high priest and

---

[34] Bruce McCormack points out that in coupling the Davidic coronation formula of Psalm 2 with the priestly appointment of Psalm 110, the author seems to imply that it was in the complex act of the resurrection and exaltation that Jesus entered into the office of Priest. Other passages, however, seem to require it to begin with His death and entry into the heavenly sanctuary (Bruce McCormack, 'With Loud Cries and Tears' in Richard Bauckham *et al.* (eds.), *The Epistle to the Hebrews and Christian Theology* [Grand Rapids: Eerdmans, 2009], p. 64).

[35] George Milligan observes, 'There is perhaps no book in the Bible in which his [viz., Jesus'] absolute sinlessness is more emphatically asserted, and yet at the same time so asserted as to show that not even here have we any limitation to that perfect oneness with humanity' (Milligan, *The Theology of the Epistle to the Hebrews*, p. 79).

[36] The contexts of all three 'perfection' passages reference this aspect: 'since he was tempted in that which he suffered, he can come to the aid of those who are tempted' (2.18); 'For we do not have a high priest who cannot sympathize with our weaknesses, but one who has been tempted in all things as we are, yet without sin' (4.15); and 'He always lives to make intercession for us' (7.25).

[37] Thus, Jesus is able to extend to us not only mercy in the sense of sympathizing with our weaknesses, but grace (4.16) as a moral factor – mercy extended to sinners (Vos, *The Teaching of the Epistle to the Hebrews*, p. 103).

perform this priestly service.[38] At his death, Jesus offered himself as an unblemished sacrifice to God (9.14), entered the holy place through his own blood (9.11), obtained eternal redemption for the transgressions of the worshipers (9.15), and became the mediator of a new covenant (9.15). His blood now cleanses our consciences from sin and dead works to serve the living God, and we who are called may receive the promise of our eternal inheritance (9.14-15).[39]

> Because Jesus was made like his brothers and sisters,
> experienced weakness, temptation, and suffering,
> was faithful and obedient,
> offered propitiation for sin, and
> was exalted to God's right hand,
>> in his role as high priest
> He is able to help us
>> by forgiving us and cleansing our conscience from dead works,
>> freeing us to serve the living God,
>> saving us and making us perfect,
>> sympathizing with us,
>> interceding for us, and
>> giving us mercy and grace.

Holiness Through the Believer's Faithful Life and Sufferings: Hebrews 10–12

In the previous section, we saw that Jesus was perfected through suffering and obedience in order to become a merciful and faithful high priest. He completely identified with his brothers and sisters, partaking of flesh and blood, experiencing life with weakness and

---

[38] Hebrews 2.17 can be taken as purpose or result: Jesus became like his brothers and sisters so that he could be a merciful and faithful high priest εἰς τὸ ἱλάσκεσθαι τὰς ἁμαρτίας τοῦ λαου – *unto* propitiation/*in order to* make propitiation for/*with the result that* he made propitiation for the sins of the people (Carl W. Conrad, 'EIS TO with Infinitive', June 22, 2000, http://www.ibiblio.org/bgreek/test-archives/html4/2000-06/0916.html). Conrad argues that this construction indicates a formal assimilation of purpose and result in light of the affinity of the ideas.

[39] In Hebrews, Jesus' death is almost always connected to cleansing and separation from sin and guilt: Jesus offered only one sacrifice, since he had no sin (7.27); the blood of sacrifices was for cleansing and forgiveness (9.23-28.); Jesus was manifested to put away sin by the sacrifice of himself (9.26); Christ was offered to bear the sins of many (9.28); the former sacrifices could not make perfect or cleanse the worshiper forever (10.1); we have been made holy through the offering of Christ's body (10.5); Christ offered one sacrifice for sin (10.12, 14, 26); and Jesus suffered as a sin offering outside the gate (13.10).

temptation, yet did not sin. In this way, he fulfilled the τελος of the Old Testament cult system, dying once for all time as a spotless sacrifice and becoming the source of eternal salvation to all those who obey him (5.9). His blood atones for sin and cleanses believers' hearts and consciences, enabling them to draw near to God in worship. From his exalted position at God's right hand, this great high priest continues to provide grace and help to believers in their weakness and temptation so that they can live holy and pleasing lives before God.

In the last unit of Hebrews (10.19–13.17), the preacher moves from heaven back to earth, from the glorious and exalted Christ to the persecuted and discouraged believers, and focuses more intently on their experiences. In chapters 10–12, the author brings into focus how the life of faithful endurance through suffering is the path to holiness. This section will examine how the author builds a case in four movements. In the last part of chapter 10, he reminds the readers of their faithfulness through past trials and exhorts them to persevere. In chapter 11, he situates the readers within a procession of witnesses to the life of faith and demonstrates that God's people have always suffered persecution and reproach. The author reaches a climax in the first few verses of chapter 12, where he presents Christ as the ultimate example of persevering through suffering to glory. Finally, in 12.5-11, he expounds on Prov. 3.11-12 to interpret sufferings in a meaningful and positive way as discipline from the hand of a loving father.[40]

Believers Become Heirs of Righteousness as they Endure Persecution (10.32–12.1)

In 10.32-39, the author reminds the believers of their trials and faithfulness in the past. These verses provide a window into the community's experience. The believers endured 'a great contest of sufferings', being put on display and exposed to public shame (θεατριζόμενοι) through reproaches and afflictions, being put in prison, and having their possessions seized (vv. 32-34). The author emphasizes that they accepted this joyfully in anticipation of a better and lasting possession (v. 34) and a great reward (v. 35). Now, they are in need of similar faith and endurance, and the author re-

---

[40] Chapter 13 also contains parallels between Jesus' life and sufferings and those of believers, embedded in a section of paraenesis (see esp. vv. 12-17).

minds them that they must persevere to obtain what was promised
(v. 36) and to preserve their souls (v. 39). This will place them in the
company of the righteous, who as Habakkuk prophesied, will live
by faith (Hab. 2.4).

From 10.39 to 12.1, the author continues this trajectory as he affirms the readers' solidarity with God's people throughout the ages.
He calls to their attention that the life of faith has always been one
marked by suffering and reproach. He champions men and women
who lived as aliens and wanderers, who were destitute and afflicted,
who were tortured and mistreated. These overcame fear, scorned
the ephemeral pleasures of sin, and endured fiery trials because their
lives were anchored to unseen realities. The author invokes them as
witnesses of the possibilities of the life of faith; in a sense, their lives
serve as a seal of conviction that the author's message is trustworthy.[41] In this way, the author both normalizes and honors the readers' sufferings. He also italicizes the outcomes of the continual faith
that the pioneers exercised: they gained God's approval, obtained
God's testimony that they were righteous and pleasing to him, and
became heirs of the righteousness that is according to faith (11.2-7).

Just as the faith that the author envisions through chapter 11 is
not a momentary act but a continual choice, the righteousness that
results is more than a forensic declaration. The context implies both
a continual faith and a process of growing in holiness and righteousness. The experiences and decisions of these exemplars are
parallel to those of the righteous who live by faith (presented in
chapter 10) and those of God's sons and daughters, who are trained
by his fatherly discipline and come to share in his holiness (in chapter 12). Through the fire, they were purified; as they ran with perseverance, they were conditioned; and as they trained themselves to
distinguish right from wrong, they became mature. Throughout
chapters 12 and 13, the author will insist that the readers, in like
manner, should persevere through trials to share in God's right-

---

[41] F.F. Bruce, *Hebrews* (NICNT; Grand Rapids: Eerdmans, rev. edn, 1990), p.
333. See also Ceslas Spicq, 'μάρτυς', in *Theological Lexicon of the New Testament*
(trans. and ed. James Ernest; Peabody: Hendrickson, 1994), II, n. 12, pp. 449-51.
He observes that this is one of the early examples of the beginning of the semantic shift in which the ordinary word for witness acquired a distinctive Christian
sense of 'martyr'. See pp. 333-34 for discussion of association between the concepts of 'faithful witness' and 'martyrdom'.

eousness and holiness (ch. 12) and live in a way that pleases God (ch. 13).

Believers Follow Jesus Through Sufferings and Reproach to Glory (12.1-3)

After reminding his readers of the faithful lives of their patriarchs and before reframing suffering as divine discipline, the author pauses to consider the supreme paradigm of endurance in suffering – Jesus. The author has been building up to this moment, and now he reaches the summit of his rhetorical and theological trajectory.[42] Jesus is the One in whom believers obtain the promises (9.15) and achieve perfection (10.4). Using the metaphor of a race that requires focus and endurance, the author offers Jesus' life and death as a model for how to endure suffering and be formed by it according to God's will. If the readers will continually remember Jesus' focus on the prize, his endurance, his decisive disregard for worldly honor, and his ultimate exaltation, they will be able to follow in his footsteps to glory.

There are several noteworthy points in this passage related to how believers address suffering, sin, and other earthly difficulties. As they *look away from* any distraction, they must *fix their gaze intently* on the author and perfecter of faith – Jesus (12.2).[43] The word ἀφοράω connotes both an exclusivity of attention and a sustained reflection on its object. The Christian runner must not have eyes for 'anyone or anything except Jesus',[44] and as the runner continues to meditate on the passion of Jesus, she will find the model for her own conduct and the source of her endurance.

In addition, Jesus is the ἀρχηγός, the author or originator of faith. As Bruce contends, this refers to faith *in general* and should not be translated with a possessive pronoun (KJV, ERV, RSV).[45] Faith signifies the salvation that begins and ends with Jesus, and is thus parallel to the author's earlier assertions that Jesus is the author of salvation (2.10), the source of salvation (5.9), the one who will

---

[42] Croy, *Endurance in Suffering*, p. 168.

[43] Ceslas Spicq, 'ἀφοράω', *Theological Lexicon of the New Testament* (trans. James D. Ernest; Peabody: Hendrickson, 1994), I, p. 247. See also Thompson, *Hebrews*, p. 248.

[44] Neil R. Lightfoot, *Jesus Christ Today: A Commentary on the Book of Hebrews* (Grand Rapids: Baker, 1976), p. 229.

[45] Bruce, *Hebrews*, p. 337.

appear a second time for salvation (bringing to completion what he started (9.28), and the one who has opened a new and living way to God for believers (10.20). Jesus is also the ἀρχηγός in the sense of one who takes the lead or sets the example. He is the forerunner, pioneer, captain, 'pathfinder', and trailblazer (6.20).[46] Jesus has run the race of faith ahead of believers and draws them after himself; he leads all who follow him to glory (2.10).[47] Thus, believers both receive salvation from him and follow in his footsteps (12.2-3). Through his suffering, Jesus became the source of this faith; through his suffering, he showed believers how to run the race of faith. Both of these senses are in continuity with the author's emphases throughout the epistle.

Jesus is also the τελειωτής or perfecter of faith. The writer apparently coined this term, as it is used only here in the New Testament and is unattested in other ancient literature. Friberg indicates that it portrays Jesus as 'the one who brings faith to its highest attainment, either in himself as an example or in others through his high priestly ministry'.[48] This allows it to complement ἀρχηγός both as the perfecter of our salvation – who having 'laid the foundation of faith in our hearts' brings it to completion[49] – and the one who has manifested faith to the end (Rieger), who has attained to perfection in faith (Bleek, De Wette), and in whom perfected faith appears (Ebrard).[50] He is the source of faith and its destination; he is the alpha and the omega (Rev. 1.8; 21.6; 22.13).[51] Through this

---

[46] Bruce, *Hebrews*, p. 337.

[47] Delitzsch, *Commentary on the Epistle to the Hebrews*, p. 303.

[48] Timothy Friberg, Barbara Friberg, and Neva F. Miller, *Analytical Lexicon to the Greek New Testament* (Baker's Greek New Testament Library; Grand Rapids: Baker, 2000), BibleWorks, v.8.

[49] Kistemaker, *Exposition of the Epistle to the Hebrews*, p. 368. He cross-references Phil. 1.6, 'He who began a good work in you will perfect it until the day of Christ Jesus'.

[50] Delitzsch, *Commentary on the Epistle to the Hebrews*, p. 304.

[51] Revelation 21.6-7 and 22.13-14 explicitly connect this title with the gift of salvation:

> It is done. I am the Alpha and the Omega, the beginning and the end. I will give to the one who thirsts from the spring of the water of life without cost. He who overcomes will inherit these things, and I will be his God and he will be my son'; and 'I am the Alpha and the Omega, the first and the last, the beginning and the end. Blessed are those who wash their robes, so that they may have the right to the tree of life, and may enter by the gates into the city.

redemptive power, Jesus has given his faithful ones the assurance of final victory.[52]

Finally, the author features how Jesus' actions reflect his attitude toward eternal and earthly values and rewards. The readers are to consider how Jesus endured the cross 'for the joy set before him' and 'scorning shame'. First, Jesus looked ahead to the result of his suffering. While it is possible grammatically to interpret 'ἀντὶ τῆς προκειμένης αὐτῷ χαρᾶς' as 'instead of the joy set before him' (i.e. Christ renounced his pre-incarnate bliss), the context supports 'because of/in order to secure the joy set before him' (i.e. Jesus endured the cross in anticipation of the joy he would have in bringing others into God's kingdom).[53]

Second, Jesus despised shame.[54] Καταφρονέω means to despise, scorn, disdain, or consider of little worth.[55] It is not that Jesus steeled himself against any emotion in stoic fashion; along with agonizing pain, the weight of sin, and the feeling of utter abandonment, Jesus was acutely sensitive to the hostile opposition, false accusations, blasphemy, and ridicule that he endured.[56] He was hung on a cross as a criminal – naked, bruised, and cursed. Yet he did not allow these feelings to stand between him and the will of God.[57] As deSilva comments, Jesus refused to define honor and shame according to the criteria of a sinful society; he chose to 'disregard society's evaluation of his actions in answer to a higher court of opin-

---

[52] Delitzsch, *Commentary on the Epistle to the Hebrews*, p. 304.

[53] See Bruce, *Hebrews*, p. 332; Daniel B. Wallace, *Greek Grammar Beyond the Basics: An Exegetical Syntax of the New Testament* (Grand Rapids: Zondervan, 1996), pp. 336-38, BibleWorks, ver. 8. Compare 1 Pet. 1.1; Heb. 2.10.

[54] The article here could justify either a pronominal interpretation, 'its shame', or the broader concept of shame itself. The latter seems preferable, as it is more inclusive – the humiliation that began by sharing in flesh and blood came to a climax on the cross.

[55] Friberg, Friberg, and Miller, *Analytical Lexicon to the Greek New Testament*.

[56] For example, in Gethsemane, he was grieved and distressed 'to the point of death' (Mt. 26.37-38); Luke adds, 'And being in agony he was praying very fervently; and his sweat became like drops of blood, falling down upon the ground' (Lk. 22.44). On the cross, Jesus cried out asking why God had forsaken him (Mt. 27.46).

[57] James A. Moffatt, *A Critical and Exegetical Commentary on the Epistle to the Hebrews* (ICC; Edinburgh: T & T Clark, 1975), p. 197.

ion'.[58] In doing this, Jesus became the supreme model of faith. Moreover, God rewarded him for submitting to a suffering death by exalting him to God's right hand.[59]

Believers Share in God's Holiness by Partaking of His Fatherly Discipline (12.4-11)

In 12.4-11, the author moves from the metaphor of an athletic race to one of parental discipline.[60] Verses 3-5 serve as a transition, and he mildly rebukes his readers on two accounts. First, he reminds the audience that in their striving against sin, they have not yet resisted to the point of shedding blood – yet they have grown weary.[61] The

---

[58] David A. deSilva, *Despising Shame: Honor Discourse and Community Maintenance in the Epistle to the Hebrews* (SBL Dissertation Series 152; Atlanta: Scholars Press, 1995), p. 169.

[59] Delitzsch, *Commentary on the Epistle to the Hebrews*, p. 305. The epistle consistently presents Jesus' exaltation as the reward for His sufferings, compare esp. 1.3; 2.4-10.

[60] James Sanders traces the Old Testament background on suffering and discipline. He examines the usage of the primary Hebrew root for discipline (יסר, 'to discipline, chasten, or admonish'), which leads him to conclude that it always conveys the idea of teaching or learning a lesson. He finds that many texts (e.g. Pss. 51.9-10; 119.71; the book of Jeremiah) espouse a positive view of divinely inflicted sufferings, even denoting that sufferings should be 'sought or cherished'. These passages testify to the consummate purposefulness of suffering and the profound love of God that one may encounter in hardship. Sanders asserts, however, that the recipients of all disciplinary suffering were implicitly blameworthy in some way prior to the instruction (James A. Sanders, *Suffering as Divine Discipline in the Old Testament and Post-Biblical Judaism* [Rochester, NY: Colgate Rochester Divinity School, 1955], pp. 41, 91, 94). N.C. Croy draws on the research of Sanders and others as he questions whether this 'orthodox' retributive perspective of ancient Judaism is indeed what the author has in mind in Hebrews 12. Croy studies Jewish and Greco-Roman literature and concludes that παιδεία reflects a non-punitive frame of reference and was used almost exclusively with non-punitive connotations in Greco-Roman society. In the New Testament, the noun form appears outside of Hebrews 12 only twice, and in both cases, the connotation is one of discipleship. Further, the internal evidence in Hebrews that the community's source of trials is external and religiously motivated, which is beyond their control and certainly not to their discredit (N. Clayton Croy, *Endurance in Suffering: Hebrews 12:1-13 in its Rhetorical, Religious, and Philosophical Context* [SNTS Monograph Series 98; Cambridge: Cambridge University Press, 1998], pp. 130-33; 157; 162-64; 197-98). deSilva concurs that the author is not addressing illness, domestic abuse, financial hardship *per se*, or living under an oppressive government, but the reproach, insult, abuse, and deprivations that believers were suffering directly because of associating with Jesus and God's people. (deSilva, *Perseverance in Gratitude*, pp. 449-50).

[61] Their striving against 'sin' here should be taken as parallel to Jesus' enduring hostile opposition against himself by 'sinners' (v. 3); this is confirmed by the reference to 'shedding blood', which would be inappropriate in reference to re-

author challenges the readers to compare their sufferings with those of Jesus, who endured hostile opposition against himself on their behalf. Second, he reprimands them for forgetting the exhortation that is 'addressed to them as sons' (12.5). This is the beginning of a section in which the author probes suffering from a different perspective, as something 'divinely purposeful and personally beneficial'.[62] Here we find the clearest link in the book of Hebrews between believers' sufferings and their holiness.

The discourse begins with a quotation from Prov. 3.11-12: 'My son, do not regard lightly the discipline of the Lord, nor faint when you are reproved by him; for those whom the Lord loves he disciplines, and he scourges every son whom he receives' (12.5-6).[63] In its original context, this constitutes the final of four exhortations on relating to God. Since it presents discipline as cherished evidence of God's love for his children, Beale and Carson refer to it as the 'the crowning exhortation of the unit in Proverbs'.[64] As he does elsewhere (e.g. with Psalm 110 in ch. 2), the author includes a strategic portion of the original text and supplements it with more subtle allusions that would not have been lost on the Scripture-versed reader.[65]

---

sisting internal temptations. Alternatively, perhaps the author is thinking of their struggle against the sins of neglect, becoming weary, refusing to listen to the one who is speaking, and hardening their hearts, which would be connected to their struggle with sinners more indirectly.

[62] Croy, *Endurance in Suffering*, p. 2. Guthrie divides the exposition of the proverb into three movements: First, 12.7-8 suggests that discipline serves to validate the hearers' relationship with God as father. Second, in 12.9 the author explains proper response to God's discipline. Third, 12.10-11 gives encouragement by pointing out the benefit of discipline: it leads to holiness (Guthrie, 'Hebrews', loc. 36235).

[63] This follows the LXX (vs. the MT, which has 'as a father [corrects] every son in whom he delights' (Guthrie, 'Hebrews', loc. 36260). Croy notes that as the author has done elsewhere in the Epistle, he makes a forceful application of the OT text to the readers, pluralizing the singular number and 'recontextualizing the generic statement of the original for the very particular circumstances of the community' (Croy, *Endurance in Suffering*, p. 195).

[64] Guthrie, 'Hebrews', loc. 36251.

[65] In Hebrews 12, the author systematically (although not rigidly) expounds on themes from Proverbs 3 (e.g. discipline, profit, life, peace, righteousness, healing to bones, straight paths, and not stumbling). For example, both speak of life and peace as the results of discipline and correction (Prov. 3.2; Heb. 12.9, 11); Prov. 3.5 has 'The Lord making your path straight', and Heb. 12.13 has 'make straight paths for your feet'; Prov. 3.8 speaks of 'healing to your body/refreshment to your bones', and Heb. 12.13 of the lame limb not being put out of joint,

The quotation from Proverbs 3 consists of two imperatives followed by two phrases that provide the basis for the desired actions. These two verses are structured as couplets of roughly synonymous parallelism. First, the Teacher advises, 'My son, do not regard lightly the discipline of the Lord, nor faint when you are reproved by him' (Prov. 3.11; Heb. 12.5). The emphases of these verbs are slightly different: ὀλιγωρέω (to think lightly of; regard as having little worth) concerns the receiver's attitude toward the value of the discipline, whereas ἐκλύω (to become weary or discouraged; lose heart) addresses the receiver's physical or emotional response to the reproof.[66] The subsequent reason *why* the one undergoing discipline should take heart is, 'the Lord disciplines those whom he loves, and he scourges every son whom he receives' (Prov. 3.12; Heb. 12.6).[67] As the author of Hebrews reprises in 12.7, believers should *endure* with hope and confidence *because* they know that God is dealing with them as beloved and accepted sons and daughters.[68] The readers's hardships are not evidence of God's neglect or indifference, as

---

but rather healed; both passages speak of the profit gained through discipline, Prov. 3.13-18 of wisdom and Heb. 12.10 of sharing in God's holiness; Prov. 3.16-18, 22 describe long life, paths of peace, and a tree of life, and Heb. 12.9, 14 speak of peace and 12.11 of the fruit of righteousness; Prov. 3.27-32 give advice for living peacefully with neighbors, and Heb. 12.14 instructs believers to 'live at peace with all men'; finally, Prov. 3.32-33 promise that the Lord is intimate with the upright, and Heb. 12.14-15 urges believers to 'pursue holiness, without which no one will see the Lord'. Perhaps further study could explore this as *midrash*.

[66] Friberg, Friberg, and Miller, *Analytical Lexicon to the Greek New Testament*.

[67] deSilva observes that the author reinforces his instructional conception of discipline by repeating παιδεία but never reintroducing the aspects of the OT text that tend in a punitive direction (μαστιγόω, 'scourge', and ἐλέγχω, 'reprove'.) Furthermore, the author highlights educative rather than punitive discipline, in the terms he chooses and in his return to athletic imagery (v. 11) (deSilva, *Perseverance in Gratitude*, pp. 448-50).

[68] Translating this as an imperative, as did deSilva ('endure for the purpose of educative discipline'), Kistemaker ('endure hardship as discipline'), and the NRV/NIB is preferable to translating it as an indicative, as did Thompson, the NAS, NAU, ERV, and ESV ('It is for discipline that you endure'). The earlier hortatory subjunctive in v. 1 and imperative in v. 3, together with the 'shall we not much rather be subject' in v. 9 point to the paraenetic tone of the passage; the author is trying to motivate the readers to endure. See deSilva, *Perseverance in Gratitude*, p. 447; Kistemaker, *Exposition of the Epistle to the Hebrews*, p. 376; and Thompson, *Hebrews*, p. 254. Also, Croy argues that the ὡς in v. 7 is not just a comparative (as if a parent might address a child), nor is it contrary to fact (as if they were sons), but it is predicative, addressing them *as sons,* which in fact they are (Croy, *Endurance in Suffering*, p. 195).

they might think. To the contrary, sufferings serve as confirmation that the readers are legitimate children of God. The contrapositive is also true: 'If you are without discipline' – and here the author adds that the readers have indeed all partaken of God's discipline – 'then you are illegitimate children, not sons'.[69] Furthermore, in maintaining that this discipline is a necessary component of a parent-child relationship, the author frees discipline from necessarily punitive connotations.[70]

In verse 9, the author advances his comparison one step further with an *a fortiori* (lesser to greater) argument before changing to contrast in verses 10-11: if we respected our earthly fathers who disciplined us, shall we not much rather submit to the father of [our] spirits? Believers should do more than 'respect' our divine disciplinarian – we should submit ourselves to him, knowing that those who endure the suffering will live.[71]

This *life* could refer to the life of faith that the author presented in 10.37-39 and chapter 11: the righteous person 'lives' by faith as he is delivered from eschatological judgment and 'lives' with God in the world to come.[72] However, it would also be natural for the author to be drawing on the correlation of discipline, instruction, and life that saturates Proverbs.[73] In fact, Proverbs 3, which the author quoted earlier, identifies life and peace as fruit of God's instruction (v. 2). This points to a life that preserves the soul throughout one's time on earth and is consummated in the eschaton (as in Heb. 10.29).

In verse 10, the author elaborates on his human-divine contrast: not only is God worthy of greater honor, God's discipline is of greater benefit to his children. The discipline of earthly fathers is for

---

[69] It is possible to interpret this generally as the discipline of which all children have become partakers, since the verb γεγόνασιν is 3rd person plural. However, πάντες can be used substantially for 'all of you' (e.g. Mt. 26.27); the author is making the point that 'if you are without discipline ... you are illegitimate children'; and the author frequently employs μέτοχος (sharer and partaker, along with its corresponding verb) throughout the epistle with specific reference to his readers' experience. This specific reading also adds to the parallel of the readers' sharing in God's holiness (v. 10).

[70] Croy, *Endurance in Suffering*, p. 199.

[71] Thompson, *Hebrews*, p. 255.

[72] deSilva, *Perseverance in Gratitude*, p. 452.

[73] For example, Prov. 6.23 advises, 'Reproofs for discipline are the way of life', and 16.22 echoes this: 'Understanding is a fountain of life to one who has it, but the discipline of fools is folly'.

a short time (perhaps signifying *incomplete*) and according to their limited judgment; however, the discipline of the heavenly father is always to the child's advantage and has enduring benefits, including participation in God's holiness. This assertion that holiness proceeds from a special association or identification with God harmonizes with the author's conception of holiness throughout the epistle, and the partitive genitive of direct object (τῆς ἁγιότητος αὐτου) reinforces that believers share God's holiness in a derived and partial way.[74]

As with the life in verse 9, there are indications within Hebrews that the readers already share in God's holiness and righteousness. First, after describing Jesus' perfection and work as high priest in chapter 2, the author emphatically opens chapter 3 with 'Therefore, holy brothers [and sisters], partakers of a heavenly calling'. The author specifically highlights what he has demonstrated in the previous passage: that Jesus has made believers *holy* and that Jesus now calls believers his *brothers and sisters*. Just as he partook (μετέσχεν, 2.14) of flesh and blood, they are now partakers (μέτοχοι, 3.1) in his heavenly calling.[75] Second, in the warning of 6.4-5, the author assumes that believers have tasted of the heavenly gift, the Holy Spirit, and the powers of the age to come. Third, throughout chapter 11, the author contrasts how the patriarchs and others obtained God's witness of their faith and became heirs of righteousness, although they died without receiving the promises (11.7, 13). This implies that they received the righteousness while they were alive. Through their obedience and perseverance in trials, they found ongoing favor with God that resulted in the preserving of their souls (10.39).

The second indication is the author's use of athletic and familial disciplinary analogies. This adds to the argument that the recipients begin to benefit from the training after a short time and in increasing measure. As the athlete continues to build strength and endurance, her body becomes accustomed to the exercise and it becomes less difficult and painful. As a child grows and matures, his parents' discipline shapes his character and his own choices reinforce what

---

[74] Wallace, *Greek Grammar Beyond the Basics*, p. 133.

[75] Cf. Phil. 3.14-15, 'I press on toward the goal for the prize of the upward call of God in Christ Jesus. Let us therefore, as many as are perfect, have this attitude'.

he has learned. He requires less and less correction and is able to reap the rewards of his earlier discipline. Likewise, a healthy believer becomes increasingly mature. As the author expresses in 6.12, the readers must show diligence so that they will realize the full assurance of hope until the end, not being sluggish, but imitating those who through faith and patience inherit the promises.[76]

The third indication is found in verse 11. The author acknowledges that discipline is never pleasant at the time, but painful. Here, the author revisits athletics to speak of being 'trained' or 'exercised' by the discipline (γεγυμνασμένοις).[77] Like athletes who beat their bodies and subdue them to be fit for competition (1 Cor. 9.27), believers must walk through suffering and persecution to be transformed into the image of Christ (Rom. 8.29; 2 Cor. 3.18). The author encourages the struggling believers that this process is rigorous and difficult, unpleasant and uncomfortable, but neither pointless nor profitless because in time it will bear fruit. Here, the author weaves in additional imagery and from Proverbs 3 (understanding is 'a tree of life', vv. 17-18; the ways of instruction are peace, vv. 27-33) to emphasize that steadfast endurance through suffering will *yield* or *bring back* to them the peaceful fruit of righteousness.[78] The

---

[76] This same logic is found in 2 Pet. 1.3-8:

His divine power has granted to us everything pertaining to life and godliness, through the true knowledge of him who called us by his own glory and excellence. For by these he has granted to us his precious and magnificent promises, so that by them you may become partakers of the divine nature, having escaped the corruption that is in the world by lust. Now for this very reason also, applying all diligence, in your faith supply moral excellence, and in your moral excellence, knowledge, and in your knowledge, self-control, and in your self-control, perseverance, and in your perseverance, godliness, and in your godliness, brotherly kindness, and in your brotherly kindness, love. For if these qualities are yours and are increasing, they render you neither useless nor unfruitful in the true knowledge of our Lord Jesus Christ.

[77] Wallace identifies this as an intensive/resultative perfect, which is often better represented by the English present tense (Wallace, *Greek Grammar Beyond the Basics*, p. 575).

[78] I am assuming here that *discipline* is what produces the fruit; *righteousness* is the fruit itself (i.e. δικαιοσύνης is an epexegetical or appositional genitive); and *peaceful* is a description of this fruit. In addition, righteousness is functioning in a synonymous or complementary way to holiness. A theology such as that of Frank Macchia would provide the framework for this – he speaks of justification and sanctification as overlapping, complementary, and comprehensive metaphors or lenses. He contends that justification is more than a divine disposition or declaration; it is a transformative gift as well as a reality rooted in God 'apart from us'. It

connotation is that suffering is a reliable and profitable investment, and those who endure will surely reap the benefits of it after some time. At the end of the path lie the prize and the harvest.

Summary

In this section, we observed how the author used experiences of the readers, of the community of God's people, and of Jesus to encourage the readers to run the race of faith with perseverance until the end. The author reminded them that Jesus suffered and ran with endurance, and through these sufferings was perfected and learned obedience so that he became a merciful and faithful high priest and was exalted to God's right hand. If they would only lay aside sin and distractions, set their eyes on Jesus, and exchange society's standards of honor and shame for those of a higher 'court of reputation,' they would be able to endure sufferings and bear the reproach of Christ (13.13) without growing weary and losing heart. They, like the heroes of chapter 11, would become heirs of righteousness by faith.

The author also reframed the experiences of the readers to help them accept their hardships as discipline from the hand of a loving father – discipline that was always to their advantage and that would yield the precious and enduring fruit of holiness, righteousness, and life. He taught them that through their trials, believers are refined, acquire the character they need to fulfill God's will, and eventually, reach glory. The readers' experiences of reproach and hardship do not subject them to victimization that should lead them to waver in their convictions and cede to the pressures of society. Rather, they represent an opportunity to compete for the prize and become heirs of God's promised life and righteousness.[79]

Reflections

As the contemporary Pentecostal community reflects on this masterful epistle, we should be asking questions similar to those that

---

involves liberating, reordering, 'righteousing', renewal, new creation, and redemptive power; it is revealed in God's saving acts; and it is participated in by faith in Christ (Frank D. Macchia, *Baptized in the Spirit: A Global Pentecostal Theology* [Grand Rapids: Zondervan, 2006], pp. 27, 129-37). See also Frank D. Macchia, *Justified in the Spirit: Creation, Redemption, and the Triune God* (Pentecostal Manifestos; Grand Rapids: Eerdmans, 2010).

[79] deSilva, *Perseverance in Gratitude*, p. 427.

concerned the author and first readers of Hebrews: How do the Scriptures explain and give meaning to our experiences? Where does our story fit in God's overarching plan of salvation history? In light of Scripture, are there attitudes or beliefs that we need to change? As we consider these questions, I would like to offer some possible ways for us to appropriate the teaching of Hebrews, with an eye toward holiness and suffering.

First, as we evaluate the doctrine of sanctification and how we should embody holiness in our contemporary contexts, let us strive to elucidate the doctrine in holistic ways. Hebrews reveals that holiness has many dimensions: it has both a positive, participatory aspect and a negative, abstention-oriented one; it is both completed and ongoing; it is both something God works in us and something we pursue;[80] it has both individual and corporate elements; it has both moral and ethical implications; and it affects both our relationship with God and our interactions with others (Heb. 12.14).[81]

Second, Hebrews presents a largely *positive* theology of holiness.[82] Conspicuously absent in the epistle is the vocabulary of *abstention* that defines holiness in some Pentecostal circles. The author of Hebrews warns of only five out of eighty vices listed in the New Testament: being evil, unbelieving, immoral, disobedient, and worldly or profane.[83] The author focuses instead on enjoining the

---

[80] Perhaps we could say it has both positional, forensic, and transformational elements.

[81] I will not address all of these, but present some observations that relate to them.

[82] The frequent imperatives in the letter indicate the author's concerns for the readers – that they not harden their hearts, fall away, be sluggish, forsake the assembly, abandon their confidence, regard the Lord's discipline lightly, and refuse the one who is speaking (3.8, 13, 15; 4.7, 11; 6.12; 10.25; 12.5). Rather, the author enjoins them to be diligent, hold fast their confession, draw near with confidence, press on to maturity, draw near with a sincere heart, consider how to encourage one another, go to Christ outside the camp, and run with endurance (4.11, 14, 16; 6.1; 10.22, 23, 24; 12.1, 28; 13.13).

[83] Words compiled from vice lists in Mt. 15.19; Mk 7.21; Rom. 13.13; 1 Cor. 5.11; 6.9; 2 Cor. 12.20; Gal. 5.19; Eph. 4.31; 5.3; Col. 3.5, 8; 1 Tim. 1.9; 2 Tim. 3.2; Tit. 3.3; Jas 3.15; 1 Pet. 2.1; 4.3, 15; Jude 1; Rev. 9.21; 21.8; 22.15. The author searched in Hebrews for all forms and derivatives of the Greek words. Of all the letters of the New Testament, only Philippians, 1–2 Thessalonians, and Philemon of Paul's letters; Hebrews; Jude; and 1–3 John do not contain vice lists. It is not surprising that Philemon and 1–3 John should contain no vice lists, considering their brevity and specific purposes. So it seems significant that the remaining

believers to be diligent, hold fast their confession, draw near with a sincere heart and assurance of faith, press on to maturity, consider how to encourage one another, go to Christ outside the camp, and run with endurance. This shows how the readers's circumstances guided the Preacher as he instructed the believers on how to live as God's special and holy people. Hebrews points to a theology of holiness that involves appropriating God's grace, committing to God's purpose, persevering through trials, learning obedience as God's children, and sharing in God's nature. Our theology of holiness should reflect these multifaceted concerns.

Third, some Pentecostals tend to emphasize the individual, on-going and transformational, more 'cooperative' side of holiness and overlook its positional, corporate, and ethical dimensions. Let us be thankful for our positional holiness; Hebrews affirms that Jesus' redemptive suffering on the cross provided cleansing, atonement, and freedom from sin for believers. Because of the faithfulness of Christ (2.17; 3.2, 6; 10.23), we have been made holy and we are Jesus' holy brothers and sisters (3.1). Second, the church body also constitutes God's holy people – we embody God's way of being in the world.[84] Finally, just as Israel's worship, institutions, feasts, and conventions pointed to God's character and God's will, the church's presence and practices represent God and instantiate his grace, his justice, and his holiness.[85] Like the first readers, we practice holiness as we show hospitality to strangers, care for prisoners and the oppressed, honor marriage, teach sound doctrine, remain content and free from the love of money, offer praise to God, bear reproach, live at peace with everyone, endure trials and persecution, submit to our leaders, and share with others (Heb. 13.1-17).

Jesus completely identified with us, partaking of flesh and blood, experiencing life with weakness and temptation, yet did not sin. In this way, he fulfilled the τελος of the Old Testament cult system, dying once for all time as a spotless sacrifice and becoming the source of eternal salvation to all those who obey him. As we en-

---

Epistles are those written especially to suffering believers (Phil. 1.30; 2 Thess. 1.4).

[84] See Luke Timothy Johnson, *Prophetic Jesus, Prophetic Church: The Challenge of Luke–Acts to Contemporary Christians* (Grand Rapids: Eerdmans, 2011).

[85] See John Howard Yoder, *The Politics of Jesus* (Grand Rapids: Eerdmans, 1994).

counter sufferings, we should neither focus on them and accord them 'ultimate' status nor dismiss earthly existence as contemptible or trivial. Rather, let us fix our eyes on Jesus – Jesus who was tempted, Jesus who prayed with loud cries and tears, Jesus who endured the cross, Jesus who bore the contempt of society, Jesus who experienced the hostility of sinners – and ask for grace in our time of need. His blood atones for sin and cleanses believers' hearts and consciences, enabling us to draw near to God in worship. From his exalted position at God's right hand, this great High Priest continues to provide grace and help to believers in our weakness and temptation so that we can live holy and pleasing lives before God. Jesus walked this path ahead of us and made it possible for us to walk it.

Fifth, let us acknowledge that the life of faith is one of sufferings, and this is neither insignificant nor incidental. There is a substantive relationship between perseverance and righteousness, trials and perfection, suffering and holiness, and discipline and eternal life. Sufferings do not derive from a lack of faith, but provide a means for exercising faith and receiving God's approval (Heb. 11.2). The presence of suffering in our lives confirms our legitimacy as children of God and demonstrates his love for us. Our sufferings can be a means of blessing and fellowship with God, and provide opportunities to draw believers closer to one another as we sympathize with others.

Finally, our sufferings can nourish in us the hope of future victory and vindication. Throughout Hebrews, the author presents Jesus' suffering as the basis for his exaltation. He encourages the struggling believers that as they follow the example of their Pioneer, they will through faith and patience inherit the promises (6.11). As Paul notes, if believers suffer with Christ, we will also be glorified with him (Rom 8.16-17). One day, we will reap the harvest of our sufferings, sharing in God's holiness and life. We will be among the spirits of the righteous made perfect and receive a kingdom that cannot be shaken (12.28)!

5

LET THE HOLY YET BE HOLY: HOLINESS IN THE APOCALYPSE

DAN MORRISON[*]

Introduction

The last book of the Christian canon, the Apocalypse of John, serves as the focus of much popular eschatology. The forthcoming movie 'Left Behind', based on the series co-authored by Tim LaHaye and Jerry Jenkins, presents a future that contains a series of post-Rapture, worldwide, cataclysmic events. This 'Left Behind' re-boot, as well as many other films and writings, have led to a theology that places the divine judgments of Revelation at the center of the work. No matter the timing of such events, if they are to be read literally, the book of Revelation offers much more than a sequence of calamities that mark the end of the world.

The text of the Apocalypse identifies the writing as prophecy (Rev. 1.3; 22.7, 10, 18-19).[1] As such, John, the author of the work, sees himself as part of the ongoing prophetic tradition within the

---

[*] Dan Morrison (MDiv, Assemblies of God Theological Seminary) is a PhD student at McMaster Divinity College, Ontario, Canada.
[1] R. Waddell, *The Spirit of the Book of Revelation* (JPTSup 30; Blandford Forum: Deo, 2005), p. 124; D.E. Aune, *Apocalypticism, Prophecy, and Magic in Early Christianity: Collected Essays* (Grand Rapids: Baker Academic, 2008), p. 178; M.A. Knibb, 'Prophecy and the Emergence of Jewish Apocalypses', in R. Coggins *et al.* (eds.), *Israel's Prophetic Tradition* (Cambridge: Cambridge University, 1982), pp. 155-80 (156); S. Tonstad, *Saving God's Reputation: The Theological Function of Pistis Iesou in the Cosmic Narratives of Revelation* (London: T & T Clark, 2006), p. 18; H.B. Swete, *The Apocalypse of St. John* (New York: Macmillan, 1906), p. 3; G.K. Beale, *The Book of Revelation: A Commentary on the Greek Text* (Grand Rapids: Eerdmans, 1999), p. 181. Waddell also notes that Rev. 19.10 possibly contributes to this understanding.

Jewish-Christian heritage.[2] As with most writings following the prophetic traditions of their canonical predecessors – the Old Testament prophets – John uses his work to do more than discuss future events; he 'seek[s] to have an effect on the audiences that will hear Revelation, to move them to remain in or adopt certain courses of action and to continue to embody certain values'.[3] One such value is the embrace of holiness.

As John brings the Apocalypse to a close, he presents his audience with a four-fold exhortation, ὁ ἀδικῶν ἀδικησάτω ἔτι καὶ ὁ ῥυπαρὸς ῥυπανθήτω ἔτι, καὶ ὁ δίκαιος δικαιοσύνην ποιησάτω ἔτι καὶ ὁ ἅγιος ἁγιασθήτω ἔτι ('let the evildoer yet do evil, and the unclean yet be unclean, and the righteous yet do righteousness, and the holy yet be holy', Rev. 22.11). As with many things in the Apocalypse, New Testament scholars express disagreement concerning the purpose/meaning of the text. Dean Flemming asserts that the statement serves as a rhetorical warning and challenge for people to decide whether they will have a part in the holy city,[4] which required they be holy people. H.B. Swete and R.H. Mounce note the imminence of the end, signifying the lack of time for any change to occur.[5] As a result, both the holy and the unholy would remain in their present states and receive the respective rewards noted in the text. J.R. Michaels explains that the statement does not function on an individual level, but on a corporate one, noting the possibility of people changing, but the continuation of good and evil.[6] Finally, Rob Wall explains that the text refers to the fact that the contents of the prophecy will occur, no matter people's actions.[7] Despite the

---

[2] J. Fekkes, *Isaiah and Prophetic Traditions in the Book of Revelation: Visionary Antecedents and Their Development* (JSNTSup 93; Sheffield: JSOT press, 1994), p. 38.

[3] D.A. deSilva, 'Rhetorical Functions of Intertexture in Revelation 14:14-16:21', in D.F. Watson (ed.), *The Intertexture of Apocalyptic Discourse in the New Testament* (SBL Symposium Series 14; Atlanta: Society of Biblical Literature, 2002), p. 216.

[4] D. Flemming, '"On Earth as It Is in Heaven": Holiness and the People of God in Revelation', in K.E. Brower and A. Johnson (eds.), *Holiness and Ecclesiology in the New Testament* (Grand Rapids: Eerdmans, 2007), pp. 343-62 (349).

[5] Swete, *Apocalypse of St. John*, p. 302; R.H. Mounce, *The Book of Revelation*. (Grand Rapids: Eerdmans, 1998), p. 406.

[6] J.R. Michaels, *Revelation* (IVP NTC; Downers Grove: InterVarsity, 1997), pp. 252-53. This view seems to gain support from the writing of Flemming, who asserts that that primary focus concerning holiness addresses corporate, not individual holiness (Flemming, '"On Earth as It Is in Heaven"', pp. 347-49).

[7] R.W. Wall, *Revelation* (NIBC; Peabody: Hendrickson, 1991), pp. 264-65.

differing views, the final portion of the statement, 'let … the holy yet be holy', emphasizes the continued holiness of the people of God. Such an exhortation raises questions concerning an initial call to holiness for these individuals. No explicit call to holiness, such as that in 1 Pet. 1.16, exists within the Apocalypse. This lack of an explicit call raises questions concerning the book's call to holiness and how the writing communicates this call.

John's oracles call people to repentance and to a life exhibiting the holiness God has given them.[8] The lack of an explicit call to holiness raises questions concerning how the author of Revelation does this. In this essay, I will demonstrate that John incorporates verbal and conceptual allusions to the Old Testament that present 'the holy' and 'the unholy' in terms recognizable to those familiar with the Old Testament, calling his audience to function as the ancient Israelites should have – a holy people that lived in a different fashion than the pagans surrounding them.

Approach and Methodology

In order to demonstrate John's use of Old Testament images to communicate and encourage holy living among the churches of Asia Minor, as well as later audiences, I will utilize an intertextual approach in my study of John's use of Old Testament texts.[9] I use the term 'approach' because 'intertextuality is not a method'.[10] As a result, this theory provides the lens through which the text is analyzed. Admittedly, the term 'intertextuality' has been used many different ways.[11] In New Testament studies the term refers to little

---

[8] P.L. Redditt, 'History of Prophecy', in M.J. Boda and J.G. McConville (eds.), *Dictionary of the Old Testament Prophets* (Downers Grove: InterVarsity, 2012), p. 587; T.E. Fretheim, 'Repentance in the Former Prophets', in M.J. Boda and G.T. Smith (eds.), *Repentance in Christian Theology* (Collegeville, MN: Liturgical Press, 2006), pp. 25-46 (26).

[9] G. Allen, *Intertextuality* (New York: Routledge, 2000). This work provides a brief introduction to the concept.

[10] S. Moyise, 'Intertextuality and Historical Approaches to the Use of Scripture in the New Testament', *Verbum Ecclesia* 26 (2005), pp. 447-58 (447).

[11] W. Irwin, 'Against Intertextuality', *Philosophy and Literature* 28 (2004), pp. 227-42 (28); S. Moyise, 'Intertextuality and Biblical Studies: A Review', *Verbum Ecclesia* 23 (2002), pp. 418-31. While Irwin asserts the term has 'almost as many meanings as users' (p. 227), Moyise explains that different forms of intertextuality exist, requiring individuals using the term to explain to their readers what they mean by their use of the term or abandon the use of the term.

more than discussions of the use of the Old Testament in the New. Despite this misappropriation of the term, which has caused Julia Kristeva, the person credited with coining the term, to employ an alternative term – transposition,[12] this study will utilize the word with regard to more than a study of John's sources. I seek to examine both the source text and the present text in order to determine what new meaning John assigns to the text used, based on the new context in which he composes the Apocalypse.[13]

According to Kristeva, every text, whether spoken, thought, or written, serves as a mosaic of absorbed and transformed preceding texts and influences.[14] This understanding leads to the idea that John's use of source texts within the writing of Revelation does not mandate that those texts bear only the historical meaning possessed within their ancient contexts.[15] Instead, his use of a text has the ability to function actively and possess meaning, as expressed by John, given the new context in which both John and his audience find themselves.

This study will commence with a brief discussion regarding the state of Israel after the exodus and their initial call to holiness in the Old Testament. Given the explanation above regarding a shift in context providing potential for the creation of new meaning, attention will be given to the historical context of the Apocalypse. After this, I will proceed with analysis of selected texts in order to determine if they function as allusions. Once it has been determined if such allusions exist, both the original text and the text of the Apocalypse will be analyzed. Following this, discussion will commence regarding the relationship between the two texts and how

---

[12] J. Kristeva, *The Revolution in Poetic Language* (trans. Margaret Waller; New York: Columbia University, 1984), pp. 59-60.

[13] E. Van Wolde, 'Trendy Intertextuality', in S. Draisma (ed.), *Intertextuality in Biblical Writings: Essays in Honor of Bas Van Iersel* (Kampen: Kok, 1989), pp. 43-49 (47). Van Wolde explains that writers have the capacity to create meaning, based on the new context in which the author places the text.

[14] J. Kristeva, 'Word, Dialogue and Novel', in *The Kristeva Reader* (New York: Columbia University, 1986), pp. 34-61 (37).

[15] *Contra* W.C. Kaiser, 'The Single Intent of Scripture', in G.K. Beale (ed.), *The Right Doctrine from the Wrong Text?: Essays on the Use of the Old Testament in the New* (Grand Rapids: Baker Academic, 1994), pp. 55-69 (69). *Contra* G.K. Beale, 'Questions of Authorial Intent, Epistemology, and Presuppositions and Their Bearing on the Study of the Old Testament in the New: A Rejoinder to Steve Moyise', *IBS* 21 (1999), pp. 151-80.

John gives new meaning to the Old Testament texts in light of his present and his visionary experiences.

Definition of Terms and Examples

The myriad of discussions regarding the use of the Old Testament in the New Testament have led to the lack of precision when addressing the presence of allusions in in New Testament writings.[16] Based on the work of William Irwin, an allusion is 'a reference that is indirect in the sense that it calls for associations that go beyond mere substitution of a referent'.[17] When he explains that an allusion does not simply substitute referents, he notes that the knowledge of the reader should go beyond the basic information. He adds that in order for an allusion to be accurately understood, 'one must make certain [accurate] associations to assemble correctly the pieces of the allusion puzzle'.[18] Irwin also calls for the intention of the author in presenting the allusion and the possibility of detection by the audiences.[19] Despite Irwin's demand for the intention of the author, it must be admitted that individuals unconsciously allude to texts, phrases, and works, but do not realize they have done so, until others have made them aware of the connection.[20]

Though Irwin provides a good definition for identifying an allusion, he fails to provide much detail regarding what an allusion does, which seems vital to understanding what an allusion is. Stanley Porter explains that an allusion's function 'involves the invoking

---

[16] S.E. Porter, 'The Use of the Old Testament in the New Testament: A Brief Comment on Method and Terminology', in C.A. Evans and J.A. Sanders (eds.), *Early Christian Interpretation of the Scriptures of Israel: Investigations and Proposals* (Sheffield: Sheffield Academic Press, 1997), pp. 79-96 (80-88).

[17] W. Irwin, 'What Is an Allusion?' *JAAC* 59 (2001), pp. 287-97 (293).

[18] Irwin, 'What is an Allusion?', p. 288.

[19] Irwin, 'What is an Allusion?', pp. 293-94. With regard to the possibility of detection by the audience, this work does not assert that this discussion addresses all allusions related to the topic of holiness, but acknowledges that the presentation of allusions is not only limited by space, but also in relation to the knowledge of the author concerning the various works from which the author may have gathered data. In order to aid in accurately identifying allusions and potential sources, I will employ the use of computer-aided searches in order to expand the scope of possible source texts.

[20] S.E. Porter, 'Further Comments on the Use of the Old Testament in the New Testament', in T.L. Brodie *et al.* (eds.), *The Intertextuality of the Epistles: Explorations of Theory and Practice* (NTM 16; Sheffield: Sheffield Phoenix, 2006), pp. 98-110. Porter explains that an allusion may or may not be consciously intentional.

of a person, place or literary work'.[21] As a result, the combination of Irwin's and Porter's explanations provides both the criteria and function of allusions. With this, attention will be given to two types of allusions this essay will explore – verbal allusions and conceptual allusions.

Verbal Allusions

For this study, a verbal allusion may be defined as a reference to a preceding text via the use of distinctive words or phrases that collocate with other terms or concepts that demonstrate a relationship between the two texts.[22] The words and phrases appearing in both texts have the capacity to prompt the discussion of a potential allusion's presence, but the presence of those allusions must be substantiated, especially when there exists the possibility of more than one source text. One such example appears in the relationship between Rev. 1.5 and Psalm 88.

Revelation 1.5 and Psalm 88

Revelation 1.5 presents a manifold description of Jesus Christ. The text notes him as ὁ μάρτυς, ὁ πιστός, ὁ πρωτότοκος τῶν νεκρῶν καὶ ὁ ἄρχων τῶν βασιλέων τῆς γῆς ('the faithful witness, the firstborn of the dead, and the ruler of the kings of the earth'). If searching for the terms πιστός and μάρτυς, one will discover multiple potential referent texts that describe the same entity (Ps. 88.38 LXX; Prov. 14.5; 14.25; Jer. 49.5). Psalm 88 describes the moon as a faithful witness, while the two texts found in Proverbs simply provide general statements regarding faithful witnesses. The Jeremianic text provides information regarding God serving as a faithful witness against the people if they fail to keep the words of the Lord spoken to them. This reference of the text to God makes it a likely referent for the passage.

Further investigation reveals that a search for the term πρωτότοκος also appears in Ps. 88.27. The presence of the term πρωτότοκος in the same psalm as πιστός and μάρτυς lends weight to the idea that John may have been using the psalter as his source. In his analysis of the text, Marko Jauhiainen reminds readers that

---

[21] Porter, 'Further Comments on the Use of the Old Testament', p. 12.
[22] P. Mallen, *The Reading and Transformation of Isaiah in Luke–Acts* (London: T & T Clark, 2008), p. 24.

John refers to ὁ πρωτότοκος τῶν νεκρῶν, a concept with which people in the early church would have been familiar (cf. Col 1.18).[23] Though Jauhiainen makes a noteworthy observation, those analyzing the text should recognize that Ps. 88.27 also contains the term βασιλεύς (a term that also appears in Rev. 1.5), noting κἀγὼ πρωτότοκον θήσομαι αὐτόν, ὑψηλὸν παρὰ τοῖς βασιλεῦσιν τῆς γῆς ('and I will establish him firstborn, highest over the kings of the earth').

The primary difference between the psalm and the Revelation text resides in the difference between the use of the term ὑψηλὸν in the psalm and ἄρχων in Revelation. The relationship between the terms πρωτότοκος and βασιλεύς in the psalm lends weight to the possibility of the psalm, instead of the Jeremainic text, serving as the source for John's text. The distinction between the use of the term ὑψηλὸν in the psalm and John's choice of ἄρχων may find resolution in the foundational concept presented in Psalm 88.

Psalm 88 functions as a scriptural commentary on the unilateral, everlasting nature of the Davidic covenant.[24] Recognizing that God is the one who establishes the kingdom of this ruler (2 Samuel 7), the presentation of Jesus in this manner demonstrates John's recognition of Jesus as the ultimate Davidite who fulfills the expectations of the covenant God made with David.[25] The relationship between the terms πιστός, μάρτυς, πρωτότοκος, and βασιλεύς in Rev. 1.5 and Psalm 88 supports John's appeal to the psalter and provides adequate support for the use of the text.

Though there are words that appear in relation to one another in both passages, signifying a relationship between the texts, verbal allusions can also exist in other ways. In the example above, both the terms used and the referents remain the same (given the understanding of Jesus Christ as the seed of David). At the same time, other allusions exist where verbal parallels exist, but the referents in

---

23 M. Jauhiainen, *The Use of Zechariah in Revelation* (Wissenschaftliche Untersuchungen zum Neuen Testament 199; Tübingen: Mohr Siebeck, 2005), p. 113.

24 M.L. Strauss, *The Davidic Messiah in Luke-Acts: The Promise and Its Fulfillment in Lukan Christology* (JSNTSup 110; Sheffield: Sheffield Academic Press, 1995), p. 97.

25 G.D. Fee, *Revelation* (New Covenant Commentary Series; Eugene: Cascade Books, 2011), pp. 7-8. Cf. Psalm 2.

the texts are different. One such example appears in the relationship between Rev. 2.27 and Ps. 2.9.

Revelation 2.27 and Psalm 2.9

Revelation 2.26-28 provides a promise to the overcomer, a portion of the promise is that ποιμανεῖ αὐτοὺς ἐν ῥάβδῳ σιδηρᾷ ('he shall rule them with a rod of iron', 2.27a). When surveying the texts of the Septuagint and the Greek New Testament in order to find the terms ῥάβδος ('rod') and σιδηροῦς ('iron'), one finds three texts outside of the Apocalypse that contains these terms – all of which occur in the Septuagint (Ps. 2.9; Ps. 17.24; Mic. 4.13). A quick survey of these texts reveals Ps. 2.9 as the source for John's text, as it is the only text that discusses anyone ποιμαίνω ('ruling') others ἐν ῥάβδῳ σιδηρᾷ ('with a rod of iron').

Though the use of exact verbiage here would likely constitute a quotation or paraphrase, this text functions as an indirect reference that presents a change in referent from the promised Davidite, who also functions as the son of God (Ps. 2.7), to all who overcome. This shift in referent reveals that New Testament writers did not always preserve the meaning of the texts from which they drew,[26] though they maintained their foundations in the preceding biblical writings, while they revealed new insights pertaining to those texts.[27] In this context, such a shift appropriates a promise for a Davidite to all who follow Christ.

Recognizing allusions that present verbal parallels, including those with modified referents, the question of texts that invoke a person, place, or literary work, while not maintaining verbal parallels with any identifiable texts, also demands attention. When this happens, I will refer to it as a 'conceptual allusion'. Conceptual allusions are those that convey the same idea as earlier material but do not use the same terms as the source text.[28] It becomes necessary to explore this idea because the establishment of the use of one text by another becomes problematic when the relationship is limited only

---

[26] S. Moyise, 'Respect for Context Once More', *IBS* 27 (2006), pp. 24-31 (25).

[27] M.J. Boda and M.H. Floyd (eds.), *Tradition in Transition: Haggai and Zechariah 1-8 in the Trajectory of Hebrew Theology* (Library of Hebrew Bible 475; New York: T & T Clark, 2008), p. xiii.

[28] K. Kyoung-Shik, *God Will Judge Each One according to Works: Judgment according to Works and Psalm 62 in Early Judaism and the New Testament* (Berlin: Walter de Gruyter, 2010), pp. 36-37.

to verbal parallels.[29] This issue becomes especially apparent when a New Testament author utilizes an Old Testament Hebrew text instead of the Greek,[30] though conceptual allusions can occur even when the written text and its source are in the same language.

Matthew 2.15 and Hosea 11.1

Though not in the context of the Apocalypse, a popular example of this appears in Matthew's quotation of Hosea 11.1.

Hos. 11.1 (MT)	Mt 2.15	Hos. 11.1 (LXX)
מִמִּצְרַיִם קָרָאתִי לִבְנִי	ἐξ Αἰγύπτου ἐκάλεσα τὸν υἱόν μου	ἐξ Αἰγύπτου μετεκάλεσα τὰ τέκνα αὐτοῦ
Out of Egypt I called my son.	Out of Egypt I called my son.	Out of Egypt I called his children.

As becomes more apparent in the translation, the text of Mt. 2.15 more closely parallels the Hebrew text. The greatest difference between the Matthean text and that of Hosea (LXX) appears in the calling of 'my son' and 'his children'.[31] Though a verbal parallel cannot be established across languages, Matthew's reference to Hosea demonstrates the potential for New Testament writers to use the Hebrew Old Testament instead of the Greek Old Testament.

These multiple forms of allusions that have been presented provide a foundation for this study by which we can effectively focus this study on Revelation's allusions to preceding texts. Given the wide array of topics in Revelation, the focus will be placed upon those texts that relate to an understanding of holiness among the people of God.

Revelation in History

Though often sought when studying the Gospels, Acts, and the Epistles, the historical setting of the Apocalypse is often ignored in more popular studies, evidenced by the futuristic ideas regarding the

---

[29] J. Paulien, 'Elusive Allusions: The Problematic Use of the Old Testament in Revelation', *BibRes* 33 (1988), pp. 37-53 (44); M.J. Boda, *Praying the Tradition: The Origin and Use of Tradition in Nehemiah 9* (BZAW 277; Berlin: Walter de Gruyter, 1999), p. 3.

[30] Paulien, 'Elusive Allusions', p. 42.

[31] R.T. France, *The Gospel of Matthew* (NICNT; Eerdmans, 2007), p. 80.

text. When exegetes give attention to its historical setting, the text comes 'to be seen, not as a prophecy of the modern reader's future, but as a response to Roman persecution of Christians near the end of the first century'.[32] Such a statement in no way denies the prophetic nature of the work, but does highlight the prophetic activity of forthtelling – the proclamation of divine communication that calls for a response from the audience.[33] Understanding the nature of the communication and response requires inquiry regarding the dating and historical setting of the Apocalypse. It is in contrast to the context of ancient Israel that the historical setting of Revelation allows us to determine the extent to which John is preserving or creating new meaning in his composition.

Dating of Revelation

With regard to the dating of the book, the earliest external evidence concerning the dating of the Apocalypse comes from Irenaeus. Though he does not refer directly to the writing of the text, he asserts that the visions took place at the end of Domitian's reign,[34] which occurred from 81 to 96 CE. This would place the vision, if not the writing itself, during the mid-90s CE. Though other writings provide alternative dates for the composition of the Apocalypse, R. H. Charles raises doubts regarding their reliability.[35]

The internal evidence for the work primarily revolves around the use of the name 'Babylon'. The destruction of this city appears six times throughout the book (14.8; 16.19; 17.5; 18.2, 10, 21). It seems highly unlikely that the text is referring to the Babylon of the sixth century BCE. When comparing the concept of Babylon in Revelation to the Old Testament, readers will find that oracles concerning Babylon in the Apocalypse maintain a dependence upon Old Tes-

---

[32] A.Y. Collins, *Crisis and Catharsis: The Power of the Apocalypse* (Philadelphia: Westminster, 1984), p. 14. Despite the commendation of those at Pergamum for 'hold[ing] fast to [Christ's] name' during the time at which Antipas was killed, there is no evidence to corroborate the idea of Christian persecution across the Empire.

[33] Beale, *The Book of Revelation*, p. 184; M.L. Strauss, *How to Read the Bible in Changing Times: Understanding and Applying God's Word Today* (Grand Rapids: Baker, 2011), p. 126.

[34] Irenaeus of Lyons, 'Against Heresies', in A. Roberts *et al.* (eds.), *The Ante-Nicene Fathers: The Apostolic Fathers With Justin Martyr and Irenaeus* (Vol. 1; New York: Cosimo, Inc., 2007), 5.30.5.

[35] R.H. Charles, *A Critical and Exegetical Commentary on the Revelation of St. John.* (ICC; Edinburgh: T & T Clark, 1920), I, p. xcii.

tament oracles against the nations, primarily Babylon, 'the symbol of a proud idolatrous empire which flaunts its power at the expense of others and scoffs at the thought of its own downfall or judgment', and Tyre, 'a symbol of international trafficking, opulent wealth and commercial hegemony' – both descriptions of the Roman Empire.[36] In addition to this, the use of Babylon as a designation for Rome was common after 70 CE, given the destruction of the temple occurring at the hands of Rome (just as Babylon had in 587 BCE).[37]

Idolatry and Economics: Threat to the Churches of Asia

With regard to believers in Asia Minor, two issues impacted John's writing: the activity of the imperial cult and the economic pressures associated with the trade guilds.[38] Though the imperial cult may not have been a strong force across the entire empire during the first century CE,[39] 'the repression of persons who would not support this cult' was a reality.[40] Though Jews received exemptions with regard to participation in the imperial cult, the synagogues began to perform the task of determining when Jewish sects no longer functioned as such, causing Christians to be exposed to the requirements placed on non-Jews by the imperial cult.[41]

Like John, many early Christian writers coupled the discussion of idolatry, of which imperial worship is an example, with the topic of economics.[42] Given the large amount of commerce and the activities of the trade guilds in the area, participation in these organizations would prove fiscally beneficial for one's future.[43] The problem with participation in these groups stemmed from the pagan practices associated with them, including the acknowledgement of

---

[36] Fekkes, *Isaiah and Prophetic Traditions*, pp. 86-88; K.H. Jobes, *1 Peter* (Baker Exegetical Commentary on the New Testament; Grand Rapids, MI: Baker Academic, 2005), p. 322.

[37] J.N. Kraybill, *Imperial Cult and Commerce in John's Apocalypse* (JSNTSup 132; Sheffield: Sheffield Academic Press, 1996), p. 33.

[38] D.A. deSilva, 'The Social Setting of the Revelation to John: Conflicts Within, Fears Without', *WTJ* 54 (1992), pp. 273-302 (289).

[39] deSilva, 'Social Setting of the Revelation', p. 289.

[40] T.B. Slater, 'On the Social Setting of the Revelation to John', *New Testament Studies* 44 (1998), pp. 232-56 (238).

[41] deSilva, 'Social Setting of the Revelation', p. 290.

[42] Kraybill, *Imperial Cult and Commerce in John's Apocalypse*, p. 17.

[43] I. Smith, 'The Economics of the Apocalypse: Modelling the Biblical Book of Revelation', *JITE* 155 (1999), pp. 443-57 (449-50).

the guilds' patron deities.[44] For Christians in the empire, fiscal prosperity, as possessed by the Laodiceans (Rev. 3.17a), likely stemmed from compromising with their surrounding culture.[45] Despite the persecution experienced by some Christians, 'the greatest threat was the temptation to compromise with the dominant Roman culture'.[46]

Holiness in the Old Testament

After the deliverance of the Hebrews from the bondage of Egyptian slavery, the Lord calls them to function as a holy nation to him (Exod. 19.6). While the people are at Sinai, they receive the word of the Lord through Moses regarding what it means for them to be holy. As early as Lev. 11.44-45, the Israelites learn that their call to be holy results from the holiness of the one who called them.[47] In addition to the call to holiness, the expectation that they would abide by this calling rests on God's delivering this people. Walter J. Houston asserts that readers should recognize the deliverance as 'a change of masters', instead of freedom.[48] The Israelites then faced the question of what it means to live out the holiness to which they have been called.

The concept of holiness maintains an intrinsic relationship with the idea of separateness and communicates the otherness of God.[49] In the same way, that which is holy serves the purpose of God's use. Therefore, the Israelites recognized that holy people, things, and places were dedicated to the Lord's service. The Israelite understanding of holiness functioned on a cline that covered three categories: holy, clean, and unclean (Lev 10.10).[50] The potential for movement along this cline maintained association with certain activities. Cleansing and sanctifying served as movement toward holi-

---

[44] deSilva, 'Social Setting of the Revelation', p. 291; S.J. Friesen, 'Satan's Throne, Imperial Cults and the Social Settings of Revelation', *JSNT* 27 (2005), pp. 351-73 (369); Smith, 'The Economics of the Apocalypse', pp. 450-51.

[45] J.C. Thomas, *The Apocalypse: A Literary and Theological Commentary* (Cleveland: CPT Press, 2012), p. 190.

[46] Flemming, 'On Earth as It Is in Heaven', p. 344.

[47] W.J. Houston, 'The Character of YHWH and the Ethics of the Old Testament: Is Imitatio Dei Appropriate?' *JTS* 58 (2007), pp. 1-25 (8).

[48] Houston, 'Character of YHWH', p. 10.

[49] M.J. Boda, *A Severe Mercy: Sin and Its Remedy in the Old Testament* (Siphrut, 1; Winona Lake: Eisenbrauns, 2009), p. 51; J.A.D. Weima, '"How You Must Walk to Please God": 1 Thessalonians', in R.N. Longenecker (ed.), *Patterns of Discipleship in the New Testament* (Grand Rapids: Eerdmans, 1996), pp. 98-119 (102).

[50] Boda, *A Severe Mercy*, p. 51.

ness, while profaning and defiling functioned as movement toward
uncleanness. These categories not only existed within an Old Testament context, but also persist in various New Testament writings.

A Kingdom, Priests

The opening chapter of the Apocalypse contains a doxology that
describes both John and his readers. He identifies them as
βασιλείαν, ἱερεῖς ('a kingdom, priests', Rev. 1.6, cf. 5.10). A search
of the LXX and the Greek New Testament reveal that the terms collocate in six verses outside of the Apocalypse, all of which appear in
the LXX. Though the terms βασιλεία and ἱερεύς appear together in
six verses (1 Kgs 2.22; 2.35; 2 Chr. 29.21; 1 Esdr. 8.10; Ezra 7.13;
Neh. 12.22), they do not reflect the idea presented in Rev. 1.6.
Based on this, it would appear that Rev. 1.6 does not function as a
verbal allusion to any texts. As a result, it becomes necessary to
search for conceptual allusions.

The Revelation text uses the terms to refer to the same group. In
addition, the group functions as such in relation to God. These features of the Revelation text serve as the foundation of the conceptual allusion. The only place in the Old Testament where the terms
'kingdom' and 'priests' refer to the same entity is Exod. 19.6.

Exod. 19.6 (MT)	Rev. 1.6	Exod. 19.6 (LXX)
וְאַתֶּם תִּהְיוּ־לִי מַמְלֶכֶת כֹּהֲנִים וְגוֹי קָדוֹשׁ...	καὶ ἐποίησεν ἡμᾶς βασιλείαν, ἱερεῖς τῷ θεῷ καὶ πατρὶ αὐτοῦ	ὑμεῖς δὲ ἔσεσθέ μοι βασίλειον ἱεράτευμα καὶ ἔθνος ἅγιον
And you shall be to me a kingdom of priests and a holy nation...	And he made us a kingdom, priests to his God and father, to him be glory and dominion forever. Amen	And you shall be to me a royal priesthood and a holy nation...

When recognizing this group as a kingdom of priests,[51] one must
recognize that priests were counted as holy unto God (Lev. 21.7).
In the same way that the priests function as mediators on behalf of

---

[51] C.L. Seow, *A Grammar for Biblical Hebrew* (Nashville: Abingdon Press, rev.
edn, 1995), pp. 116-23. The understanding provided results from translating the
Hebrew text with the understanding that מַמְלֶכֶת כֹּהֲנִים serves as an indefinite
construct chain.

the Israelites, the nation of Israel was to function on behalf of the nations.[52]

As can be seen in the chart above, all of the texts note that this group maintains their function in relation to God. The Lord speaks in Exodus 19 with reference to the future, while John speaks with references to God's completed action in Revelation 1. Based on these features, the text reflects the idea appearing in both versions of Exod. 19.6,[53] though John's writing appears to maintain stronger parallels with the construction of the Hebrew text. This text lacks verbal parallel, but its translation presents a conceptual parallel.

In addition to the description of this group as 'kingdom of priests' the Exodus text provides an additional description of the group – ἔθνος ἅγιον ('a holy nation'). Given the presence of this designation in Exodus, it seems likely that both John and his read-ers were familiar with this concept (Acts 15.21),[54] recognizing that as a kingdom of priests they were to function as a holy people. John's elimination of this designation in his writing may have re-sulted from his knowledge that he and his audience were aware of the concept, thus eliminating the need to communicate it explicit-ly,[55] or it may have resulted from the fact that he would later explain that this group of people was comprised of people ἐκ πάσης φυλῆς καὶ γλώσσης καὶ λαοῦ καὶ ἔθνους ('from every tribe and language and people and nation', Rev. 5.9).

---

[52] W.C. Kaiser, *Mission in the Old Testament: Israel as a Light to the Nations* (Grand Rapids: Baker, 2000), p. 23; C.G. Bartholomew, *A Royal Priesthood?: The Use of the Bible Ethically and Politically: A Dialogue with Oliver O'Donovan* (Grand Rapids: Zondervan, 2002), p. 2.

[53] F.L. Fisher, 'New and Greater Exodus: The Exodus Pattern in the New Testament', *Southwestern Journal of Theology* 20 (1977), pp. 69-79 (78); Swete, *Apoca-lypse of St. John*, p. 8; G.R. Osborne, *Revelation* (BECNT; Grand Rapids: Baker Ac-ademic, 2002), pp. 64-65; Flemming, 'On Earth as It Is in Heaven', p. 347; Mounce, *The Book of Revelation*, p. 50; M. Himmelfarb, *The Apocalypse: A Brief Histo-ry* (Malden: Wiley-Blackwell, 2010), pp. 83-84; Beale, *The Book of Revelation*, p. 193. Beale explains that there is some question regarding the rendering of the text in 19.6, with regard to the question of if it should be understood to be 'royal priest-hood' or 'priestly kingdom'. Ultimately, the questions surrounding this bear no major significance, as both renderings provide the understanding the individuals fulfill both a royal and priestly role.

[54] B. Witherington, *Grace in Galatia* (London: Continuum, 2004), p. 20.

[55] N. Fairclough, *Analysing Discourse: Textual Analysis for Social Research* (New York: Routledge, 2003), p. 40.

The Sinai Covenant served as a foundation for the existence of the Old Testament people of God.[56] John's incorporation of the text of Exod. 19.6 into Rev. 1.6 provides believers in Asia Minor with a new perspective on what it means to be the covenant people of God. Jews who had not embraced the idea of Jesus as the Messiah proclaimed that those who were Christians, including Christian Jews, were not really Jewish.[57] The presence of Exod. 19.6 in Revelation's text, addressed to those who believe in Christ, transforms the text for believers. He appropriates the Exodus language and applies it to the new covenant people of God.[58] Given the place of believers as 'a kingdom, priests', he also indicts those who would make such accusations against believers, referring to them as 'a synagogue of Satan' (Rev. 2.9; 3.9).[59] This highlights the idea that those of the 'synagogue of Satan' may retain their place in the synagogue, but they are not truly Jews (cf. Rom. 2.29). Such recognition by the recipients of the Apocalypse would undoubtedly recall the Old Testament mandate of holiness that accompanies the privilege of functioning in a royal and priestly fashion.

Beyond the declaration of this people as a priestly kingdom, John also draws on the concept of the exodus. The legal stipulations discussing the holiness of the people present the deliverance of the people from Egypt as the purpose for their need to obey.[60] Israel's obligation to obedience results from God's act of deliverance.[61] Just as the Old Testament provides this reminder, the Apoc-

---

[56] J.I. Durham, *Exodus* (WBC; Waco, TX: Word Books, 1987), III, p. 262. Durham explains, 'An affirmative response to Yahweh's "if" on the part of the people of Israel will mean the birth of "Israel" as Yahweh's people. Within that affirmative response, indeed, there would have been only "sons of Israel," the descendants of Jacob. With the affirmative response, "Israel," a community of faith transcending biological descendancy, could come into being.'

[57] Collins, *Crisis and Catharsis*, pp. 85-86.

[58] S. Pattemore, *The People of God in the Apocalypse: Discourse, Structure, and Exegesis* (SNTS Monograph Series 128; Cambridge: Cambridge University, 2004), p. 112.

[59] P.L. Mayo, *'Those Who Call Themselves Jews': The Church and Judaism in the Apocalypse of John* (Princeton Theological Monograph Series; Eugene: Pickwick, 2006), p. 53; A.Y. Collins, 'Vilification and Self-Definition in the Book of Revelation', *HTR* 79 (1986), pp. 308-20 (313).

[60] R. Rendtorff, *The Covenant Formula: An Exegetical and Theological Investigation* (London: Continuum, 1998), p. 41.

[61] B. Schramm, 'Exodus 19 and Its Christian Appropriation', in A.O. Bellis and J.S. Kaminsky (eds.), *Jews, Christians, and the Theology of the Hebrew Scriptures* (Atlanta: Society of Biblical Literature, 2000), p. 336.

alypse provides a similar premise, noting that the people have been λύσαντι ἡμᾶς ἐκ τῶν ἁμαρτιῶν ἡμῶν ἐν τῷ αἵματι αὐτοῦ ('loosed from their sins by [Christ's] blood' Rev. 1.5). The text repeats this idea in Rev. 5.9, noting that Christ ἠγόρασας ('purchased') people with his blood, making them his own.

Temple: The Holy Place of Worship

Revelation 11 explains that John receives κάλαμος ὅμοιος ῥάβδῳ ('a measuring rod like a staff', v. 1), with which he is to measure three things – the temple, the altar, and the worshipers. He explains that he was not to measure the outer court of the temple, ὅτι ἐδόθη τοῖς ἔθνεσιν ('for it is given over to the nations', Rev. 11.2). The discussion of measuring the temple leads some scholars to focus their attention on Ezekiel's last vision as the background for this passage.[62]

Though some parallels appear in the concept of measuring, John's receipt of the rod and the instruction to measure stands against Ezekiel observing the measurements taken by another being and reporting them. In addition, Revelation 11, does not reveal whether or not John even measures those things which he is instructed to measure. The difference between these texts seems great enough that Moyise, when describing Rev. 11.1-2, states, 'the function is quite different from Ezek. 40-43'.[63] It would appear most individuals who relate this text to Ezekiel do so because the end of the preceding chapter draws on Ezekiel's text, and the first few verses of chapter 11 continue the call narrative.[64]

Zechariah 2.1-5 has also been presented as a possible Old Testament source for Rev. 11.1-2,[65] asserting that the measuring of the temple serves as protection. Marko Jauhiainen notes the lack of lex-

---

[62] Fekkes, *Isaiah and Prophetic Traditions*, p. 71; Fee, *Revelation*, p. 148; Mounce, *The Book of Revelation*, p. 213; R. Herms, *An Apocalypse for the Church and for the World: The Narrative Function of Universal Language in the Book of Revelation* (BZNW 143; Berlin: Walter de Gruyter, 2006), pp. 39-40.

[63] S. Moyise, *The Old Testament in the Book of Revelation* (JSNTSup 115; Sheffield: Sheffield Academic Press, 1995), p. 78.

[64] D.E. Aune, 'An Intertextual Analysis of the Apocalypse of John', in *Apocalypticism, Prophecy and Magic in Early Christianity: Collected Essays* (Tübingen: Mohr Siebeck, 2006), pp. 120-49 (132); M. den Dulk, 'Measuring the Temple of God: Revelation 11.1-2 and the Destruction of Jerusalem', *New Testament Studies* 54 (2008), pp. 436-49 (440).

[65] Waddell, *The Spirit of the Book of Revelation*, p. 165; R. Bauckham, *The Climax of Prophecy: Studies on the Book of Revelation* (Edinburgh: T. & T. Clark, 1993), p. 269, n. 46.

ical connections between the texts and argues for little support of 'thematic or contextual connectors'.[66] The lack of verbal and conceptual allusions to any specific Old Testament passage leads to the recognition that Rev. 11.1-2 does not utilize any specific text as a source, but likely draws on the general understanding that the temple in Jerusalem was holy.[67] Despite Rev. 11.1-2 functioning as an allusion for this study, John does provide an example by contradiction – the unholy place of Babylon.

Babylon: The Dwelling Place of Demons

Holiness requires separation from the surrounding culture by word and deed (Lev. 18.3).[68] Though practically lived out in slightly different ways, based on social context and culture, the call to be different than the surrounding culture continues for New Testament believers (1 Pet. 1.14-16). As seen in the Old Testament, God calls his people to be separate from those around them (Num. 16.23-24; Isa. 48.20, 52.11; Jer. 27.8; Zech. 2.10-11 LXX). Revelation 18.4-8 provides that same kind of call for God's people in the Empire. Revelation 18 consists of a conflation of allusions with the Old Testament writings of Isaiah and Jeremiah,[69] all of which present the downfall of ancient Babylon.[70] Such recognition of the use of multiple texts and images reflects the practice of ancient Israelite prophets;[71] it does not require a reader acknowledge only one source when the text demands otherwise of a passage.[72] The table below highlights John's use of Old Testament sources.

Concept	MT	Revelation	LXX
Declaration of Babylon's Fall	Isa. 21.9	Rev. 18.2	Isa. 21.9
The Call to Separate from Babylon	Jer. 51.45	Rev. 18.4	----------

---

[66] Jauhiainen, *The Use of Zechariah*, p. 68.

[67] Dulk, 'Measuring the Temple of God', p. 441. The author goes so far as to assert that 'the presence of the temple' itself makes the hallows the holy city.

[68] N. Koltun-Fromm, *Hermeneutics of Holiness: Ancient Jewish and Christian Notions of Sexuality and Religious Community* (New York: Oxford University, 2010), p. 46.

[69] Fekkes, *Isaiah and Prophetic Traditions*, p. 87.

[70] Fekkes, *Isaiah and Prophetic Traditions*, p. 87.

[71] M.J. Boda, 'Hoy, Hoy: The Prophetic Origins of the Babylonian Tradition in Zechariah 2:10-17', in Boda and Floyd (eds.), *Tradition in Transition*, p. 180.

[72] Waddell, *The Spirit of the Book of Revelation*, pp. 165-66.

The Severity of Babylon's Sin	Jer. 51.9	Rev. 18.5	Jer. 28.9
Repayment for Deeds	Jer. 50.29	Rev. 18.6	Jer. 50.29
Boasting of Babylon	Isa. 47.8	Rev. 18.7	Isa. 47.8
Consummation of Judgment	Isa. 47.9	Rev. 18.8	Isa. 47.9

Comparison of Revelation's text with that of the Hebrew Bible and the Greek Old Testament reveal the Hebrew Bible as the most likely source for his allusions. One significant example of this appears in Rev. 18.2. This text explicitly uses the term πίπτω ('to fall') and Βαβυλών ('Babylon') in collocation. The Septuagint contains only two passages where these terms collocate and discuss the fall of Babylon (Isa. 21.9; Jer. 28.8 LXX).

Isa. 21.9 (MT)	Rev. 18.2	Isa. 21.9 (LXX)
נָפְלָה נָפְלָה בָּבֶל	Ἔπεσεν ἔπεσεν Βαβυλὼν ἡ μεγάλη	Πέπτωκεν Βαβυλών

The Revelation text contains a unique feature in which the term πίπτω appears in repetition. The Septuagint does not contain this feature when speaking of Babylon's fall, but the Hebrew Bible does (Isa. 21.9). Though written in different languages, John's vocabulary in Rev. 18.2 parallels the Hebrew Bible more than the Greek Old Testament,[73] constituting a conceptual parallel.

Understanding that John uses the Hebrew Bible as his source when writing Rev. 18.2, allows for the possibility of Rev. 18.4 alluding to Jer. 51.45, a text that does not appear in the Septuagint.

Jer. 51.45 (MT)	Rev. 18.4
צְאוּ מִתּוֹכָהּ עַמִּי	Ἐξέλθατε ὁ λαός μου ἐξ αὐτῆς

Just as the term ἐξέρχομαι means to go/come out, יצא, the term appearing in the Hebrew text, can have the same meaning.[74] Furthermore, the third person singular feminine suffix הָ corresponds to the αὐτῆς of Rev. 18.4. When analyzing both of these texts, it seems most likely, that John provides a likely translation of Jer. 51.45.

---

[73] D.E. Aune, *Revelation 17-22* (Dallas: Word Books, 1997), 52c, p. 985. Despite the 'literal rendering of the Hebrew', Aune asserts John's use of an alternate Greek source that contains the double use of the verb.

[74] W.L. Holladay and L. Köhler, *A Concise Hebrew and Aramaic Lexicon of the Old Testament* (Grand Rapids: Eerdmans, 1971), p. 139.

Besides the conceptual allusions that have been established, readers will find that John's description of the city alludes to Old Testament descriptions of things that are unholy. Babylon is a place for demons and the unclean. Since the holy and unholy must not come into contact with each other, Babylon must therefore be an unholy city. For this reason, God calls his people – his holy people – to come out of the city.

When comparing the text of Revelation to the Old Testament texts from which John collects material, an issue that must be addressed is whether the call to 'come out' functions literally or figuratively. In the Old Testament, the call to holiness and separation functioned as both physical and spiritual.[75] Within a New Testament context, believers are called to live separately from those around them, while living in the midst of non-Christian cultures. If Rome was considered the known world to Paul's listeners, John's recipients would have nowhere to which to go in the process of fleeing Rome. At the same time, the possibility of a literal separation of believers from the Empire should not be completely ignored.[76] Despite the lack of clarity as to whether or not John creates new meaning regarding the people of God physically separating from the surrounding culture, analysis does reveal that John appropriates Old Testament language of destruction for the Roman Empire, noting they function as ancient Babylon.

Holy Presence
Just as God serves as the ultimate origin of his people's holiness, it also finds reward in him. As the Apocalypse comes to a close, John centers his attention on God's holy presence among his people.[77] Revelation 21.3 presents a voice from the throne proclaiming, Ἰδοὺ ἡ σκηνὴ τοῦ θεοῦ μετὰ τῶν ἀνθρώπων, καὶ σκηνώσει μετ᾽ αὐτῶν, καὶ αὐτοὶ λαοὶ αὐτοῦ ἔσονται, καὶ αὐτὸς ὁ θεὸς μετ᾽ αὐτῶν ἔσται [αὐτῶν θεός] ('behold, the tabernacle of God is with humanity, and he shall dwell with them, and they shall be his people, and God himself shall be with them their God'). The term σκηνόω ('to dwell') finds rare use in the New Testament, appearing a total of

[75] C. Simone *et al.* (eds), 'The Jewish Tradition and Civil Society', in *Alternative Conceptions of Civil Society* (Princeton: Princeton University, 2002), pp. 151-71 (158).
[76] Thomas, *Apocalypse*, p. 525.
[77] Fekkes, *Isaiah and Prophetic Traditions*, p. 170.

five times in the Johannine corpus. One becomes immediately aware of the lack of verbal parallel, given the occurrence of the term only once in the LXX (Gen. 13.12). This requires that conceptual parallels be considered.

When examining the LXX for the idea of God dwelling among his people, two passages come to the fore – Ezek. 37.27 and Zech. 2.14-15. Analysis reveals that John conflates these two sources.

Ezek. 37.27 (LXX)	Rev. 21.3	Zech. 2.14-15 (LXX)
καὶ ἔσται ἡ κατασκήνωσίς μου ἐν αὐτοῖς, καὶ ἔσομαι αὐτοῖς θεός, καὶ αὐτοί μου ἔσονται λαός.	καὶ ἤκουσα φωνῆς μεγάλης ἐκ τοῦ θρόνου λεγούσης, ᾿Ιδοὺ ἡ σκηνὴ τοῦ θεοῦ μετὰ τῶν ἀνθρώπων, καὶ σκηνώσει μετ αὐτῶν, καὶ αὐτοὶ λαοὶ αὐτοῦ ἔσονται, καὶ αὐτὸς ὁ θεὸς μετ αὐτῶν ἔσται [αὐτῶν θεός]	τέρπου καὶ εὐφραίνου, θύγατερ Σιων, διότι ἰδοὺ ἐγὼ ἔρχομαι καὶ κατασκηνώσω ἐν μέσῳ σου, λέγει κύριος. καὶ καταφεύξονται ἔθνη πολλὰ ἐπὶ τὸν κύριον ἐν τῇ ἡμέρᾳ ἐκείνῃ καὶ ἔσονται αὐτῷ εἰς λαὸν καὶ κατασκηνώσουσιν ἐν μέσῳ σου, καὶ ἐπιγνώσῃ ὅτι κύριος παντοκράτωρ ἐξαπέσταλκέν με πρὸς σέ

Although the texts do present the idea of God dwelling among his people, it is important to note that John uses the term σκηνὴ instead of Ezekiel's κατασκήνωσίς; he also uses σκηνόω instead of Zechariah's κατασκηνόω.

Once again, John utilizes Scriptural materials and appropriates them for a different group than did his Old Testament predecessors. The Ezekielic and Zecharianic writings note that God will dwell among the people of Israel (Ezek. 37.21-22; Zech. 2.14), while John universalizes this group among which God will dwell by identifying them as λαοὶ ('peoples').[78] John's use of the term reflects the prophecy of Zechariah where he continues by noting many nations taking refuge in the Lord and being his people (Zech. 2.15, LXX). This supports the idea of John communicating that 'the nations are not just spectators but are fully part of the city' where God dwells with his people.[79]

With regard to the holiness of this group that experiences God's divine presence, Ezekiel functions as a backdrop for this discussion. Ezekiel 37.28 (LXX) notes God as the one who makes this people holy when his holiness is among them forever. John explains that the dwelling place of God is with humanity in the holy city. When describing the city in detail, he notes the impossibility of anything unclean or those who perform detestable acts entering into the presence of that which is holy (Rev. 21.27). The background of Ezek. 27.28 also reminds the recipients of the Apocalypse that the holiness they have results from God making them holy.

Conclusion

This study has evaluated a topic that has received little attention in Revelation studies – holiness. I have contended that John utilizes Old Testament images that discuss holiness in order to urge his recipients to live a holy life within their present context of their present situation. Though many presentations of holiness appear in the Apocalypse, I have focused on three specific topics: people, places, and God's presence. Though the text of Revelation presents these ideas by contrast to that which is being encouraged, audiences of the Apocalypse – past, present, and future – the rewards and punishment associated with behavior should continually urge God's people to live holy lives.

---

[78] D. Mathewson, *A New Heaven and a New Earth: The Meaning and Function of the Old Testament in Revelation 21.1-22.5* (JSNTSup 238; London: Sheffield Academic Press, 2003), p. 48.

[79] Moyise, *Old Testament in the Book of Revelation*, p. 82.

6

HAVE WE BEEN SANCTIFIED?: RENEWING THE ROLE OF EXPERIENCE IN INTERPRETING THE BIBLICAL TEXT

SCOTT A. ELLINGTON[*]

Baffled and Bemused

I remember just sitting there, reading the same line over and over again and feeling just a bit dim witted. How many were 'sanctified'? This was my very first Monthly Minister's Report as a newly minted Exhorter in the Church of God and I wanted to get it right. I knew what it meant to be saved, to be filled with the Holy Ghost, and to be added to the church, but how was I to figure out how many people I'd seen 'sanctified' during the preceding month. I knew about Wesley's experience of being 'perfected in love'. I knew that some early Pentecostals shared a kinship with Methodists and that my own church held it to be the second of three distinct works of grace. But what did 'being sanctified' look like? I'd experienced a dramatic rededication to faith after a turbulent time of backsliding in my own life and also knew what it was to hear a call of God to missionary service. I'd been exhorted to holiness many times growing up in the church and had had many experiences of God, but to the best of my knowledge I'd never seen anyone sanctified.

So I asked older and more experienced ministers for help, but that simply added to my uncertainty. They could direct me to scriptures that call us to holiness, could talk about experiences of victory over sin, and could point to the Church's Doctrinal Commitments

* Scott Ellington (PhD, University of Sheffield) is Professor of Christian Ministries at Emmanuel College in Franklin Springs, GA.

where I read that we believe in 'sanctification subsequent to justification'. Some, though not all, could testify to a personal experience of sanctification, but none were able to offer a particularly clear description of the experience or practical advice on how to know it when I saw it.

In considering the future of holiness in the Pentecostal movement for this present study, then, I looked forward finally to exploring the breadth and depth of Pentecostal scholarship on the subject and silencing at last the niggling suspicion that I was being asked to affirm something that was no longer universally witnessed to in my church and that I had not experienced myself. But if I expected an epiphany, I was destined for only partial gratification.[1] Contemporary biblical studies on holiness and sanctification, particularly in Pentecostal circles, are scarce on the ground.

First of all, asking about holiness from the perspective of biblical scholarship is itself a vexed inquiry. That God is holy, that we are called to holiness, that we are called saints, and that we are to progress in sanctification are all affirmed in Scripture. Anglican scholar David Peterson rightly points out that 'First and foremost, holiness in Scripture is a description of God and his character',[2] so that what we can say about sanctification derives from what we are able to say about God. But less apparent is the idea that, like Holy Spirit baptism, the Wesleyan understanding of sanctification is a momentary experience that we first have and then seek to understand through our study of Scripture. Baptism in the Holy Spirit as an event distinct from regeneration is attested to in the book of Acts, while sanctification, which is a frequent topic particularly in Paul's writings, is not so obviously marked out as a crisis event. The doctrine of sanctification as a pivotal experience and a distinct work of grace, more fully than that of Holy Spirit baptism, rests first and foremost

---

[1] A number of studies by Pentecostals emerged approximately 25 years ago, including Stanley M. Burgess (ed.), *Reaching Beyond: Chapters in the History of Perfectionism* (Peabody: Hendrickson, 1986); Stanley M. Horton, 'The Pentecostal Perspective', in Stanley N. Gundry (ed.), *Five Views of Sanctification* (Grand Rapids: Academie Books, 1987), pp. 103-35; and Russell P. Spittler, 'The Pentecostal View', in Donald L. Alexander (ed.), *Christian Spirituality: Five Views of Sanctification* (Downers Grove, IL: InterVarsity Press, 1988), pp. 133-70; but scholarly production has been more sparse since then.

[2] David Peterson, *Possessed by God: A New Testament Theology of Sanctification and Holiness* (Grand Rapids: Eerdmans), 1995, p. 18.

on experience and only derivatively are biblical arguments sought to underpin it.

Secondly, when we consider the importance of holiness in the life of the believer and the need to grow in its appropriation we might expect an extensive body of research on the subject, but in fact the list of Pentecostal scholars currently exploring that essential aspect of our life in Christ is short indeed. And small comfort can be drawn from the realization that Pentecostals are not alone in this neglect. David Peterson opens his own study of holiness in the New Testament by echoing J.I. Packer's assertion that holiness is a 'neglected priority' in the wider church and a 'faded glory' among Evangelicals. Peterson points out,

> Very little attention is given to the subject in academic circles. Popular studies appear from time to time, but these often lack biblical insight and theological depth. Serious teaching about the theme is rarely heard in our churches. Meanwhile, much of our contemporary church life seems superficial, self-indulgent and compromised.[3]

The company of biblical scholars engaging issues of holiness and sanctification is particularly select and the conclave of Pentecostal biblical scholars who have taken up discussion of these crucial doctrines as we move into a postmodern ethos is positively intimate.

Silence on the topic of holiness and the Holy Spirit's role in bringing it to full harvest in the life of each believer, though, comes at a bad time. As the last vestiges of cultural Christianity begin to dissipate in the West and an individualistic syncretism of the heart becomes for many the greater moral good, we need with renewed energy and hunger to pursue Spirit-led holy lives.

In the discussion that follows I will consider the interplay of experience and biblical text that has always stirred Pentecostal reflections of Christian living. I will then consider the work of Pentecostal biblical scholars in the areas of the need to extend the conversation beyond traditional Wesleyan and Finished Work roots, the community nature of sanctification and the value of exploring Old Testament concepts of holiness more extensively.

---

[3] Peterson, *Possessed by God*, p. 11.

Pinning Down Experience

Pentecostal conversations about holiness and sanctification have been largely shaped by our Wesleyan inheritance, as that bequest was both uncritically adopted by some and largely set aside by others. Two related issues were introduced into Pentecostal language through the Wesleyan-Holiness branch of the family, holding onto the doctrine of sanctification as a *second distinct work of grace* and identifying *entire sanctification* with that work as something that can be experienced fully by every believer in this life.

Almost from its inception, Pentecostals could not agree on the relationship between the experiences of sanctification and empowering for service as distinct works of the Spirit. As the baptism in the Holy Spirit with the evidence of new tongues took center stage defining the movement, some sought to hold onto the crisis experience of sanctification which for many paved the way for the crisis experience of Spirit baptism, so that Spirit baptism added a third rung in the ladder of Christian ascent. For others, though, sanctification as a separate, unique occurrence proved to be only a temporary steppingstone, the need for which subsided with the newer, fuller experience of Holy Spirit baptism. Now that the Day of Pentecost had fully come, immediate sanctification could best be subsumed back into the finished work of Christ's regeneration. The first notable controversy in Pentecostalism, then, was over the theological fate of a transformative experience of holiness.

The need to discuss the Finished Work vs. Second Work of Grace debate that divided nascent Pentecostalism in the exploration of the biblical roots of holiness rests in the experiential emphasis that anchors so much of both biblical and theological reflection for Pentecostals, just as it did for our Wesleyan cousins before us. Our hermeneutic leans heavily on what we experience. John Wesley's experience of a heart strangely warmed is the result not of biblical study and theological reflection reaching for experience, but rather of first encountering God and then of reading the text with new eyes.[4] Without the experience of encounter and transformation, it is

---

[4] Melvin Dieter points out that while Wesley was convinced of the need for holiness long before his Aldergate experience, but that experience altered fundamentally his thinking. 'Only after his own experience of personal faith in Christ, in what is now know as his "Aldersgate experience," did he see that one's relationship with God was established by the merit of Christ rather than the merit of

hard to conceive either of Wesley formulating a doctrine of crisis perfection in love or of early Pentecostals adopting it in describing their own experiences of Spirit encounter. Holiness is to be experienced and appropriated, not merely understood.

For Pentecostals, though, questions about immediate sanctification as a second work of grace were present from the very beginning. Stanley Horton expresses the twin stumbling blocks of insufficient biblical warrant and inconsistent testimony to experience eloquently.

> The early Pentecostals continued to teach sanctification as a second definite work of grace, believing that the baptism in the Holy Spirit represented a third experience. Many, however, especially among those of Baptist or Reformed background, had scriptural questions about this teaching. Many others, like my mother, could not distinguish a second definite work in their own experience.[5]

Finished Work Pentecostal and many Evangelical[6] scholars alike have identified the crisis element of sanctification with conversion. But while a variety of texts affirm a *positional* sanctification at the time of new birth, there has been little attempt to identify an *experiential* element of sanctification in conjunction with regeneration. This merging of sanctification as a crisis experience with that of regeneration, though, fails to create adequate space for the experiential element of the Spirit. Here, I think, is the principal loss resulting from a strict Finished Work perspective, the setting aside of any expectancy that the Spirit might routinely offer a pivotal sanctifying experience to punctuate her[7] ongoing work of sanctification in the life of believers. But are our choices, I wonder, reduced to either

---

personal good works'. Melvin Dieter, 'The Wesleyan Perspective', in Gundry (ed.), *Five Views of Sanctification*, p. 20.

[5] Stanley M. Horton, 'The Pentecostal Perspective', in Gundry (ed.), *Five Views of Sanctification*, pp. 103-135 (107).

[6] Gordon Fee, *God's Empowering Presence: The Holy Spirit in the Letters of Paul* (Peabody: Hendrickson, 1994), p. 79; and Peterson, *Possessed by God*, 1995.

[7] The English language is impoverished by it inability to offer a personal pronoun that is both relational and not tied to a specific gender. While referring to the Spirit with the feminine personal pronounce is far from an adequate solution to that problem, it reflects my attempt both to acknowledge that God cannot be described by a single gender and that references to God should continually press for personal expression.

holding to a Second Work experience to which many Pentecostals today cannot attest or abandoning focused experience altogether? And is our experience of the role of the Spirit in our sanctification to be limited to process rather than crisis, a steady strengthening, but never a consuming fire? Can Pentecostals affirm one or more crisis experiences of sanctification, subsequent to regeneration, without adopting a Second Works theology as its foundation?

Writing on the Wesleyan understanding of sanctification, Melvin Dieter has credited American revivalism with creating an inappropriate emphasis on the crisis element of sanctification that does not reflect Wesley's view of what Dieter calls the 'process-crisis-process continuum' understanding of sanctification.

> Revival preaching emphasized immediate and definable turning points in personal experience as essential to the Christian's life. Holiness preaching clustered the elements of Wesley's teaching on sanctification around the second crisis of faith, subsequent to justification, commonly called *entire sanctification*.[8]

In particular, Dieter maintains, Phoebe Palmer's stress on the immediate acquisition of full sanctification departs from Wesley's own view.

> It is obvious in her [Palmer's] message that the 'moment' of revivalist appeal, the immediacy of response anticipated (lest the hearer demonstrate unbelief and fall into condemnation by delay), and the entire cleansing in the moment of total consecration all tended to shift the point away from the balance that Wesley had maintained.[9]

Crisis experience, Dieter argues, is only a single element in something larger. It punctuates a lifelong process rather than defining a spiritual state.

> Entire sanctification for Wesley was the moment of the believer's perfection in love, but only in a qualitative sense. Quantitatively, the lure of divine love was so immeasurable that the lifestyle of the sanctified believer was always that of a pilgrim and not that of a settler. There was no stopping place in the constant

---

[8] Dieter, 'The Wesleyan Perspective', p. 38.
[9] Dieter, 'The Wesleyan Perspective', p. 40.

quest for personal spiritual growth and witness in love – in relationship with God and others.[10]

Dieter's critique suggests that an unbalanced view, rather than establishing a doctrine of experiential, crisis sanctification more firmly, in fact made it more vulnerable to being minimized or dismissed altogether. The process-crisis-process model of Wesley has become a regeneration-process-parousia understanding with no room for sanctification to be experienced as a definitive, free standing event this side of heaven.

But Dieter's corrective also suggests that a sharp polarization between sanctification as a single event and as an essentially undifferentiated process is perhaps too stark. If we can speak of a baptism of the Spirit with subsequent fillings, should our understanding of our experience of sanctification be limited to a single conspicuous pinnacle encounter and a largely featureless landscape coloring the remainder of our spiritual pilgrimage? What would be the equivalent of subsequent fillings when speaking of sanctification? If the empowering Spirit is active throughout the life of the believer in both crisis and process, why should that not be the case for the sanctifying Spirit? Perhaps these questions are linked to a diminished emphasis on the role of the Spirit in sanctification by Pentecostals.

Ralph Del Colle points to two trends within classic Pentecostalism that have led to a less direct association of the Spirit with sanctification. First, the shift of Holy Spirit baptism language that developed within the Wesleyan-Holiness tradition to describe the experience of enduement with power and the evidence of tongues meant a diminished, though still acknowledged role of the Spirit in the second experience of grace, sanctification.[11] Secondly, the Finished Work doctrine that tied sanctification to regeneration meant that the former became a more Christologically than pneumatologically

---

[10] Dieter, 'The Wesleyan Perspective', p. 41.

[11] The identification of a crisis experience of sanctification with New Testament references to the baptism in the Spirit are found, for example, in Donald S. Metz, *Studies in Biblical Holiness* (Kansas City: Beacon Hill Press, 1971), pp. 111-21 and Alex R.G. Deasley, 'Entire Sanctification and the Baptism with the Holy Spirit: Perspectives on the Biblical View of the Relationship', *Wesleyan Theological Journal* 14.1 (Spring 1979), pp. 27-44.

centered event.[12] So, for example, Lyle Story notes, 'It is interesting that in the International Pentecostal-Holiness Church, their Doctrinal Amplification contains a section on the Holy Spirit, with no mention made of the role of the Spirit in sanctification' and that in the Assemblies of God's 16 truths, 'Sanctification is one of the 16 truths, but is expressed as separation from evil, life of holiness, power for becoming holy, with identification with the death and resurrection of Christ', with no direct mention of the role of the Spirit.[13] Del Colle argues that personal transformation and Christian mission are inseparable, so that sanctification must be understood as a principal activity of the Spirit that cannot be limited to her role in regeneration. 'In this respect', says Del Colle, 'there is some wisdom in the older Wesleyan-Holiness doctrine that Spirit-baptism includes both sanctification and enduement with power'.[14] In insisting on the legitimacy of the experience of Spirit Baptism as more than just an experience of Christian perfection, have Pentecostals perhaps gone too far, disassociating the experience of sanctification for the empowering of the Spirit that brings about holiness in our lives? The transformative aspect of regeneration does not and should not close the door to the subsequent crisis experiences of transformative power affected by the Spirit. And if sanctification is not simply the poor cousin of power baptism in the family of the Spirit's activity in our lives, it is both undesirable and unwise to deny the potential for and aptness of ongoing experiences of Christian perfection, including a continued association of sanctification with Holy Spirit baptism. And just as crisis experiences of the Spirit are described as both initial baptism and subsequent fillings, it is, I suggest, neither necessary nor possible to limit crisis encounters with the sanctifying Spirit to a single event. Put differently, a crisis experience of sanctification need not preclude subsequent experiences, nor need it be qualitatively different existentially from that initial experience.

---

[12] Ralph Del Colle, 'The Pursuit Of Holiness: A Roman Catholic-Pentecostal Dialogue', *Journal of Ecumenical Studies*, 37.3-4 (Summer-Fall 2000), pp. 301-20 (306-307).

[13] J. Lyle Story, 'Pauline Thoughts about the Holy Spirit and Sanctification: Provision, Process, and Consummation' *Journal of Pentecostal Theology* 18 (2009), pp. 67-94 (75).

[14] Del Colle, 'The Pursuit Of Holiness', pp. 315-16.

Closely tied to the exploration of sanctification as crisis experience is that of entire sanctification. The tension here is between a positional and actualized understanding in which entire sanctification is seen either as something established positionally at regeneration or as a goal to which we move, but which is fully actualized only in the *parousia*. Moving away from a Second Works understanding of sanctification has all too often meant a retreat from engaging an experience of entire sanctification as well. Stanley Horton, for example, notes the dropping of 'entire' for the Assemblies of God language about sanctification in its 1961 assembly. To the extent that entire sanctification language is still used by Assemblies writers, says Horton, it refers to one of three understandings, to believers 'living up to the light that they have', to the reality that, though we continue to sin, through the Spirit we are now enabled not to do so,[15] and to the transformation that awaits us at Christ's return.[16] Story identifying entire sanctification with the third of these, points out;

> God's provision of sanctification is inextricably bound up with the divine commitment and engagement with the human process of bringing sanctification to consummation at the time of the Parousia … The human response belongs to the process wherein imperatives and exhortations follow on the heels of statements of divine provision, which also look to completion at the Parousia.[17]

Story's focus in this life is on initiation and process, not completion. So, for example, he notes that 'Other passages, which contain biographical material, reveal Paul's awareness of his own divided self (Romans 7; Phil. 1.6; 2.12-18; 3.12-15). Paul is ever aware that he

---

[15] Dieter identifies this second view with Wesley's own understanding; sanctified Christians 'would never be free from the *possibility* of deliberate, willful sinning in this life. They could, however, be delivered from the *necessity* of voluntary transgression' ('The Wesleyan Perspective', p. 14). But this understanding suggests that the power of sin is not broken at regeneration, so that Christians continue to live of necessity as slaves to sin even after a salvation experience. Were that the case, there could be no process preceding the crisis experience of sanctification and no liberty from sin for those Christians who had not experienced a transformation to holiness.

[16] Horton, 'The Pentecostal Perspective', pp. 123-25.

[17] Story, 'Pauline Thoughts about the Holy Spirit and Sanctification', p. 69.

has not attained complete sanctification'[18] Entire sanctification for Story is something toward which we move and which has been isolated from our ongoing experiences of the Spirit.

In Search of Lost Community

One of the more extensive studies of holiness undertaken in recent years by a Pentecostal biblical scholar has been offered by J. Ayodeji Adewuya. He acknowledges both the crisis and process aspects of sanctification, linking the former with the conversion experience rather than with a distinct second work of grace or with the *parousia*.

> Two inferences may be drawn from this study. First, although conversion is a genuinely sanctifying divine work, as initial sanctification, it is only the beginning. Second, if lives of holiness were the inevitable result of Christian conversion, much of Paul's writings would not only be unintelligible but also superfluous. Overall, Paul presents holiness both as momentary and progressive.[19]

In his study of sanctification language in Romans 8 he also draws a clear distinction between the crisis aspect of sanctification and the experience of Holy Spirit baptism. Rather than develop a supporting line of reasoning for this differentiation, though, he is content with an argument from silence.

> Two important conclusions emerge from this short study. First, there is nothing in the passage that suggests that the believer, because of his or her experience of sanctification, no longer needs to 'receive the Holy Spirit'. The second conclusion logically follows from the preceding. Sanctification is not to be confused with the baptism with the Holy Spirit.[20]

Since the first conclusion is implied from what the passage doesn't say about baptism rather than from demonstrating what it does and the second is drawn from the first, Adewuya's inferences are tenuous at best. His argument, of course, is in service of not also col-

---

[18] Story, 'Pauline Thoughts about the Holy Spirit and Sanctification', p. 91.
[19] J. Ayodeji Adewuya, *Transformed by Grace: Paul's View of Holiness in Romans 6-8* (Eugene, Oregon: Cascade Books, 2004), p. 99.
[20] J. Ayodeji Adewuya, 'The Holy Spirit and Sanctification in Romans 8.1-17', *Journal of Pentecostal Theology* 18 (2001), pp. 71-84 (84).

lapsing Spirit baptism into the regeneration experience, but the result is both a de-emphasizing of the experiential aspect of the momentary element of sanctification and a dissociating of it from the baptizing work of the Spirit. Here again the close identification of momentary sanctification with regeneration and its being somewhat eclipsed by receiving the Holy Spirit has served to sideline the experiential aspect of sanctification.

Having downplayed the crisis element of sanctification, Adewuya nonetheless argues for the need to revitalize our teaching of the prospect of entire sanctification, that is, true freedom from sin in this life, though he discusses this in terms of process rather than crisis. Drawing on the 'slavery' language of Romans 8, Adewuya's denies the possibility of both being in Christ and remaining in sin: 'Paul uses the slavery metaphor to show the absurdity of a believer's remaining under the control of sin'.[21] He acknowledges both divine action and human effort in the ongoing process of sanctification and, though he stops short of speculating on the state of grace of a believer who does not actively pursue holiness, he makes it clear that the sanctification of the believer is both possible and essential. He looks at Romans 6-8 as a unit and uses a contextual argument to insist that Paul's confession of warring natures within him in 7.13-25 refers not to his current state as believer, but rather to his unregenerate life when he was still a slave to sin. Thus Adewuya champions a notion of entire sanctification in the life of the believer based on freedom from slavery to sin, though he does not explore fully the tension between the reality of that freedom and the struggle that Christians experience as they try to live in it.

Most intriguing, though, is Adewuya's exploration of the corporate nature of sanctification. In his study of 2 Cor. 6.14–7.1, he focuses on the 'my people' language, seeing in its use an allusion to the covenant community of the Old Testament. He draws a series of parallels between 2 Corinthians and the Holiness Code summarized in Leviticus to undergird his argument. 'These points of contact are to be seen in Lev. 19, (Lev. 19:19 = 2 Cor. 6:14) a chapter that emphasizes social conduct, and in the sermonic conclusion to

---

[21] Adewuya, *Transformed by Grace*, p. 19.

the HC, (Leviticus 26), (Lev. 26:11-2 = 2 Cor. 6:16)'.[22] Adewuya finds in Corinthians generally a series of metaphors that highlight the corporate nature of the church.

> The web of metaphors that Paul weaves in the Corinthian corre-
> spondence is remarkable. The metaphors, both rich and varied,
> reinforce a corporate or communal vision of the church. Among
> these are: 'the temple of God,' (1 Cor. 3:16-17; 6:19; 2 Cor. 6:16),
> 'the body of Christ' (1 Cor. 12:4-31), 'bride of Christ' (2 Cor.
> 11:2), metaphors which are of significant relevance to the under-
> standing and articulation of the nature of the Christian commu-
> nity and the task of Christian living – communal holiness or cor-
> porate sanctification.[23]

Hannah Harrington has pointed out that the understanding of the people of God coming to represent and take the place of the temple of God is not unique to Christian writers, but is also found in the Qumran community. 'The idea that a community of believers could replace the Temple Service', she asserts, 'was already put forward by the Jews of Qumran, largely a community of ex-priests who had rejected the Jerusalem Temple in its corrupt state'.[24]

Adewuya argues that holiness is essentially relational in nature. He writes, 'However, my contention is that relationship should be treated as an element in sanctification. The relationship of believers to others is so inextricably bound with their relationship with God that they cannot be separated (Cf. 2 Cor. 6:14-18)'.[25] Lyle Story echoes this conviction, connecting the corporate nature of the people of God with the two-fold command that defines the nature and function of the Spirit-formed and sustained community.

> True holiness is found within the sphere of Christ's body and is
> to be channeled through that body. Holiness is lived out in the
> context of the dual love-commandments: love for God and love
> of the neighbor, which naturally cohere as one commandment.

[22] J. Ayodeji Adewuya, *Holiness and Community in 2 Cor 6:14 – 7:1: Paul's View of Communal Holiness in the Corinthian Correspondence* (New York: Peter Lang, 2003) p. 92.

[23] Adewuya, *Holiness and Community*, pp. 171-172.

[24] Hannah Harrington, *Holiness: Rabbinic Judaism and the Graeco-Roman World* (London: Routledge, 2001) p. 58.

[25] Adewuya, *Holiness and Community*, p. 188.

Through a faith-union experience with Christ, one is incorporated into the Body of Christ; this is the sphere of the Spirit wherein holiness as love is expressed.[26]

While Adewuya's and Story's models affirm the centrality of community in both Old and New Testament, it should be pointed out that they remain somewhat in tension with Pentecostalism's North American heritage that, in many contexts, affirms individualism. Russell Spittler remarks of the somewhat uncomfortable truth of this reality.

> Though it may seem awkward to identify individual experience as a dimension of spirituality, the spirituality of Pentecostalism cannot be grasped without comprehending the lofty role of personal religious experience among Pentecostals. Individualism, long identified as a mark of revivalist sects and often deplored within enlightened religious circles, is clearly a virtue among Pentecostals.[27]

It remains to be seen whether individual experience is integral to Spirit encounter or if, in fact, Spirit encounter takes place in spite of what may prove to be a Western cultural anomaly. Can holiness happen in a relational vacuum? Tom Hank's role in the film *Castaway* models for us the peculiar twists and turns that relationship takes when we are isolated from those who rub against our egos, shaping and forming us. His only companion, Wilson the volleyball, is simply a projection of his own fears and needs. Perhaps the decisive lack of holiness manifested in the Western church springs from our accented individualism and our decidedly Wilsonian vision of our commitment to the faith community. Certainly the corporate aspects of experiences of the Spirit have yet to receive much attention in our conversations about holiness.

Adewuya concludes that 'Holiness, for Paul, is in its essence social holiness. The Christian life is not to be conceived merely as an individual struggle for perfection. Instead, it ought to be seen as a community project, and that in an important sense'.[28] Perhaps one of the more important challenges for western Pentecostalism in the

---

[26] Story, 'Pauline Thoughts about the Holy Spirit and Sanctification', p. 84.

[27] Russell P. Spittler, 'The Pentecostal View', in Alexander (ed.), *Christian Spirituality: Five Views of Sanctification*, pp. 133-54 (141).

[28] Adewuya, *Holiness and Community*, p. 196.

immediate future is to adjudicate this tension between individual experience and corporate identify and function.

Listening to Our Elders

One area of study suggested by Adewuya's notion of relational holiness is a more thorough exploration of antecedents found in the Old Testament. For Pentecostal scholars this has normally meant a diminished role for the Spirit. As James Muilenburg has pointed out, a clear association between the Spirit and sanctification is essentially a New Testament phenomenon.

> But what distinguishes the NT preoccupation with holiness from the OT more than aught else is its predication of holiness to the Spirit of God ... The OT employs the expression 'holy Spirit' only three times (Ps. 51:11 – H 51:13; Isa. 63:10-11), whereas the NT has it more often than all other occurrences of the word 'holy,' about ninety times. Sanctification plays a correspondingly great role.[29]

But the Spirit's role, while less prominent, is certainly not eclipsed when considering Israel's holiness. And interestingly, in the first of the two contexts in which the Spirit is called holy, Psalm 51, cleansing and restoration of the individual from sin is the focus, while in the second, Isaiah 63, it is the recreation and restoration of the exiled people of God. The Spirit as creator and re-creator suggests some promising connections. Second Isaiah takes up the theme creation, adopting both creation and exodus imagery to animate the prophet's message of Judah's redemption from exile. The God who created for himself a people in the exodus will now create them anew and gather them back from where they have been scattered. Isaiah 44.2-3 speaks both of God creating his people and of the Spirit sustaining that creation:

> Thus says the Lord who made you
> And formed you from the womb, who will help you,
> 'Do not fear, O Jacob My servant;
> And you Jeshurun whom I have chosen.
> 'For I will pour out water on the thirsty land

---

[29] George Buttrick *et al.* (eds.) 'Holiness', in *The Interpreter's Dictionary of the Bible* (New York: Abingdon Press, 1962), II, pp. 616-25 (623).

And streams on the dry ground;
I will pour out My Spirit on your offspring
And My blessing on your descendants.

The gift of the Spirit calls to mind that which is most basic to life, water in desert places. Exodus language is also recalled in Isaiah 63:

In all their affliction He was afflicted,
And the angel of His presence saved them;
In His love and in His mercy He redeemed them,
And He lifted them and carried them all the days of old.
But they rebelled
And grieved His Holy Spirit;
Therefore He turned Himself to become their enemy,
He fought against them.
Then His people remembered the days of old, of Moses.
Where is He who brought them up out of the sea with the shepherds of His flock?
Where is He who put His Holy Spirit in the midst of them,
Who caused His glorious arm to go at the right hand of Moses,
Who divided the waters before them to make for Himself an everlasting name,
Who led them through the depths?
Like the horse in the wilderness, they did not stumble;
As the cattle which go down into the valley,
The Spirit of the Lord gave them rest.
So You led Your people,
To make for Yourself a glorious name (Isa. 63.9-14).

As I have suggested, the other mention of God's spirit as holy, found in Psalm 51, speaks of God's re-creation not of the exiled nation, but of the exiled human spirit:

Create in me a clean heart, O God,
And renew a steadfast spirit within me.
Do not cast me away from Your presence
And do not take Your Holy Spirit from me.
Restore to me the joy of Your salvation
And sustain me with a willing spirit (Ps. 51.10-12).

Here God's presence to recreate and renew are expressed through the ongoing gift of his Holy Spirit to sustain and renew life. The

Spirit as creator, redeemer and life-giver adds depth to the New Testament association of the sanctifying and regenerating Spirit.

Future Directions

So how should Pentecostals respond to the question 'Who has been sanctified?' I find in my own life and Spirit-led journey a hunger for more, for a more fundamental experience of the sanctifying Spirit. I acknowledge that I became a saint of God when the Spirit first made her home in my heart and that I am called and empowered to move steadily toward journey's end at the Parousia. But I desire to know more fully moments of life-altering encounter with the sanctifying Spirit where progress in that journey is not measured in mere inches.

This current study suggests a number of conclusions and trajectories for further research.

1) While Pentecostals may not agree on the shape of sanctification, there should be agreement on the ongoing need for the empowering Spirit to create a holy people. Holiness is a work of the Holy Spirit.

2) Pentecostals should explore more fully experiential aspects of sanctification without the need either to limit them to a single crisis experience or to tie that experience solely to a first, second or third experience of grace. It is counter productive to segregate sanctifying experiences, limiting them to either regeneration or the Baptism of the Holy Spirit. Limiting crisis sanctification to the regenerative work of the Spirit leaves inadequate space to consider its experiential aspects. And since sanctification is as much process and crisis, it seems arbitrary to limit specific crisis experiences. Future research should consider the questions such as 'Should we continue to talk about sanctification as essentially experiential?' and if so, 'How is sanctification experienced in our communities of faith today?'

3) The communal aspects of sanctification should be explored more fully and a clearer understanding of how this might impact church teaching on the pursuit of holiness should be considered. Certainly the dialogue should extend beyond the western Church to include the testimonies of and reflections on the sanctifying Spirit in less individualistic cultures.

4) Though the Old Testament has been drawn on in articulating the communal nature of sanctification, more work remains to be

done. Creation, redemption and restoration are works of the Spirit associated with the people of God and with being restored to God's presence in the aftermath of sin and separation. More could be said of the sanctifying work of the Spirit in the Old Testament.

Continuing conversations about the future of sanctification will point the Pentecostal community to a rediscovery of the experience of sanctification, to a broadening of our understanding of the Spirit's role in holiness, and to an openness to consider the diverse nature of experience in both crisis and process as we think about those who have been, are being, and remain to be perfected in the love of Christ.

PART TWO

THEOLOGY

7

'NOT I, BUT CHRIST': HOLINESS, CONSCIENCE, & THE (IM)POSSIBILITY OF COMMUNITY

CHRIS E.W. GREEN[*]

Introduction

True to our pietist roots, we Wesleyans and Pentecostals are people not only of the Spirit but also of the spirit.[1] Typically, our traditions speak of the individual's 'heart' is a (or even *the*) primary locus of the divine activity,[2] and, naively or not, many of us assume that we can and should trust at least to some degree our personal sense of what God is saying and doing to and through us at the deep center of our own being.[3] We also hold that this capacity for self-transcendence – that is, 'spirit' – entails the responsibility to exercise, by God's grace, power over ourselves, to live a life of Spirit-empowered self-control – just as Jesus did. At the risk of overgeneralizing, one might say that Wesleyan and Pentecostal traditions

---

[*] Chris E.W. Green (PhD, Bangor University) is Assistant Professor of Theology at the Pentecostal Theological Seminary in Cleveland, TN, USA.

[1] For the relationship of Pentecostalism and Pietism, see Roger E. Olsen, 'Pietism and Pentecostalism: Spiritual Cousins or Competitors?' *Pneuma* 34.3 (2012), pp. 319-44.

[2] For an argument against the idea that Pietism is necessarily individualistic and otherworldly, see Christian T. Collins Winn, Christopher Gehrz, G. William Carlson, and Eric Holst (eds.), *The Pietist Impulse in Christianity* (Eugene, OR: Pickwick, 2013). For the purposes of this paper, I am using 'pietism' as shorthand for a kind of spirituality that is in fact individualistic, even if it proves to be true that not all forms of pietism fit such a description.

[3] As Olsen ('Pietism and Pentecostalism', p. 327) puts it, for P/pietists, 'the emphasis is on *experience* of God in the "inner person" – a powerful, transforming, immediate work of God that changes a person's affections away from sin and toward the "things of God"'.

understand holiness primarily in individualistic, interiorist, and per-formative terms. If we think ecclesially at all, we tend to do so by assuming that the church-community is transformed only as the individual believers who constitute the church's being are them-selves transformed – one by one, from the inside out, as they per-sonally progressively conform their lives to God's revealed will.[4]

For most of us, I suspect, this pietistic way of engaging the world and experiencing God is simply second nature.[5] But what if this is at least in part an unwise way to live? The question driving my concern in this paper is simply stated: What if our pietistic way of being-in-the-world makes the *churchly* life called for by the Scrip-tures impossible? Perhaps so long as we think of the individual be-liever's relation to Christ as basic to the church's being – rather than the other way around – and describe holiness and sanctification in predominately individualist terms, regarding the believer's con-science as an alternative, more trustworthy witness to God's Word than the church's teaching and pastoral ministries, then the kind of community Scripture mandates for us will prove always elusive, re-maining at best an 'ideal' that haunts our attempts at life together. Or, to ask the question yet another way, what if this breed of pie-tism does not, in the final analysis, quite square with the witness of Scripture, the work of the Spirit, the call of the *ecclesia*, and the na-ture of human being-in-community?

With all of that in mind, perhaps the time has come for those of us influenced by the pietistic impulse – and that includes nearly all forms of Christianity in the West, and certainly most Wesleyans and Pentecostals – seriously to reconsider and, where necessary, radical-ly to reconfigure the way we interpret our experiences of God, neighbor, and self; our understandings of churchly existence; and the call, personal and corporate, to holiness. What follows, then, is

---

[4] Olsen ('Pietism and Pentecostalism', p. 335) contends that 'both Pietism and Pentecostalism were and are movements to deepen individual's spirituality and renew church life through inward, unmediated, transforming experience of God'. This way of framing the truly Christian life is vividly illustrated in the arrange-ment of Richard Foster's much lauded *Celebration of Discipline*. He begins with the individual, 'inward' disciplines and moves through the 'outward' disciplines to the 'corporate' disciplines.

[5] So I cannot quite agree with Olsen ('Pietism and Pentecostalism', p. 343) when he suggests that pietists specialize in the 'interior domain' while pentecos-tals specialize in the 'expressive domain'.

an initial, tentative attempt at such reconsideration and reconfiguration.

Conscience and/or Church?

In the early works of Martin Luther, we perhaps catch a glimpse of two decisive shifts in Christian thinking about the conscience: first, a move away from will as the anthropological locus of divine activity, as Augustine and Aquinas had assumed, to conscience (*synteresis/conscientia*);[6] second, a turn from the church's teaching offices to the individual's self-judgment as the final arbiter of truth-claims. Luther himself did not invent these moves or determine these shifts. But without them, one might argue, the Reformation would not have been possible. And it seems clear that as the events and teachings of the Reformation(s) worked their way into the imagination of Christians in the West, it became more and more apparent that one would have to decide whether the church's *magisterium* or the individual's faith would have the final word in matters of discernment. Cardinal Ratzinger has argued, quite brilliantly, that no such tension necessarily exists.[7] I am deeply sympathetic with Ratzinger's contentions, I am nonetheless convinced that in practice the issue is more problematic than he allows. In short, I am convinced that we must attend to what has become for many a strictly either/or matter: either we trust our own conscience or we trust some external, churchly authority. In this paper, I hope to begin the work of reframing this either/or by reimagining the pursuit of holiness as fundamentally and essentially *ecclesial* calling – a calling that cannot be met without ongoing transfiguration of the individual's conscience through the ascetical and kenotic suffering-in-joy of churchly life-together in and for the world. By contrasting John Wesley's view of conscience with the view of Dietrich Bonhoeffer, I hope to bring the crucial issues into relief, and then to offer at least a few provisional revisionary proposals.

---

[6] Jason Goroncy, 'The Human Conscience in Martin Luther, Immanuel Kant and Frederick Denison Maurice', Unpublished Paper (Nov 11, 2012), p. 1.

[7] Joseph Cardinal Ratzinger, *On Conscience* (San Francisco: Ignatius Press, 1984).

Conscience and Immediacy:
John Wesley on Self-Knowledge in/and the Spirit

In his sermon 'On Conscience', Wesley articulates his view by offering, first, a rough definition: 'Conscience, then, is that faculty whereby we are at once conscious of our own thoughts, words, and actions; and of their merit or demerit, of their being good or bad; and, consequently, deserving either praise or censure'.[8] He goes on to describe what he takes to be conscience's threefold office:

> It is a *witness* – testifying what we have done, in thought, or word, or action. It is a *judge* – passing sentence on what we have done, that it is good or evil. It, in some sort, *executes* the sentence, by occasioning a degree of complacency in him that does well, and a degree of uneasiness in him that does evil.[9]

Conscience as (In)Fallible Witness

Perhaps most importantly, Wesley understands conscience as a trustworthy witness. The moral striving he believes necessary is only possible insofar as one's conscience can be expected to speak with sufficient veracity about one's standing before God and neighbor.[10] Insofar as it is shaped continually by Scripture and Christian conversation, the conscience remains a more or less sufficiently trustworthy witness.[11] Indeed, it speaks with God's voice. A good conscience, he says, is '*divine* consciousness of walking in all things ac-

---

[8] 'On Conscience' §I.3. As Wesley sees it, a Christian conscience is 'that faculty of the soul' that 'by the assistance of the grace of God' makes it possible for one to know oneself, to discern one's own 'tempers, thoughts, words, and actions', and to know whether or not one is living in conformity to the Divine purpose.

[9] 'On Conscience' §I.7.

[10] As Kevin T. Lowery (*Salvaging Wesley's Agenda: A New Paradigm for Wesleyan Virtue Ethics* [Eugene, OR: Pickwick, 2008], p. 276) explains, for Wesley 'moral purity requires a clear conscience, and this requires some type of immediate assurance'. For Wesley's use of Pietist thought, see Kenneth Collins, 'John Wesley's Critical Appropriation of Early German Pietism', *WesTJ* 27 (1992), pp. 57-92.

[11] In his commentary on Song of Songs 3.1, Wesley suggests that God withdraws his 'manifestations' from the believer for (only?) one or the other of two reasons: 'either because I had not sought him diligently, or because I had abused his favour'. Thomas Oden (*John Wesley's Scriptural Christianity: A Plain Exposition of His Teaching on Christian Doctrine* [Grand Rapids: Zondervan, 1994], p. 236) explains Wesley's view in this way, 'A Christian conscience void of offence is a conscience living by faith on the sole foundation of Christ's atoning work, instructed by the revealed and written Word, *capable of self-examination*, able without pretense (sic) to confess before God one's sin ...'

cording to the written word of God'.[12] Of course, walking in everything required/forbidden by the Word is possible only if one has a
tender conscience, which 'observ[es] *any* deviation from the word of
God, whether in thought, or word, or work; and immediately feels
remorse and self-condemnation for it'.[13] The truly sanctified believer, being conformed to the rule of Scripture, enjoys a 'habitual', persistent 'inward consciousness' of right-standing with God. In other
words, the believer's Scripture-formed conscience is more or less
perfectly sensitized and so more or less perfectly dependable. In his
sermon on the witness of the believer's spirit, Wesley insists

> ... the joy of a Christian does not arise from any blindness of
> conscience, from his not being able to discern good from evil.
> So far from it, that he was an utter stranger to this joy, till the
> eyes of his understanding were opened; that he knew it not, until
> he had spiritual senses, fitted to discern spiritual good and evil.
> And now the eye of his soul waxeth not dim: He was never so
> sharp-sighted before: He has so quick a perception of the small-
> est things, as is quite amazing to the natural man. As a mote is
> visible in the sun-beam, so to him who is walking in the light, in
> the beams of the uncreated Sun, *every* mote of sin is visible. Nor
> does he close the eyes of his conscience any more: That sleep is
> departed from him. His soul is *always* broad awake: No more
> slumber or folding of the hands to rest! He is *always* standing on
> the tower, and hearkening what his lord will say concerning him;
> and *always* rejoicing in this very thing, in 'seeing him that is invis-
> ible'.[14]

---

[12] 'On Conscience' §I.12.

[13] In good Anglican *via media* fashion, Wesley seeks to avoid extremism. So he
finds that the *tender* conscience lies exactly between a *hardened* conscience, on the
one side, and a *scrupulous* conscience, on the other. To have a scrupulous conscience is to find 'fear where no fear is', to condemn oneself without cause.
Those inflicted with a hyperactive conscience err by 'imagining some things to be
sinful, which the Scripture nowhere condemns; and supposing other things to be
their duty, which the Scripture nowhere enjoins'. With acute pastoral sensitivity,
Wesley encourages believers to 'yield to [the scrupulous conscience] as little as
possible', giving themselves instead to 'earnest prayer' so they can be 'delivered
from this sore evil, and may recover a sound mind'. He also observes that nothing helps tame the hyperactive conscience more than truthful conversation with a
'pious and judicious friend' ('On Conscience' §II.3).

[14] 'The Witness of Our Own Spirit' §18. Emphasis mine. Wesley did, from
time to time, temper his descriptions of 'full assurance', and over the course of

Faith – the 'evidence, conviction, demonstration of things invisible – has opened the 'eyes of understanding' so that 'divine light' is 'poured in' enabling believers to see the wonders of God's law, 'the excellency and purity of it; the height, and depth, and length, and breadth thereof, and of *every* commandment contained therein'.[15] Through faith that beholds 'the light of the glory of God in the face of Jesus Christ', believers 'perceive, as in a glass, *all* that is in ourselves, yea, the *inmost* motions of our souls'.[16] Because God's love is shed abroad in our hearts, we are enabled 'to love one another as Christ loved us'. Because God's law, as promised, has once again been engraved on the heart, there is in the soul 'an *entire* agreement with his holy and perfect law', so the believer is in fact capable of 'bringing into captivity *every* thought to the obedience of Christ'.[17]

Because he needs conscience to do superhumanly dependable work, Wesley goes out of his way to insist that

> ... it is not *nature*, but the *Son of God*, that is 'the true light, which enlighteneth every man that cometh into the world'. So that we may say to every human creature, 'He,' not nature, 'hath showed thee, O man, what is good'. And it is his Spirit who giveth thee an inward check, who causeth thee to feel uneasy, when thou walkest in *any* instance contrary to the light which he hath given thee.[18]

Christ himself is the light that enlightens conscience, for the true and the good, so that the knowledge that conscience brings to bear is in effect *divine* knowledge, which means that the witness of conscience is sufficient for knowing truly, if not fully, whether or not we are satisfactorily fulfilling the divine will. Such self-knowledge is possible only through the 'assistance of the Spirit of God', whose power alone can free from sinful self-love and 'every other irregular

---

his life, he may have developed a more nuanced teaching. Even late in life, however, he could at least on occasion revert to the strongest language. See Collins, *The Theology of John Wesley,* pp. 131-36.

[15] 'The Witness of Our Own Spirit' §8.

[16] 'On the Witness of Our Own Spirit' §8.

[17] 'On the Witness of Our Own Spirit' §8. As Oden (*John Wesley's Scriptural Christianity*, p. 236) explains it, 'The regenerated, Christ-shaped conscience does not let us off cheaply. It tells us the truth about ourselves. When we listen to it with sincerity, we either hear it acquitting or accusing us. Paul would not have commended a conscience void of offense if that were wholly impossible'.

[18] 'On Conscience' §I.5.

passion'. 'In all the offices of conscience, the 'unction of the Holy One' is indispensably needful.[19] Without this, 'neither could we clearly discern our lives or tempers; nor could we judge of the rule whereby we are to walk, or of our conformity of disconformity to it'.[20] For Wesley, moral stirrings are God's own work. There can be no question of a point or purpose to the moral life apart from a relationship with God.[21]

The Law Written on the Heart

In his antinomian works, Wesley is careful to insist that the conscience is *not* infallible. For example, in his sermon 'The Original, Nature, Property, and Use of The Law' (§I.4) Wesley argues that before the Fall, the law – a 'divine copy' of God's mind, 'a complete model of all truth, so far as is intelligible to a finite being' – was impressed upon Man so that it was in fact 'coeval with his nature'.[22] Adam's sin, however, 'wellnigh effaced' the law from the heart, which meant that 'the "eyes of his understanding" [were] darkened in the same measure as his soul was "alienated from the life of God"'. When, through faith, the law is newly written on the heart, the believer's experience is wondrous:

---

[19] As Wesley sees it, it is *impossible* to live the holy life unless and until one has the full assurance of having been forgiven and the awareness of abiding in moment-to-moment communion with God. This assurance must precede all our knowing and reasoning: it must be the ground and source of all our experiences. To that end, the witness of the Spirit is always given 'to and with' the believer's own spirit so that the truly Christian life is one marked by the 'perceptible' effects of the Spirit evidenced first and generatively in the believer's affections – through the incessant eruption of a supernatural abiding love, peace, hope and joy – and then naturally also in the believer's embodied life. In his own words ('The Witness of the Spirit II', §3.5):

> That the 'testimony of the Spirit of God' must, in the very nature of things, be antecedent to the 'testimony of our own spirit,' may appear from this single consideration: we must be holy in heart and life before we can be conscious that we are so. But we must love God before we can be holy at all, this being the root of all holiness. Now we cannot love God, till we know he loves us: 'We love him, because he first loved us'. And we cannot know his love to us, till his Spirit witnesses it to our spirit. Till then we cannot believe it; we cannot say, 'The life which I now live, I live by faith in the Son of God, who loved me, and gave himself for me'.

[20] 'On Conscience' §I.11.
[21] Robin W. Lovin, 'Moral Theology', in William J. Abraham and James E. Kirby (eds.), *The Oxford Handbook of Methodist Studies* (Oxford: Oxford University Press, 2011).
[22] 'The Original, Nature, Property, and Use of The Law' §I.4.

The fruits of the law of God written in the heart are 'righteousness, and peace, and assurance for ever'. Or rather, the law itself
is righteousness, filling the soul with a peace which passeth all
understanding, and causing us to rejoice evermore, in the testimony of a good conscience toward God.[23]

Still, glorious as the experience of the believer may be, the experience is never in this life everything it was before the Fall. The law,
Wesley says, is in '*some measure* ... re-inscribed' in the heart of the
'dark, sinful creature'.[24] As the believer matures in Christlikeness the
law, inscribed both in Scripture and in the conscience, mirrors with
increasing but never absolutely perfect clarity the believer's failings.
'... he sees daily, in that divine mirror, more and more of his own
sinfulness. He sees *more and more clearly*, that he is still a sinner in all
things, – that neither his heart nor his ways are right before God;
and that every moment sends him to Christ'.[25] Of course, much
rides on how one reads the 'some measure' and the 'more and
more'. Without question, however, Wesley does hold that the witness conscience is sufficiently clear: the believer knows enough to
live obediently, and to move deeper and deeper into conformity
with God's will.

Failings of conscience are especially frequent for the new, imma-
ture believer. Wesley suggests that the transformation wrought by
the initial experience of the Spirit's immediacy effects a kind of
shock, so to speak, to the moral system that renders the regenerate
person incapable of reading her own sinfulness accurately:

How naturally do those who experience such a change imagine
that all sin is gone; that it is utterly rooted out of their heart, and
has no more any place therein! How easily do they draw that in-
ference, 'I *feel* no sin; therefore, I *have* none: it does not *stir*; therefore it does not *exist*: it has no *motion*; therefore, it has no *being*!'[26]

---

[23] 'The Original, Nature, Property, and Use of The Law' §II.12.
[24] 'The Original, Nature, Property, and Use of The Law' §I.4.
[25] 'The Original, Nature, Property, and Use of The Law' §IV.5.
[26] 'The Scripture Way of Salvation' §I.5. Wesley quotes Macarius in support of
this view, 'How exactly did Macarius, fourteen hundred years ago, describe the
present experience of the children of God: 'The unskilful', or unexperienced,
'when grace operates, presently imagine they have no more sin. Whereas they that
have discretion cannot deny, that even we who have the grace of God may be
molested again. For we have often had instances of some among the brethren,

Before long, however, the believer is 'undeceived' and comes to realize 'two principles' warring within the heart. Knowing that, the justified believer is freed to submit to the gradual work of sanctification, waiting in the means of grace. Presumably, on the far side of 'perfection in love' the conscience is no longer deceived in these ways because the love of God enlightens the understanding perfectly.

Summary & Conclusion

We see, in summary, a few of the defining marks of Wesley's theology of conscience: (a) conscience is a natural faculty lost through original sin but re-activated, at least to some of its original capacity, by the Spirit; (b) conscience is kept from fatal error only by constant conformity to Scripture in the discipline of Christian conversation; (c) although all believers enjoy sufficient awareness of God's will for necessary obedience, maturing believers can and should expect to have intensified sensitivity to the Spirit and increasing clarity of purpose. In the final analysis, then, perhaps Wesley's view is best described as arising from an 'optimism of graced nature'.[27]

While Wesley himself sought to correct those who relied overmuch on their own conscience, trusting too simply in the workings of their own spirit, many of Wesley's followers lost touch with his insistence on the means of grace and warnings against enthusiasm.

---

who have experienced such grace as to affirm that they had no sin in them; and yet, after all, when they thought themselves entirely freed from it, the corruption that lurked within was stirred up anew, and they were well nigh burned up.'

[27] Ann Taves (*Fits, Trances, and Visions: Experiencing Religion and Explaining Experience from Wesley to James* [Princeton, NJ: Princeton University Press, 1999], pp. 48-54) contends that Wesley's view of religious experience is similar to if not as developed as Jonathan Edwards'. Both defined 'true religion' – a religion of the heart – as something different from both 'formalism' and 'enthusiasm'. They both defended 'the possibility of a direct and immediate experience of the Spirit of God' and insisted that 'authentic experience must be tried and tested in practice'. They differed in just a couple of respects. First, Edwards was less sanguine about experience than was Wesley. Second, Edwards developed a philosophy of experience that differentiated between 'natural and supernatural affections in order to isolate the supernatural affections as the true distinguishing marks of the Spirit'. Wesley, conversely, made no distinction. Following Outler and Gunter, Taves argues that Wesley's 'witness of the Spirit' was linked to a 'spiritual sense' in the *regenerate*, rather than the 'natural', person. In her words, 'The presence or activation of the spiritual sense (a result of the new birth) enabled converts to intuitively apprehend the witness of the Spirit with their spirit that they were children of God (the experience of new birth)'. However, apart from the evidence of the fruit of the Spirit, this internal sense was deemed necessarily mistaken.

Under the influence of Phoebe Palmer and others, 19th century American Methodists intensified the optimistic elements already at work in Wesleyan thought,[28] and this optimism has continued to find expression in 20th and 21st century Wesleyan, Holiness, and Pentecostal spiritualties.

Self-Address, Idolatry, and Community: Bonhoeffer on Conscience and Churchly Life

Dietrich Bonhoeffer's vision differs in almost exaggerated fashion from Wesley's. For Bonhoeffer, conscience belongs to fallenness, and human self-address 'remains a move within the essential estrangement of human being from the sociality of pure, unbroken creation'.[29] As Clifford Green explains, in Bonhoeffer's theology conscience 'is in *no way* the voice of Christ'. Instead, it is the voice of 'sinful self-reflection'. In fact, conscience can be and often is opposed to faith, for faith 'looks solely to Christ (*actus directus*) and away from the self'.[30]

> The call of conscience in natural man is the attempt on the part of the ego to justify itself in its knowledge of good and evil before God, before men and before itself, and to secure its own continuance in this self-justification ... Thus the call of conscience has its origin and its goal in the autonomy of a man's own ego.[31]

Conscience as Idolatrous Substitute for Christ

For Bonhoeffer, human being-in-the-world is always already disrupted so that every one of us suffers inescapable 'disunion with God, with men, with things' and with ourselves.[32] Conscience is 'the voice of the apostate life which desires at least to remain one with itself'.[33] Having become like God (*sicut deus*) through the 'knowledge

---

[28] See Douglas M. Strong, 'Sanctified Eccentricity: The Continuing Relevance of the Nineteenth Century Holiness Paradigm', *WesTJ* 35.1 (Spring 2000), pp. 9-21.

[29] Wesley D. Avram, 'The Work of Conscience in Bonhoeffer's Homiletic', *Homiletic* 39.1 (2004), pp. 1-14 (p. 2).

[30] Clifford Green, *Bonhoeffer: A Theology of Sociality* (Grand Rapids: Eerdmans, 1999), p. 97.

[31] Bonhoeffer, *Ethics*, p. 239.

[32] Bonhoeffer, *Ethics*, p. 24.

[33] Bonhoeffer, *Ethics*, p. 28.

of good and evil', we determine to be both God and neighbor *for ourselves*. 'In conscience and remorse [man] always seeks to feign the presence, the reality of another in his life; man accuses, torments and glorifies himself only in order to escape by lying from the dreadful loneliness of an echo-less solitude'.[34] Personal *integrity* is not, then, a Christian aim. What is needed, instead, is Christ-like *character*. And this comes only in and by kenotic life-in-community.

It follows from these insights that sin must be the hubristic attempt to address ourselves as *Thou*, to play creator to and for ourselves, to be our own judge and savior. So long as I am trying to 'find myself', I remain lost to Christ and so to others. So long as I am attempting to at-one myself, to justify my own existence, I remain at odds with both God and neighbor.[35] As the young Bonhoeffer argues in his *Sanctorum Communio*,

> Whereas in the primal state the relation among human beings is one of giving, in the sinful state it is purely demanding. Every person exists in complete, voluntary isolation; everyone lives their own life, rather than all living the same life in God. Now everyone has their own conscience.[36]

If the conscience is a substitute for the voice of God and neighbor, a kind re-placing of the now-absent other, then Christ (who is to us both God and neighbor and who therefore possibilizes our relation to them) is the substitute for the conscience. He replaces it as the other who makes God and neighbor present to us again and finally.

Bonhoeffer quotes Luther to this effect: 'Seek thyself only in Christ and not in thyself, then wilt thou find thyself eternally in him'. To which Bonhoeffer adds: 'Here the man *in se conversus* is torn away from the attempt to remain alone with himself and is turned towards Christ'.[37] In sin, I seek to be a law unto myself. However, when Christ, the 'Lord of conscience', becomes in faith 'the point of unity of my existence', then my autonomy is mercifully undone. Jesus alone is the *nomos* who orders my existence before God in the

---

[34] Dietrich Bonhoeffer, *Creation and Fall: A Theological Interpretation of Genesis 1-3* (London: SCM Press, 1959), pp. 92-93.

[35] Bonhoeffer treats this problem at length in his *Life Together* (San Francisco: Harper, 1954).

[36] Bonhoeffer, *Sanctorum Communio*, p. 108.

[37] Bonhoeffer, *Act and Being*, p. 170.

world. He names me, and so gives me myself. 'Jesus Christ has become my conscience'.[38] And just so he 'sets [my] conscience free for the service of God and of our neighbor'.[39] In that freedom, I come into being, into what might be called abundant life.

The Fallibility of Conscience

Bonhoeffer learned by harsh experience the inextricable difficulties of living from and by one's conscience. 'The man with a conscience', he says 'fights a lonely battle against the overwhelming forces of inescapable situations which demand decisions'.[40] He is 'torn apart' by these conflicts. 'Evil comes upon him in countless respectable and seductive disguises', and he is unable always to discern rightly the good from the bad. The fractured complexity of worldly reality is simply too much for the human spirit – itself also fractured and impenetrably complicated – to process rightly.

Not only as a theologian, but also as an experienced pastor, Bonhoeffer understood that reliance upon one's own conscience spells danger for the *community*. Trusting in one's own self-address belongs to what Bonhoeffer names as 'private virtuousness' – the death of ecclesial life together. Such 'private virtuousness' fundamentally distorts the nature of true holiness. The person strictly committed to never offending his or her own conscience will not commit flagrant sins, of course, and will not do or leave anything undone that violates his or her controlling and controllable sense of right and wrong. However, such a person remains necessarily 'blind and dead to the wrongs' which inevitably surround him or her, and this means that personal blamelessness *always* comes at the price of 'responsible action in the world'.[41] 'Responsibility for our neighbor is cut short by the inviolable call of conscience'.[42] Not only that, but most sins remain unperceivable to the one sinning, so even if one were to obey one's conscience perfectly, one would not therefore by holy with the holiness God is and offers. In any case, it is unwise for the Christian individual to be 'constantly feeling his spiritual pulse'.[43] Such infatuation with one's 'health' subverts patience, hu-

---

38 Bonhoeffer, *Ethics*, p. 240.
39 Bonhoeffer, *Ethics*, p. 240.
40 Bonhoeffer, *Ethics*, p. 68.
41 Bonhoeffer, *Ethics*, p. 69.
42 Bonhoeffer, *Ethics*, p. 238.
43 Bonhoeffer, *Life Together*, p. 30.

mility, and gratitude, and just so threatens the only legitimate ground for Christian community. It is above all this community-threatening consequence of pietistic self-concern that Bonhoeffer seeks to expose and defeat.

Although deeply indebted to Luther's insights on conscience, Bonhoeffer differed from him on at least one key point. Luther, as Clifford Green explains, was a late medieval theologian concerned above all with 'the hypertrophy of the negative conscience'. Bonhoeffer, conversely, was a modern theologian concerned primarily with the distribution of power in human social relations.[44] Lutheran soteriology 'is focused on the guilty conscience'.[45] Bonhoeffer's soteriology focuses instead on Christ's de-throning of conscience in a call of the sinner away from self-awareness to love of God and neighbor. In Luther, the bad conscience prepares the way for the hearing of the Gospel. In Bonhoeffer, the voice of conscience makes one deaf to the call of Christ to life in community and just so inhibits the saving work of God.

The Need for Self-Judgment

It would be a misreading of Bonhoeffer to think he means Christians ought not to judge themselves at all. It is not a question of *if,* but a question of *how* that judgment takes place – from what source and to what end – and a question of *what* that judgment is taken to mean. For the Christian, the only criterion of judgment is Christ himself. 'Jesus Christ occupies within him exactly the space which was previously occupied by his own knowledge of good and evil'.[46] Therefore, 'self-examination will always consist precisely in our delivering ourselves up entirely to the judgment of Jesus Christ, not computing the reckoning ourselves but committing it to Him of whom we know and acknowledge that He is within ourselves'.[47] Self-judgment, then, is only ever *penultimate.* The most that conscience can do – even as it is freed in Christ – is open us toward the judgment Christ is and offers through his self-giving in the church's life and ministries. 'Conscience freed in Christ is conscience freed by Christ, in the church, for others'.[48]

---

[44] Green, *Bonhoeffer*, p. 124.
[45] Green, *Bonhoeffer*, p. 286.
[46] Bonhoeffer, *Ethics*, p. 45.
[47] Bonhoeffer, *Ethics*, p. 45.
[48] Avram, 'The Work of Conscience in Bonhoeffer's Homiletic', p. 4.

Precisely because believers cannot trust themselves to their own interpretation of the Spirit's leading, in the life of Christian community 'reproof is unavoidable'.[49] While this happens most often in the context of the preached Word and the giving and receiving of the Sacrament, members can and must also venture words of 'admonition and rebuke'. When rightly given and received, such admonition is *graceful*: 'Then it is not we who are judging; God alone judges, and God's judgment is helpful and healing'.[50] Plain speaking of the Word is 'a ministry of mercy, an ultimate offer of genuine fellowship' and, most importantly, is not our work, but God's. The members of the church-community must decide not to offer their own counsel, but only *God's* word. As they proclaim God's word faithfully, Christ presents himself to the hearer(s) as judge so that they, in turn, have no need any longer to trust to their own independent judgments. This means freedom for the community, freedom to be for and with one another without fear of condemnation. Only in such freedom is authentically Christian community possible.

Bonhoeffer and Wesley: Fundamental Differences?

Perhaps now we can begin to see some of the drastic differences that divide Wesley's and Bonhoeffer's visions of conscience. First, there are apparently conflicting accounts of the nature of human being and personhood in Christ. Wesley – perhaps a man too much of his own (Enlightened) times? – seems at times to voice a *de facto* individualism that cannot adequately address the noetic and structural effects of sin and, even more importantly, fails to account adequately for the communal nature of personhood-in-Christ. When coupled with his perfectionistic theology of grace, such a doctrine of conscience threatens to dissolve into an extremely sanguine account of the trustworthiness of human self-transcendence and self-address, as it arguably does in the thought and practice of many of his followers. Bonhoeffer – of course, equally a man of his times – took the noetic effects of sin with deadly seriousness. He suspected, like St Augustine and many others before him, that even the re-

---

[49] Bonhoeffer, *Life Together*, p. 107.
[50] Bonhoeffer, *Life Together*, p. 107.

deemed/sanctified heart remains by and large unreadable.[51] And so for Bonhoeffer the need for church-community has an ontological depth one does not find in Wesley's thought.

Anthony Baker contends that Wesley's dependence on Locke proved disastrous at just this point. Wesley remains faithful to Locke, according to Baker, because 'Locke gives him a framework for describing the *sine qua non* of Protestantism: we are justified by faith in God's work, not by anything within us'.[52] Locke does this by an account of *immediacy* that 'avoids all the interruptions of language and ideas'.[53] On Baker's reconstruction, however, Wesley's Lockean frame of reference and pietistic commitments led him to believe that 'true deliverance from sin, and the perfection that comes of having the love of God shed abroad in one's heart, cannot occur without a *full consciousness* that it has in fact occurred'.[54] And Baker holds that this becomes particularly problematic when it comes to aligning an understanding of perfect salvation with Locke's highest form of knowledge: knowledge of our rightness with God must come 'entirely unmediated by temporality and community'.[55] This is the rub: Wesley's doctrine of immediacy, when coupled with his optimistic view of conscience, can make it so that the individual believer has her existence independently from the church's life. She may *choose* to belong to this or that body of believers as she wills, because her life does not depend on them. If the Church is mother in any real sense, she is a surrogate mother whom, having given birth to the child, cannot be expected to raise it. This is why Baker suggests that it is an 'eroded sense of Christian community' that convinces Wesley that 'the witness of the Spirit is primarily and finally a matter of personal conviction'.[56] Insofar as Baker is right in his critique, a serious reconsideration of Wesley's theology of conscience is needed. But we cannot, in my opinion, follow Bonhoeffer

---

[51] Mildred Wynkoop ('The Theological Roots of Wesleyanism's Understanding of the Holy Spirit', *WesTJ* 14.1 [Spr 1979], pp. 77-98 [94]), insists that this pessimism is at work for Wesley too – 'No one can properly judge the value of his own sense of "unction"'. But as we have seen, Wesley does not talk in this way consistently.

[52] Baker, *Diagonal Advance*, p. 280.

[53] Baker, *Diagonal Advance*, p. 283.

[54] Baker, *Diagonal Advance*, p. 279.

[55] Baker, *Diagonal Advance*, p. 280.

[56] Baker, *Diagonal Advance*, p. 282.

all the way, either. If Wesley's account of graced nature is too optimistic – and at least for some of his followers, bordering on Pelagi-
anism – Bonhoeffer's account of graced nature is perhaps too Au-
gustinian, failing to recognize the ways in which God can and does
break through our deafness and blindness, making possible our synergistic collaboration with God's saving us.

What way forward then? We need a vigorously synergistic model
of the Christian life that both deeply appreciates the eccle-
sial/relational nature of human personhood and takes seriously the
'not-yet' reality of our eschatological being-on-the-way.[57] As people
committed to holiness and the life of the Spirit, we need to re-think
the nature and function of conscience, specifically, and, more
broadly, the relation of the human spirit to the divine Spirit. We
also need to take more seriously the ways in which finitude and sin,
personal and structural, (mal)form our knowing of ourselves and
God.

'I Do Not Even Judge Myself':
Rethinking Conscience, Personhood, and Holiness Ecclesially

1 John 3.18-20 reassures us that we can and should put the pangs of
our conscience to rest because 'God is greater than our hearts'. Similarly, Paul insists that he not only refuses the Corinthians' condemnation but also does not even judge himself, trusting instead entirely
in the judgment of Christ, given once-for-all at the End (1 Cor. 4.3-
5). So, the apostles agree: conscience, whatever service it might offer, cannot claim the ultimacy that belongs to Christ alone. Christ
alone tells the whole truth about us, and not until the Last Judgment is the truth truly set out plainly for one and all. Knowing this,
we have to keep the claims of conscience 'under authority' – ready
to submit to them insofar as they conform to the gospel, and ready
to defy them when they do not.

---

[57] Michael J. Hyde, *The Call of Conscience: Heidegger and Levinas, Rhetoric and the
Euthanasia Debate* (Columbia, SC: University of South Carolina Press, 2001), p. 3.

With the Scriptures, then, one learns that the workings of conscience are intimately connected with the fabric of human emotion as well as with our
hermeneutic or interpretive capacity to come to terms with the meaning and
significance of our situations and actions. However, owing to this connection,
rooted as it is in the contingency of experiential reality, the call of conscience
may end up communicating errors in judgment.

Paul makes a related move in his instructions about eating 'meat offered to idols' in 1 Corinthians 8 and Romans 14. As Radner explains, whatever 'self-knowledge' (syn-eidesis) Paul has in mind is 'deeply constrained', calling for 'tenderness and sensitivity in the face of its "weakness" in a brother or sister Christian'. In the final analysis, then, Paul expects believers to surrender their rights and to crucify their consciences 'for the sake of another's conscience and for the goals of "peace"'.[58]

From these brief reflections, we can take away at least two claims: (a) self-knowledge and self-judgment, short of the Last Judgment, is necessary but also merely provisional, and (b) conscience's purpose is always only to enable the believer to engage faithfully in the churchly life of unity-in-Christ. Radner says it exactly: 'Christian conscience is unceasingly relearned as the Christian … is restlessly reordered in and for the sake of "life together"'.[59] A truly Christian conscience, then, is nothing more or less than the expression of God-like kenotic, transfiguring love. Which means that self-judgment, insofar as it is faithful, always already opens out to include neighbor and enemy, for we are members not only of Christ but also of one another. Any understanding of conscience that assumes we need only a personal relationship to God and do not need the judgment and grace of our brothers and sisters in Christ *must* be wrong.

Radner correctly sees that the truth to which conscience is purposed to witness is nothing other than the character of Christ's own person. *He* is the truth, as Scripture says (Jn 14.6). 'Hence, the "true" person is the person whose individual humanity, unique in every way, yet human and ordered by the perfect humanity of Christ, is given over to the self-giving of Jesus'.[60] True 'individuality' is possible only in and through Christ,[61] and faithfulness to one's conscience is in the final analysis nothing more or less than allowing one's life to be given over to the neighbor and to Christ so that the Spirit can make the Body one with God's own oneness. Knowing

---

[58] Ephraim Radner, *A Brutal Unity: The Spiritual Politics of the Christian Church* (Waco: Baylor University Press, 2012), p. 378.

[59] Radner, *A Brutal Unity*, p. 380.

[60] Radner, *A Brutal Unity*, p. 418.

[61] As Radner (*A Brutal Unity*, p. 418) puts it, 'every person is properly and truthfully "found" only and wholly "in Christ"'.

that, we see that holiness is not a personal matter, but a way of living with others so churchly life is made that much more possible. And we discern that conscience is a gift one receives for the other's sake. In submitting one's self-judgment to Christ's lordship, one is being fitted for ecclesial existence. Learning to say, with Paul, 'not I, but Christ in me' (Gal. 2.20), we are learning to 'pursue peace with everyone' and just in this way to discover before the world the holiness without which 'no one shall see the Lord' (Heb. 12.14).

8

THE *PENTECOSTAL TRIPLE WAY*: AN ECUMENICAL MODEL OF THE PENTECOSTAL *VIA SALUTIS* AND SOTERIOLOGICAL EXPERIENCE

MONTE LEE RICE*

Introduction

Reflecting postmodern deconstruction on the homogenising pull of globalized meta-narratives that marginalise local interpretive voices, ongoing research in global Pentecostalism is rectifying earlier North American and European historiographical hegemony over local Pentecostal historiographies and theologies worldwide. Yet research continues towards identifying theological distinctives of global Pentecostalism. Notable are two fielded reasons. One motive reflects George Lindbeck's thesis on the determinative role of doctrinal language towards spiritual experience.[1] Another reflects drives towards ecumenical engagement, which premises the sharing of communal gifts reflected in a tradition's theological distinctiveness.

I suggest that the early Wesleyan-Pentecostal *via salutis* comprising the Pentecostal threefold soteriological experiences of redemption, sanctification, and Spirit baptism implicitly exists as another theological core within the Pentecostal primordial psyche. In this paper, I will therefore revisit Steven Land's and Simon Chan's earli-

* Monte Lee Rice (MDiv, Asia Pacific Theological Seminary) is an itinerant minister who has served within some 15 nations in Southeast Asia and Africa. Monte and his wife, Jee Fong, live in the Republic of Singapore, Southeast Asia.
    [1] George A. Lindbeck, *The Nature of Doctrine: Religion and Theology in a Postliberal Age* (Louisville, KT: John Knox Press, 1984), pp. 18-23, 69, 113-24.

er envisioning of Pentecostal spirituality as a *spiritual theology* according to the classical Christian idea of human life formed on the way to union with God (*theosis*).[2] I will also retrieve Chan's earlier patterning of the Pentecostal threefold experience to the 'Three Ways' of purgation, illumination, and union, which he retrieved from the ascetical/mystical spiritualities resident within Roman Catholicism and Eastern Orthodoxy.[3] In doing so, I propose an analogous patterning of the Pentecostal threefold experience to a constructivist understanding of the Three Ways, which I believe, may make the earlier Pentecostal threefold experience more theologically appealing to Keswickian as well as Wesleyan Pentecostals and Charismatics.[4] What results is a *via salutis* model that clarifies the Pentecostal threefold experience as a *constructivist functioning, trinitarian imaging,* and *narrative shaping* Pentecostal soteriology, broadly cohered through the Pentecostal metaphor of Spirit baptism – as an integrating core of global Pentecostal spirituality and experience. I call this the Pentecostal Triple Way (PTW) model.

In part one I will establish two theological warrants for the PTW model: first, converging appreciation towards soteriology as a global theological core, and second, how prominent Pentecostal theological methods nuance the experiential multidimensionality of Pentecostal soteriological experience. In the first section of part two, I will demonstrate how the model re-envisions Land's earlier soteriological envisioning of the Pentecostal threefold experience, noting its merits and limitations via ongoing trends in Pentecostal theology. Then in section two, I will delineate the model according to its triadic-integrative methodology and structure. In part three I will

---

[2] Steven J. Land, *Pentecostal Spirituality: A Passion for the Kingdom* (JPTSup 1; Sheffield: Sheffield Academic Press, 1993; Cleveland, TN: CPT Press, 2010), pp. 11-12, 67-69, 74, 112-13; Simon Chan, *Pentecostal Theology and the Christian Spiritual Tradition* (JPTSup 21; Sheffield: Sheffield Academic Press, 2000), pp. 12, 31-36, 73-77.

[3] For a brief overview of the Three Ways, see the following articles by Thomas D. McGonigle in Michael Downey (ed.), *The New Dictionary of Catholic Spirituality* (Collegeville, MN: Liturgical Press, 1993): 'Three Ways', pp. 963-65; 'Purgation, Purgative Way', pp. 800-802; 'Illumination, Illuminative Way', pp. 529-31; 'Union, Unitive Way', pp. 987-88.

[4] I am following Amos Yong's designation of the term 'Keswickian', to Pentecostals historically representative of William H. Durham's 'finished work' two-stage scheme and 'Keswick "higher Christian life" revivalism'; *In the Days of Caesar: Pentecostalism and Political Theology* (Grand Rapids, MI: Eerdmans, 2010), pp. 28, 168-71.

conclude by delineating how in response to 21st-century contextual issues, the PTW model projects two key trajectories towards Pentecostal spirituality. The first trajectory delineates how the model contributes to integration of power, holiness, and love in Pentecostal spirituality. The second trajectory delineates what I call the soteriological scripting of apostolic testimony in Pentecostal life history.

Part One: Theological Warrants

Converging Proposals Toward a Theological Core of Global Pentecostalism

The model's first theological warrant arises from proposals respectfully suggested by Frank Macchia and Dale Coulter towards identifying core theological distinctives of global Pentecostalism. Macchia suggests that warrant for this ongoing research stems from Lindbeck's thesis that doctrinal language and theological constructs significantly shape faith communities.[5] For two reasons Coulter shares Macchia's sentiment – first of which is ecumenical responsibility towards other Christian traditions, which enjoins us towards giving and receiving gifts that reflect our respective communal giftedness. Through ecumenical dialogue we thus more clearly learn who we are, as we discover 'theological resemblance' with other Christian spiritualities both present and past.[6] Linked to the 'problem of finding doctrinal coherence among global micro-Pentecostalisms', Coulter's second reason is that Pentecostals worldwide have uncannily articulated their theologies via 'inherited theological models' that history and critical reflection prove incongruent to Pentecostal spirituality. Hence, Coulter stresses the need for 'developing alternative theological models' that resonate better with Pentecostal spirituality.[7]

---

[5] Frank D. Macchia, 'Baptized in the Spirit: Towards Global Theology of Spirit Baptism', in Veli-Matti Kärkkäinen (ed.), *The Spirit and Word: Emerging Pentecostal Theologies in Global Contexts* (Grand Rapids, MI: Eerdmans, 2009), pp. 3-20 (3).

[6] Dale M. Coulter, 'What Meaneth This? Pentecostals and Theological Inquiry', *Journal of Pentecostal Theology* 10.1 (2001), pp. 38-64 (39-40, 51).

[7] Dale M. Coulter, '"Delivered by the Power of God": Toward a Pentecostal Understanding of Salvation', *International Journal of Systematic Theology* 10.4 (October 2008), pp 447-67 (448); *idem*, 'What Meaneth This', pp. 51-52. Roman Catholic theologian Jeffrey Gros similarly suggested that Pentecostals would benefit from seeking commonalities with Christian traditions that lie deeper in the collective history of the Church; 'Dialogue: Ecumenical Connections Across Time: Medie-

Macchia meanwhile believes that currently fielded suggestions boil down to two basic answers. Hollenweger's research exemplifies the first answer: a holistic experience of the Spirit, coupled with how Pentecostals express this through oral modes of theologising.[8] The second answer comprises several proposals, each offering some form of 'doctrinal coherence' (e.g. five/fourfold gospel framework, eschatology).[9] Macchia then reiterates his thesis earlier argued in his work, *Baptized in the Spirit: A Global Pentecostal Theology*: the Pentecostal metaphor of Spirit baptism as the integrating, 'crown jewel' of Pentecostal theology.[10] To resolve the fragmenting of holiness from vocational-charismatic power in past understandings of Spirit baptism, Macchia argues for 'expanding the boundaries of Spirit baptism', describing it as a fluid metaphor comprising the entire soteriological scope of human life, even the eschatological renewing of creation.[11] In doing so, I believe that Macchia indelibly shifts the question of what is theologically distinctive about Pentecostalism to *soteriology*.

Coulter has more specifically argued that we appreciate soteriology as the theological core of global Pentecostal theology, which he further proposes 'be expressed in terms of two dominant metaphors: acquisition of God's life and deliverance'. He clarifies these metaphors as depicting a life-long deliverance from sin through 'increasing acquisition of God's triune life', a description that I find as highly resonant to the PTW model.[12] It seems then that Macchia's

---

val Franciscans as a Proto-Pentecostal Movement?' *Pneuma* 34 (2012), pp. 75-93 (76).

[8] Macchia, 'Baptized in the Spirit', pp. 12, 15; see Walter J. Hollenweger, *Pentecostalism: Origins and Developments Worldwide* (Peabody, MA: Hendrickson, 1997), pp. 18-20, 196.

[9] Donald W. Dayton, *Theological Roots of Pentecostalism* (Peabody, MA: Hendrickson, 1987); William Faupel, *The Everlasting Gospel: The Significance of Eschatology in the Development of Pentecostal Thought* (JPTSup 10; Sheffield: Sheffield Academic Press, 1996); Land, *Pentecostal Spirituality*.

[10] Macchia, 'Baptized in the Spirit', pp. 13-15, 20; *idem*, *Baptized in the Spirit: A Global Pentecostal Theology* (Grand Rapids, MI: Zondervan, 2006), pp. 17-18, 20, 25-26, 22, 57.

[11] Macchia, *Baptized in the Spirit*, pp. 18, 26, 46, 57, 59-60, 61-88 (ch. 3: 'Expanding the Boundaries of Spirit Baptism'), pp. 90-91, 154.

[12] Coulter, 'Delivered by the Power of God', pp. 447, 449. Coulter substantiates this thesis by noting amongst Roman Catholics, Methodists, and Pentecostals a 'shared soteriological substructure' enunciated through their mutual pneumatologies; *idem*, 'Baptism, Conversion, and Grace: Reflections on the "Underlying

thesis of Spirit baptism as the integrating 'crown jewel' of Pentecostal theology now reinforces Coulter's argument that what is theologically distinctive about Pentecostalism is its distinctive soteriology. I have concluded that fusing together Macchia's and Coulter's respective discussions, suggests good warrant for appreciating the Pentecostal theological distinctives of Spirit baptism and soteriology as referring to the same dynamic and a viable theological core to global Pentecostalism. I believe that as this study proceeds further, these trajectories shall point towards the timely relevance of the PTW model for ongoing developments in Pentecostal soteriology.

Convergences in Prominent Pentecostal Theological Methods
The second warrant for the PTW model arises from how prominent Pentecostal theological methods nuance the experiential multidimensionality of Pentecostal soteriological experience. I gathered this premise from reflection on Peter Neumann's recent study, *Pentecostal Experience: An Ecumenical Encounter*. Several variables make Neumann's work crucially relevant. First, his work freshly confirms Hollenweger's thesis that Pentecostalism is foremost an 'experiential tradition'. Second, Neumann explores how three notable Pentecostal theologians, namely Macchia, Chan, and Amos Yong, demonstrate three divergent examples on how 'the appeal to experience of God' is currently pursued in Pentecostal theology'. Third, Neumann's utilisation of the Wesleyan Quadrilateral (Scripture, tradition, reason, and experience) as an evaluative framework to their theological projects shows how each accents one of the 'three traditional media of the Spirit: Macchia accenting Scripture (more broadly, "Word"), Chan, the Christian tradition, and Yong, reason'.[13] Most important *though not explicitly developed*, is that Neumann's analysis infers that all three theologians stress the multi-dimensional, soteriologically fielded dynamics of experiencing the Holy Spirit, while also appreciating Pentecostal spirituality as a cultural-linguistic mediating ethos.

Beginning with Yong, I will briefly survey their respective soteriological themes to note how they converge towards PTW model. In

---

Realities" Between Pentecostals, Methodists, and Catholics', *Pneuma* 31 (2009), pp. 189-212 (190).

[13] Peter D. Neumann, *Pentecostal Experience: An Ecumenical Encounter* (Princeton Theological Monograph Series 187; Eugene, OR: Wipf and Stock Publishers, 2012), pp. 1-5, 14, 331.

his book, *The Spirit Poured Out on All Flesh: Pentecostalism and the Possibility of Global Theology*, Yong articulates a 'world pentecostal and pneumatological soteriology'.[14] Anchored upon a Lukan prioritised hermeneutic, Yong delineates the 'multidimensionality of salvation', comprising 'seven dimensions of salvation'; namely, personal, family, ecclesial, material, social, racial, class, gender, cosmic, and eschatological salvation. Yong then delineates a four-step scheme, beginning with the patristic understanding of Christian initiation as a prolonged process.[15] Step two broadens the Spirit baptism metaphor towards the experiences of justification, sanctification, and the Pentecostal nuance on empowerment for service. Step three adapts the Wesleyan dynamic *via salutis* notion, thus appreciating both maturational processes and 'crisis-event' experiences that move believers through phases of spiritual maturity. Step four incorporates Donald Gelpi's 'multidimensional' conversion theology (religious, intellectual, affective, moral, and sociopolitical types of conversion). The four steps lead Yong to conclude that the New Testament Spirit baptism metaphor encompasses the whole field of soteriology, and varied experiences that foster ongoing conversion in multidimensional manners.[16]

Macchia suggests a 'Trinitarian structure of Spirit baptism' comprising a 'full-orbed soteriology', by framing ongoing experiences in Spirit baptism via the *loci* of justification, sanctification, and charismatic empowerment for service. This triad of 'ongoing experiences', thus demonstrates God's 'Trinitarian involvement' in the human salvific journey. Macchia remains averse however to clearly demarcated salvific 'stages' (described as a 'fracturing' of 'life in the Spirit'), which he believes has too often construed Christian life as a series of disconnected 'crisis moments' lacking coherency.[17] Finally, Macchia stresses how this comprehensive theology of Spirit bap-

[14] Yong, *The Spirit Poured Out on All Flesh: Pentecostalism and the Possibility of Global Theology* (Grand Rapids, MI: Baker Academic, 2005), p. 82.

[15] Yong, *The Spirit Poured Out*, pp. 98-100. See Killian McDonnell and George T. Montague, *Christian Initiation and Baptism in the Holy Spirit: Evidence from the First Eight Centuries* (Collegeville MN: Liturgical Press, 2nd edn, 1994).

[16] Yong, *The Spirit Poured Out*, pp. 91-108, 118-19. See Donald L. Gelpi, *The Conversion Experience: A Reflective Process for RCIA Participants and Others* (New York, NY: Paulist Press, 1998), pp. 26, 42-57.

[17] Macchia, *Baptized in the Holy Spirit*, pp. 18, 27-31, 77; *idem*, 'Baptized in the Spirit', pp. 19-20, 27-30.

tism reinforces ecumenical consensus that justification and sanctification should not be construed as salvific stages but rather as 'two overlapping metaphors'.[18]

Chan's proposal to pattern the Pentecostal threefold experience to the 'Three Ways', derives from his broader project towards initiating a Pentecostal 'traditioning process' that situates Pentecostal spirituality within the older Christian ascetical/mystical tradition. He premises this project on what he calls the 'Pentecostal reality', encompassing a 'cluster of experiences' cohered together via the Pentecostal Spirit baptism metaphor. Like Macchia and Yong, Chan appreciates Spirit baptism as signifying the full scope of soteriology, conjoined to the dynamics of holiness and sanctification. Finally, he also describes experiences of Spirit baptism as revelatory encounters with the Triune life of God.[19] Therefore, I have concluded through this survey that Neumann's study infers how Keswickian oriented Pentecostal scholarship is developing in manners that subsume the entire Pentecostal threefold experience under the rubric of soteriology. I thus conclude that the divergent projects of Yong, Macchia, and Chan demonstrate growing convergence towards appreciating a multi-dimensional, experiential soteriology as a compelling option towards articulating a theological centre of Pentecostal tradition.

Part Two: The Pentecostal Triple Way Model

A Re-envisioning of Steven J. Land's Pentecostal Threefold *Via Salutis*

I will now demonstrate how the PTW model comprises a re-envisioning of Land's envisioning of Pentecostal soteriology, by critiquing its merits and limitations via an assessment of Yong's, Macchia's, and Chan's respective soteriological projects. Land's aim was pastorally oriented towards overcoming unhealthy dichotomies between holiness, love, and power, which he described as the 'unfinished theological task of Pentecostalism'. Building on this purpose, Land argues that through the three soteriological crisis-event experiences, God infuses believers with 'apocalyptic affections' that comprise the 'core of Pentecostal spirituality'.[20] He then coalesces

---

[18] Macchia, *Baptized in the Spirit*, pp. 129, 140; *idem, Justified in the Spirit: Creation, Redemption, and the Triune God* (Grand Rapids, MI: Eerdmans, 2010), p. 8.

[19] Chan, *Pentecostal Theology*, pp. 7, 10, 21.

[20] Land, *Pentecostal Spirituality*, pp. 11-12.

these affections of *gratitude, compassion*, and *courage* to the theological virtues of *faith, hope*, and *love* signifying the transformative coming of God's kingdom (regeneration: righteousness → *faith* → 'gratitude'; sanctification: peace → *love* → 'compassion'; Spirit baptism: joy → *hope* → 'courage').[21]

Land accentuates the 'category of crisis' in spiritual progress, but complements it by stressing how the trinitarian life of God patterns the Pentecostal threefold experience not as an *'ordo salutis'* but rather 'as a *via salutis'*.[22] Hence, Land suggests that the soteriological experiences of redemption, sanctification, and Spirit baptism may together comprise a 'developmental process with three dimensions'; hence, sources of 'continuing direction'.[23] However, he schematises this Pentecostal *via salutis* via the 'trinitarian dispensationalism' exemplified by Joachim of Fiore.[24] Land thus seeks to follow Jürgen Moltmann's appropriation of Joachim's trinitarian reading of salvation history. Yet Moltmann cautioned that appropriating Joachim's scheme bears the risk of minimising the perichoretic roles of the Father and the Son within the Spirit's own salvific mission.[25] Land may have inadvertently proceeded in this direction. Therefore, while he described his project as a Pentecostal *via salutis*, he could not fully shift from a maturational/linear perception of the Pentecostal threefold experience. I believe that Land thereby limited his project towards bridging the very thing he wanted to achieve, which was to establish a 'theological coherent case for the normativity' of Pentecostal experience(s).[26]

I suggest that still lacking in Land's project is a coherent apologetic for the plethora of spiritual crisis-events and experiential dynamics that characterise Pentecostal spiritual life. Macchia captures this need in response to the Pentecostal revivalistic penchant for construing the spiritual life as a 'series of separate, disconnected

---

[21] Land, *Pentecostal Spirituality*, pp. 67, 74-75, 120-21, 133-35.

[22] Land, *Pentecostal Spirituality*, pp. 67, 112, 114, 173, 200.

[23] Land, *Pentecostal Spirituality*, pp. 203.

[24] Land, *Pentecostal Spirituality*, pp. 197-98; *idem*, 'The Triune Center: Wesleyans and Pentecostals Together in Mission', *Wesleyan Theological Journal* 34.1 (1999), pp. 83-100 (85, 89); published simultaneously in *Pneuma* 21.2 (1999), pp. 199-214.

[25] Jürgen Moltmann, *The Spirit of Life: A Universal Affirmation* (trans. Margaret Kohl; Minneapolis, MN: Fortress Press, 2001), pp. 232, 295, 297-98.

[26] Land, *Pentecostal Spirituality*, pp. 71, 112, 203-204; *idem*, 'The Triune Center', pp. 84, 88, 96-98.

experiences'. He does so by arguing the need for 'a *more integral un-derstanding* [emphasis mine] of conversion, sanctification, and char-ismatic spirituality/empowerment that does not separate these di-mensions of spirituality into distinct stages', while recognising their 'theological distinctions', and our formative need for consciously desiring these diverse experiences.[27] However, while Macchia, Yong, and Chan mutually stress the ongoing multidimensionality of spir-itual experience and renewal within the broad soteriological rubric of Spirit baptism, my reflections on the narrative structure of both Christian soteriology and human experience, suggests that we need a more explicit narratological framework that clarifies their distinc-tives, which I am attempting to provide through the PTW model.

The PTW model addresses Macchia's call for better integrating the three Pentecostal soteriological experiences in manners that nar-ratively structure diverse renewing experiences in Pentecostal spirit-uality. It does so by incorporating two missing methodological in-gredients to the preceding soteriological discussions: *constructivism* and *narratology*, which I have coalesced to the trinitarian missions of the Spirit. With these ingredients, the PTW model blends together the common theological core options of holistic experience *cum* oral theologising, Spirit baptism, and soteriology, into a comprehensive descriptive of a global Pentecostal theological core, by moreover envisioning a trinitarian coherency to the experiential multidimen-sionality that characterises global Pentecostalism.

Explication of the PTW Model via its Triadic Methodology

Constructivist Functioning Soteriology

I will now explicate the PTW model according to its triadic-integrative methodology. Following Chan's lead, I will delineate throughout this discussion relevant dynamics of the Three Ways, suggesting how we may appropriate these toward a fresh envision-ing of the Pentecostal threefold *via salutis* in an ecumenical model of spiritual and life formation. I begin by focusing on how the PTW model comprises a constructivist approach to the Pentecostal three-fold soteriological experience. First to note is that discussions on

[27] Macchia, Frank D., 'Theology, Pentecostal', in Stanley M. Burgess and Ed-uard M. van der Mass (eds.), *The New International Dictionary of Pentecostal and Char-ismatic Movements* (Grand Rapids, MI: Zondervan Publishing House, rev. edn, 2002), pp. 1120-41 (1129, 1131).

the Three Ways classify such triadic salvific-developmental schemes as either constructivist or maturational paradigms that stress chronological stages.[28] Second, varied assessments have observed implicit roots of early North American Pentecostal multiple-stage salvific schemes to patristic and medieval multi-stage soteriologies along with the Eastern Orthodox concept of *theosis*. Highly relevant is David Bundy's thesis that early Pentecostal multiple-stage spiritualities (e.g William J. Seymour, Minnie Abrams, Thomas Ball Barratt) evidence a clear retrieving from the Alexandrian maturational three-stage salvific journey scheme (*praktiké*/'beginner', *theorétik-os*/'proficient', *gnosis*/*theologia*/'perfect'), along with Eastern Orthodox *theosis* themes via Wesleyan and Holiness influences.[29] Bundy's study provides a crucial congruence between Pentecostal soteriology and the Three Ways, although his discussion pertains only to its maturational expressions.

We can best appreciate a constructivist understanding of the Three Ways by also noting that constructivism is an ancient though contemporary meta-theoretical perspective that emphasises construction of life and/or meaning through ordering and patterning processes. Constructivist psychology thus stresses that people construct meaning to their lives through discovering patterns that provide coherence to their life experiences.[30] Contemporary life, moral, and faith developmental models also generally reflect constructivist premises.[31] Similarly, constructivist understandings of the Three Ways generally postulate the model as three concurrent, repeatable,

---

[28] Richard Woods, 'Three Ages', in *The New Dictionary of Catholic Spirituality*, p. 963; McGonigle, 'Three Ways', in *The New Dictionary of Catholic Spirituality*, p. 964. Biblical precedence for the maturational paradigm arises from themes signifying stages in spiritual progress, especially in the Pauline and Johannine literature; Richard Byrne, 'Journey (Growth and Development in Spiritual Life)', in *The New Dictionary of Catholic Spirituality*, pp. 565-77 (569).

[29] David Bundy, 'Visions of Sanctification: Themes of Orthodoxy in the Methodist, Holiness, and Pentecostal Traditions', *WesTJ* 39.1 (Spring 2004), pp. 104-36 (105-106, 127-35). Research on *theosis* themes within Pentecostalism have blossomed over the past decade: Veli-Matti Kärkkäinen, *One with God: Salvation as Deification and Justification* (Collegeville, MN: Unitas Books; Liturgical Press, 2004), pp. 108-15; Edmund J. Rybarczyk, *Beyond Salvation: Eastern Orthodoxy and Classical Pentecostalism on Becoming like Christ* (Milton Keynes: Paternoster Press, 2004).

[30] Michael J. Mahoney and Donald K. Granvold, 'Constructivism and Psychotherapy', *World Psychiatry* 4.2 (June 2005), pp. 74-77 (74-75).

[31] James W. Fowler, *Stages of Faith* (San Francisco, CA: Harper & Row, 1981), pp. 99, 99, 274-75, 288-91.

and spiralling processes leading towards union with God. This constructivist approach is most notably associated with the 13th century Franciscan theologian Bonaventure's soteriological model titled, *De Triplici Via* (*The Triple Way*; ad 1259-1260).[32] It seems that contemporary analysis within both Roman Catholicism and Eastern Orthodoxy generally favours the constructivist paradigm.[33]

Trinitarian Imaging Soteriology

The PTW model also projects a narratological framework that explicitly clarifies Macchia's reference to the 'Trinitarian structure of Spirit baptism', by more closely coalescing the three Pentecostal soteriological experiences to the respective soteriological missions of the Trinity. My proposal builds on Bonaventure's teaching that the Three Ways comprises the trinitarian structure of soteriology, through which God restores human similitude to His Triune personhood. In their restored state, humans stand erect, facing outward.[34] Hence, Bonaventure described sin as *incurvatus* ('bent over'); hence, sin bends humans in towards themselves. Salvation via the Three Ways thus describes the human journey from this dysfunctional state to uprightness through union with God.[35] Therefore, trinitarian spirituality implies restored human personhood as iconic of God's Triune personhood. Trinitarian spirituality thus depicts salvation as a salvific journey from dysfunctional *incurvatus* to union with God in His outward moving mission towards humanity and creation.[36] I suggest describing this soteriological aim as *imaging*.

---

[32] J.M. Hammond, 'Bonaventure, St', in Thomas Carson and Joann Cerrito (eds.), *New Catholic Encyclopedia* (Washington, DC: The Catholic University of America, 2nd edn, 2003), II, pp. 479-93 (481-82, 491); E.E. Larkin, 'Three Ways, The', in *New Catholic Encyclopedia*, vol. 14, pp. 65-66 (65); McGonigle, 'Three Ways', p. 964.

[33] Robert Davis Hughes III, 'The Holy Spirit in Christian Spirituality', in Arthur Holder (ed.), *The Blackwell Companion to Christian Spirituality* (Malden, MA: Blackwell Publishing Ltd, 2005), pp. 207-22 (213, 220). For an Eastern Orthodox constructivist approach see Kallistos Ware, *The Orthodox Way* (Crestwood, NY: St Vladimir's Seminary Press, 2001), pp. 106-107.

[34] Bonaventure, *The Enkindling of Love* ('The Triple Way'), trans. Regis J. Armstrong, http://john114.org/Docs/T_SB_Enkindling%20of%20Love3.htm; Hammond, 'Bonaventure, St', p. 488.

[35] Hammond, 'Bonaventure, St', p. 491.

[36] Catherine Mowry LaCugna and Michael Downey, 'Trinitarian Spirituality', in *The New Dictionary of Catholic Spirituality*, pp. 968-82 (969).

Commentaries on the Three Ways often note how the 'way' metaphor intrinsically infers this journey towards *theosis* (divinisation; union with God), and accompanying ascetic motifs characteristic of the spiritual life.[37] So in going out from ourselves in mission with God, humans show themselves as Moltmann suggests, created in the image of the Triune God (*imago Trinitatas* = *imago Dei*).[38] Appreciating the Pentecostal threefold experience as a spiralling rhythm thus reinforces Miroslav Volf's description of the salvific journey as one comprising movement from the self-referencing self to a self opened up towards others through 'the Spirit of embrace'.[39] From the premise that Spirit baptism comprises the entire salvific journey, the PTW model thus strongly suggests the social orientations of justification and holiness. As Macchia notes, this means that through the Spirit's embrace at the very horizon of spiritual regeneration, one is justified and hence set apart as participants in 'God's Triune, perichoretic life and mission'.[40]

A helpful resource towards appreciating the Pentecostal threefold experience as the trinitarian structure of Spirit baptism, is Robert Davis Hughes' own constructivist understanding of Three Ways. In his model, the Three Ways signify in human development, the greater 'three-fold' mission of the Spirit towards creation, whereby the Spirit executes the three roles of God's Triune personhood.[41] The purgative way signifies the 're-turn' of all things back to the Father.[42] In human life, it comprises redemptive awareness and experience. Comprising experiences of cleansing, it infuses the theological virtue of *faith*. The illuminative way signifies the transfiguring of human life into the pattern of the Son. Comprising experiences of dislocation leading to awakening, it infuses the theological virtue of *love*. Pointing to the Spirit's mission proper, the unitive way signifies our union to God's aims for all creation. It comprises increasing revelation of the Trinity, and eschatological awareness arising from

---

[37] Byrne, 'Journey', in *The New Dictionary of Catholic Spirituality*, p. 565; LaCugna and Downey, 'Trinitarian Spirituality', pp. 972-73.

[38] Moltmann, *Spirit of Life*, p. 221.

[39] Miroslav Volf, *Exclusion and Embrace: A Theological Exploration of Identity, Otherness, and Reconciliation* (Nashville, TN: Abingdon Press, 1996), p. 66.

[40] Macchia, *Justified in the Spirit*, pp. 4-5, 8-12, 214, 254-56, 293-94, 301-302, 306, 311.

[41] Hughes III, 'The Holy Spirit', p. 219.

[42] Hughes III, 'The Holy Spirit', pp. 213-14.

infusion with the theological virtue of *hope*. This hope is deeply missiological, because it signifies intensified longing for both the receiving and *giving* of love, arising from encounter with the perichoretic life of the Trinity.[43]

I find Hughes' model helpful towards patterning the Pentecostal threefold experience to a constructivist understanding of the Three Ways. First, his approach resonates with Land's delineation of the Pentecostal affections of gratitude, compassion, and courage. Second, Hughes' model clarifies Spirit baptism as the entire soteriological field that comprises these trinitarian missions in human life. It thus moreover helps us appreciate Peter Hocken's description of Spirit baptism as intermediacy into the Trinity.[44] From this premise, we can thus appreciate the PTW model as a trinitarian categorising of Spirit baptism experiences, in that it describes how Spirit baptism restores to people their true eschatological horizon arising from intermediacy into God's trinitarian pathos and mission. Moreover, these discernible similarities between the Pentecostal threefold experience and the historical Three Ways, helps link Pentecostal spirituality to traditions of theological resemblance within the Church Catholic.

Narrative Shaping Soteriology

The third dynamic of the PTW model describes the threefold Pentecostal experience as a narrative shaping soteriology, thus pointing to the implicit storying structure and rhythm resident within a robust Pentecostal spirituality. This rhythm of storied Pentecostal experience, scripts in believers redemptive testimonies and an eschatological horizon that fosters a providential sense of destiny. Perhaps an important though broader context to this discussion may be that the human salvific quest for union intrinsically drives human aestheticism, such as exemplified in the Western philosophical triad of the good, true, and beautiful, which clarifies our need for identifiable patterns and coherency. We may thus aptly identify human-

---

43 Hughes III, 'The Holy Spirit', pp. 216-19.

44 Peter Hocken, *The Glory and the Shame: Reflections on the 20th Century Outpouring of the Holy Spirit* (Surrey: Eagle; Inter Publishing Service, 1994), pp. 7, 49, 60-61.

kind as *homo narrans*, or even *homo poeta*.[45] Alasdair MacIntrye argues
that the human quest for a coherent life, meaning the 'unity of a
human life', is essentially 'the unity of a narrative quest'.[46] This quest
thus characterises the teleological and I would say, a crucial soteriological aim of human life. As Michael Root points out, we may
therefore better articulate the doctrine of soteriology, as well as our
soteriological experiences, via these intrinsic narrative qualities of
tension and resolution that characterise human life.[47] Therefore,
presuming all human experience as 'inherently narrative' and the
aesthetic quality that describes all good 'sacred stories' in their power to evoke poetry, I will now suggest that we can aptly describe the
Pentecostal threefold soteriological experience as the poetics of
Spirit baptism.[48]

   Pentecostalism has historically celebrated the poetics of Spirit
baptism through its oral liturgies, which often comprise the sharing
of personal testimony.[49] Pentecostal spirituality thus fosters an oral
ethos, which creates an open space wherein one can freely anticipate invasive, ministerial manifestations of the Holy Spirit. Arguing
for the epistemological role of orality in global Pentecostal spirituality, James Smith describes this as an *'affective, narrative epistemology'*.
This epistemology stresses the 'role of experience' and shared 'testimony' in Pentecostal spirituality and theologising. Hence, he calls
attention to the 'narrative function of testimony' whereby Pentecostals 'enact an identity by writing themselves into the larger story of
God's redemption'.[50] Meanwhile, Chan affirms as a crucial 'traditioning' resource in Pentecostal tradition, the 'powerful narratives'

---

[45] Fowler, *Stages of Faith*, p. 24; Walter R. Fisher, 'Narration as a Human Communication Paradigm: The Case of Public Moral Argument', *Communication Monograph* 51 (March 1984), pp. 1-22 (6).

[46] Alasdair MacIntyre, *After Virtue: A Study in Moral Theory* (Notre Dame, IN: University of Notre Dame Press, 3rd edn, 2007), p. 219.

[47] Michael Root, 'The Narrative Structure of Soteriology', in Stanley Hauerwas and L. Gregory Jones (eds.), *Why Narrative? Readings in Narrative Theology* (Grand Rapids, MI: Eerdmans, 1989), pp. 263-78 (263, 268-74); originally published in *Modern Theology* 2.2 (January 1986), pp. 145-57.

[48] Steven Crites, 'The Narrative Quality of Experience', in *Why Narrative*, pp. 65-88 (66, 69); originally published in *Journal of the American Academy of Religion* 49.3 (September 1971), pp. 291-311.

[49] Hollenweger, *Pentecostalism*, pp. 302, 327, 329.

[50] James K.A. Smith, *Thinking in Tongues: Pentecostal Contributions to Christian Philosophy* (Grand Rapids, MI: Eerdmans, 2010), pp. xxi-xxiii, 12, 43-44, 51.

that characterise Pentecostal 'testimonies'.[51] Finally, Cheryl Bridges Johns suggests that the conscientization power in Pentecostal spirituality derives from this 'oral-narrative' liturgical dynamic, as believers discover they have a 'voice' towards the making of 'holy history'.[52] This poetics of Spirit baptism thus fosters the eschatological impulse in Pentecostal spirituality, endowing believers with a heightened 'sense of history' and calling to God's historical purposes.[53]

The PTW model illustrates the poetics of Spirit baptism by demonstrating how we may appreciate the threefold Pentecostal soteriological experience(s) as a spiralling narrative shaping framework that fosters in believers' lives coherency and ongoing testimonies to God's involvement in their lives. These emerge from the storying rhythm intrinsic to ever-new transitions through the Pentecostal threefold soteriological experience. I discovered how this threefold experience can be approached as a narrative shaping, soteriological framework through synthesising relevant insights from narrative methodology in personality psychology, Paul Ricoeur's threefold hermeneutical circle, and Walter Brueggemann's thesis that the genres comprising the Old Testament Psalter testify to a repetitive threefold growth pattern that engages people of biblical faith.

Psychotherapists utilizing narrative methodology presume that a healthy self-concept and self-identity, emerges through developing a coherently structured self-narrative, thus reflecting the storied nature of human existence.[54] Donald Polkinghorne thus defines self-concept as 'narrative configuration'. Hence, the 'self' evolves through the 'shaping and forming' of time in manners that lead to coherence of one's life – a coherently narrated life-story. Failure to produce such narrative configuration, commonly results in a sense of self-fragmentation, and experiences of '*angst* and despair' given that one is unable to identify a plot that coheres life events into an

---

[51] Chan, *Pentecostal Theology*, p. 20.

[52] Cheryl Bridges Johns, *Pentecostal Formation: A Pedagogy among the Oppressed* (JPTSup 2; Sheffield: Sheffield Academic Press, 1993), pp. 87, 89.

[53] Land, *Pentecostal Spirituality*, pp. 59-61; Macchia, *Baptized in the Spirit*, pp. 38-42.

[54] Donald E. Polkinghorne, 'Narrative and Self-Concept', *Journal of Narrative and Life History* 1.2-3 (1991), pp. 135-53 (136, 151).

'integrated experience of self'.[55] Ongoing narrative configuration follows the typical three stage narrative structure of beginning, middle, and end of any single episode. Yet the process of developing a coherent 'life story' is a lifelong task.[56]

A highly relevant study undertaken within the past two decades led narrative psychologists to identify a life-story form, which they call the 'redemptive self'. This 'redemptive self' narrative was observed amongst mid-life people scoring high on measures of 'generativity', referring to a high maturation stage at which one is willing to commit one's self to the well-being of future generations. Adults who articulated their life as a 'narrative of redemption', generally expressed a narrative structure in which the protagonist experiences deliverance from suffering to an enhanced status or stage, leading to a heightened sense of gratitude, destiny, and desire to seek the betterment of others.[57] The 'redemptive self' narrative to some extent resembles the broad aims of life maturation which varied 'three ways' models typically point to – the development of compassion towards others that emerges from movement towards union/*theosis* and deepening acquisition of the theological virtues of faith, hope, and love.

Ricoeur similarly refers to the '*pre-narrative quality of human experience*', which comprises the '*search of a narrative*'. Once found the perceived plot makes one's life understandable, leading to a 'narrative identity'. Ricoeur describes this process as 'emplotment'.[58] Related to his theory of emplotment is Ricoeur's hermeneutical circle, comprising the three stages of: 1. Pre-figuration/pre-understanding; 2. Configuration; 3. Re-figuration. In this scheme, 'pre-figuration/pre-understanding' refers to receiving an understanding of the world through our available cultural structures and symbols. 'Configuration' refers to initiation of the 'emplotment' process. 'Re-figuration' refers to a process in which the newly constructed narrative trans-

---

[55] Polkinghorne, 'Narrative and Self-Concept', pp. 143-44, 151.

[56] Polkinghorne, 'Narrative and Self-Concept', pp. 141, 145.

[57] Dan P. McAdams, 'The Role of Narrative in Personality Psychology Today', *Narrative Inquiry* 16.1 (2006), pp. 11-18 (16-17).

[58] Paul Ricoeur, 'Life in Quest of Narrative', in David Wood (ed.), *On Paul Ricoeur: Narrative and Interpretation* (New York: Routledge, 1991), pp. 21, 29, 33.

figures previous perceptions of reality through entirely new understandings.[59]

Through appropriation of Ricoeur's work, Brueggemann argued
that the Psalter testifies to a repetitive threefold life rhythm that engages people of biblical faith. He describes this pattern as 1. Orientation; 2. Disorientation; and 3. New orientation. Brueggemann
thus suggests that we first note how some of the Psalms illustrate
situations of secure orientation with a sense of 'equilibrium'; hence,
times when life most makes sense with God in charge. However,
most of the Psalms reflect the second stage. Here people become
'overwhelmed' through disorienting experiences. These drive them
to profound depths of prayer, sometimes in the form of lament,
and sometimes in manners inferring the limits of spoken speech in
verbalising our prayers of disorientation. Yet finally, disorientation
transitions to new orientation. This comprises the emergence of joy
through gaining a radically new revelation of God's reign, coupled
with new understandings of the world before us.[60]

I will now bring these theoretical strands together. First, we can
fuse the three preceding resources as one narrative cycle, moreover
correlated to a constructivist appreciation of the Pentecostal threefold soteriological experience(s). Second, Brueggemann's triadic 'life
passages' cycle closely resonates with Land's delineation of the three
Pentecostal affections and three forms of Pentecostal prayer,
emerging from the threefold Pentecostal experience(s).[61] Synthesising all these variables together leads to the following narrative
scheme.

1. *Redemptive* experiences/processes (story setting):
   Pre-figuration/equilibrium → 'gratitude' → 'prayer with
   words'.
2. *Sanctifying* experiences/processes (rising tension):
   Configuration/disorientation → 'compassion' → 'prayer
   without words'.
3. *Empowering* experiences/processes (resolution):

---

[59] Ricoeur, 'Life in Quest of Narrative', p. 28; *idem*, 'Time and Narrative:
Threefold Mimesis', in *Time and Narrative*, vol. 1 (trans. Kathleen McLaughlin and
David Pellauer; Chicago, IL: The University of Chicago Press, 1984), pp. 53-71.

[60] Walter Brueggemann, *Praying the Psalms: Engaging Scripture and the Life of the
Spirit* (Eugene, OR: Wipf & Stock Publishers, 2nd edn, 2007), pp. 2-12.

[61] Land, *Pentecostal Spirituality*, pp. 47, 134-35, 139, 154-55, 163, 170-71; 183.

Re-figuration/new orientation → 'courage' → 'tongues speech'.

Integrating Hughes' identification of the trinitarian missions to the Three Ways (and infusion of the theological virtues) correlates to the beginning of the narrative cycle, the Father's 'converting' mission (purgation → 'faith'); to the middle, the Son's 'transfiguring' mission (illumination → 'love'); to the end, the Spirit's 'perfecting' mission (union → 'hope'). Finally, we can note that by narratively patterning the Pentecostal threefold experience(s), the PTW model thus projects a narratological framework that more explicitly clarifies Macchia's reference to the 'Trinitarian structure of Spirit baptism'. It does so by more closely coalescing the three Pentecostal soteriological *loci* to the respective soteriological missions of the Trinity, as exemplified in Hughes' delineation of the Three Ways.

Part Three: Concluding Trajectories

Integrating Power, Holiness, and Love
In this final section, I will delineate two key trajectories the PTW model projects towards Pentecostal spirituality. The first trajectory delineates how the model contributes to integration of power, holiness, and love in Pentecostal spirituality. The second trajectory delineates what I call the soteriological scripting of apostolic testimony in Pentecostal life history. Through its perceived rhythm of redeeming, sanctifying, and empowering experiences that together narrate in Christian life the soteriological aims of Spirit baptism, the PTW model significantly contributes towards ongoing efforts in overcoming the past bifurcation of holiness and power in Pentecostal tradition. In their respective insights towards the multidimensionality of Pentecostal soteriological experience, Yong, Macchia, and Chan each address this problematic, through their mutual stress on Spirit baptism as comprising the whole soteriological field of Christian experience.[62]

While pursued through three divergent theological methods, all three theologians project Spirit baptism as nothing less than a baptism in the love of God. Macchia pursues this thesis as the heart of

---

[62] Macchia, *Baptized in the Spirit*, pp. 18, 46, Chan, *Pentecostal Theology*, pp. 68, 86-87; Yong, *Spirit of Love: A Trinitarian Theology of Grace* (Waco TX: Baylor University Press, 2012), pp. 40, 42, 60-64.

his whole theology of Spirit baptism.[63] In his recent text, *Spirit of Love: A Trinitarian Theology of Grace*, Yong draws heavily from Land's and Macchia's preceding works to argue that early holiness Pentecostal assumptions that sanctifying experiences should precede tarrying for Spirit baptism, provides a relevant resource for reinvigorating Pentecostal spirituality (with particular concern towards the Keswickian stream) as a missiologically aimed, love-producing spirituality.[64] While Chan does not explicitly associate Spirit baptism with love, his attempt to correlate the Pentecostal threefold experience with the Three Ways dovetails with Macchia's and Yong's more intentional associations. This is because common understandings within ancient ascetical and mystical traditions normally stress perfected love or charity (along with compassion) towards others, as an ultimate result of maturation through the Three Ways.[65] Chan thus argues that the bifurcation of holiness and power largely stems from detaching experiences of Spirit baptism from a believer's awareness of any prior '*discernible*' progress in 'sanctification', which a constructivist understanding of the Pentecostal threefold experience overcomes by premising spiritual growth as prerequisite to power for service.[66] Chan thus argues that that we can better check behavioural expressions of over-realised eschatology if the 'prerequisite of sanctity' is structurally coalesced along periodic experiences of spiritual power.[67]

I directly retrieved Chan's patterning of the Pentecostal threefold experience to a constructivist understanding of the 'Three Ways', having concluded that indelibly imprinted within the psyche of early North American Pentecostalism was the intuitive conviction that consecration to a holy life should precede Spirit baptism as endued charismatic power for service. One clear influence to this assumption was of course the Wesleyan-Holiness influence on early North American Pentecostalism. A classic example often cited is the quote

---

[63] Macchia, *Baptized in the Spirit*, pp. 16, 60, 257-82.

[64] Yong, *Spirit of Love*, pp. 60-67, 72, 86-90, 104-10.

[65] Steven Chase, *Contemplation and Compassion: The Victorine Tradition* (Traditions of Christian Spirituality Series; London: Darton, Longman and Todd Ltd, 2003), pp. 13-15, 98, 119-20, 148-50; Hughes III, 'The Holy Spirit', pp. 218-19.

[66] Chan, *Pentecostal Theology*, pp. 68, 70-77, 87-89; *idem*, 'Evidential Glossolalia and the Doctrine of Subsequence', *Asian Journal of Pentecostal Studies* 2.2 (July 1999), pp. 195-211 (208-209).

[67] Chan, *Pentecostal Theology*, pp. 62-64, 68-77.

from the first issue of *The Apostolic Faith* (Azusa Street), which argued that Spirit baptism is 'a gift of power upon the sanctified life'.[68] Yet a cursory review of early Assemblies of God literature illustrates continuity of this assumption, even after that movement shifted towards more Keswickian understandings of sanctification. E.N. Bell for instance stressed consecration as a prelude to Spirit baptism, advising that, 'self has to be surrendered and every heart ... cleansed ... before it can be filled with the Holy Spirit'.[69] Stanley Frodsham similarly insisted on the need for consecration prior to Spirit baptism, stating, 'When ... we present our bodies a living sacrifice, holy and acceptable ... the fire of God's Spirit will fall'.[70] Citing the Pentecost narrative in Acts, Donald Gee stressed the same theme: 'Repentance is the prerequisite of the Baptism in the Holy Spirit. I am wondering if that is not why some of our present-day baptisms are so shallow – lack of repentance'.[71] While usually evidencing a strong Reformed approach to discussions on sanctification, William Menzies describes the early Assemblies of God ethos stating, 'holiness was more than a theological concept ... regardless of what school of thought was entertained about the doctrine of sanctification, there remained a great concern about holiness of life'.[72]

I therefore suggest that even amongst early Keswickian oriented Pentecostals, the ongoing assumption that consecration to a holy life should precede Spirit baptism, served a *functional purpose* for awakening *believers to* the eschatological horizon imparted via experiences of Spirit baptism, understood as empowerment for missiological witness and service. Without necessarily implying the older three-stage soteriological understanding, expressions of consecration to God thus provided amongst early Keswickian oriented Pentecostals, a healthy ongoing rhythm that integrated experiences of

---

[68] 'The Apostolic Faith Mission', *The Apostolic Faith* 1.19 (September 1907), p. 2 (author unknown).

[69] E.N. Bell, *Questions and Answers* (Springfield, MO: Gospel Publishing House, 1945), p. 55.

[70] Stanley Frodsham, *Rivers of Living Water: The Secret of a Perpetual Pentecost* (Springfield, MO: Gospel Publishing House, 1947), p. 21.

[71] Donald Gee, *After Pentecost* (Springfield, MO: Gospel Publishing House, 1945), p. 55.

[72] William W. Menzies, *Anointed To Serve: The Story of the Assemblies of God* (Springfield, MO: Gospel Publishing House, 1971), p. 57.

redemption, consecration, and vocational power for service. The PTW model thus seeks to conceptualise a renewed appropriation of this early 20th century North American Pentecostal assumption that consecration to a holy life should precede Spirit baptism for missiological witness – not in manners necessarily implying chronological stages but rather primarily as a spiralling rhythm within the human salvific journey.

A crucial manner, however, in which the PTW model diverges from Chan's earlier proposal is in its description of the third experience not as Spirit baptism per se, but rather more specifically as missionally empowering experiences. Three variables account for this description, first of which is increasing recognition that the Pentecostal metaphor of Spirit baptism should be appreciated as comprising the entire human salvific journey, within which as earlier mentioned, Macchia integrates the three soteriological 'elements' of 'justification, sanctification and charismatic empowerment'. Second, what I have consistently observed in descriptions of the unitive way is, besides the idea of relational union to God, a growing cosmic awareness and hence, union with God in His mission towards creation. Third, I have sought to correspond this aspect of the Pentecostal threefold experience to the crucial role that the traditional Pentecostal hermeneutical prioritising of Luke–Acts plays in shaping the Pentecostal psyche, mission consciousness, and communal giftedness.

Chan similarly corresponds the unitive way to the third Pentecostal experience as an 'empowerment for mission'. Yet in wanting to stress empowerment as resulting from spiritual growth, he consistently argues against any viable role for the traditional Pentecostal Lukan-prioritised hermeneutic.[73] He especially faults the exegetical projects of Roger Stronstad and Robert Menzies as contributing to the bifurcation of holiness and power, given that their arguments for a Lukan pneumatology stresses the coming of the Spirit as an missiological empowerment without soteriological function.[74] There

---

[73] Chan, *Pentecostal Theology*, pp. 43-50, 71, 73-74, 85-87.
[74] Chan, *Pentecostal Theology*, pp. 42, 85-86. See Roger Stronstad, *The Charismatic Theology of St Luke* (Peabody, MA: Hendrickson, 1984); Robert P. Menzies, *Empowered for Witness: The Spirit in Luke–Acts* (JPTSup 6; Sheffield: Sheffield Academic Press, 1994); *idem, The Development of Early Christian Pneumatology with Spiritual Reference to Luke–Acts* (JSNTSup 54; Sheffield: JSOT Press, 1991).

are certainly limitations to their readings of Luke's pneumatology, notwithstanding their positive role towards Pentecostal readings of Scripture. Yet from the perspective of Lindbeck's cultural-linguistic principle, I find it crucial to integrate the PTW model with the historical Pentecostal Lukan-prioritised hermeneutic. Yong provides helpful direction by how he premises his 'pneumatological soteriology' upon this hermeneutical lens, noting its role towards shaping the Pentecostal imagination, while conversely stressing Stronstad's limitations.[75]

I suggest two key terms that clarify this trajectory: the Roman Catholic conciliar slogan *aggiornamento*, and Cheryl Bridges Johns' description of Pentecostalism as a movement of *conscientization* and hence, 'social transformation'. Noting its reference to the 'development of theological resources' that may 'provide a coherent critique of the culture of modernity', Wolfgang Vondey suggests that *aggiornamento* aptly describes the crucial role which life at the grassroots level plays within global Pentecostalism in fostering the role that 'orthopathy' plays in shaping contextualized though 'critical, countercultural' dynamics of Pentecostal liturgy.[76] Meanwhile, in her book *Pentecostal Formation: A Pedagogy among the Oppressed*, Johns argues that 'Pentecostalism as a movement offers a social-spiritual climate for conscientization' in the context of a robust Pentecostal worshiping ethos.[77] Working from South American educator Paulo Freire's educational conscientization paradigm which he purposed towards the social uplift of lower socio-economic communities, Johns defines *conscientization* as 'the process whereby persons become aware of the socio-cultural reality which shapes their lives', yet also of 'their ability to transform that reality'.[78] Johns thus argues that Pentecostalism is communally gifted with a 'dual prophetic role: denouncing the dominant patterns of the status quo and announcing the patterns of God's kingdom', by providing 'symbols of

---

[75] Yong, *The Spirit Poured Out*, pp. 83-91.

[76] Wolfgang Vondey, *Beyond Pentecostalism: The Crisis of Global Christianity and the Renewal of the Theological Agenda* (Grand Rapids, MI: Eerdmans Co, 2010), pp. 159-65; citing Tracey Rowland, *Culture and the Thomist Tradition after Vatican II* (London: Routledge, 2003), p. 19.

[77] Johns, *Pentecostal Formation*, pp. 12-13, 62.

[78] Johns, *Pentecostal Formation*, p. 13.

hope' that empower people towards experiences of both spiritual and social transformation.[79]

I suggest that to some extent, the Pentecostal experience of Spirit baptism mediated through the cultural-linguistic ethos of Pentecostal communities that are in turn shaped by the traditional Lukan-prioritised hermeneutic, fosters these crucial Pentecostal dynamics of '*aggiornamento*' and 'conscientization' within Pentecostal liturgical ethos. I also suggest then that there are core elements within Pentecostalism which when held together, comprise a spiritual tradition that demonstrates salient affinity within a tradition exemplified in Luke–Acts, which distinctively draws upon themes conversely reflecting the Old Testament prophetic tradition. Hence, the historical prioritising of Luke–Acts has particularly informed perennial contours of Pentecostalism, such as its nuance on shared narrative identity with the first-century apostolic church, its perennial oral ethos, democratisation of ministry, redemptive appeal towards the marginalised and nuances towards themes of social, racial, and demographic inclusiveness, and reconciliation. Pentecostal experiences of Spirit baptism thus empower, especially the previously voiceless, with a newfound prophetic imagination that makes them witnesses to God's coming kingdom in ways that radically subvert prevailing realities.

In arguing that Luke stresses the Church as the foretold eschatological 'prophethood of believers', I thus believe that Stronstad intuitively articulated themes deeply primal to the communal giftedness of the Pentecostal tradition worldwide.[80] These dynamics altogether contribute to the communal giftedness of Pentecostalism, which it should ecumenically offer back to the broader Church Catholic. This Lukan-prioritised hermeneutic grants Pentecostalism its communally *epicletic* giftedness towards fostering personal and communal consecration to social holiness and God's mission. No longer of course can we narrowly define Spirit baptism to just these themes. Yet perhaps we can attribute these themes to what we might better describe as a 'pentecostal experience of Spirit baptism',

---

[79] Johns, *Pentecostal Formation*, pp. 65-70.

[80] Stronstad, *The Prophethood of All Believers: A Study in Luke's Charismatic Theology* (JPTSup 16; Sheffield: Sheffield Academic Press, 1999; Cleveland, TN: CPT Press, 2010), p. 28.

which I would correlate to the unitive way, hence – missionally empowering experiences.

Soteriological Scripting of Apostolic Testimony

I will now conclude by delineating what I define as the soteriological scripting of apostolic testimony in Pentecostal life history. This pertains to how the PTW model may inform the traditional Pentecostal stress on seeking transformative encounters with the Holy Spirit through congregational dynamics of worship. Daniel Castelo argues that sustained moral witness necessitates the discerning of altar experiences within the interpretive Pentecostal '*way of being-in-the-world*' as an 'epicletic community'. By 'epicletic', Castelo refers to Pentecostal appreciation towards the '*presence, prompting, and empowerment* of the Holy Spirit'.[81] Translating the PTW model to congregational experience affirms this timely envisioning of Pentecostal spirituality, through its soteriological understanding of Pentecostal experiences(s) as an ongoing life-narrative-shaping rhythm of *redeeming, sanctifying,* and *missionally* empowering experiences and processes initiated through the Holy Spirit.

As an ecumenically rooted yet uniquely Pentecostal way of spiritual and life formation, the PTW model describes the ongoing narrative structuring of the Christian 'self' within the ascetical structure and identity-forming context of Christian community. Helpful towards clarifying this trajectory is Dean Blevins's suggestion that we reorientate the postmodern socially constructed self to a theologically grounded 'self-in-harmony' with the trinitarian life of God.[82] Ideally, congregational worship dramatises this life-formation through its threefold liturgical movement of doxology, consecration, and epiclesis.[83] Through a constructivist approach to the threefold Pentecostal soteriological experience(s), we can correlate liturgical doxology to redemptive experiences/processes, liturgical expressions of consecration to sanctifying experiences/processes, and liturgical expressions of epiclesis to missionally empowering experiences/processes. The threefold movement within congregational worship thus consecrates one's self towards periodic and ongoing

---

[81] Daniel Castelo, *Revisioning Pentecostal Ethics: The Epicletic Community* (Cleveland, TN: CPT Press, 2012), pp. 2-3, 22. (emphasis original)

[82] Dean G. Blevins, 'A Wesleyan View of the Liturgical Construction of the Self', *Wesleyan Theological Journal* 38.2 (Fall 2003), pp. 7-29 (22-23, 28).

[83] Blevins, 'A Wesleyan View', pp. 23, 26-27, 29.

storying rhythms of the Pentecostal threefold soteriological experiences as we discern through the Spirit their emergence.

The PTW model also envisions a relevant Pentecostal vision of holiness and Christian *telos*, responsive to the 21st-century problematics of contingent social systems, virtual-human interface, protean selfhood, psychic fragmentation, and postmodern narcissism by accentuating holiness in terms of integrity, unity, wholeness, and completeness. In doing so, the model suggests the scripting of ongoing identity formation and identity narratives of people united with God for His mission towards creation in the recapitulatory pattern of the Son through the power of the Holy Spirit. Accentuating holiness via the Wesleyan insight of sanctifying/perfecting grace, the model also points to the Pentecostal notion of restored apostolicity or apostolic vocation and experience, which Pentecostals generally interpret as restored intermediacy with the first church in its life experience, giftedness, and mission.[84] A common theme within early Pentecostal literature describes sanctification as preparatory to restored 'apostolic faith'.[85] In early Pentecostalism, this strong sense of restored apostolicity thus in turn clarified early Pentecostal self-identity as 'holiness people'.[86] What thus qualifies us as 'holiness people' is that we identify ourselves as people *set apart* as missionary witnesses to God's kingdom.

We saw how the PTW model describes the threefold Pentecostal experience as a narrative shaping soteriology, thus pointing to the implicit storying structure and rhythm resident within a robust Pentecostal spirituality. This structural rhythm lends to the orality that has historically hallmarked Pentecostal congregational ethos, liturgy, and its distinctive way of theologising. This narrative understanding of Pentecostal soteriology thus describes how the Triune God uses this spiralling rhythm of redeeming, sanctifying, and empowering experiences to script in us – ever-new stories and testimonies of

---

[84] Kärkkäinen, '"The Leaning Tower of Pentecostal Ecclesiology": Reflections on the Doctrine of the Church on the Way', in John Christopher Thomas (ed.), *Toward a Pentecostal Ecclesiology: The Church and the Fivefold Gospel* (Cleveland, TN: CPT Press, 2010), p. 270.

[85] Macchia, *Baptized in the Spirit*, p. 229; Land, *Pentecostal Spirituality*, pp. 51-52.

[86] Kimberley Ervin Alexander, 'The Holiness of the Church: An Analysis of Wesleyan-Pentecostal Thought', *International Journal for the Study of the Christian Church* 11.4 (November 2011), pp. 269-78 (271-72).

God's faithfulness, that shape our missional witness of Jesus through the power of the Holy Spirit.

The PTW model therefore suggests that the conceptual link which these experiences and processes provide between Pentecostal spirituality and its implicit soteriological message, accounts for the power that Pentecostalism historically demonstrates towards restoring to people a sense of 'voice', providential awareness, and historical consciousness. This restoration especially proves evident for people who have suffered deep experiences of deprivation in all forms. Such broken people find their true eschatological horizon towards the shaping of history, as the Spirit consecrates them towards apostolic intermediacy into God's Trinitarian pathos and mission. Hence, they especially discover that their lives help shape history towards the coming fullness of God's kingdom, as the Holy Spirit scripts in them ongoing testimonies of God's hand on their lives. In this Pentecostal *via salutis*, believers therefore experience restored primal human vocation as 'storytellers' of God's new creation.

To conclude, the Pentecostal Triple Way model projects a Pentecostal *via salutis* and a Pentecostal *theologia viatorum* ('wayfarer's theology'), comprising a lifelong spiralling rhythm of *redeeming, sanctifying*, and *missionally* empowering experiences and processes initiated through the Holy Spirit on holy ground. This rhythm projects a soteriological narrative that perfects believers in mission with God for the perfecting of all creation, while leading them in their salvific journey towards *theosis*. This narrative envisioning of Pentecostal soteriology also points to an implicit triadic storying rhythm resident within a robust Pentecostal spirituality. This rhythm of storied Pentecostal experience, scripts in believers redemptive testimonies and an eschatological horizon that fosters a providential sense of destiny in shaping history towards the coming fullness of God's kingdom.

9

HOLINESS AND ECONOMICS: TOWARDS RECOVERY OF EUCHARISTIC BEING IN A MARKET-SHAPED WORLD

DANIELA C. AUGUSTINE[*]

Introduction: From the 'Sacredness' of the Market to the Sacredness of the World

The world is a market. Hardly anyone would contradict such a statement today. The process of globalization, as the technological-ly-induced compression of time and space, has landed a true sense of omnipresence to Western neoliberal capitalism and its all-commodifying market logic. Global economic integration has insured that the entire world may share the devastating impact of the latest crisis engineered at the prosperous stock markets of the West by unholy trading and lending practices. The global economy has absorbed and 'equitably' distributed the negative outcome of Wall Street's moral irresponsibility, making everyone pay for the greedy appetites of a few. It could be argued that every person in the world has been subjugated in one way or another to the effects of this economic crisis (e.g. through the loss of 'investments, retirement, college savings; a home lost to foreclosure or a job lost to cutbacks; or simply the increased debt burden'[1] of national governments as well as through the reduction of charitable giving towards international and domestic projects, etc.).

---

[*] Daniela C. Augustine (DTh, University of South Africa) is Associate Professor of Theological Ethics at Lee University in Cleveland, TN USA.
[1] Rebecca Todd Peters, 'Examining the Economic Crisis as a Crisis of Values', *Interpretation* (April 2011), pp. 154-66 (p. 154).

Yet, we are told that moral values are irrelevant to the market – that markets are morally neutral and navigated by scientifically assessable economic laws of production, consumption, and exchange. The claim of neoliberal economics is that everything can potentially be commodified and sold at the market, and that since the market is neutral, impersonal, and automatic it can function 'without systems of justice based on natural law'.[2] As M. Douglas Meeks points out, 'the great fascination of the market is the assumption that we have finally found a way to organize mass human behavior without dominion, authority and coercion'.[3] However, the father of neoliberal (or 'neo-classical') economics, Adam Smith utilized rather morally-charged language in developing his political economy. He insisted that the common good is an eventual outcome of the personal pursuit of wealth and economic self-interest. Smith asserted the guidance of society by 'the invisible hand' of divine providence in accomplishing the betterment of all while indulging individual interests and desires.[4] Other thinkers of the time affirmed Smith's idea

---

[2] M. Douglas Meeks, *God the Economist: The Doctrine of God and Political Economy* (Minneapolis, MN: Fortress Press, 1989), p. 38.

[3] Meeks, *God the Economist*, p. 38.

[4] Adam Smith, *The Theory of Moral Sentiments* (New York, NY: Augustus M. Kelley Publishers, 1966), p. 304. In this particular work Smith advocates a connection between human greed and divine providence in God's 'care of the universal happiness of all rational and sensible beings' (p. 210). For further reading on Smith's ideas about the function of self-interest see his work, *An Inquiry into the Nature and Causes of the Wealth of Nations* (London: William Benton Publisher, 1955). While a superficial reading of his work in economics may give an impression of a secular rationale in support of his analyses and corresponding conclusions, many researchers have suggested that we view Smith as a 'life-long moral philosopher, who never casts aside his earlier concerns about human morality in his later pursuit of economic truths'. Kathryn D. Blanchard, *The Protestant Ethic or the Spirit of Capitalism: Christians, Freedom, and Free Markets* (Eugene, OR: Cascade Books, 2010), p. 57. Such an understanding of Smith necessitates keeping in dialectical tension his two main works, namely, *The Theory of Moral Sentiments* and *An Inquiry into the Nature and Causes of the Wealth of Nations*, and it assumes that the second text is somehow informed and shaped by the first. If this is true, 'then Smith can be seen as promoting an economic model that is based on socially sanctioned ethical norms supported by appropriate and just social institutions' (Blanchard, *The Protestant Ethic or the Spirit of Capitalism*, p. 57) Some authors go as far as to suggest that Smith is in fact a moral theologian and that his elaboration on the 'invisible hand' is 'his particular contribution to eighteenth-century theodicy'. Lisa Hill, 'The Hidden Theology of Adam Smith', *European Journal of the History of Economic Thought* 8.1 (2001), pp. 1-29 (p. 22). Hill articulates the various interpretations of function of 'the invisible hand' in Smith's work, e.g. lexical and metaphorical, critical and ironic, evolutionary Darwinian, theological assertion of

that personal greed functions as a virtue in this model of market economy since its final end leads to a richer society as a whole.[5]

Neoliberal economics claim that profit and efficiency 'are the end goals of any rational economy', yet deny the fact that these goals function as moral values in society 'by guiding behavior and decision-making'.[6] As Rebecca Todd Peters asserts,

> By establishing that economic theory does, in fact, privilege certain values, we are able to ask why these values are more important than justice, compassion, and environmental sustainability. Thus, we open up the possibility for the important conversation about what values ought to guide decision-making in economic theory and in the business community.[7]

Awareness of the fact that economics are not morally neutral raises the important question regarding the legitimacy of the undiscerning marriage between Western Christianity and the neoliberal market economy. Christianity has lent its spiritual authority to the market – hallowing its values, partaking (often indiscriminately) in its commodifying practices, and benefiting by its mechanism of turning speculative promises into easy money. As William E. Connolly (Krieger-Eisenhower Professor of political theory at Johns Hopkins University) has observed, neoliberalism in America 'lives off the larger cultural ethos within which it is embedded, without committing itself publically to all aspects of it'.[8] Neoliberalism feeds off

> the spiritual support of constituencies that claim that the market is divinely inspired, that state support of ecological and egalitarian practices constitutes an attack on the divine order, and that microeconomic experiments with the property form, consump-

---

divine providence, etc.

[5] Munyaradzi Felix Murove, 'Perceptions of Greed in Western Economic and Religious Traditions: An African Communitarian Response', *Black Theology* 5.2 (2007), pp. 220-43.

[6] Peters, 'Examining the Economic Crisis as a Crisis of Values', p. 160.

[7] Peters, 'Examining the Economic Crisis as a Crisis of Values', p. 160.

[8] William E. Connolly, 'Capitalism, Christianity, America: Rethinking the Issues', *Political Theology* 12.2 (2011), pp. 226-36 (p. 228).

tion practices, and the work process assault American exception-alism.[9]

The irony of joining the conviction of divinely ordained and guided capitalism with 'the neoliberal faith in the market as nearly self-sufficient, self-equilibrating system' is that these are mutually contradictory ideas. While global society is now painfully aware that there is no such thing as totally self-regulating market, the problematic union of these two convictions is further fortified through the assertion made by proponents of neoliberalism (e.g. Milton Friedman) that 'because profit-making is the essence of democracy', any government that pursues stricter market-regulation policies 'is being anti-democratic'. [10] Paradoxically, however, as Robert W. McChesney has argued, the assertion of the 'sacredness' of the market actually has had a demoralizing and deconstructive effect on the democratic process because it eventually depoliticizes the citizens. 'If electoral democracy affects little of social life, it is irrational to devote much attention to it'.[11] Therefore, regardless of change of governments, no essential change can be expected within the economic system. McChesney further insists that

> Neoliberal democracy with its notion of the market *über alles*, takes dead aim at this sector. Instead of citizens, it produces consumers. Instead of communities, it produces shopping malls. The net result is an atomized society of disengaged individuals who feel demoralized and socially powerless.[12]

Western Christianity cannot keep ignoring that both neoliberal economic theory and its application are morally charged, often in ways that stand in conflict with the foundational values of Scripture and Christian Tradition.[13] Christianity cannot afford to be indifferent in the face of the comprehensive 'objectivity' of the market that prioritizes profit over people and remains blind to the creation of a non-marketable populace which is alienated from the cycle of production and consumption, by virtue of lacking market value. The

---

[9] Connolly, 'Capitalism, Christianity, America: Rethinking the Issues', p. 229.

[10] Robert W. McChesney, 'Introduction', in Noam Chomsky, *Profit over People: Neoliberalism and Global Order* (New York, NY: Steven Stories Press, 1999), p. 9.

[11] Robert W. McChesney, 'Introduction', p. 10.

[12] Robert W. McChesney, 'Introduction', p. 11.

[13] Peters, 'Examining the Economic Crisis as a Crisis of Values', pp. 156-58.

weak, the young, the elderly and the handicapped are among this 'surplus'[14] humanity excluded from the bliss of market society.

While critically reexamining the moral values of neoliberal capitalism, Western Christianity could employ its own spiritual resources in re-envisioning the function of *okonomia* within the global *oikos* – the planetary household – by summoning economics to moral responsibility and emphasizing the importance of moral and social values in economic development.[15] Meeks defines *oikos* as 'access to livelihood'.[16] For home

> is where everyone knows your name. Home is where you can always count on being comforted, forgiven, loved, and cared for. Home is where there is always a place for you at the table. And, finally, home is where you can count on sharing what is on the table.[17]

If we apply this poetic definition of home to planet Earth as the *oikos* of contemporary global society, we may conclude that almost two-thirds of the planet's population is homeless, for they live in poverty – in sub-human conditions with scarce access to livelihood.[18] As Daniel G. Groody remarks, when looked at from 'below', 'it becomes all the more evident that economic development in the global village has not always led to greater human development. Most of the world lacks the basic necessities for dignified human life'.[19] Economic justice has become the central question of the *oikonomia* of the global village, and receiving justice is receiving 'access to home'.[20] The inadequacies of economic development are further highlighted by the growing awareness of the interdependence between ecological, economic and social sustainability. Therefore, concerns for economic justice have become closely linked with

---

[14] In his work M.D. Meeks develops the concept of 'surplus people' who do not fit in the logic and cycles of market economy. See 'The Church and the Poor in Supply-Side Economics', *Cities* 1 (Fall 1983), pp. 6-9.

[15] H.A.H. Bartholomew I, Archbishop of Constantinople and Ecumenical Patriarch, *Encountering the Mystery* (New York, NY: Doubleday, 2008), p. 161.

[16] Meeks, *God the Economist*, p. 33.

[17] Meeks, *God the Economist*, p. 36.

[18] For statistics on poverty in the global village see Daniel G. Groody, 'Globalizing Solidarity: Christian Anthropology and the Challenge of Human Liberation', *Theological Studies* 69 (2008), pp. 250-68.

[19] Daniel G. Groody, 'Globalizing Solidarity', p. 258.

[20] Meeks, *God the Economist*, p. 36.

the demand for ecological justice as authors like Sallie McFague have identified nature as the 'new poor' in the North Atlantic economies and called for its emancipation and inclusion in the planetary household.[21]

The Eastern European experience has proven that neither socialism nor capitalism hold the answer to solving issues of economic justice and sustainability in the world. As Nicolas Berdyaev asserts, both capitalism and socialism are ultimately motivated by individualism, and their displays of concern for the common good cannot be separated from this prioritizing of self-interest.[22] Both capitalism and socialism have substituted the spiritual goals of life with material means; both economic models are therefore unable to sustain authentic human rights and freedom (since these represent high spiritual goals and have a spiritual origin).[23] Berdyaev points out that 'the historical material force is a part of the spiritual historical reality' and that 'the entire economic life of humanity has a spiritual base, a spiritual foundation'.[24] Therefore, the spiritual root of economic injustice resides in the reversal of the natural hierarchism between spirit and matter, between spiritual and economic life, which manifests itself in the individualist inversion of social vision, and the secularization and fetishism of materialism and economics.[25] Economic individualism has substituted truth with Mammonism. 'Economic Materialism', in turn, has declared the entire spiritual life of the humanity 'as being an illusion and a fraud',[26] has obscured the spiritual nature of the world, demystifying it and depriving it of wonder. In view of this, according to Berdyaev, 'socialism is only a further development of the industrial capitalist system; it is

---

[21] Sallie McFague, 'An Ecological Christology: Does Christianity Have It?' in Dieter T. Hessel and Rosemary Redford Reuther (eds.), *Christianity and Ecology: Seeking the Well-Being of Earth and Humans* (Cambridge, MA: Harvard University Press, 2000), pp. 29-45 (p. 30). See also McFague's work, *Life Abundant: Rethinking Theology and Economy for A Planet in Peril* (Minneapolis, MN: Fortress Press, 2001), pp. 33-37.

[22] Nicolas Berdyaev, *The New Middle Ages*, vol. 2 of *Collected Works* (Sofia: Zachari Stoyanov, 2003), p. 526, pp. 530-31.

[23] Nicolas Berdyaev, *Philosophy of Inequality* (Sofia: Prozoretz, 1923), p. 110, p. 116.

[24] Nicolas Berdyaev, *The Meaning of History*, vol. 2 of *Collected Works* (Sofia: Zachari Stoyanov, 2003), p. 313.

[25] Nicolas Berdyaev, *The New Middle Ages*, p. 531.

[26] Nicolas Berdyaev, *The New Middle Ages*, p. 531.

the final celebration of its beginnings and a triumph of their universal spread'.[27] Therefore, any expectation of social transformation
that facilitates authentic human freedom and socio-economic justice
would demand a 'revolution of the Spirit'[28] resulting in a renewed
vision of the world that recaptures its spiritual identity and purpose.[29]

On the day of Pentecost the socio-political and economic reality
of the Kingdom of God is birthed in the womb of the Church by
the Spirit. What the Spirit creates is holy for it is the social form of
the Trinitarian communal life embodied within humanity – it is the
life of the Holy God translated within the human *socium*. The economics of the Spirit transform the community of faith into God's
household so that, in return, it may make the world into a home for
all. The Spirit exposes the unsanctified nature of the market and
reveals the sacredness of the world, created and given to humanity
as a gift toward a holy communion with God and neighbor. In the
last Adam humanity experiences the restoration of its ontological
essence as a Eucharistic being with a priestly mandate within the
cosmos. This renewed ontology reunites economics with their spiritual foundations in the new Christ-like consciousness of the believers.

Undoubtedly, Christianity can contribute its theological resources towards inspiring and building a new global economic ethos
that prioritizes justice, compassion, and sustainability as guiding
principles of economic management to the benefit of all God's
creatures. After all, if attaining the likeness of God is the aim of the
spiritual life, it means that sanctification involves perfect 'love for

---

[27] Nicolas Berdyaev, *The New Middle Ages*, p. 531.

[28] Nicolas Berdyaev, *The New Middle Ages*, p. 522.

[29] As Berdyaev points out, only the Spirit creates a brotherhood and sister-
hood that are a realization of true freedom – as freedom in Christ. In the Christ-
centered spiritual togetherness (*sobornost*) there is no 'mechanical equality'. There
is also no contradiction and difference between 'a right and an obligation' (Nicolas Berdyaev, *Philosophy of Inequality*, p. 115). The *sobornost* of the faith community
is the work of the Spirit who translates the communal life of the Trinity within
the community of believers, making possible sharing life with the other in all of
its wholeness. The personal freedom in the Spirit's *sobornost* does not contradict
the freedom of the other, for it is not based on competition for the limited resources of the material reality. It is based rather on the eternal and infinite reality
of divine love and grace. In this divinely initiated and infused *sobornost*, the hospitality of God is incarnated in the community of Christ as a gift of the Spirit, a gift
of freedom to the other to be and to become.

all of creation' (St. Isaac the Syrian).[30] In light of the Church's eschatological destiny of union with God in *theosis*, her fundamental
social (and thus, also economic) program in the world should be the
doctrine of the Trinity, of 'God in communion, a social God'.[31] As
H.A.H. Bartholomew asserts, every form of human community 'has
as its vocation to become, each in its own way, a living icon of the
Trinity'[32].

In light of the above, the remainder of the present essay offers a
theological reflection on some potential building blocks toward a
new Spirit-inspired political economy. The text highlights the reality
of the world as Eucharistic sacrament, thus offering a vision of the
cosmos that can shift society's focus from a 'sacred market' to a
sacred world. The text examines the ontology and vocation of humanity as royal priests and stewards of the cosmos and takes a look
at the correlation between Pentecost, holiness, and economics in
the restoration of humanity's Eucharistic priesthood in the world.
Finally, the essay offers an understanding of the Eucharist as pedagogy of disciplining desires and an antidote to consumerism.

The World as Eucharistic Sacrament

If the ongoing human project of world-making has its ontogenesis
in God's infinite creative energies, then it is not accidental that human life unfolds into a procession of time organized into weeks as a
perpetual memorial of the divine creative act. Each time-segment of
seven days becomes a cosmic echo of that event, resonating within
the social fibers of the human community, casting forth all human
life as a cultic replica of creation. God creates nature and gifts it to
humanity, which in turn creates culture[33] by taking nature and add-

---

[30] H.A.H. Bartholomew I, *Encountering the Mystery*, p. 94.

[31] H.A.H. Bartholomew I, *Encountering the Mystery*, p. 133.

[32] H.A.H. Bartholomew I, *Encountering the Mystery*, p. 133.

[33] We have come to define culture as 'what we make of the world'. See Andy
Crouch, *Culture Making: Recovering Our Creative Calling* (Downer Grove, IL: IVP
Books, 2008), p. 23. Therefore, while nature is the creation of God, culture is the
creation of humanity. See also Kathryn Tenner, *Theories of Culture: A New Agenda
for Theology* (Minneapolis, MN: Fortress Press, 1997), pp. 28-29, and H. Richard
Niebuhr, *Christ and Culture* (New York, NY: Harper&Row Publishers, 1975), pp.
32-34. Niebuhr concludes that 'Culture is the "artificial, secondary environment"
which man superimposes on the natural. It comprises language, habits, ideas,
beliefs, customs, social organization, inherited artifacts, technical processes, and

ing to it its own life in the form of daily work illumined by creative imagination, that in a limited way recalls the divine creative act. The first seven days of the cosmic time-space continuum become the measure that marks all of time as its internal intentionality and driving principle. Thus, for the cycle of human productivity enwrapped in the liturgical anamnesis of everyday life, the experience of time appears as a sequence of six days of work as worship culminating in the seventh day of 'rest *as* worship'.[34] This weekly movement creates a rhythm of life in which human world-making preserves the primordial memory of the cosmos emerging out of nothing as a materialization of the divine will under the bespeaking power of God's uncreated energies. Marked by the seven days of divine creation, weekly life becomes a liturgy that evokes the teleological procession of time and matter – from eternity toward eternity, from the Spirit toward the Spirit. In its sacramental substance, time guides the world towards its final consummation beyond its own boundaries into a new, never-ending 'eighth day' that frames the gates of eternity – where the cosmos experiences 'the gathering together and transformation of matter into spirit'.[35]

This understanding of time and matter unveils the sacramental essence of the cosmos as being itself an exquisitely choreographed Eucharistic liturgy intended to shape humanity into the likeness of the Creator. By participating in it, human beings learn solidarity with others in the shared cosmic nature that each one of them hypostatizes and yet all have in common. Therefore, as Dimitru Staniloae insightfully suggests,

> A separation of cosmic nature taken to the limit between human individuals is impossible. Too great or too unequal a separation of nature brings about war between persons and indeed war within human nature itself or else makes of the latter its slave. Precisely for this reason, everyone is able to contribute to the

---

values' (p. 32). 'The world so far as it is man-made and man-intended is the world of culture' (p. 34).

[34] John Dominic Crossan, *God and Empire: Jesus Against Rome, Then and Now* (Ney York, NY: Harper One, 2007), p. 54.

[35] Dimitru Staniloae, *The Experience of God: Orthodox Dogmatic Theology*, vol. 2 *The World: Creation and Deification* (Brookline, MA: Holy Cross Orthodox Press, 2005), p. 6.

corruption not simply of a nature that belongs to himself [herself] personally, but also of that nature which belongs to all.[36]

Therefore, the God-given limitations of the material world are part of the intentional pedagogy of becoming like Him – they press us to share life and grow spiritually out of selfishness into communal solidarity with others, realizing that the only way matter can meet all existential needs is through the generosity of the Spirit. The liturgical nature of life as matter in communion with the Spirit, is a pedagogical tool that teaches humanity to see the world otherwise – as a sacred space for an encounter with the divine, as a cathedral where the life of God is seeded and gardened by the Spirit until it is fully grown into the materiality of the cosmos. This illuminated perspective cultivates human communal life of 'work and sacrifice'[37] as an inspirited imaging of the Trinity's divine communal reality. It faces the limited resources of the world with the mandate for a new asceticism of surrender to solidarity in reverent consumption that gives to others 'the possibility for development'[38] and flourishing. This is a mark of Eucharistic existence that differentiates between the present stage of the world and its destiny in God, and provides an antidote to the passions and desires that commodity the world by making it and end in itself.[39] A Eucharistic consciousness nurtures a God-like self-sacrificial attitude for the life of the world (Jn 6.51). It shapes humanity into the form of Christ who mends the world with His own life and offers it back to the Father whole, healed and renewed.

In the act of creation, God gives the world to humanity in self-sharing as a gift of life so that humanity may, in turn, learn to share it with the other and the different. The world is a gift with a pedagogical function – helping humanity 'to grow spiritually'[40] – to grow in the likeness of God. This pedagogy develops through the 'dialogue of the gift' between the recipient and the giver in which the world is to be continually received with gratitude and offered back

---

[36] Staniloae, *The Experience of God*, p. 2.

[37] Staniloae, *The Experience of God*, p. 7.

[38] Staniloae, *The Experience of God*, p. 7.

[39] Alexander Schmemann, *For the Life of the World* (Crestwood, New York: St Vladimir's Seminary Press, 1983), p. 17.

[40] Dimitru Staniloae, *The Experience of God*, p. 22.

to God in a gesture of self-sacrificial giving.[41] Therefore, since humanity does not have anything of its own to give to God, it learns to give back to the Creator from the Creation (e.g. the tithe, the Sabbath). The greatest gift in this exchange is that of giving oneself, giving one's own life. This ultimate call to the likeness of God for humanity is communicated in God's self-giving in Christ.

According to the paradoxical dialectic of the 'complete dialogue of the gift',[42] through the continual receiving and offering in return of the gift between two persons, they are drawn closer to one another until, in the words of Staniloae,

> ... the gift becomes something common and comes to be the transparent means for the fullest communion between persons. And not only is the gift something common, but it is also increased though the life which the persons communicate to one another through love manifested in the gift they make; in this way the persons give themselves as gift, and through this giving they grow spiritually.[43]

According to this logic, the world cannot be kept for oneself – it is made to be shared as a Eucharistic communion with the other. Trying to keep the world for oneself – reducing it to a personal possession intended to satisfy one's own appetites and desires – distorts its meaning and purpose as a communion of matter and Spirit. Divorced from its spiritual dimension, the world is commodified and made an end in itself, and its material limitations are exposed together with the impossibility to satisfy the ever-present human demand for more of the world. The realization that the world is not enough to satisfy the greed and self-indulgence of all

---

[41] Staniloae, *The Experience of God* (p. 22):

The paradox [of the return of the gift] is explained by the fact that the gift received and returned draws the persons close to one another to such an extent that the object of the gift becomes something common and comes to be the transparent means for the fullest communion between persons. And not only is the gift something common, but it is also increased through the life which the persons communicate to one another through the love manifested in the gift they make; in this way the persons give themselves as a gift, and through this giving they grow spiritually.

'The dialogue of the gift between God and the human person lies in the fact that each bestows himself upon the other' (p. 23).

[42] Staniloae, *The Experience of God*, p. 22.

[43] Staniloae, *The Experience of God*, p. 22.

causes alienation from and violence against the other, viewed now as a competitor for finite material resources. As a pedagogy on becoming like God and a gift towards communion with Him, the world becomes enough only when seen as having its origin, meaning, and end in God. The world is enough only when it is blessed and shared as a Eucharistic gift with joy and gratitude, with the reverence of 'liturgical *askesis*'[44] and self-giving for the life of the world.

Therefore, in its true nature, the world is given as a gift by God, so that it may draw humanity closer to Him, but also that it may be shared by fellow humans as the means/element of full communion with the other, for when we gift it to the other we are offering it back to God (Mt. 25.31-46). Part of the Christoforming pedagogy of the gift is that we are to give to the other more than what we have received from God (Mt. 25.14-30) – we add to the gift our very life in the form of creative work that increases the value of what we have received as nature (e.g., grain and grapes are transformed through the *askesis* of human work into bread and wine before being offered Eucharistically to God). This makes our offering a sacrifice for the life of the other. We give from ourselves to the other and as they receive this gift we become partakers in their life. In a way, we receive the world from God, in order to join our life to it and offer it back to God in a Eucharistic surrender to the form and content of His own communal life. In this offering we become

---

[44]For the purposes of the present essay 'liturgical *askesis*' is understood as an act of *praktikē* (ascetic struggle) within the context of liturgy. As Margaret Pfeil asserts, *paraktikē* takes place 'as the Christian worshiper's graced and free response to God's gratuitous love celebrated in Christian liturgy. First, liturgical asceticism springs from and seeks to nourish the life of the Christian worshiping community, and second, it implies an eschatological horizon in which the ultimate *telos* of *askesis* consists in the fullness of life in God'. Margaret R. Pfeil. 'Liturgy and Ethics: The Liturgical Asceticism of Energy Conservation', *Journal of the Society of Christian Ethics*, 27.2 (Fall/Winter, 2007), pp. 127-49 (pp. 127-28). As David Fagerberg states, if liturgy means 'sharing the life of Christ' and 'if *askesis* means discipline (in the sense of forming), then liturgical asceticism is the discipline required to become an icon of Christ and make his image visible in our faces'. David Fagerberg, 'A Century on Liturgical Asceticism', *Diakonia* 31.1 (1998), p. 41. Liturgical asceticism 'involves a contemplative awareness of the practices of the worshiping community as *leitourgia*, the work of the people of God at the service of the world' (Pfeil, 'Liturgy and Ethics', p. 134). Traditionally, however, *askesis* is not understood only as the means of becoming like God, but as a mark of *theosis* (e.g. in the hagiographies of the saints). *Askesis* is imitation of God in Christ-likeness, by applying the cross to the totality of one's life. Ultimately, it is fasting from oneself for the sake of the other, motivated by self-giving love.

like God in flesh – we become like Christ – the perfect Eucharistic being who through the incarnation took into Himself the world to the cross, 'circumscribing all that have their origin in Him'[45] in order to welcome them into His resurrection. Therefore, the world is intended to lead the human being toward God and the resurrection (life eternal) as a renewed life of partaking in the divine nature. As Staniloae remarks, 'In this sense all things found in the middle between God and the human person call for the cross'[46] through which humanity detaches itself from the gift in order to be united with the giver. 'By returning to God the gift of nature transformed by the *askesis* of our work and through the imprinting of the cross', we sanctify the cosmos and refuse to continue making it an end in itself, thus also sanctifying ourselves. In doing so, we recognize our destiny in God and enact it in self-giving to the other. We become like Him – we become holy with His communal holiness of self-giving love.

In the first chapter of Genesis, we see God creating within the divine communal self not only a sanctuary for the possibility and flourishing of the other but also building a home for them.[47] He takes time in carefully crafting and furnishing this home according to the physical needs of His creatures so that they may truly have access to life more abundant. He personally dwells there with them (Gen. 3.8) providing not only shelter and material sustenance but also fellowship in communal belonging. Thus, God meets the distinct human need of sociality, for a human life without community of unconditional acceptance is not life to the fullest; it is not life abundant for those created in the image of God. Yet Scripture asserts that because the earth is not just any dwelling place but home in the presence of God, all creatures depend on the generous unconditional hospitality of the Creator whose providential care sustains their very life (Job 12.10, 34.14-15, Mt. 6.26, Lk. 12.24-28, Acts 17.25).

The unconditional hospitality of God in the act of creation culminates in the establishing of the Sabbath as a day of rest. Time is both an outcome of creation and the canvas on which God spreads

---

[45] St. Maximus the Confessor, *Gnostic Chapters,* 1.67, PG 90.11108B.

[46] Staniloae, *The Experience of God*, p. 25.

[47] For an exposition on God as an architect building and furnishing a house see Crossan, *God and Empire*, pp. 51-52.

the universe. Therefore, John Dominic Crossan invites us to consider, 'It is not humanity on the sixth day but the Sabbath on the seventh day that is the climax of creation. And therefore our "dominion" over the world is not ownership but stewardship under the God of the Sabbath.'[48] Therefore, the Eucharistic nature of the world as a shared communion with God and neighbor is clearly visible in the reality of the Sabbath. The seventh day is a day of rest for all of God's creatures. This is the day in which God gives humanity relief from its labor and commands it to do likewise to the other. Both the anthropic and the non-anthropic creation is to enjoy the unconditional care of God in the Sabbath rest, a gesture of all-encompassing cosmic hospitality provided by the divine host for His creatures. Yet, this hospitality is justice and the recipients of the divine welcome are to extend it to others as an act of 'God's own distributive justice'.[49] Therefore, Sabbath rest is commanded for one's entire household and all of his/her dependents – sons and daughters, male and female servants, farm animals and livestock. The Sabbath is justice as radical equality from which even the resident alien who lives in Israel is not exempted (Deut. 5.14). The Sabbath logic as all-comprehensive justice of divine hospitality is further translated into the Sabbath Year and the Sabbath Jubilee. Indeed, this is not just 'rest *for* worship but rest *as* worship'[50] in recognition of the ownership of God upon all of creation, including time, and of the creatures' full dependence on the divine grace as hospitality.

The Eucharistic nature of the cosmos, intended to cultivate humanity in the divine likeness, transforms everyday work of world-making into a home-building for the other. Human creative labor becomes a priestly sacramental enactment of God's love for His creation – the very love which hosts the cosmos in self-sacrificial nurture and care for all creatures and demands the same of humanity as a faithful stewardship of God's household.

---

[48] Crossan, *God and Empire*, p. 53.
[49] Crossan, *God and Empire*, p. 54.
[50] Crossan, *God and Empire*, p. 54.

Royal Priests and Stewards of the Cosmos

The ontology of humanity, embodied in the first Adam before the fall, is that of a community of priests in the cathedral of the cosmos, bearing the image and growing into the likeness of the communal Trinity amidst the material world. As a priest before God, Adam stands as the embodiment of the cosmic communion of matter and Spirit, representing in his very being a sacrament in which the icon of the cosmos and the icon of God are united together as an evocation of the destiny of the world where God is to be all in all (Eph. 1.21). Thus, human ontology is to be the materialization of the sacred story of the world, joining together the primordial memory of its beginning with the anticipation of its eschatological unfolding. In the words of St. Gregory the Theologian,

> The Word of God wanted to reveal that humanity participates in both worlds, namely in invisible as well as in visible nature ... Therefore, Adam was placed on this earth as a second world, a large world within a small world, like an angel that worships God while participating in the spiritual and material worlds alike. Adam was created to protect and preserve the visible world, while at the same time being initiated into the spiritual world.[51]

Scripture preserves the reminder that both the material and spiritual components of humanity have their origin in God. Matter is spoken forth out of nothing by the Word as an act of the Creator's 'self-limitation' in opening space for the existence of creation.[52] This image epitomizes the essence of divine love as reflexive re-spacing of the self, fasting from one's own being on behalf of the existence of the other. Consequently, the earth/nature (in a way, following the example of its Creator) gives itself in sharing her material body with humanity so that the human body may rise from her under the craftsmanship of the divine creative energies. Further, the human spirit comes forth as the very breath of God – as His self-sharing with the other. Matter is indwelt with the divine presence as the human body becomes a temple of the spiritual reality on earth. Therefore, the creation of the world is an act of divine love ex-

---

[51] H.A.H. Bartholomew I, *Encountering the Mystery*, p. 96.
[52] Jürgen Moltmann, *The Trinity and the Kingdom* (Minneapolis, MN: Fortress Press, 1993), p. 59.

pressed as both the Trinity's *askesis* and *kenosis*. On the one hand, in an ascetic expression of self-giving love, God fasts from Himself in order to create within His eternal omnipresence space and time for the existence of the other. In a gift of unconditional hospitality, God becomes the immediate dwelling place of the other as the very environment in which they live and move and have their being (Acts 17.28). On the other hand, God pours Himself in the *kenosis* of the Word and the Spirit into the other so that they may come to be. Thus, in the act of creation we see the Trinity as an ascetic community of self-sharing with the other – this is the materializa- tion of God as love – a communal life of radical hospitality (*philoxe- nia*) marked by unconditional love for the other, the different, the absolute stranger. As the very outcome/fruit and cosmic expression of the divine reality of love, humanity is created to be an icon of the Trinity on earth and to exhibit the same communal life marked by *askesis* (self-fasting) and *kenosis* (self-sharing) in relation to the other. Humanity is placed amidst the cosmos as a priestly, Eucharistic, communal reality, in order to serve as an agent/mediator of the world's transfiguration into the likeness of God's communal life until the divine community becomes all in all.

Humanity is created in the image and for the likeness of God.[53] Therefore, from the beginning the spirit of *askesis* (fasting from oneself on behalf of the other) is to be cultivated in the human be- ing through abstaining from some of the fruit of the world (Gen. 3.2-3) for the sake of communion with God and nature. The priest- ly vocation of humanity involved the Eucharistic discernment of the world as a divine gift of substance and beauty for the sake of cultivating a community of shared life with the other – with God and (both the anthropic and non-anthropic) neighbor. Therefore, as Orthodox theologians have suggested, we can understand the 'orig-

---

[53] A number of the Early Fathers of the Church differentiated between the 'image' and the 'likeness' of God in humanity as His creation. The image is un- derstood as a God-given potentiality of likeness, while the likeness, culminating in union with God, is seen as the final goal and destiny of human existence. The likeness is an outcome of cooperation and alignment of the free human will with the will of God. Thus, attaining the likeness is a process and an empowering ped- agogy on becoming like God by choosing to love and will like Him. It is a call to perfection substantiated by uncreated grace that makes humanity partaker in the divine nature. Vladimir Lossky, *The Mystical Theology of the Eastern Church* (Crest- wood, NY: St. Vladimir's Seminary Press, 1997), pp. 114-21.

inal sin' also in terms of humanity's rejection of its priestly vocation in the cosmos, forfeiting its Eucharistic existence and reducing the world from a divine gift of encounter and communion with God and neighbor to a utility toward one's own self-indulgence, thus making it an end in itself. To proclaim the world as an end in itself is to deny its contingency on God and therefore, its created essence as originating in Him. By denying matters' causality in God, humanity commits the idolatry of substituting God with matter. 'For what is an end in itself is also without a cause',[54] and such is God alone. If the human being is created not only as *homo sapiens* or *homo faber*, but first and foremost as '*homo adorans*',[55] as a priest standing in the center of the world in order to unify it with the fulfillment of its destiny, then humanity worships what it perceives as having an end in itself and look for its own fulfillment in it. As a worshiping creature, humanity is created with an inherent longing for a union with God – for its self-realization in *theosis*. The peculiarity of the dialectic of worship, however, is that we worship what we love and we become what we worship. Worship is a transfiguring pedagogy on becoming like God. Therefore, humanity is instructed to love God with the entirety of one's being (Deut. 6.5, Mt. 22.37, Mk 12.30, Lk. 10.27) so that it may worship Him alone and therefore, be transformed into His likeness. Thus, idolatry endangers humanity's destiny by forming it into something else than God. By making the world an end in itself, the human being misdirects its ontological hunger and longing for the Creator towards the creation and surrenders to a never-satisfied-consumption of the world that deforms its purpose and meaning to the detriment of all of its creatures.

The act of creation as God's loving *askesis* and *kenosis* is an external expression of the internal reality of the divine communal life as *perichoresis*. The Orthodox tradition describes the *perichoresis* of the communal Trinity as 'three divine persons united with one another in the unceasing movement of mutual love'.[56] In the last Adam redemption makes humanity partaker in this divine communal life (2 Pet. 1.4), placing the human creature under the gentle carving flow of this all-engulfing love until it has been re-created into the perfect embodied image of God – the image of Christ – for 'to be human is

---

[54] St. Maximus the Confessor, *The Ambigua*, PG 91.1072B-C.
[55] Schmemann, *For the life of the World*, p. 15.
[56] H.A.H. Bartholomew I, *Encountering the Mystery*, p. 133.

to be Christlike'[57] – the perfect image of God in human flesh (Col. 1.15). Attaining Christlikeness is restoration of authentic human freedom to be and to become, to love and to be loved. Yet, in accordance with the Trinitarian communal image in humanity, as H.A.H Bartholomew asserts, this true freedom is 'never solitary but always social'.

> We are only free if we become a *prosopon* – to use the Greek word for 'person', which means literally 'face' or 'countenance' – only if we turn towards others, looking into their eyes and allowing them to look into ours. To turn away, to refuse to share, is to forfeit liberty. Freedom is expressed as encounter.[58]

The Christoforming work of God in the human being turns his/her face towards the other, being summoned to responsibility to provide what is lacking but needed in the other's life so that they may truly flourish. Therefore, the divine perichoretic reality enfleshed within the human community is manifested as *philanthropia* (self-giving as love for the fellow human – emphasizing the shared sameness of humanity) and *philoxenia* (self-sharing in hospitality as love for the stranger – highlighting the unique, irreproducible otherness of each human being). As God's redemptive love turns humanity's face towards the other, he/she becomes an unavoidable encounter with the image of God. Perhaps the earth's spherical form can be understood as providential underlining of the world's reality as a sacrament towards communion with the other. In the words of Immanuel Kant, the fact that the earth is a globe means that we cannot be 'infinitely scattered, and must at the end reconcile ourselves to existence side by side'[59] with the other. Even when we turn our back to them and their need, the curve of the globe takes us on a journey back face to face with the other, denying the possibility for infinite distance. The saving grace of God leads humanity back to the beginning, to the encounter of the face – the image of God facing itself in the other until a person sees themselves in the other as in a mirror and thus, is capable to love the other as oneself (Lev. 19.18, Mt. 19.19). The human journey back to God becomes

---

[57] H.A.H. Bartholomew I, *Encountering the Mystery*, p. 132.
[58] H.A.H. Bartholomew I, *Encountering the Mystery*, p. 132.
[59] Immanuel Kant, *Perpetual Peace: A Philosophical Essay* (trans. M. Campbell; New York: Grand Publishing 1972), p. 138.

pedagogy of discerning Him in the other. Apart from seeing God's image in the other one cannot see God. Apart of loving the other one cannot love God (1 Jn 4.20). Salvation becomes a way of seeing God disguised in the body and face of the other despite their socio-economic, cultural, ethnographic, racial, gender and language otherness. Thus, the process of discerning Christ in the other, even in his/her most distressful condition (Mt. 25.31-46) becomes the Christoforming power in one's life that ultimately allows them to see God. Seeing Christ in the other makes one like Christ – makes them a renewed Eucharistic being. Each human being stands in the face of the other imprinted with the same origin and destiny – Christ Himself – the beginning and the end. In this sanctified/deified perspective, the face of the other meets us as the future of the world – as the full potentiality of the fullness of life more abundant in, with and through God. There is no future, no salvation, no world without the other.

Pentecost, Holiness, and Economics: The Restoration of Humanity's Eucharistic Priesthood in the World

Attaining the likeness of God as *theosis* in Christ-likeness is the ultimate calling and purpose of all humanity.[60] The path towards the likeness of God demands one's continual Christic transfiguring which calls for sanctification of personal will and desires, for fasting from oneself on behalf of the other in expression of an incarnated love towards God and neighbor. The freedom of human will in the image of God is a prerequisite for attaining the divine likeness. As Lossky asserts, it takes one will to create humanity, but two to sanctify it. 'A single will to rise up the image, but two to make the image into a likeness'.[61] Therefore, sanctification demands the synergistic collaboration between the divine and human will. This synergy is impossible apart from Christ's incarnation, crucifixion, resurrection. and ascension. He is the Way (Jn 14.6) that bridges the chasm between humanity and God – the chasm of 'death, sin and fallen [hu-

---

[60] Christophoros Stavropoulos, 'Partakers of Divine Nature', in Daniel B. Clendenin (ed.), *Eastern Orthodox Theology: A Contemporary Reader* (Grand Rapids, MI: Baker Books, 1995), pp. 183-92 (pp. 183-84).

[61] Vladimir Lossky, *Orthodox Theology: An Introduction* (Crestwood, New York: St. Vladimir's Seminary Press, 1978), p. 73.

man] nature'.[62] His incarnation overcomes the abyss of fallen nature; His crucifixion overcomes the chasm of sin; and as death is
exhausted by His resurrection, the One who is the Resurrection and
the Life (Jn 11.24) overcomes and destroys 'the last enemy' (1 Cor.
15.26).[63] Finally, in His ascension Christ unites heaven and earth as
their ultimate destiny in and with God, bringing humanity within
the *koinonia* of the Trinity as 'partakers of the divine nature' (2 Pet.
1.4) and making possible its transfiguring into God's likeness. This
vision of human destiny extends beyond the necessity of salvation
into the eschatological goal of union with God in the Cosmic Christ
(Eph. 1.10). United with Christ, humanity participates in the imma-
nence of His second coming, experiencing the transfiguration of the
cosmos in 'the eternal splendor of the kingdom'.[64]

Therefore, sanctification as attaining the likeness of God manifests itself only as a result of the work of Christ (1 Cor. 1.30) – as an
outcome of divine grace in and through the agency of the Holy
Spirit (1 Pet. 1.2). 'The Holy Spirit is the main and essential beginning of sanctification'[65] – the One who applies what is objectively
accomplished in Christ to the life of the individual believer and the
community of faith, forming Christ's Body on earth.

Pentecost inaugurates the beginning of the sanctifying work of
the Holy Spirit in the *koinonia* of redeemed humanity.[66] Therefore,
Pentecost is not merely a continuation of the Incarnation or its se-
quel. It is its result and purpose. 'The creature has become fit to
receive the Holy Spirit'[67] and be the dwelling place and in-fleshed
reality of the Trinitarian *koinonia* in the cosmos. Therefore, as St.
Basil asserts, the empowerment of the Holy Spirit is for 'perfection
in holiness' as 'an unyielding, unchangeable commitment to goodness' – holiness as God-likeness that 'is impossible without the Spirit'.[68]

In the last Adam, heaven and earth (matter and Spirit) are
brought once again into an ontological communion and the re-

---

[62] Stavropoulos, 'Partakers of Divine Nature', p. 188.
[63] Stavropoulos, 'Partakers of Divine Nature', p. 188.
[64] Lossky, *Orthodox Theology: An Introduction*, p. 85.
[65] Stavropoulos, 'Partakers of Divine Nature', p. 188.
[66] Lossky, *Orthodox Theology: An Introduction*, p. 85.
[67] Lossky, *The Mystical Theology of the Eastern Church*, p. 159.
[68] St. Basil the Great, *On the Holy Spirit* (Crestwood, NY: St. Vladimir's Seminary Press, 1980), p. 63.

deemed human *socium* is reestablished as the icon of the Trinity on earth. On the day of Pentecost, the Spirit conceives Christ in the community of faith transforming it into His own communal Body on earth. The Church is born as the *theophorous* (God-bearing) and *theophanic* (God-manifesting) Body of Christ doing the will of the Father in the power of the Spirit. As the Spirit descends upon His own – the Son in His communal embodied form – the priestly, royal and prophetic dimensions of the Messianic anointing are transferred upon His disciples transforming them into a royal priesthood and prophethood of all believers.[69] In Christ, the community of faith becomes the restoration of humanity's ontology and vocation according to God's original creative intent.

The Spirit-saturated community enfleshes the Trinitarian life in all aspects of its existence, including its *oikonomia*. In the words of St. Gregory the Theologian, the first Adam 'was destined to serve as a royal steward'[70] (*basileus oikonomos* – a royal economist) over creation. The economic and priestly responsibilities of humanity coincide in their purpose of labor in love for the life of the world which is the household of God. Therefore, the economic management of the world is to be the *oikonomia* of household based on sharing the family resources for the equal benefit of all its members. No wonder, the ethos of household sharing becomes visible in the economics of the Spirit embodied in the Pentecost-marked life of the Christian community.

Like the non-anthropic Creation,[71] the economic model of Pentecost follows the pattern of sharing versus trading of goods and labor – it follows the pattern of the Creator's self-sharing. The communal composition of the Pentecost model moves from the social-economic predicament of the market to that of the household. The relationships of the household are not based on the

---

[69] On the prophethood of the Pentecost Community see Roger Stronstad, *The Prophethood of All Believers* (JPTSup 16; Sheffield: Sheffield Academic Press, 1999), pp. 65-70.

[70] H.A.H. Bartholomew I, *Encountering the Mystery*, p. 96.

[71] If we look closely at the function of Creation within the economic process we will notice a different form of economic participation that does not follow market logic. Creation is not compensated for its contribution; therefore, it does not participate in the economic exchange, but follows a model of sharing itself (and its resources) with humanity. It follows the model of the self-sharing and hospitality of its Creator.

amount of capital or possessions the members have, but on their family bonds. In contrast to the market, the household does not produce and maintain class structure. The social position of the members of the household is based upon family roles and any privileges that pertain to these are appropriated within the understanding of mutual calling to one another as a part of the same family. The members belong to one another: they are each other's brothers, sisters, mothers, children, etc. They are called together in a shared family identity. The family's wealth is the wealth of all its members, who share freely in its benefits. Household material possessions are utilized by the household members for the common benefit of the household unit. The wellbeing of the household as a whole guarantees the wellbeing of all its members. It is not accidental that the family table is the centerpiece of the household and its economic model. It symbolizes sharing of the fundamental necessities of life between equals in identity and purpose. The family is nurtured and sustained as its members break bread together and share possessions – they share life and make life together.

The community of Pentecost as the household of God exhibits this family-like pattern of sharing life which also naturally includes sharing of possessions. Their identity as children of God, born into one family by the same Spirit, outweighs any particularities of gender, ethnicity, and economic class. It establishes instead the dynamic of the traditional family roles, including care-giving, nurture, protection, and provision for the needs of all.

The household of God includes all creation. The household image, therefore, summons to responsibility the members of the family of God to care for creation and its needs. The well-being of the entire household demands this care. The household of God extends beyond the visible and brings together heaven and earth into one Spirit-community. Care, compassion and love, in the context of recognition of mutual belonging are characteristics of the family bonds in the household.

Therefore, the response to the other as an act of economic and social justice in Pentecost's communal economics is not an outcome of socio-political persuasion but of spirituality that extends one's participation in the life of God and His presence on earth in the community of faith. This spirituality prioritizes the needs and well-being of the other as indispensable from the well-being of the entire household while exercising discernment between personal needs and desires and disciplining ones desires toward the likeness of God.

There is a sense of spontaneity in the communal sharing of possessions manifesting the life of the invisible Spirit now made visible within the Body of Christ.[72] The sharing of possessions is an external expression of the believers' renewed ontology. This is their way of being in the world as new humanity – the material enfleshment of their spiritual identity as a communal extension and continuation of Christ's own life on earth.[73] What they do is who they are – the resurrected Christ incarnated by the kenotic agency of the Spirit into the redeemed community. Their corporeal life, as the life of God within the human *socium*, follows a Trinitarian logic of *perichoresis* that translates itself in all aspects of human existence (including economics). For indeed, in the all-comprehensive reality of the incarnation, nothing remains outside the reach of salvation, 'nothing can be taken away from the Son of man'.[74] Christ takes upon himself the totality of human existence in order to redeem it. As the Greek Patristic tradition affirms in the words of St. Gregory of Nazianzus,

---

[72] Martin Hengel, *Property and Riches in the Early Church* (Philadelphia, PA: Fortress Press, 1974), p. 32.

[73] The incarnationalist view of Pentecost for which I have argued in previous works, also allows us to consider the possibility of looking at the remainder of Acts as rooted in Christ's extended presence on earth in His Body. Therefore, if the Gospel of Luke represents the first volume of 'all that Jesus began to do and teach' (Acts 1.1), the book of Acts can be seen as the second volume outlining 'the continuation and fulfillment of what Jesus did and thought'. Matthias Wenk, *Community-Forming Power: The Socio-Ethical Role of the Spirit in Luke–Acts* (JPTSup 19; Sheffield: Sheffield Academic Press, 2000), p. 242. The author points to the outpouring of the Spirit at Pentecost as a clear example that the ministry of Christ (the Baptizer with the Holy Spirit) continues in Acts (p. 243) He mentions also the passages of Acts 9.5, 10; 13.39; 7.55-56; 17.7; 18.10; 19.15; and 25.19 as indicative of Jesus' acting upon the disciples. Another example is the healing of the beggar in Acts 3.1-16 'presented as a continuation of Jesus' healing ministry (Acts 4.30)' (p. 245). Beverly Gaventa's work also supports the view of the book of Acts as presenting a continuation of the ministry of Jesus. See her commentary *The Acts of the Apostles* (Abingdon New Testament Commentaries; Nashville, TN: Abingdon Press, 2003), pp. 34, 62-63.

[74] Alexander Schmemann, 'The Missionary Imperative in the Orthodox Tradition', in Daniela B. Clendenin (ed.), *Eastern Orthodox Theology: A Contemporary Reader* (Grand Rapids, MI: Baker Books, 1995), pp. 195- 210 (p. 201).

For that which He [Christ] has not assumed He has not healed; but that which is united to His Godhead is also saved. If only half Adam fell, then that which Christ assumes and saves may be half also; but if the whole of his nature fell, it must be united to the whole nature of Him that was begotten, and so be saved as a whole.[75]

Therefore, if 'possessions are symbolic expressions of ourselves because we both are and have bodies',[76] then surrendering our possessions to Christ is redemptive accepting of His identity (and that of His Body) as our own. The Fathers of the Church saw the image of God in humanity as incorporating the totality of the human being – of its spiritual and material existence.[77] Therefore, the likeness of God also cannot exclude the body and its material extension of possessions. Scripture continually emphasizes the reality of the body when articulating the mandate for sanctification (1 Thess. 4.3-8, 5.23, Heb. 9.13-14, Rom. 6.19). The sanctifying work of the Spirit involves the totality of the human existence with all of its social and material expressions in actions, relationships, and desires.

The Eucharistic priesthood of the last Adam reestablishes the *perichoretic* economics of the Spirit within the community of faith. Yet, this pattern of sanctified economic relationship to the other is also present in the earthly ministry of Christ prior to His death and resurrection. The Gospel narrative of the feeding of the multitudes reminds the reader of Christ as the perfect Eucharistic being unveiling the economic manifestation of the embodied Trinitarian communal life on earth. What God has provided (bread and fish) is offered back to Him in a liturgy of gratitude; it is broken to be shared with the other in a Eucharistic meal in which nature gives itself to the other in the elements of communion blessed and multiplied by God Himself to feed His household. He is the host of this banquet in which all who desire to partake are given access to life – not only to the children of Israel, but also to the Gentiles as in the feeding at Decapolis (Mk 8.1-10) – where Christ offers 'the bread of God's

---

[75] St. Gregory of Nazianzus, *Epistle CI. To Cledonius the Priest Against Apollinarius.*

[76] Luke T. Johnson, *Sharing Possessions: Mandate and Symbol of Faith* (Philadelphia: Fortress Press, 1981), p. 40.

[77] Lossky, *Orthodox Theology: An Introduction*, p. 71, Stavropoulos, 'Partakers in the Divine Nature', p. 186.

table to people of all nations'.[78] They are all God's offspring – they are all His family.

This is a radical transformation of humanity's vision of the world. Not as a place of savage competition for limited material resources, but as a household where one shares freely his/her life with the other. It is, indeed, the transformation of the world from a market into a home.

In the economics of the Spirit within the community of faith there is no one needy among them (Acts 4.34). Classism is abolished by the radical equality of the Trinitarian *perichoretic* life to which humanity stands emancipated as partaker of the divine nature (2 Pet. 1.4). The Pentecost community, as an outcome of the socio-transformative work of the Spirit, becomes the embodiment of God's hospitality and self-sharing with the other in the present (Acts 2.43-47). This divine hospitality is an all-inclusive justice. It reunites economics with their spiritual foundations in the new Christ-like consciousness of the believers. The consequence is a new form of economic relationships, i.e. relationships that embrace the other and provide for their need out of one's own resources. The result is 'having all things in common' (v. 45) and sharing possessions as a visible material expression of the *oikonomia* of God's household. These new economic relations set the Pentecost community apart from the economics of the world. Thus, one encounters in the midst of the world the doing of the Spirit[79] who has birthed the believers into the socio-political reality of God's Kingdom and has transformed them into an extension of that reality on earth. The Spirit is the one who initiates and sustains the conditions that make this radical economic justice possible, for such justice is an outcome of one's act of worship in Spirit and Truth. Therefore, as was proven by the Eastern-European Marxist experiment, the secularization of this vision is destined to failure.

---

[78] Brian K. Blount, 'The Apocalypse of Worship: A House of Prayer for all Nations', in Brian K. Blount and Leonora Tubbs Tisdale (eds.), *Making Room at the Table: An Invitation to Multicultural Worship* (Louisville, KY: Westminster John Knox Press, 2001), p. 21.

[79] Miroslav Volf, *Exclusion and Embrace: A Theological Exploration of Identity, Otherness, and Reconciliation* (Nashville, TN: Abingdon Press, 1996), pp. 228-29. For an extensive study on the spiritual mandate of sharing possessions, see Johnson, *Sharing Possessions: Mandate and Symbol of Faith*. The author discusses the topic also in relation to the event of Pentecost (p. 21).

Breaking bread together (v. 46) as both daily commensality and
Eucharistic celebration of the unity of the Body of Christ becomes
a symbolic centerpiece of living out the just socio-political reality of
the Kingdom within the household of God.[80] The architectural
placement of the communal dining table in the Eastern Orthodox
monasteries is an intentional reminder and a symbolic enactment of
this reality. The dining table is positioned in a way which presents it
as an extension of the sanctuary's altar. Therefore, the daily commensality of the community is viewed as a continuation of its
communion around the table of the Lord. Each table becomes the
Lord's table, for He is the host that gives sustenance to all. His
presence is invited and the meal is offered and blessed in His name
with gratitude in recognition of being a gift from God as 'our daily
bread' (Mt. 6.11, Lk. 11.3). Indeed, we are forever His guests. Yet,
this is also our family table – the table of our Father – and we are at
home, for we are His children and members of His household.
Here we all have access to life that is shared as a sacrament for the
consecration of the entire cosmos.

This redemptive eschatological union with God in the Cosmic
Christ is both experienced and anticipated in the 'liturgical anamnesis'[81] of the community of faith. The anamnesis of Christ (1 Cor.
11.24-25) is not a mental recollection, but an enacted likeness. It is
choosing 'to be' and 'to do' like Him, becoming His extension on
earth through the incarnational agency of the Holy Spirit. Through
the Body of Christ, heaven descends on earth and restores the unity

---

[80] In her book *Of Widows and of Meals: Communal Meals in the Book of Acts*
(Grand Rapids, MI: Eerdmans, 2007), Reta Halterman Finger offers an in-depth
study of the daily commensality of natural and fictive kin groups in first century
Palestine. She examines the passages in Acts concerning the economic life of the
early Christians on the background social economic practices of the day and from
the contextual view-point of the poor (especially widows and their daughters who
were one of the most economically destitute demographic groups). She emphasizes the communal daily breaking of bread both as sharing between kin in a
communal eating as well as a sacramental practice the originating of with is in the
meals Jesus shared with both Jews and Gentiles. Some authors have distinguished
between the *koinonia* in Acts 2.42 and the breaking of bread as between communal and Eucharistic meals. However, it is the presence of Jesus Christ that transforms a meal into a Lord's Supper. Therefore, the sacramental nature of sharing
the meal in the name of the Lord in evocation of His presence in the unity of His
Body on earth in thanksgiving is translated in both daily commensality and the
Eucharist.
[81] Pfeil, 'Liturgy and Ethics', p. 136.

of the Creator with His creation as the liturgical celebration translates the foretaste of the divine fullness of life in and through the Spirit-baptized *koinonia.*

The Eucharist as Pedagogy of Disciplining Desires and an Antidote to Consumerism

The Eucharist is the focal point of the liturgical celebration of Christ's oneness with His Body. As Meeks points out, the Eucharist

> is God's economic act par excellence in the household of Jesus Christ. In it is made present God's own self-giving, God's own economy by which God intends to make the world into a home.[82]

The Eucharist asserts the innocence of the non-anthropic[83] creation which comes to the table of God prior to the human community and welcomes it as the visible form of divine nourishment in the household of God. Through its inclusion within Christ in the act of the incarnation, created matter enters redemptive participation in the life of the Trinity. In the materiality of the Son's body, matter is sanctified and sanctioned as an instrument of grace in the consecration of the cosmos.[84]

The Eucharist provides pedagogy of discerning and liturgical anamnesis of the ontological, soteriological, and eschatological interrelation between humanity and the rest of creation. It instructs us towards disciplining our desires in prioritization of the well-being of others and points us to the practice of liturgical asceticism of reverent consumption (1 Cor. 11.27-34).

The Eucharist effectively deconstructs the logic of free-market consumerism, for as the individual partakes in the Eucharistic elements, she

> does not simply take Christ into her-self, but is taken up into Christ ... The act of consumption is thereby turned inside out:

---

[82] Meeks, *God the Economist,* p. 45.

[83] I am using 'non-anthropic' as a synonym to 'not human' in designation of the part of creation that does not incorporate the human *socium* and includes all of rest of the terrestrial created things and being.

[84] See Daniela C. Augustine, *Pentecost, Hospitality, and Transfiguration: Toward a Spirit-inspired Vision of Social Transformation* (Cleveland, TN: CPT Press, 2012), pp. 56-59.

instead of simply consuming the body of Christ, we are consumed by it.[85]

As 'we all partake of the one bread' (1 Cor. 10.17) we stand as one Body, for we have all become partakers of Christ and in Him—of each other. Therefore, prioritizing one's personal desires over against the needs of others, and consuming the other for one's own self-gratification within the Body of Christ becomes devouring oneself.

The ultimate challenge of the Eucharistic logic and pedagogy is that by becoming the Body of Christ, we 'must become food for others'.[86] Schmemann contemplates this extroverted missionary orientation of the Eucharist in reflecting upon the three liturgical movements of its celebration. It starts with a movement of ascent as the church is carried by the Spirit to heaven in 'its entrance into the new eon'.[87] The church experiences the fullness of the life of the community of the Trinity at the table of the Lord, and being filled and illumined by the divine presence she is called to descend back to earth. This second movement of descent is part of her missiological identity, for unless the church reenters this world there will not be 'heaven on earth'. Yet, the church returns on earth for the sake of the world and her final liturgical movement is from the interiority of the temple to the exteriority of all the world – even to its 'uttermost' parts – the farthest, the darkest, the most different from us. Therefore, 'the Eucharist transforms the church into what it is, transforms it into mission'.[88] In fulfilling her calling, the church enters the cosmos as the living Gospel in the Body of Christ that gives itself daily to feed and heal a starved and broken world.

The Eucharist detoxifies us from the dehumanizing poisons of unrestrained consumerism and helps us to build immunity towards its seductive lure. It cultivates the community of faith as a dissident force of resistance against the commodification of market logic and forms it as an incarnated critique of the utilitarian objectification of God's creation.

---

[85] William T. Cavanaugh, *Being Consumed: Economics and Christian Desire* (Grand Rapids, MI: Eerdmans, 2008), p. 54.

[86] Cavanaugh, *Being Consumed*, p. 55.

[87] Schmemann, 'The Missionary Imperative', p. 200.

[88] Schmemann, 'The Missionary Imperative', p. 200.

In many Eastern European Pentecostal communities the Eucharistic liturgy is followed by an agape feast. While the Eucharist takes place in heaven, the agape feast takes place on earth. It embodies the ultimate purpose of the Eucharistic pedagogy – it is the life of heaven on earth captured by the household table of the family of God where all share their resources and freely receive access to life so that there is not a single one left hungry and needy among them. They are all children in their Father's house and equal beneficiaries of His loving homebuilding on behalf of all of creation.

Many Eastern European Pentecostal communities spend time in fasting prior to celebrating the Eucharist. The believers commit to the fast as part of their spiritual hygiene, cleansing themselves from blind submission to the urge for consumption and learning to differentiate between their legitimate needs and self-indulgent desires. Further, the fast sharpens the believer's spiritual vision, helping them to discern the Body of Christ and to partake in the Lord's Supper in a worthy manner (1 Cor. 11.26-28). It opens his/her eyes to recognize Christ in the other and to embrace them as an organic part of the same family, as members of the same household. The fast prompts the believers to examine their minds and hearts for any negation of Christ expressed as a negation of the other. Therefore, the Eucharist liturgy includes private and public (individual and corporate) confessions and responsive articulation of forgiveness directed towards healing of one's relationship to the other – for, a separation from them is a separation from Christ, from His communal Body. The Cristoforming work of the Eucharistic liturgy cultivates in the believer the holiness without which no one shall see God (Heb. 12.14). This social holiness that starts with discerning Christ in the other – even in His most radically different and unrecognizable appearance (Mt. 25.31-46) brings the believers face to face with God now, as they share possessions with the other in benevolent actions towards those in need. Therefore, seeing the face of God in the face of the needy on this side of the *eschaton* brings them before His face in eternity as heirs of the Kingdom prepared for them by the Father 'before the foundations of the earth' (Mt. 25.34).

Therefore, the Eucharist transforms the Church into a 'passage' to heaven, 'from the old into the new, from this world into the "world to come"".[89] It teaches us, as Schmemann points out, that we were created as Eucharistic beings,

> as celebrants of the sacrament of life, of its transformation into life in God ... We know that real life is 'eucharist', a movement of love and adoration toward God, the movement in which alone the meaning and value of all that exists can be revealed and fulfilled.

This is a powerful antidote to the deformities of the free market's secular liturgies that have distorted our vision of the world. It is a redemptive recapitulation of humanity's economic life into God's economy of household.[90]

Instead of Conclusion: Holiness and Moral Economic Responsibility

As the Incarnation, so also Pentecost affirms the ontological relationship between matter and Spirit and opens the door to understanding 'the material condition of others as a spiritual matter'.[91]

The economic paradigm of the Pentecost community affirms this understanding and outlines the social responsibilities of holiness as an extension of the life of the Spirit in human flesh. Saintliness manifests itself as serving the material needs of others with one's own possessions. Sharing possessions, therefore, becomes an expression of participation in the life of God and a materialization of shared spirituality.

Edith Wyschogrod offers the following identifier of sainthood:

> A saintly life is defined as one in which compassion for the Other, irrespective of cost to the saint, is a primary trait ... Their [the saints'] lives exhibit two types of negation: the negation of self and the lack of what is needful but absent in the life of the Other.[92]

---

[89] Schmemann, *For the Life of the World*, p. 31.

[90] Schmemann, *For the Life of the World*, p. 34.

[91] Sallie McFague, 'Epilogue: The Human Dignity and the Integrity of Creation', in Darby Kathleen Ray (ed.), *Theology that Matters: Ecology, Economy and God* (Minneapolis, MI: Fortress Press, 2006), pp. 199-212 (p. 209).

[92] Edith Wyschogrod, *Saints and Postmodernity: Revisioning Moral Philosophy* (Chicago, IL: University of Chicago Press, 1990), p. xxi.

Sallie McFague argues that personal material possessions can blind humanity for the material needs of others as being a spiritual matter. She asserts that 'self-emptying, self-denial, allows us to see differently and hence to live differently ... it is often the first step toward universal love of others, toward seeing others as valuable and all as interrelated'.[93]

Viewed as self-denial on behalf of the others, the acts of sharing possessions stand among the gestures and images that summon our moral response through the hagiographies of the saints as imitators of Christ. Their redeemed humanity is defined not 'by consumption but by *kenosis*' that flows out of 'participation in the fullness of the Trinitarian life' – of mutual self-giving and receiving.[94] As the saints empty themselves in the Body of Christ they become His Body on earth and are transfigured into His New Humanity taking the form and shape of their destiny and mission in Christ-likeness. This imitation is interpreted as a fulfillment of the broader mission of the community of faith – the ministry of reconciliation (2 Cor. 5.18). The peace-making of the sons and daughters of God in this world is clearly not limited to the cessation of war and physical violence. It points to shalom of comprehensive justice that involves all humanity and the rest of creation. Therefore, the definition of peace also includes 'providing the earth and its people with the basics of existence',[95] and thus, affirming their dignity and identity as being part of our own common destiny.

The contrast between the Pentecost's economics of the Spirit and the market logic of global economic neoliberalism expose the profound need of the sanctification of humanity and its desires and point to the internal struggle of human consciousness when faced with the vision of the Kingdom in the midst of the temptation and promises of this world's economic systems. As Cavanaugh asserts, our temptation is to spiritualize our union and solidarity with the poor, the oppressed, the suffering,

> ... to make our connection to the hungry a sentimental act of imaginative sympathy. We could then even imagine that we are already in a community with those who lack food, whether or

---

[93] MacFague, 'Epilogue ...', pp. 209-10.
[94] Cavanaugh, *Being Consumed*, p. 86.
[95] MacFague, 'Epilogue ...', p. 209.

not we actually meet their physical needs. We might even wish to tell ourselves that our purchases of consumer goods do in fact feed others – by creating jobs. But we have no way of knowing if such jobs create dignity or merely take advantage of others' desperation ...[96]

Economics are a spiritual matter and an external expression of the individual and communal inner life. This is why poverty, as class-related reality, may be viewed as an outcome of a given spirituality that ushers and sustains economic models which maintain and deepen disparities and further class-division. This spirituality stands in contrast to the therapeutic measures in the Old and the New Covenants, aimed against further class-dislocation and towards restoring moral economic and civic responsibility in society at large. The concept of Jubilee is a striking example of the demand for a social covenant that executes economic justice and sustains human dignity. The forgiveness of debt and restoration of personal freedom are pointers to the spiritual destiny of the covenant people and their social bonds.[97]

The event of Pentecost induces an economic model of distributive justice as a witness of Christ's resurrected life in the Spirit-filled community (Acts 4.32-33). As Marcia Riggs states,

> ... corporate good requires sustainability. The means toward sustainability is the sharing of resources – that is distributive justice. Distributive justice means that all have the basics to survive and flourish.[98]

This model is based on reverent consumption, which shares the concern of wellbeing for all (Acts 4.34-35). Historically, Marxist thinkers have questioned the sustainability of this model and have identified the sharing of products without sharing the means of production as the primary reason for its decline and eventual disappearance.[99] The primary issue in the Act's account, however, is con-

[96] Cavanaugh, *Being Consumed*, p. 56.

[97] For a study of the Jubilee theme in the Synoptic Gospels and its implication for ethics see Sharon H. Ring, *Jesus, Liberation and the Biblical Jubilee: Images for Ethics and Christology* (Philadelphia, PA: Fortress Press, 1985).

[98] Marcia Y. Riggs, 'The Globalization of Nothing and Creation Ex Nihilo', in Ray (ed.), *Theology that Matters*, pp. 141-53 (p. 148).

[99] Rosa Luxemburg, 'Socialism and the Churches', *Marxist Classics*, http://www.newyouth.com/archives/clssics/luxemburg/socialismandthechurches.html.

cerned with sustainability of unity, human dignity, and love as being the fundamental bonds of the Pentecost social covenant and tangible expression of the participation of the faith community in the communal life of the Trinity.

The pouring of the Spirit on all flesh gives a global dimension to the eschatological vision of Pentecost. All flesh is bonded together in and through the life of the Spirit and made participant in its socio-economic reality. This globalized ethos is indispensable from the anticipation of the planetary spread of the Kingdom of God – the reality of the life of God translated in the socio-political and economic dimensions of material existence on earth. This is a reality in which economics become an outcome and an extension of the divine life through the agency of the Holy Spirit. As such, economics is an extension of justice as the fundamental relationship to the other (things and beings). Through the Spirit all flesh is brought into this comprehensive justice that realigns matter with its spiritual origin and purpose. This is a radical transfiguring of the fundamental relationships that construct the human *socium*. From material want and desires undergirding production and consumption in the context of anxious awareness of the depletion of material and energy resources, to spiritual life that permeates redemptively all material existence and translates it in the comprehensive shalom of the Kingdom. This is life in the Spirit that is more abundant. It is life free from fear and competition for survival – a life in which there is a home for all (Jn 14.2).

While reflecting on the Old Testament idea of 'the cities of refuge' (Numbers 35) Emmanuel Levinas makes the important observation that Western society – free and civilized – enjoys riches and privileges, often at the expense of the rest of the world, causing the suffering and depravation of others (e.g. through neo-colonial exploitation or through unrestrained consumption of 'cheap' goods produced in sweat shops within the developing world). With ignorant innocence we participate in manslaughter and act surprised when the anger of the world rages against us. In light of this volatile reality of our societal conscience, Levinas questions, 'does not all this make our cities cities of refuge or cities of exiles?'[100] Perhaps

---

[100] Emmanuel Levinas, *Beyond the Verse: Talmudic Readings and Lectures* (London: Continuum, 2007), p. 40.

this is why the arrival of the stranger in our midst makes us more anxious than ever – we are not sure if they are not 'the avenger of blood' (Num. 35.19). After all, driven by political and economic interests we have continually lied to the rest of the world that the level of material prosperity, proudly advertised as 'the American way' of life, can be made universal. Yet, though 'the United States comprises only 5 percent of the world's population, we consume somewhere between 23 and 26 percent of the world's energy'.[101] As James K.A. Smith observes, this way of life is destructive to creation and cannot be feasibly extended to others. It perpetuates 'a system of privilege and exploitation', and the only way to continue enjoying it 'is to keep it to ourselves'.[102] While offering to the rest of the global dwellers empty promises of sustainable Western-style consumerism, the seductive glamor of the West rested for decades upon its arrogant claim for autonomy from the rest of the world and a guardianship of human freedom as unapologetic individualism that worships self-indulging desires at the expense of nature and human community. The current global economic and environmental crisis has shattered our self-delusions for autonomous existence and has summoned us to moral responsibility for the sickness and poverty of the world. Practicing benevolence as indulgences for our consumer addictions is not enough to mend a broken world. Global healing demands a global vision of the world as a sacrament shared with the other, as a communion with God and neighbor. This vision has to be coined with a Eucharistic spirituality of priestly existence in the cosmos marked by *askesis* and *kenosis* for the life of the world. This is a spirituality cherishing this world as God's household and a sanctuary in which all of His creatures are to have access to life. For as the economics of the Spirit remind us, ultimately, 'the glory of God is every creature fully alive'.[103]

---

[101] James K.A. Smith, *Desiring the Kingdom: Worship, Worldview, and Cultural Formation* (Grand Rapids, MI: Baker Academic, 2009), p. 101.

[102] Smith, *Desiring the Kingdom*, p. 101.

[103] This is a paraphrase of St. Irenaeous' statement, 'the glory of God is man fully alive'. The text continuous: '... moreover man's life is the vision of God: if God's revelation through creation has already obtained life for all the beings that dwell on earth, how much more will the Word's manifestation of the Father obtain life for those who see God' (*Adversus Haereses*, IV, 20, 7). The paraphrase captures the spirit of the text and was made famous by Sallie McFague's writings, especially, *Life Abundant: Rethinking Theology and Economy for a Planet in Peril* (Minneapolis, MN: Augsburg Fortress, 2001), p. 3.

10

LIBERATING HOLINESS FOR THE OPPRESSED AND THE OPPRESSORS

PATRICK ODEN[*]

Introduction

There are certain standard critiques concerning the theology of Moltmann which tend to show up in any general discussion of his work. Among the most common is the charge that he does not have a very well developed concept of personal sin.[1] This is a significant charge indeed, as a concept of personal sin goes well beyond a narrow category of ways in which humans fail. A concept of sin also involves the doctrine of salvation – what are we being saved from and how this is accomplished; and it also involves the doctrine of sanctification – what are we being saved from and what we are being saved into. In my readings of his work, I have seen a mostly implicit concept of sin that is very reminiscent of the theology on sin by his colleague Wolfhart Pannenberg. Moltmann and Pannenberg both seem to understand the issue of sin being, at the core, an issue of misplaced identity, but while Pannenberg has noted this expressly in his anthropology, I have not found it stated quite as directly in Moltmann. So, I will bring up Pannenberg's understanding of sin and identity and ask how Moltmann understands this. His answer forms the basis of what follows.

---

[*] Patrick Oden (PhD, Fuller Theological Seminary) is Adjunct Professor at Azusa Pacific University and Fuller Theological Seminary.
[1] See, for example, Joy McDougal, *Pilgrimage of Love* (New York: Oxford University Press), pp. 147-51.

He agrees with Pannenberg, but notes that Pannenberg's concept of egotism as the contrast of human identity in God is a 'very male sort of sin'.[2] Pannenberg, he notes, developed his understanding in the 1960s, before a strong feminist perspective brought insight about broader issues of identity and sin in society. 'To let go your identity', Moltmann notes, 'is a very feminine sort of sin. Girls are educated to serve, to forget about themselves. But there is a healthy form to being yourself. So, there is egocentrism on the one side, apathy on the other side.'[3] In both of these we discover the roots of more visible aspects of sin, as a person either wants to express themselves through dominance or hide themselves in the dominance of another or other non-God reality. Some do not really even seem to have an option. They are in societies where dominance and competition is expected of all people or they are in contexts where they suffer under structural forms of oppression.

In these situations (personal or structural) we also discover the roots of a more holistic understanding of holiness, one that avoids both hiding and dominance, one that pushes against competition and domination – one that is expressed by those who have been outcasts becoming participants and one that is expressed by those who have misplaced expressions of identity letting these go and letting go forms of power and dominance that defines them over and against others. The way of the Kingdom offers an alternative to societal patterns of life and this alternative is called holiness. Holiness, then, can be expressed in forms of participating and in forms of letting go, with Moltmann emphasizing the former in his overall theology and Pannenberg the latter.

More theologically, we can see these expressions of holiness as reflecting elements of Trinitarian life, with holiness involving both a *perichoretic* and a *kenotic* expression. Our particular contexts affect which element is more emphasized in our process of sanctification. This is because our contexts affect in radical ways the kinds of sins we are tempted towards and the kinds of sins that affect us. Being freed from such sins is an expression of liberation and so we can see holiness itself as being defined as the result of liberation in our specific context. Moltmann writes that liberation has to happen

---

[2] Jürgen Moltmann, interview with the author, Tübingen Germany, May 17, 2011.

[3] Moltmann, interview … May 17, 2011.

from both sides. If liberation happens for the oppressed and the oppressors, then there is a transformed status in each as they experience this process of sanctification. How do we know when someone is liberated from their particular bondage? This is the status of holiness – being made whole in light of God's transformative work. In what follows I will develop these thoughts further.

I will begin by discussing liberation in a way that Moltmann has emphasized – that liberation must be for both the oppressed and the oppressors. I will then discuss briefly the ideas of *perichoresis* and *kenosis*, showing how these are involved in our becoming whole with and for God. After that I will utilize Moltmann's conception of holiness as a way of propounding liberation as *perichoresis*, and following that I will use Pannenberg to help elucidate liberation as *kenosis*. Together, these will fill out a more holistic understanding of holiness, one that can be expressed in forms of liberation and one that brings together the oft separated approaches of Pentecostalism and Holiness movements.

Liberation for the Oppressed and Oppressors

'Oppression', Moltmann writes, 'always has two aspects: on the one side stand the oppressors, on the other the oppressed'.[4] On both sides, humanity is destroyed. The oppressed are destroyed by being prevented from full expression of their own life and being exploited, used, and de-humanized. The oppressors are destroyed by assuming they can carry out such exploitation without consequence; they justify their behavior through the pursuit of identities that are contrary to the law of love that should orient all people in the identity of God. Humanity is destroyed in both directions, through evil and through suffering, the one causing the other, each resonating death against life. In being inhuman – oriented towards death – the oppressor dehumanizes the oppressed, ruining communion, magnifying violence. This is why both must find liberation, as both the oppressed and the oppressors are in need of a restored humanity.

---

[4] Jürgen Moltmann, 'The Liberation of Oppressors', *Journal of the Interdenominational Theological Center* 6.2 (1979), p. 69. Cf. Jürgen Moltmann, *Experiences in Theology* (trans. Margaret Kohl; Minneapolis: Fortress Press, 2000), pp. 185-88. More recently on this topic, see also Jürgen Moltmann, 'Sun of Righteousness Arise! The Freedom of a Christian – Then and Now – for the Perpetrators and for the Victims of Sin', *Theology Today* 69.1 (2012), pp. 7-17.

The need for liberation of the oppressed is obvious, and the ways of liberation are often likewise obvious: the particular form of oppression must end. Those caught in oppression must be let go from their oppression – a path of freedom expressed so clearly in the exodus narrative. In their freedom, they can then be led into a new expression of participation. 'Through hope and struggle the oppressed enter upon the way to freedom', Moltmann writes.[5] This expression of freedom cannot be turned around to be used in the service of a new form of oppressing, but should be expressed in a freedom that is freeing for all, a freedom in which communion and community find new expression. 'The history of which men and women are to be the subject must have as its goal justice, peace, and the integrity of creation, in expectation of the coming kingdom of God, which will complete history and put everything to rights'.[6] This kingdom is expressed in the prisoners being set free, the blind becoming able to see, and, in general, the blessing of God upon all those who had previously suffered, beginning a new life in hope. It is Moltmann's strong proposal that such an expression of the king-dom is not merely for a later date in the future, but that the messi-anic people are called to be bearers of this messianic reality in their contexts.

The oppressors, in contrast, are not often aware of their need for liberation, and many of the oppressed would be scandalized by hearing that such liberation goes hand in hand with their own struggles for freedom. The fact remains, however, that for freedom to be experienced in full, the oppressors must likewise find their liberation, albeit not from some perceived slight or by gaining a perverse victimhood. Instead, the oppressors must be liberated from their oppressing. 'Whoever wishes to help the oppressed to gain their freedom must begin with himself: he must cease being their oppressor'.[7] The oppressors find their freedom by discovering the ways in which they are directly or indirectly participating in op-pression and letting go these forms of involvement. This liberating conversion involves the oppressor becoming oriented towards the discipleship of the cross, no longer having to establish their own self or identity, instead finding this wholly in Christ. This liberation

---

[5] Moltmann, 'The Liberation of Oppressors', p. 70.
[6] Moltmann, *Experiences*, p. 298.
[7] Moltmann, 'The Liberation of Oppressors', p. 70.

is the counter-image to a liberation of the oppressed, letting go instead of taking up, making space and freeing others to participate.

Moltmann notes three particular ways in which oppressing is expressed: racism, sexism, and capitalism.[8] The latter might indicate Moltmann's occasional Marxist leanings, yet to dismiss him – or to agree with him – because of this would be to miss his particular emphasis. In each of these, the issue is primarily one of identity and anxiety. Finding one's identity in a false narrative of dominance indicates and provokes anxiety – which then is confronted by trebling the oppression. In racism, one's identity is found in the perceived cultural superiority of one's own race, with the right to domination seen as an inherent right, legitimized in structural and in often indirect ways. 'In racism one's own identity is always defined by means of discriminating against other races. For the racist identity is a negative, cramped, and aggressive identity'.[9] With sexism, identity is established in contrast to the other gender, generally men towards women.[10] Being a complete human can be achieved only through being completely one gender.[11] Masculine sexism 'entails self-justification for the sake of self-assertion and self-assertion for the sake of world-mastery'.[12] Moltmann goes on to note that this 'superhuman pride is in truth nothing other than an expression of an inhuman anxiety'.[13]

The third particular way of oppressing is that of capitalism. The impact on those who must bear the burden of capitalistic econo-

---

[8] Moltmann, 'Liberation of Oppressors', pp. 71-76.

[9] Moltmann, 'Liberation of Oppressors', p. 71.

[10] This, however, can also be seen in men establishing themselves as more 'masculine' than other males, and increasingly (though still relatively significantly less established) women establishing assumed feminine qualities as superior.

[11] I am reminded of *The Gospel of Thomas*, p. 114. 'Simon Peter said to him, "Let Mary leave us, for women are not worthy of life." Jesus said, "I myself shall lead her in order to make her male, so that she too may become a living spirit resembling you males. For every woman who will make herself male will enter the kingdom of heaven"'; From James M. Robinson (ed.), *The Nag Hammadi Library* (San Francisco, HarperCollins, rev. edn, 1990).

[12] Moltmann, 'Liberation of the Oppressor', p. 73.

[13] Moltmann, 'Liberation of the Oppressor', p. 73. He adds, on the next page, that this is likewise 'self-hatred' and 'a form of miscarried love of God'. This may be because one's own sense of deficiency is responded to by over-compensation for dominance and achievement. The idea of it being a form of miscarried love of God is especially relevant in the forms of sexism which have been so institutionalized within church and theology.

mies is well-established, with Moltmann's emphasis here more focused toward the 'self-incurred misery of the middle class'.[14] This is
because the pursuit and establishment of wealth can easily become a
primary mode of establishing identity, in which one who 'falls under
the compulsion of capitalism will in many respects be alienated
from his or her true self'.[15] In effect, competition becomes the driving reality of not only the economy but all of life, with every element of life monetized. Our societies depress people in order to let
them work, he has noted.[16] They take advantage of lack of value, so
as to propel people to prove themselves worthy. Which leads to a
great deal of anxiety in our societies. 'Ours is a society of competition. Which on the field feels good. It can be fun when playing
sports. But it must be limited', he says, adding, 'It cannot be the only way of living'.[17] Competition to get acknowledgement becomes
inherently a society of winners and losers, of the dominating and
the dominated. Even in the church, one might add, much is done
out of a sense of competition, or a quest to find identity by proving
one's worth over and against another. This comes out of an anxious
identity rather than the fullness of God.

These three ways tend to be clear, and most of us would nod
about the clear elements of oppressing that others who participate
in these exhibit. Let me add a fourth category to Moltmann's list:
education. In considering my own life, I am rejecting attitudes and
assumptions of sexism and racism, and my status as an adjunct professor certainly limit my perceived success in capitalistic assumptions about wealth. Yet, in being honest, I would categorize myself
among the potential oppressors because of my education.
Knowledge is power, as the saying goes. Knowledge, likewise, puffs
up. Education brings its own forms of dominance and insufficient
identity. This dominance is not only expressed towards students but

---

[14] Moltmann, 'Liberation of Oppressors', p. 74.
[15] Moltmann, 'Liberation of Oppressors', p. 75. Moltmann notes four ways in
which this may take place: (1) 'One will be compelled always to justify oneself by
means of work, accomplishment, profit and progress: human beings are what
they accomplish'. (2) 'One will be compelled to worship an idol, for one will find
it necessary to place one's faith and one's trust in the increase of capital'. (3) 'Ac-
cumulated riches represent a potential but unusable life' representing 'the 'appearance of human existence' but not its actuality, because these possibilities can
be hoarded only at the cost of actuality'. (4) 'Wealth isolates'.
[16] Moltmann, interview … May 17, 2011.
[17] Moltmann, interview … May 17, 2011.

to any who may be perceived as less educated, or towards colleagues who may be perceived to be more ignorant. Academia brings with it its own sustained and often vicious forms of competition that have nothing to do with wealth and much to do with other perceived indicators of success: stature and power. We too are oppressors in need of liberation and a particular form of holiness that proclaims the fullness and freedom of God in our contexts.

With these three in mind, and my fourth added to the mix, Moltmann offers his conception of sin, in which he notes that in these forms of oppressing we see the 'phenomena of aggression'.[18] And at the heart of this aggression is anxiety, and at the heart of this anxiety is 'the impulse to self-assertion'.[19] It is this impulse towards self-assertion, towards the pursuit of forms of identity that are contrasts to God, that is at the root of original sin.[20] This is why merely addressing the issues mentioned in isolation does not lead to more substantive liberation or societal transformation, as such inherent self-assertion will find other modes of expression. We have to go to the root of the problem and the root of the problem is the need for substantive liberation and transformation into a life expressing the fullness of God – a life of holistic holiness. Original sin is, at its root, miscarried love of God and distorted trust in God.[21] Thus, holiness, at its root, can be said to be the rightly oriented love of God and trust in God. Those who are oppressors must be liberated into this love and trust, from whatever it is that presently impairs this love and trust. Those who are oppressed must be invited into the experience of love and trust, finding freedom. But what kind of freedom?

Freedom should not be understood in terms of mastery. Moltmann writes, 'When we say that we are free, when we can do and accomplish what we want, we understand freedom as mastery and

---

[18] Moltmann, 'Liberation of the Oppressor', p. 76.

[19] Moltmann, 'Liberation of the Oppressor', p. 76.

[20] Moltmann, 'Liberation of the Oppressor', p. 76 notes three dimensions of original sin which, as he puts it, should not be overlooked: '(1) Human beings do not merely *have* sins; they *are* sinners. (2) Sin is not a moral error but a *compulsion*; a servitude of the will. (3) This faulted mode of being and this compulsion are universal.' (emphases in original)

[21] Moltmann, 'Liberation of the Oppressor', pp. 76-77.

orient it to the ideal of the master'.[22] This is freedom in the terms of liberalism, where each person is granted to be their own sovereign and entrepreneur, to live as an individual only constrained where one's own freedom hits the limits of someone else. Every person is thus a competitor, testing one's own freedom over and against others, to see whose claim would stand each test. 'Each is free for himself, but no one can share in the freedom of another,' Moltmann writes, adding, 'I believe that this represents the untruth of freedom'.[23] The truth of freedom – real freedom – is not found in mastery but in relationship. 'The *truth of freedom* I find in unrestricted communion [*Gemeinschaft*], for the truth of human freedom is *love*'.[24] We are free when we are free to be wholly who we are in the context of others being wholly who they are, accepting and inviting them into participation even as they accept and invite us. This is real freedom because it takes away both the elements of competition that divisive unfreedom entails and helps each person go beyond the limits of their own individuality. Instead of a barrier, the freedom of others becomes (using one of Moltmann's favored phrases) 'a wide space where there is no cramping'.[25] If we were to utilize trinitarian terms to describe such reciprocal participation in each other's life, we could describe this freedom as *perichoresis*.

Perichoresis

In John 17, we find Jesus praying to the Father, and in this prayer praying for the continuing ministry of the disciples. 'The glory that you have given me I have given them, so that they may be one, as we are one, I in them and you in me, that they may become completely one, so that the world may know that you have sent me and have loved them even as you have loved me'.[26] This is a unity that includes diversity and more than this, it is a unity that includes one within the other, describing the relationship of Jesus with the Father as being in each other, and extending this expression of unity to

---

[22] Moltmann, 'Liberation of the Oppressor', pp. 81-82. He adds, 'When we say that we are free when we are no longer determined by others but rather determine ourselves, we understand freedom as master: each person ought to be his or her own master'.

[23] Moltmann, 'Liberation of the Oppressor', p. 82.

[24] Moltmann, 'Liberation of the Oppressor', p. 82. (Emphasis original)

[25] Following Job 36.16.

[26] John 17.22-23 (NRSV).

those who are participants with Jesus. In trying to wrestle with how this might be conceived, early theologians proposed the image of a dance – a mutuality of participation.

Moltmann notes that this concept of perichoresis 'grasps the circulatory character of the eternal divine life. An eternal life process takes place in the triune God through the exchange of energies'.[27] This goes beyond simply a model for how the divine unity can be conceived, as if were merely an organizational principle. The concept of perichoresis illuminates the fullness of each Person. Moltmann writes, 'The trinitarian Persons do not merely exist and live in one another; they also bring one another mutually to manifestation in the divine glory'.[28] If, then, this is a model for people as well as for the Trinity, expressing their unity in the same way as God does, then unity in the church must be expressed by bringing 'one another mutually to manifestation'.[29] We participate together to help each other become in full who we truly are. In this self-similar expression of God's triune identity, a perichoretic ideal is an expression of being holy as God is holy. As we participate in God's energies we awaken each other to the fullness of life.

Kenosis

Moltmann realizes that while perichoresis may be the clear first task for those who are oppressed, to be lifted into participation and manifestation of their true being, for the oppressor it is not a matter of being first lifted up, but of letting go false forms of mastery, domination, and identity. 'Oppressors', he writes, 'will begin their "long march" into true freedom for the first time when they com-

---

[27] Jürgen Moltmann, *The Trinity and the Kingdom of God* (trans. Margaret Kohl; Minneapolis: Fortress Press, 1993), p. 174. He further focuses this definition, adding, 'The Father exists in the Son, the Son in the Father, and both of them in the Spirit, just as the Spirit exists in both the Father and the Son. By virtue of their eternal love they live in one another to such an extent, and dwell in one another to such an extent, that they are one. It is a process of most perfect and intense empathy.' Pannnenberg, *ST* I, p. 334, disagrees that this concept establishes the unity of God, it only manifests it, suggesting that it presupposes 'another basis of the unity of the three persons'. He adds, 'The inward and outward working together of the three persons cannot be the basis of the premise of their unity, though their essential unity, which has its basis elsewhere, can find expression in it'.

[28] Moltmann, *The Trinity*, p. 176.

[29] Moltmann, *The Trinity*, p. 176.

prehend the extent to which their perversion of freedom into mastery has imprisoned and isolated them'.[30] This comprehension, and the actions that follow, is likewise an expression of sanctification – one that involves first letting go what such people feel they are owed or deserve or must control. In this letting go, we can see another Trinitarian expression, that of *kenosis*. The term '*kenosis*' is most generally applied to the Son, emphasizing the self-emptying and self-humbling as described in Phil. 2.6-11. This self-emptying is an expression of obedience. Pannenberg writes, 'As the incarnation of the Logos was the result of the self-emptying of the eternal Son in his self-distinction from the Father, so the self-humbling of Jesus in obedience to his sending by the Father is the medium of the manifestation of the Son on the path of his earthly life'.[31] Pannenberg goes on to note that this is not surrender or negation of the Son's identity as God, rather it 'is its activation'.[32] The manifestation of the Son in his identity was through *kenosis,* a manifestation of self-emptying for the sake of communion with God and with others.[33]

This expression of *kenosis* can be seen in the activities of the other Trinitarian persons as well. Moltmann considers the act of creation a self-withdrawal of the Father, who made space within himself for others to be created and maintained in their particularity, utilizing Luria's term *zimsum,*[34] withdrawing his presence so that others may be made manifest. This is an expression of his love even before the initiating of his creation. 'This self-restricting love', Moltmann writes, 'is the beginning of that self-emptying of God which Philippians 2 sees as the divine mystery of the Messiah'.[35] The *kenosis* of the Father in creation is expressed in the *kenosis* of Jesus as Messiah,

[30] Moltmann, 'Liberation of the Oppressors', p. 82.

[31] Pannenberg, *ST,* II, p. 377.

[32] Pannenberg, *ST,* II, p. 377.

[33] Jürgen Moltmann, *God in Creation* (trans. Margaret Kohl; Minneapolis: Fortress Press, 1993), p. 89, writes, 'Through his self-emptying he creates liberation, through his self-humiliation he exalts, and through his vicarious suffering the redemption of sinners is achieved'.

[34] See Moltmann, *God in Creation*, p. 87.

[35] Moltmann, *God in Creation*, p. 88. He continues: 'Even in order to create heaven and earth, God emptied himself of his all-plenishing omnipotence, and as Creator took upon himself the form of a servant'. Moltmann goes on to, essentially, connect this expression of *kenosis* with an ultimate reality of perichoresis, in which God is 'all in all'. Cf. Moltmann, *God in Creation*, pp. 88-89.

and continues in the work of the Spirit. 'How does this come about?', Vladimir Lossky asks. He answers, 'That remains a mystery – the mystery of the self-emptying, of the κένωσις of the Holy Spirit's coming into the world'.[36] The Spirit, in essence, remains concealed, pointing towards the Son even as the Son always pointed towards the Father, manifesting the common nature of the Trinity in working to manifest others. 'He remains unrevealed, hidden, so to speak, by the gift in order that this gift which He imparts may be fully ours, adapted to our persons'.[37] This work manifests in a self-similar fashion to the other works of the Triune Persons, and in this manifestation orients a fullness of life that likewise manifests the same expression. Thus, the *kenosis* of the Holy Spirit must, then, likewise be expressed as *kenosis* in the lives of men and women, thus including this element of divine activity within the expressed liberation that is true holiness.

Perichoresis as Holiness for the Oppressed

Which brings us back to Philippians 2, where Paul introduces the hymn with, 'Let the same mind be in you that was in Christ Jesus'.[38] This same mind involves both *kenosis* and *perichoresis*, a letting go and a raising up, an exhaling and an inhaling. Each, then, is likewise an expression of a holistic holiness. Both must be included within any particular person's sanctification, yet given the context one should predominate as a way of overcoming false forms of identity and entering into a more substantive form of freedom. For those who are oppressed, who have been dehumanized and their identity stripped from them, the element of perichoresis should be prioritized, as they are given space to discover and express their burgeoning, Spirit-empowered, identity in full. Indeed, this is precisely why, I would argue, that Pentecostal churches particularly resonate in communities that are or have historically experienced oppression. The particular emphases of Pentecostal churches emphasize a broad range of participation and empower those who might otherwise be ignored or alienated. This emphasis of perichoretic holiness is also Moltmann's emphasis in discussions of sanctification.

---

[36] Vladimir Lossky, *Mystical Theology of the Eastern Church* (Crestwood, NY: St Vladimir's Seminary Press, 1998), p. 168.
[37] Lossky, *Mystical Theology*, p. 168.
[38] Philippians 2.5.

In beginning his discussion of sanctification, Moltmann focuses on the work of the Spirit in perichoretic terms. 'God's Spirit is life's vibrating, vitalizing field of entry: we are in God, and God is in us. Our stirrings towards life are experienced by God, and we experience God's living energies. In the open air of the eternal Spirit, the new life unfurls'.[39] For those in contexts of disaster, or conflict, or oppression, however, the daily struggle prevents such unfurling of life as the constraints of the context continually seek to repress. Thus, such expression of life is initiated in forms of liberation that identify, empower, and include such people in transformative contexts of participation. 'The creative power of life is to be found in its expression', Moltmann writes, and so the expression of holiness in contexts of oppression is one of discovering one's own creative contributions and being freed to utilize these in diverse ways.[40]

Sanctification today, for Moltmann, means 'the search for the harmonies and accords of life'.[41] Life can no longer be led at the expense of others and these others must be seen in their particularity and as important parts of the whole of a given context. We must perceive life as existing in interrelated sectors, from small scales to the largest, becoming sensitive to the conditions of each person and how such conditions affect their participation in God's holistic work. God who is holy works in ways which transform his people, with God inviting us and calling for our participation, no matter our past or current societal status.[42] This is grace, and grace that begins with God cannot be shunted from others. 'Sanctification as an act of God in a human being signifies a relationship and an affiliation,

---

[39] Jürgen Moltmann, *The Spirit of Life: A Universal Affirmation* (trans. Margaret Kohl; Minneapolis, MN: Fortress Press, 2001), p. 161. He continues: 'In the confidence of faith we plumb the depths of the Spirit, in love we explore its breadth, and in hope its open horizons. God's Spirit is our space for living.'

[40] Moltmann, *Spirit of Life*, p. 163. See also See also Jürgen Moltmann, 'The Church in the Power of the Spirit', in *The Holy Spirit in the World Today* (ed. Jane Williams; London: Alpha International, 2011).

[41] Moltmann, *Spirit of Life*, p. 173.

[42] Moltmann, *Spirit of Life*, p. 180 writes, 'Life is always specific, never general. Life is everywhere different, never the same. It is female or male, young or old, handicapped or non-handicapped, Jewish or Gentile, white or black, and so forth. Life is everywhere endowed. There is no such thing as unendowed life. There is only the social undervaluation of certain gifts, and the preference given to others.'

not a state in itself. What God loves is holy, whatever it may be in itself.'[43]

Thus, it is not a special act of favor that calls us to include and give space to others, it is a recognition of the work that God already is enacting in that person, recognizing God's value for them and his work in and through them. Because, as Moltmann puts it, 'Sanctification as a gift leads to sanctification as a charge'.[44] The work of holiness that God initiates is to be recognized and honored, and so the work of holiness that is sanctification in the life of believers can never be a passive experience. 'Sanctification', Moltmann writes, 'is the discipleship of Jesus and means coming to life in God's Spirit'.[45] This discipleship and coming to life is oriented by God's kingdom not societal patterns, and wherever societal patterns conflict with God's kingdom, such patterns are to be confronted and resisted.

That which is being made holy is, in essence, being made whole; 'what is holy is that which has become whole again, and is unscathed and healthy'.[46] Holiness then is about, ultimately, being freed to be who God has called each person to be. In their wholeness of being and expression they find the holiness of God's work in their life, shaping them more fully who they truly are. This understanding, then, cannot abide forms of religious manipulation that seek control and constraint, insisting on defining holiness through moral or authoritarian demands. As this holiness must, by definition, be empowered by the Holy Spirit, it does not lack a moral component, it just cannot be limited to such or limited to the oft capricious ways morality is applied to some but not others.

Holiness as perichoresis means 'being freed and justified, loved and affirmed, and more and more alive'.[47] As the life of God is experienced more and more in a person's life and in a context, this life overflows with powers and energies, expressing the divine life in the present life, marking a sharp distinction from the anemic expressions of life in the surrounding context. This is why the images of the Spirit as the light, the source, and the fruit are about illumination and growth, a growth that should not be constrained. Those

---

[43] Moltmann, *Spirit of Life*, p. 174.
[44] Moltmann, *Spirit of Life*, p. 174.
[45] Moltmann, *Spirit of Life*, p. 175.
[46] Moltmann, *Spirit of Life*, p. 175.
[47] Moltmann, *Spirit of Life*, p. 176.

who oppose such growth in a person are not opposing that person as much as they are opposing the wellspring of the Spirit working in that person. 'So', Moltmann writes, 'the "passion for life" must be awakened and the numbing spell of apathy must be broken'.[48] Those who despair of life must be led into a way of desiring life, with passion and with enacted hope. This is the way of the Spirit for all people, and should be especially emphasized among those whose experiences of life seem to contradict such a call. Such people who are in experiences of oppression find this wholeness that is holiness in 'the free space for our freedom, as the living space for our lives, as the horizon inviting us to discover life'. This is an exploration of trust, an expansion in hope, and the wideness of God's work through the breadth of God's transformative love that is all-encompassing. 'Christ's Spirit is our immanent power to live', Moltmann writes, 'God's Spirit is our transcendent space for living'.[49]

In looking at God's particular work in our life, we should not look for that which we do not have but 'must first of all discern who we are, what we are and how we are at the point where we feel the touch of God on our lives'.[50] This is a diversity that expresses the unity of the Spirit, each person unique and vital, each person called to be part of this whole work of God in a given context and into eternity. This is the perichoretic expression of holiness that is enacted in diverse ways among diverse peoples, oriented by the Spirit's always particular and always universal work. This particular and universal work is inviting all people into participation and into having a voice in their context. In the perichoretic community of the Spirit, everyone has a role and everyone has a ministry. These can be expressed in terms of charismata, understood both specifically and broadly. More broadly, 'whatever he is and brings with him becomes a charism through his calling, since it is accepted by the Spirit and put at the service of the kingdom of God'.[51] This insists that a person should not be objectified as a role in a system or

---

[48] Moltmann, *Spirit of Life*, p. 178. He adds, 'They must learn to love it with such passion that they are not prepared to adapt to the forces of destruction, and to let the trend to death take its course unchecked'.

[49] Moltmann, *Spirit of Life*, p. 179.

[50] Moltmann, *Spirit of Life*, p. 181.

[51] Moltmann, *Spirit of Life*, p. 182.

as a cog in a machine, nor should they be seen only in terms of what they can offer a specific ministry or church service. The holiness that is perichoretic holiness is holistic, encompassing the whole of life that the Spirit is enabling for that person. Each person is formed into a particular kind of person in holiness and in this holiness expresses a particularly way of living – which is unique to each person.

The diversity of the Spirit's work forms the unity of the expression of the Kingdom in that context, with the Spirit forming a particular people in a specific community through diverse expressions of holiness – ways in which the Spirit is working through them. 'The acceptance of other people in their difference and their particularity is constitutive for the community of Christ', Moltmann writes, 'Only the free wealth of individually different charismata ministers to life and its limitation. Every restriction and uniformity in ideas, words and works benumbs the community and bores other people.'[52] Holiness, in other words, that is the holy work of the Holy Spirit is understood through an expression of perichoresis.

Kenosis as Holiness for the Oppressors

What about those who already are involved, powerful, even dominating? Does such activity itself imply the state of holiness? Of course not. Indeed, for many the very source of oppression in society and the church has been those who justify such activities with some sort of divine mission. Yet, going back to the very core of the Philippians 2 hymn, the pattern of renewal we see in Christ was of an entirely different kind. Transformation came through participation with humanity and this participation was pursued not by a display of the dominance and glory of Jesus as God, but as a man among other people, lowly, then broken, then killed. Jesus let go such a display of divinity in order to be a true minister. Jesus was God, and it was his right to assert such an identity. But he did not. How then can we justify dominance and oppression by those who have no right to be gods to others? Such a pose as such often involves asserting false forms of identity, making them neither god nor even truly human.

---

[52] Moltmann, *Spirit of Life*, p. 184.

Indeed such justification for dominance and oppression is at the heart of sin, seeking to establish one's self in a way that is not in line with God's identity. Wolfhart Pannenberg writes, 'The image of the individual who takes himself or herself to be the center of his or her life aptly describes the structure of sin'.[53] Thus, for such a person the process of sanctification involves not a taking up – as it is false assertations and wrong expressions that are the problem – but a letting go, letting go assumptions about an identity that leads a person away from and into opposing God's work. This is the process of *kenosis*, for just as Jesus put aside his rightful claim to glory, in order to be truly holy as Jesus was holy so too must each person put away wrongful claims to glory. For those in contexts and situations of oppressing this would be the predominant mode of holiness – letting go and in this letting go making space for others and becoming oriented rightly, and humbly, in God's identity.

Pannenberg develops his understanding of sin based on the human drive towards exocentricity. We know who we are by being among others who are not us.[54] In this situation, the ego is driven towards ever more definition and distinction. Self-identity becomes established by defining oneself not only as distinct from others but over and against others which becomes 'the organizing principle of the unity of the individual's experience'.[55] This is not only destructive and divisive for relationships, as each ego is in constant competition with others, but it is also destructive for the particular individual. As human identity can never be truly sustainable, and in-

---

[53] Wolfhart Pannenberg, *Human Nature, Election, and History* (Philadelphia: Westminster, 1977), p. 26. Wong writes, 'sin arises out of the tension in the interplay of two natural human drives, egocentricity and exocentricity, or, as discussed earlier, self-centeredness and openness to the world. Thus, it is sin insofar as it falls into conflict with the infinite destiny of humanity, or as the ego adheres to itself rather than letting itself be inserted into a higher unity of life, beyond the individual and the community to the origin of the whole of reality. To the extent that this tension between egocentricity and exocentricity is seemingly unavoidable, sin is something that belongs to human givenness.' Kam Ming Wong, *Wolfhart Pannenberg on Human Destiny* (Burlington, VT: Ashgate, 2008), p. 107.

[54] Cf. Wolfhart Pannenberg, *Anthropology in Theological Perspective* (Philadelphia: Westminster, 1985), pp. 84-86.

[55] Pannenberg, *Anthropology*, p. 85. He continues, 'The ego continues to be constituted as exocentric, but its presence to the other now become a means for it to assert itself in its difference from the other. Presence to the other becomes a means by which the ego can dominate the other and assert itself by way of this domination.'

volves a multiplicity of contradictions and dissolutions, attempts to set oneself up as one's own defining reality always results in disintegration – we are no longer integrated with ourselves, with others, or especially with God who is the only sustaining identity upon which all others must be oriented towards.

In the face of such disintegration, a person can either be rightly oriented with God, thus being established in the true identity that is holiness or they can continue to resist, assuming that more domination or power or other forms of identity satisfaction will bring resolution to the underlying confrontation with the void.[56] 'The proud', Pannenberg writes, 'cannot easily tolerate the awareness of their own nonidentity and existential failure'.[57] Aggression against one's own self leads easily to aggression against others, with assumptions, generally implicitly, of being God's equal – able to determine their own identity, meaning and dominate others. The proud 'take pleasure in pluming themselves on this, and they take offense at any infringement upon it'.[58] Pannenberg goes on to note that this consciousness of sin is not itself a guard against falling into the dangers of establishing a false identity, with assertions of distortion and self-failure becoming a tool for more wrongly oriented efforts and, likewise, a way to assert power and control over others – the temptation of preachers and pastors – or by pursuing good works to somehow, in these works, making one's own self seem necessary. It is only in focusing wholly on God as the source of identity, rather than emphasizing the sin or failure in isolation, that such discussions can be a factor in human liberation.[59]

---

[56] See James Loder, *The Logic of the Spirit* (San Francisco: Jossey-Bass, 1998), pp. 122-24.

[57] Pannenberg, *Anthropology*, p. 153.

[58] Pannenberg, *Anthropology*, p. 153. Cf. Pannenberg, *Anthropology*, pp. 266-67.

[59] Pannenberg, *Anthropology*, p. 153. Cf. Pannenberg, *Anthropology*, pp. 480-81. Moltmann, *Spirit of Life*, pp. 201-202, writes,

But the people who throw themselves into practical life because they cannot come to terms with themselves simply become a burden for other people. Social praxis and political involvement are not a remedy for the weakness of our own personalities. Men and women who want to act on behalf of other people without having deepened their own understanding of themselves, without having built up their own capacity for sensitive loving, and without having found freedom towards themselves, will find nothing in themselves that they can give to anyone else. Even presupposing good will and the lack of evil intentions, all they will be able to pass on is the infection of their own egoism,

People who are trying to establish their own identity through some means or some other way other than God contribute to not only their own continued alienation but also the continued nonidentity of others, as such others may begin to see in an oppressor or dominant figure a source for identity. The only way towards wholeness is by putting aside such attempts at self-definition or overcoming alienation by dominance, control or actions. 'Faith in the conquest of alienation by the action of alienated human beings is a faith that is still under the spell of alienation'.[60] Only in repentance, and in foregoing such actions or identity as being themselves substantive for definition, can a person become free to be truly themselves in light of God's ultimate identity, the only identity that is sustainable through eternity, and as such the only identity that is able to sustain other identities without their collapse into ultimate disintegration.[61]

Such repentance from false attempts at identity formation and meaning must be oriented towards God and must, likewise be expressed in community, as only in community can our wrongly oriented exocentricity that establishes itself over and against others can find resolution with and among others in a new, holy exocentricity. 'Here too the goal is the restoration of community, the reintegration of the individual into the community, the removal of alienation, the "purification" of conscience from the judgment that condemns our works and keeps us imprisoned in nonidentity'.[62] This is a fundamental role of the Eucharistic community that in continually reorienting itself towards Christ for all meaning and identity offers a sustaining role for each individual members. 'Individuals recover their identity through reintegration into the community; they recover a freedom which they neither possess nor can exercise for themselves in isolation, but which they possess only as recognized members of the shared world'.[63] This recovery of true identity through the letting go of false and insufficient forms to establish identity is

---

the aggression generated by their own anxieties, and the prejudices of their own ideology.

[60] Pannenberg, *Anthropology*, p. 281.

[61] See Pannenberg, *ST*, III, pp. 640-41.

[62] Pannenberg, *Anthropology*, pp. 311-12.

[63] Pannenberg, *Anthropology*, p. 312. For a description of this process see Patrick Oden, *It's a Dance: Moving with the Holy Spirit* (Newberg, OR: Barclay Press, 2007, ch. 5.

an expression of *kenosis* that leads to true holiness in the life of the participants and in the community. [64]

Conclusion

When I was in Tübingen, Moltmann continued our conversation by noting there are two forms of sin that come out of false identity formation: hubris on the one side, apathy on the other side. Both of these have become models of virtue in our society – to be desperate to oneself, or to be desperate of oneself. Moltmann mentions Kierkegaard, who noted that this is the sickness to death. And Moltmann then emphasizes this further by saying, 'This is important'.[65] If, then, there are these two kinds of sin, there are also two kinds of associated forms of holiness that are contrasts to these expressions of sin. Apathy and hubris are confronted by emphases of *kenosis* and perichoresis. Moltmann is especially helpful in pointing towards the need for perichoretic holiness while Pannenberg is especially helpful in pointing toward the need for a kenotic holiness.

As very few are wholly the oppressed or the oppressor, with most people experiencing both forms of oppression and opportunities for oppressing, these emphases should be understood within a dynamic, holistic understanding of holiness that is both inviting and emptying. In letting go, we give space to others to participate. In their letting go, they give space to us to participate. This dual aspect to holiness can certainly be seen in the holistic ministry of John Wesley who saw social action and wide participation as going hand in hand with the active quest to overcome particular forms of sin. In our era, it seems these emphases have, more or less, been divided

---

[64] Cf. Pannenberg, *ST*, I, p. 179. Wolfhart Pannenberg, *Basic Questions in Theology: Collected Essays* (Minneapolis: Fortress Press, 1971), II, p. 248, writes,

> Whoever has been gripped by God's future surely places himself, his trust, and his hope in it. But the ontological primacy of God's future over every presently existing form of human realization remains in force even here. For man will participate in the glory of God only in such a way that he will always have to leave behind again what he already is and what he finds as the given state of his world. Man participates with God not by flight from the world but by active transformation of the world which is the expression of the divine love, the power of its future over the present by which it is transformed in the direction of the glory of God.'

Cf. Wolfhart Pannenberg, *Faith & Reality* (Philadelphia: Westminster Press, 1977), pp. 78-79.

[65] Moltmann, interview … May 17, 2011.

between the movements that have particularly emphasized the work of the Holy Spirit in the Western World. The Wesleyan Holiness movement has long emphasized the need to let go false forms of identification, to avoid sins and temptations that would otherwise provide a false sense of meaning. The Pentecostal tradition has emphasized participation, wide-involvement and empowering of each person to express fully the work of the Spirit in their lives.

While these theologians and traditions do not lack elements of their counterpart, they tend to be vulnerable in the areas the other is strong. Pentecostal churches, for instance, tend towards such problems as the health-wealth Gospel – which divinizes cultural forms of identity – and very charismatic leaders from whom their followers derive meaning and identity. The Holiness churches celebrate the work of the Holy Spirit in what they should not be doing, but struggle to illuminate the fullness of God's work in every person's life, leading towards legalism and an often passive church experience and Christian life in general. In understanding holiness as liberation from both sides, the expression of liberation for both the oppressed and oppressors, we can see how a dynamic understanding lends towards a holistic renewal of Christian community in diverse contexts, and in this renewal leading towards a holistic transformation of each context as the Spirit continues to work strongly among us all, leading each of us as individuals and as a community towards the fullness of God's life in, with, and through us.

11

A HOLY RECEPTION CAN LEAD TO A HOLY FUTURE

DANIEL CASTELO[*]

By way of highlighting this volume's guiding theme, allow me to recall a feature of my academic testimony that I have not made public before. In many ways, I pursued academic theology as a vocation because of the issue of sanctification within Pentecostalism. Or maybe I should clarify: I pursued this call largely because of sanctification being a *non-issue* within Pentecostalism. What I mean by a 'non-issue' is that sanctification was not conceptually secured for me as I grew up, so it was a precarious theological notion in my experience.

Throughout my early life, I had the opportunity to interact with a number of ministers within my family's denomination (Church of God, Cleveland), and as a teenager, I started to ask these ministers questions regarding holiness. My questions emerged from a number of sources. Most pressingly, my parents did not allow me to participate in what were deemed 'worldly' activities, including 'mixed bathing' (swimming with people of the opposite sex) and movie-going. The rationale for such prohibitions was that these were improper for holiness folk, but as a teenager who lived in hot climates and who was very captivated by a number of movie franchises, I was not entirely convinced of their impropriety. A sustained case was never made to me so that I was compelled to see the worldliness of these activities, so I took the prohibitions to be not so much

---

[*] Daniel Castelo (PhD, Duke University) is Associate Professor of Theology at Seattle Pacific Seminary and University in Seattle, WA.

resistances to the world as denials of me having innocent fun. Important here is that my family's theology was bearing into how I was being raised: I was not allowed to do certain things because of the understanding that my family was trying to lead holy lives. I never experienced a species of practical reasoning that had as its end a view of holiness as a way to pursue a beautiful and meaningful life, and so the prohibitions were in some sense meaningless and burdening to me as I grew up.

Interestingly enough, I came to realize that other people within my own denomination did not find such activities worldly at all. I started to see – again because of the interplay and tensions between the practical and the theoretical – that the situation was more complex than what my parents would have it. The disconnect I sensed between theory and praxis occasioned my first intuitive understanding of critical thinking: I started to ask, 'Who defines what is worldly and what is holy? Are these matters up for grabs depending on one's parents and location? If so, then does that not lead to an ultimate relativism at the prohibitive level?' All of these questions swirled in my head for years, especially as I saw generational gaps. Older Pentecostals were oftentimes caught up in a rigidity that seemed overbearing to me, but I also witnessed in them a level of integrity and sincerity that I found noble. At the same time, I saw newer generations delight in their newfound freedom so as not to be bound by the inflexibility of their parents and grandparents, and yet many of these people were not passionate about their faith, nor were they disposed to sacrifice for it in the way their forebears did. Of course, all of this evidence is anecdotal and perhaps idiosyncratic to me, but it nevertheless impacted significantly my theology of holiness particularly and the Christian life more generally.

Another source of my questioning came from my early studies of the Church of God's denominational history. I am not sure where I picked up the sensibility of tradition-based inquiry; nevertheless I thought it important in junior high school to read Charles W. Conn's *Like a Mighty Army*, the official denominational history of the Church of God. Reading the work so early in my life made a lasting impact upon me. I was (and continue to be) startled by the fact that this ecclesial body was a holiness group (1886) before it was a Pentecostal one by an entire decade (1896). For me, this detail alone required any serious student of the denomination to consider holiness to be part of the Church of God's past *and* future. And when I began reading other authors, especially Donald Dayton and those who follow his historical instincts and conclusions, I grew to realize that not simply the Church of God but the Pentecostal movement as a whole are best understood when situated in the milieu of the nineteenth-century holiness movement. Once again and more broadly, I came to see that holiness should be part of Pentecostalism's future because it is so vital to Pentecostalism's past.

These realizations, however, were challenged by the ongoing experiences of my life, my perpetual present so to speak. When I came to ask ministers about the precise topic of sanctification, that is, how one comes to be holy, none gave me an answer that was satisfactory to me. A pattern emerged: Many initially responded to my queries with the claim that I had stumbled upon a very difficult matter, and this gesture, I believe, was often their initial reaction because of their own confusion or indecisive outlook on the matter; I came to conclude that theirs was a strategy of deferral based on their own ignorance and disquietude related to the theme. I sensed – again practically – that the matter was indeed complicated, but historically, the issue merited, in my opinion, ongoing consideration for purposes of identity inculcation and cultivation. I could not understand how a topic so basic to Pentecostal identity could be in such disarray, and this recognition worried me. Based on my experience, I came to ask: If Pentecostals are unable to articulate a theme so crucially related to their past, then what hope exists for the tradition in terms of theological continuity? I started to retain a certain uneasiness of my own, one related to Pentecostalism's coherence across time. I still harbor that worry today.

What is the future of holiness in Pentecostalism? I think a conversation on the matter requires some working sense of the role of holiness in Pentecostalism's past. Without some awareness of where the tradition has been, no hope is available for understanding where it is today, and without some localization of the present situation, the outlook for holiness' future in Pentecostalism is dire. I am of the persuasion that at least two challenges face the future of holiness in Pentecostalism because they are ones that have yet to be resolved in Pentecostalism's past. I cannot offer a thoroughgoing reconstrual of all that is involved in these particular matters, but I do hope to raise awareness of them so that more work can be pursued to clarify their many dimensions.

1) Is holiness a moral-theological category? The reason I begin with this question is that I am not sure how Pentecostals on the whole would answer it today. On the one hand, it would make sense that Pentecostals would respond in the affirmative, that holiness is a moral-theological category, especially when testimonies are at play in which people are delivered and healed of any number of maladies and vices within the modality of Pentecostal worship. However, the prominence of the 'holiness codes' or prohibitions within some sectors of Pentecostalism have created a distaste or aversion to material, bodily, and moral expressions of holiness because of their associated abuses. In light of such extremes, some within those traditions may be tempted to turn to a 'positional' understanding of holiness, one in which holiness is more of a status of being in Christ, a view oftentimes associated (rather reductively) with the Apostle Paul.

These divergences require a reassessment of what holiness is and its shape within the biblical witness. Most certainly, moments within the biblical testimony point to holiness being a God-enabled and God-granted reality. It is God who sets apart a nation and a people. God is spoken of in various visions as surrounded by the heavenly host with the thrice-repeated proclamation that God is holy. The spirit who indwells believers and bears witness with their spirit is the Holy Spirit. And countless other examples exist. I am of the persuasion that no Christian could possibly argue that holiness is an impossibility in the Christian life, for too many authoritative materials (or what William Abraham and others would claim as the church's canonical heritage) suggest that the Trinity has made a species of holiness available to the Christian community here and now.

The difficulty resides in human agency and its relation to holiness. Can Christians sanctify themselves? Varying theological proposals have emphasized different aspects of this question. But according to the biblical witness, yes, believers can, and in fact should, sanctify themselves. My colleague Robert Wall has made the case that the depiction of holiness within the Catholic Epistles collection of the New Testament makes this precise point.[1] As believers we are to purify and sanctify ourselves through covenant-keeping practices of fidelity to the triune God of Christian confession. Christians do this through their ongoing obedience and conformity to the normative implications of the gospel. Obedience and faithfulness are sanctifying or purifying features of the Christian life. Protestants generally have a strong aversion to such reasoning because they often believe it promotes a works-righteousness approach to the Christian life. This initial reaction, if carried and sustained in an unqualified way, simply cannot account for the dynamism inherent to a covenant-bound way of life. As Christians we can participate in the new covenant brought about and established by Christ in obedience to the Father and empowered by the Spirit, but that new covenant, with the freedom and blessedness it promises, is nevertheless a covenant. In other words, a covenant-framed life comes with obligations that are intrinsic to the quality, depth, and vitality of that life itself. In a specific way, we can and ought to sanctify ourselves because God deems it right and fitting that we do so in this covenant partnership. 'Be holy' and 'be perfect' are not suggestions or recommendations; they are commands, but as with any command in Scripture, they are veiled promises[2] of God's faithfulness to help and enable us to do that which corresponds for us to do in the Christian peregrination.

All of these claims point in the direction that holiness is in some sense a moral-theological category. But if it is so, then what to do with the holiness codes of Pentecostalism's past? They in turn require some kind of renewed and sustained assessment. The value of the prohibitions is that they were attempting to maintain a workable sense of what is sacred and profane. The gospel's logic requires this kind of negotiation. If the gospel is 'good news', it is so in contradistinction to 'bad news'. Worldliness is not a harmless fiction; it is an ever-present threat not simply to a Christian's mind and soul but also to one's body and life, and this is so not just at the individual level but also at the corporate. The prohibitions were indicative of a pressing urgency on the part of early Pentecostals to secure some

---

[1] See his chapter and the biblical evidence he raises in *Holiness as a Liberal Art* (ed. Daniel Castelo; Eugene, OR: Pickwick, 2012).

[2] This is a feature of a Wesleyan logic brought to prominence repeatedly by Albert Outler.

kind of *practical* barrier between the church and the world. This gesture does not emit from a self-absorbed spirituality (as some have critiqued early Pentecostal ethics to be) but very much one that has the world in its purview as a threatening and maleficent force. In my estimation, the future of holiness within Pentecostalism requires this ongoing sense of the world's power to corrupt, harm, and destroy authentic Christian life.

The difficulty of the prohibitions, of course, is their penchant to codify holy resistances to the world's encroachments so that the activities they suggest become ends unto themselves. Rules, denials, and avoidances can become ritualistic in the worst sense of the term; they can become expressions of a kind of mindless, heartless, going-through-the-motions form of existence. *That is why the prohibitions have no place in communal forms of life apart from an enacted and sustained exercise of practical reasoning.* The 'spirit of the prohibitions' has to be on display in holy lives, holy deliberation, and holy discernment. These activities are crucial so that the form of godliness does not trump the power of godly living. Within such an ethos, the denial of something like 'mixed bathing' can be cast as a communal form of resistance to the world's tendencies to excite lust through a fashion industry that entices the objectification of human bodies by insisting and mandating the maximization of bodily exposure (especially of women, which further feeds into the worldly arrangement of patriarchy). Or within such a way of communal existence, the denial of movie-going can be framed as a holy resistance to the world's numbing encroachments to desensitize us to sin by way of exposing us to gratuitous profanity, drug-use, and violence.

When properly negotiated, the prohibitions are not so much rules or codes that need enforcement as much as working and revisable proposals by which a community comes to terms with how best to respond and resist the nefarious encroachments of worldliness. Originally, the prohibitions depicted holiness as a moral-theological category because their formulators had an intuited sense that worldliness had deleterious moral-theological consequences; what these espousers often lacked was a well-developed sense of how best to inculcate and sustain a community's holy resistance to the world. This shortcoming manifested itself not simply in terms of practical matters but also at the theological/conceptual level, which leads us to the next issue from Pentecostalism's past that requires immediate consideration and resolution if holiness is to have a future among its fold.

2) Can the 'Finished-Work' controversy be picked up once again so that it can be settled conceptually in a way that problematizes and transcends instantaneity and progressivity? In my way of thinking, the future of holiness within Pentecostalism significantly pivots on whether headway can be made on this matter since this issue has continually divided Pentecostals across denominational and theological trajectories. As a way of establishing some basis by which to advance this conversation, let me offer a set of sub-claims for consideration.

First, it is a matter of historical observation that the vast majority of early American Pentecostals were influenced or even purveyors of logics inherent to the nineteenth-century holiness movement. The particular logic I have in mind is, of course, the understanding of the 'crisis experience' or the 'definitive work of grace'. Culprits could be named all around as to this understanding's origins and popularity, but broadly, the idea had merit and efficacy within a species of American revivalism that in turn mutated into many forms all the while retaining some basic, observable characteristics. These similarities across the board would include voluntarism, the sacramentality of the altar experience, the expectation and adequacy of the immediate, and the belief that experiences were to some degree of a singular, uniform, and accessible nature – they were 'out there' to be had by each person within the proper circumstances. In these cases the details may have been different, but an intuited sense of commonality and generalizability was perpetuated and taught. These characteristics and many more have marked American revivalism for some time, and they are evident both in the holiness and Pentecostal movements. For those who upheld this logic as the primary way of encountering and being transformed by God, it was natural that the sensibilities, reasoning, and expectations forged within one movement would be carried over into the other. Without the holiness movement, the American Pentecostal movement would probably have taken shape quite differently than it did.

What to do with the logic of the 'crisis moment' or the 'definitive work of grace' understanding? I think it has to be particularized within a form of revivalist Christianity that is itself increasingly becoming particularized. The ways people experience Pentecostalism in North America is less and less in terms of something analogous to the revivalist preacher who comes for a few days to hold an old-fashioned tent-revival. If this form of 'practicing Pentecostalism' is changing, then its inherent logics and narrative mechanisms have to alter as well. Let me be clear: I do not wish to characterize the ideas of 'crisis' or 'works of grace' as useless or outdated, for they have helped perpetuate an ethos that was very significant for Pentecostal identity and self-understanding; however, this is one, and only one, model for understanding growth and development in the Christian life. The model continues to bear fruit, and for that reason, it should continue to be sustained and considered as viable. But as a singular model, it cannot account for the many dimensions, shapes, and forms of maturation inherent to an expansive depiction of the Christian life.

And if we integrate the first consideration and assume my working proposal therein, namely that holiness is a moral-theological category, then of the three crises that some Pentecostal traditions espouse (namely, salvation, sanctification, and Spirit-baptism), the most precarious one is precisely sanctification. The reason that sanctification is precarious under these conditions is that moral-theological categories require time, trial-and-error, and the cultivation of wisdom for their flourishing. The challenge here is of the burden and weight of everyday or quotidian living. The 'definitive work of grace' paradigm cannot accommodate adequately the peaks and valleys that life throws our way. Yes, it may be the case that we need to have an altar moment, whether at church, our home, or wherever. But it also may be the case that a 'touch from God' is not all that we need if that 'touch' is viewed exclusively in terms of instantaneity and immediacy. The most obvious example here is of Jesus at Gethsemane: Jesus apparently wanted in a moment to have the cup of suffering pass, but God's plan for Jesus was to go on to Golgotha. The crisis model makes sense when located within the Acts 2 narrative; it is less than compelling when one tries to negotiate Jesus' cry of dereliction.

Is what I am suggesting a capitulation to the 'Finished Work' theory? No, not at all, for William Durham still upheld the 'crisis' logic; he just maintained that two, rather than three, existed. But his reservations are indicators of a broader concern worth pursuing, namely a conversation of the adequacy of the crisis-process model itself when applied to sanctification and holiness. I wish to suggest that little headway has been made in this conversation because the terms of the discussion require not only recalibration but suspension and perhaps even replacement in particular settings.

In light of this particularization of the crisis-process model, what can be offered as an alternative? I have tried in my work to raise the ideas of improvisation and performance, ones that do not suggest 'works' per se but rather attend to the modality of Christian existence, one that is existentially conditioned by the norming vision of Christ, the empowering presence of the Spirit, and the community's epicletic disposition.[3] I have maintained this perspective in this form so as to break the dyadic or dualistic impasse that exists between instantaneity and progressivity when depictions of sanctification are on offer. In a very basic sense, this binary has to be problematized and transcended in some fashion. 'Instant versus process' thinking conceals more than it illuminates, and its relentless and dogged lodging within Pentecostal speech related to sanctification has created more problems than ways forward. With any dualism, people feel compelled that they have to choose sides, and once they do, it is hard to recognize the merits of the non-chosen side. Binaries are reductive by nature; they assume that only two formulated possibilities exist with regard to the realities they seek to illuminate. And because they are reductive in nature, binaries destroy the imagination. This situation is especially true with Pentecostal speech related to sanctification: So often the conversation is unquestionably depicted as 'either crisis or process' that people often depict the resolution to be one of balance, but rarely are the terms themselves questioned. Could it be that 'crisis' and 'process' are themselves inadequate to account for the God-enabled depth-dimensions associated with Christian existence?

What is being pointed out here is the potential bankruptcy of dyadic thinking, which I find to be only remediable in Christian terms through a pneumatological intervention. The holiness of the Christian life is not approached or cultivated strictly through lenses that depict human development as an interplay of crises and processes. Speaking developmentally, we may look back at our lives

---

[3] See, for example, Daniel Castelo, *Revisioning Pentecostal Ethics – The Epicletic Community* (Cleveland, TN: CPT Press, 2012).

and point to peaks and valleys, yet the contours of that hermeneutical process can and do shift so that our narration of these events can change as we continue to change. Analogically, the same applies to how we narrate our spiritual lives. What is crucial is not so much getting the narration 'right' but rather continually participating in a Spirit-saturated way of life so that our condition and the many narrations emitting from it are faithful. Simply applied to our matter at hand, my concern is not whether one has an experience of sanctification and in turn how one can know it; my ultimate concern relates to whether a person is living here and now within an existential modality in which holiness is understood and shown as something beautiful, desirable, and good. Holiness is more faithfully and compellingly shown rather than proclaimed, recognized rather than asserted, and embodied rather than conceptualized. For this reason, the patterns of Pentecostal speech related to sanctification ought to be recalibrated so as to reflect such commitments. Otherwise, sanctification will continue to be something endlessly debated within a vicious dyad, and such activity in itself can overshadow its instantiation within a communal form of life.

To conclude these reflections, I have tried to make the case that holiness can have a future in Pentecostalism if current-day members of the tradition have the courage to recall and repair the way holiness has been depicted in their past. Such work is tedious and demanding but nevertheless necessary if that future is to be a true future.

PART THREE
PRACTICAL THEOLOGY

TWENTY-FIRST CENTURY HOLINESS: LIVING AT THE INTERSECTION OF WESLEYAN THEOLOGY & CONTEMPORARY PENTECOSTAL VALUES

JOHNATHAN E. ALVARADO[*]

Pentecostalism, the charismatic movement, and the renewal tradition are rooted in the holiness movement from which they were birthed. The Wesleyan substrata of these spiritualities generally tend to emphasize the formation of values and virtues within the Christian community. Among the highly prioritized values for Wesleyan Pentecostals are biblical fidelity, personal and communal holiness, and the value of community over individuality. In the 21st century postmodern era, those values and virtues have come under serious question and scrutiny. This essay seeks to examine some aspects of 21st-century theology and practice in light of Wesleyan holiness sensibilities.

In this essay I will argue for a fresh appropriation of the doctrine of holiness by returning to the intersections between Pentecostalism and the Wesleyan holiness tradition. My rationale for this prescription is the notion that Pentecostal communities need to explore and rediscover the theological and practical implications of the Wesleyan holiness foundations of their faith. I will further assert that such a fresh appropriation of holiness will enable Pentecostal churches to counter trends that are represented by the House Church and Emerging Church movements and explore a few ideas in relation to

[*] Johnathan E. Alvarado (DMin, Regent University) is Professor of Theology and Dean of the Chapel at Beulah Heights University in Atlanta, Georgia

a doctrine of holiness, most particularly its pneumatological dimension.

Within Pentecostal churches in the 21st century (particularly in the west), there seems to be a diminution of theologically sound, biblically grounded, historically supported standards upon which to promote a holiness framework for Christian conduct and thus a sustainable future.[1] Though many contemporary churches do not self-identify as Emergent or House church, they share the values, attitudes, and core structures that often define these two movements.[2] This phenomenon is also true in some other Christian traditions, but the focus of this essay is mainly upon the Pentecostal tradition in the Western, or more specifically North American context.

It is my sad opinion that the House Church and the Emerging Church movements espouse relativism, deconstruction of helpful ecclesial structures, injurious individualism, and a minimization of the person of Jesus. These trends seem to result from a basic misunderstanding of the nature of the church and the Christian life, and thus are all symptoms of a larger problem firmly gripping some contemporary Pentecostal churches.[3] That problem is exacerbated by a non-emphasis of the renewing work of the Holy Spirit and the Pentecostal life,[4] which is the benchmark for a holiness framework for 21st-century Pentecostal living.

In order to be properly understood, the renewing work of the Holy Spirit within Pentecostal Christian communities must be set in dialogue with holiness aspects of the Wesleyan tradition. I believe this to be true and necessary because of John Wesley's status as the spiritual progenitor of the holiness-Pentecostal movement.[5] I also

---

[1] Kevin W. Mannoia and Don Thorsen (eds.), *The Holiness Manifesto* (Grand Rapids, MI: Eerdmans Company, 2008), p. 18.

[2] D.A. Carson, *Becoming Conversant with the Emerging Church: Understanding a Movement and its Implications* (Grand Rapids, MI: Zondervan Publishing, 2005), p. 13.

[3] Margaret Poloma, *The Assemblies of God at the Crossroads: Charisma and Institutional Dilemmas* (Knoxville, TN: University of Tennessee Press, 1989). In this text Margaret Poloma is specifically speaking of the Assemblies of God, but her work has broad implications for the Pentecostal church at large.

[4] Steven J. Land, *Pentecostal Spirituality: A Passion for the Kingdom* (JPTSup 1; Sheffield: Sheffield Academic Press, 1993), pp. 56-57.

[5] Vinson Synan, *The Holiness–Pentecostal Tradition: Charismatic Movements in the Twentieth Century* (Grand Rapids, MI: Eerdmans, 1997), p. 1. See also, Donald W. Dayton, *Theological Roots of Pentecostalism* (Peabody, MA: Hendrickson, 1987).

believe it to be true because of John Wesley's strong assertion that transformation of the human personality occurs by the Holy Spirit.[6]

Wesley believed and taught that authentic spiritual encounter in the Word, by the Spirit, and through the means of grace, resulted in a change of life called sanctification. This sanctifying work of the Spirit happens within individuals and within the community.[7] Sanctification is a distinct emphasis of Wesleyan holiness spirituality. Perhaps it is non-adherence to this foundational principle of holiness, which undergirds the Pentecostal movement, that has taken the contemporary church in directions that are ultimately narcissistic, self-destructive, and unsustainable.

When the basic framework of holiness is absent, Pentecostal churches tend to pursue pragmatic and functional utilitarianism,[8] moral relativism, accommodations, and cultural tides. One of the overarching challenges that this essay seeks to address is the influence of the postmodern and theologically uninitiated popularist voices representing the aforementioned movements. The opinions of these contemporary voices are undermining the foundation of holiness upon which the Pentecostal church is built. Their attitudes, as demonstrated in their practice of Christian living and expressed in their publications, tend to orient the church toward contemporary goals that often have little to do with the *missio dei*.

There are three presenting problems that the House and Emerging church movements represent and that this essay seeks to address briefly. Those problems are rampant individualism, the deconstruction of beneficial ecclesial structures, and worship practices that are devoid of substance and meaning. While the limited scope of this essay does not permit a full explication of all of the potential pitfalls that remain, these three danger zones are worthy of exploration and mention. Together they represent the fruit of the aforementioned absent framework of holiness in the contemporary Pentecostal church.

---

[6] Randy L. Maddox, 'Reconnecting the Means to the End: A Wesleyan Prescription for the Holiness Movement', *Wesleyan Theological Journal* 30.2 (1995), pp. 40-41.

[7] Melvin E. Dieter, 'The Wesleyan Perspective', in Stanley N. Gundry (ed.), *Five Views on Sanctification* (Grand Rapids, MI: Zondervan, 1987), pp. 12, 16-17.

[8] Barry Callen, 'The Context: Past and Present', in Kevin W. Mannoia and Don Thorsen (eds.), *The Holiness Manifesto* (Grand Rapids, MI: Eerdmans, 2008), p. 15.

I am writing about 21st-century holiness because I am trying to connect aspects of Wesleyan holiness theology with contemporary Pentecostal values as understood through renewal lenses. I seek to affirm the potentials of this intersection and to offer some limited critique of the shortcomings of the House and Emerging Church movements, and contemporary Pentecostal values. I am writing this essay in order to describe how that intersection might look. I am also writing to discover what practices of our Pentecostal faith and tradition might be enjoined or reinvigorated as a result.

Holiness Theology at the Crossroads of Wesleyanism and Pentecostalism

I tend to agree with Steven Land's assertion that, 'the whole church is Pentecostal'.[9] He purports this notion as it pertains to the ubiquity of the Spirit's presence, activity (in varying degrees), and influence upon the affective domain of all Christians in every Christian tradition. He makes this assertion and frames his explication of Pentecostal Spirituality in hopes of giving other traditions points of intersection with and simultaneously distinction from Pentecostalism. My agreement with this statement and its underlying truisms is to say that the church, ecumenically and generally, is tending in its practices and sensibilities to gravitate toward a more pneumatocentric way of being in the world.

It has been my observation that many Christian traditions are with increasing regularity embracing and practicing manners of life and worship that are germane to the Pentecostal tradition. Many churches are growing to make room for and to expect the active and discernable presence of the Holy Spirit in their services of worship. Even churches that have not been historically associated with Pentecostalism are endeavoring to respond faithfully to what they perceive to be happening by the Holy Spirit. They are living out of what James K.A. Smith calls, 'the DNA of the church'. In that, he means that the church is internally encoded to respond to the Holy Spirit's presence, power, and initiation. He agrees with Land and asserts that the church is 'genetically' Pentecostal.[10]

---

[9] Land, *Pentecostal Spirituality*, p. 7.
[10] James K.A. Smith, 'Teaching a Calvinist to Dance', *Christianity Today* 52.5 (May 1, 2008), pp. 42.

The Charismatic Renewal is an example of the ever-growing transformation of mainline and denominational churches into pneumatic centers. The fastest growing churches on the planet are Pentecostal and Charismatic, all in the renewalist tradition. Soon the movement will rival in numbers of adherents Islam in Africa and Roman Catholicism in Latin America.[11] This global, spiritual tide is influencing Christian communities everywhere. A potential danger that now appears on the horizon, particularly in the North American context, is the uncritical inculcation of cultural and/or philosophical postmodern values into the contemporary Pentecostal church. These values tend to obfuscate the holiness sensibilities upon which the Pentecostal church is built. This is the profound danger of operating without the moorings of Wesleyan holiness theology to anchor adherents to holiness as lifestyle.

This is in my opinion what is happening with the so-called Emerging Church and the House Church movements. Don Thorsen affirms this observation when he says,

> Whole church movements are considered postmodern, most notably the so-called 'emergent church' movement. However, this popular usage of postmodernism has more to do with how and to whom ministry occurs than it has to do with a philosophical and theological description of Christianity.[12]

This is because, unlike Pentecostal churches in the Wesleyan holiness tradition, these movements have adopted postmodern theological frameworks from which they operate.

Many of them have developed an ethos of resistance to all things structural, historical, and religious. That influence is now being felt within some Pentecostal churches. This is why it is necessary to cultivate a dialogue between 21st-century Pentecostal churches and Wesleyan holiness theology in order to explore the prospect of common theological themes between them. Wesleyanism and postmodernity may share some common concerns and objectives whether they are overtly articulated or not.

---

[11] Vinson Synan, *An Eyewitness Remembers the Century of the Holy Sprit* (Grand Rapids, MI: Chosen Books, 2010), pp. 202-203.

[12] Don Thorsen, 'Holiness in Postmodern Culture', *The Wesleyan Theological Journal*, 43.2 (Fall 2008), p. 130.

Wesleyan holiness tenets are important today for the Pentecostal church and other movements that are influenced by Pentecostal spirituality. This is so because these newer movements (the House and Emerging Church movements) seem to share with Pentecostal churches Wesley's appreciation for the experience of the Holy Spirit's movement within the community.[13] The experience of the Holy Spirit, however, should be accompanied by shared behavioral mores that impact the church for the better. This is not the case in many contemporary Pentecostal-like churches who have been increasingly influenced by House and Emerging church sensibilities and have become more secular. Donald Bowdle suggests: 'A debilitating secularization of holiness has too much affected the current Pentecostal denominationalism'.[14] They have desensitized the church to the holiness standards of Wesleyan heritage.

Too little emphasis is given to personal holiness, conversion, and modesty of life, while too much emphasis is given to individual prerogatives, self-actualization, and personal freedoms. Too few persons who operate from this postmodern mindset take seriously the Wesleyan imperative that 'The Christian life is a journey from sin to holiness'.[15] Much of the conversation from leaders and proponents of the movements birthed within the postmodern era speak only of how the church must embrace the newness of how people think and feel without much regard to critiquing the nature of that thinking and feeling with respect to postmodernity and its propensity to injure the church.[16]

To be sure, Wesleyan holiness theology is rooted in at least three things. First, it is rooted in the Anglican tradition from which John Wesley came. Wesley's Anglicanism informed his understanding of the church. His ministry and insistence upon remaining Anglican

---

[13] Thorsen, 'Holiness in Postmodern Culture', p. 126.

[14] Donald Bowdle, 'Informed Pentecostalism: An Alternative Paradigm', in Terry L. Cross and Emerson B. Powery (eds.), *The Spirit and the Mind* (New York: University Press of America, 2000), p. 17.

[15] William J. Abraham, *Aldersgate and Athens: John Wesley and the Foundations of Christian Belief* (Waco, TX: Baylor University Press, 2010), p. 79.

[16] Carson, *Becoming Conversant with the Emerging Church*, p. 125. See also Dan Kimball, *The Emerging Church* (Grand Rapids, MI: Zondervan Publishers, 2003). Kimball basically delineates the problems, challenges, and hang-ups that seculars have with the church. He is kind and gracious in his critique but lacks the theological substratum to proffer an ecclesial model capable of effectuating lasting reform within the church.

demonstrated his appreciation for and connection to the church, though he expanded his ecclesial practices beyond the borders of Anglicanism. This is also evident in his affinity to the sacraments as means of grace. Second, Wesleyan holiness theology is synergistic. It requires active cooperation from its adherents and participation in the communal life of the church as embodied religious practice. Finally, Wesleyan holiness theology is experiential.[17] His emphasis upon heart religion was to counter the trends for rationalistic or propositional Christianity that brought about little efficacy in the lives of believers. Wesley tended toward a theology of encounter that would dramatically and drastically change people's lives.

Postmodernism and the House and Emerging Church Movements

Defining postmodernism is a dubious task to say the least. Within the House and Emerging church movements postmodernism can be seen generally as relativism, deconstruction, and protest.[18] I have already proposed that the House and Emerging church movements simultaneously possess the potential for injury and blessing to the church. I also indicated that there were conversations being moderated by leading voices of these groups. Some of the ones who are publishing and leading these movements are, in my opinion, theologically and ecclesiologically uninitiated. The inherent danger in this dubious undertaking is that the potential exists for their adherents to move away from the bedrock of holiness living.

Some of their publications are enticing to those who have been disillusioned by life, circumstances, and the church itself. Their writers have set themselves as contemporary watchmen, leveling critiques of the church for its structure, government, worship, and hierarchy.[19] It is my sincere belief based upon my reading of some of their literature that they have at the core of their movement a genuine love for God, though the outworking of that love is, in my opinion, misguided. Their growing disdain for all things structural and their increased distancing from the institutional church is an impediment to holiness living. Wesley espoused a holiness that was

---

[17] Thorsen, 'Holiness in Postmodern Culture', pp. 127-28.

[18] Carson, *Becoming Conversant with the Emerging Church*, p. 36.

[19] Dan Kimball, *They Like Jesus But Not The Church* (Grand Rapids, MI: Zondervan Publishers, 2007).

communal in nature, fostered in the crucible of bands, classes, and societies.[20] This translates in the 21st century to involvement in the life of the church, not an isolationist community of individuals.

These two contemporary movements may have some good points in that they are creative and culturally 'relevant'; however, I am suspect as to whether they will have the sticking power to become trans-generational movements. I also question whether the type of spirituality that they espouse will produce fully devoted Christians. While the rhetoric that they employ sounds theologically cogent, a careful investigation of their baseline propositions reveals that they are often laden with error, empty, and hollow. Only time will tell whether or not their claims for an improved ecclesiological methodology so detached from history and so fraught with novelty will usher the church into a new era.

My critique of them is not leveled with the intent to discount completely their contribution to the contemporary church. Neither is it to diminish what we can legitimately learn from them. But rather, my criticism is to expose the barriers to holiness that these movements tend to foster. Since the movements tend to be anti-structural in nature, they take on multiple forms and have overlapping tenets. Thus, my descriptions of each will be general in nature.

Before I begin discussing these two movements individually, a word on postmodernity is in order. The brevity of this study does not permit me the time to fully explicate the tenets of postmodernism, but suffice it to say that it is the cultural and sociological substratum of the 21st century. Postmodernism is the lived reality and the epistemological framework including the mind-set, affections, priorities, idiosyncrasies, and will of individuals and systems of this era. Postmodernity is epitomized in two phenomena: cyberspace and the global market.[21] It is not exclusively a secular predisposition for many in the church have adopted its tenets and inculcated them into their lives as the primary referent for living.

Douglas Meeks interestingly links cyberspace with the global market and characterizes them as both the arena and the attitude of

---

[20] Howard A. Snyder, *The Radical Wesley and Patterns for Church Renewal* (Eugene, OR: Wipf and Stock Publishers, 1980), pp. 116-32.

[21] M. Douglas Meeks, 'Wesleyan Theology in a Postmodern Era: The Spirit of Life in an Age of the Nihil', *The Wesleyan Theological Journal* 35.1 (Spring 2000), pp. 22-40 (24).

postmodern thought and affections.[22] He describes the 21st century as the age of commodification and even stretches this characterization to describe human communities via the worldwide web and emblazoned with the marks of cyber-ethos, as transactional and even disposable. Thus, everyone and everything is a commodity, a transaction, 'for sale', even the human communities themselves.[23] This notion has tremendous implications for a Wesleyan vision of holiness for Pentecostal Christians in the 21st century. This is especially true in light of the fact that both Wesleyan Christianity and Pentecostal Christianity are most authentically fleshed out in communities of believers rather than in individual persons transacting 'religious business' through cyberspace.

Stanley Grenz articulated a revealing insight into the nature of the postmodern era when he said, 'At the heart of postmodern philosophy is a sustained attack on the premises and presuppositions of modernism'.[24] His comment takes on increased potentiality when seen in light of his correlating proposition stated thusly, 'Evangelicalism shares close ties with modernity'.[25] The corollary between the age of modernism and evangelicalism is stark and telling. In light of this notion, perhaps one can discern how postmodernity is intrinsically predisposed to resist all things evangelical because of evangelicalism's connection to modernity. This would tend to include evangelicalism's link with the historic church, its roots in the holiness tradition, and its affinity to orthodoxy.

Meeks agrees with Grenz in that he asserts that the postmodern prescription

> is to undermine every logo centrism holding together the modern self. Everything that bears traces of homogeneity in civil, legal, and pedagogical institutions must be expelled. Any kind of totality and closure which would distort the full expression of the particular and concrete has to be subverted and left behind as modern detritus.[26]

---

[22] Meeks, 'Wesleyan Theology in a Postmodern Era', p. 25.
[23] Meeks, 'Wesleyan Theology in a Postmodern Era', p. 26.
[24] Stanley J. Grenz, *A Primer on Postmodernism* (Grand Rapids, MI: Eerdmans, 1996), p. 123.
[25] Grenz, *A Primer on Postmodernism*, p. 161.
[26] Meeks, 'Wesleyan Theology in a Postmodern Era', p. 28.

This truism concerning the postmodern mindset has tremendous bearing upon the postmodern predisposition and reluctance toward the church as institution.

Postmodernity is chiefly characterized by relativism, consumerism, and secularism that produce secular liturgies, coupled with anti-establishment tendencies.[27] It seeks to reorient human desires around worldly, cultural, and narcissistic pursuits through consumerism, reprioritization of affections, and desire.[28] In my opinion, it fosters an individualistic spirit within communities of persons whose goal and expectation for life is to maximize their individual potentials! This dichotomous way of being typifies the postmodern ethos and is the crucible within which the House and Emerging Church movements have been forged. I have cast the furtherance of my comments in light of this brief definition and expose of postmodernity.

The Organic or House Church Movement and the Emerging Church materialized during the era of post-modernity. They both exhibit qualities reminiscent of the general cultural values and ethos of North American 'postmodern pilgrims', to borrow from Leonard Sweet.[29] As we have discovered, the postmodern mind generally tends toward relativism, anti-structuralism, and even narcissism. This is especially true with respect to the individual Christian's relationship with God and to the church. The cultural climate and societal ethos of postmodernity provides these movements the necessary incubator in which to germinate their ideologies. It is no surprise that they have gained traction advancing their agenda for the church fueled by the cultural times in which we live.

An author, speaker, and self-proclaimed House Church expert Frank Viola is championing the Organic or House Church Movement currently. The movement is based upon his presupposition

---

[27] For a fuller treatment and explanation of postmodernism and its affect upon the church as seen through evangelical lenses see Millard J. Erickson, *Postmodernizing the Faith: Evangelical Responses to the Challenge of Postmodernism* (Grand Rapids, MI: Baker Books, 1998), and J. Richard Middleton and Brian J. Walsh, *Truth is Stranger Than it Used to Be: Biblical Faith in a Postmodern World* (Downers Grove, IL: InterVarsity Press, 1995).

[28] Smith, *Desiring the Kingdom*, p. 88.

[29] Leonard Sweet, *Post-Modern Pilgrims: First Century Passion for the 21ˢᵗ Century World* (Nashville, TN: Broadman Holman Publishers, 2000).

that the way church is being done today is far afield from the way he reads the New Testament. He states in his recent text,

> Something deep within me longed for an experience of church that mapped to what I read about in my New Testament. And I couldn't seem to find it in any traditional church I attended. In fact, the more I read the Bible, the more I became convinced that the contemporary church had departed far from its biblical roots.[30]

Thus in 1988 he left the institutional church to begin the work of organizing individuals, many of whom like him were disenchanted with the institutional church, into house churches.

These churches have no leaders, liturgies, choirs, staff, or sermons.[31] They, like Viola himself, are self-directed and 'organic' in their spiritual growth and development. The churches are independent, non-connectional, and without the benefit of spiritual covering. Though they gather together, the spirit of their gathering appears to be critical, anti-institutional, and isolationist. They are in a very real sense communities of individuals who operate without any responsibility to the larger body of Christ to walk as 'members one of another'. This, Viola submits, is authentic Christianity.

With all of the biblical and historical inaccuracies in his books set aside (there are too many to enumerate), the fundamental challenge that exists in Viola's texts is his insistence upon deconstructing the institutional church in the name of building a so-called Organic Church. The basic problem of this 21st-century construct is the tendency to separate from the larger body of Christ in favor of individualistic pursuit of so-called 'authentic' church. I contend that this mentality turned into House Church polity is fueled by the rampant individualistic ethos that has subsumed the postmodern culture.

I further contend that Viola's contempt for the institutional church and preference for the Organic Church does not foster holiness within the constituent members of the church. Randy Maddox, Ayo Adewuya, Kenneth Collins, Henry Knight, James Bowers, and Mildred Bangs Wynkoop all affirm that holiness according to

---

[30] Frank Viola, *Reimagining Church: Pursuing the Dream of Organic Christianity* (Colorado Springs: David C. Cook Publishing, 2008), p. 11.

[31] Frank Viola and George Barna, *Pagan Christianity? Exploring the Roots of our Church Practices* (Carol Stream, IL: BarnaBooks, Tyndale House Publishing, 2002).

John Wesley is a level of Christian maturity that is only attained in connectional community.[32] This is one of the principle points of divergence between these movements and Wesleyan holiness spirituality. Viola's way of being church is contradistinctive to Wesleyan theology and practice, though it is very much in line with a postmodern ethos of self-governance, self-identity, and self-direction.

The so-called Emerging Church movement in the United States began in the 1990's as a reaction against the institutional evangelical protestant church.[33] It is characterized by the postmodern sensibilities that frame its existence. There are four major aspects of postmodernity that fit broadly under philosophical and cultural mores and are attributable to the so-called Emerging Church. They are: rejection of the metanarrative so characteristic of modernity, theological pluralism that rejects neat theological categorizations, the perceived need for the church to change in order to speak to the culture, and passion for the present.[34] It is evident that at least two of these four will not bode well with Wesleyan Holiness theology.

One of the major tenets of the so-called Emerging Church is its rallying cry of creating religion without religion.[35] Emerging Church adherents tend toward an anti-structural organizational ethos that purports to create a new way of being the church but in actuality deconstructs the church it says it is reproducing. It deepens its own dilemma by disinheriting itself from the rich, two thousand year history of the church from which it is derived. Finally, the so-called emerging church has a difficult time delineating between cultural postmodernism, characterized by advocacy for and use of technol-

---

[32] See Randy Maddox, *Responsible Grace: John Wesley's Practical Theology* (Nashville, TN: Abingdon Press, 1994); Ayo Adewuya, *Holiness and Community in 2 Cor. 6:14-7:1 – A Study of Paul's View of Cmmunal Holiness in the Corinthians Correspondence* (New York: Peter Lang Publishers, 2001); Kenneth J. Collins, *The Theology of John Wesley: Holy Love and the Shape of Grace* (Nashville, TN: Abingdon Press, 2007); James Bowers, 'A Wesleyan-Pentecostal Approach to Christian Formation', *Journal of Pentecostal Theology* 6 (April 1995), pp. 55-86; and Mildred Bangs Wynkoop, *A Theology of Love: The Dynamic of Wesleyanism* (Kansas City, MO: Beacon Hill Press, 1972).

[33] Kevin Corcoran, 'The Emerging Church', in Scot McKnight *et al., Church in the Present Tense: A Candid Look at What's Emerging* (Grand Rapids, MI: Brazos Press, 2011), p. xii.

[34] Corcoran, 'The Emerging Church', pp. xiii-xiv.

[35] Corcoran, 'The Emerging Church', p. 4.

ogy, and philosophical postmodernism, characterized by the questioning of the metanarrative.[36]

The overlapping tendencies of postmodernity with the so-called Emerging Church make it difficult to frame a nuanced argument in the brevity of one essay. Suffice it to say that media and sound bites characterize postmodernity as a primary means of disseminating information. Though this is co-opted into the so-called emerging church ethos with the use of blogs, multi-media, tweets, and other social media, it does not provide them a platform from which to launch a cogent theological argument to support their movement. Their wholesale embrace of this aspect of postmodernity is in many ways undermining them as a legitimate ecclesiological movement.[37]

The so-called Emerging Church has made at least two theological commitments that make it impossible for it to be informed by Wesleyan holiness sensibilities. The first is the commitment to self-made religious identity.[38] The second is a commitment to the individual over and against the church.[39] These two axioms create serious problems for those in the Pentecostal church who are experimenting with any potential positive aspects of the so-called Emerging Church. These two theological impasses are formidable to say the least, and they call into question this church's sustainability.

This church's commitment to self-made religious identity makes it nearly impossible to maintain any religious community or theological identity. This 'anything goes' approach to religious identity opens the movement up to scrutiny in that it has no definable characteristics so as to call it Christian. In fairness to the movement, they offer an explanation of 'belonging before believing' to address the lack of theological commitments, and this has merit.[40] I only wish that while maintaining their openness to visitors, they would confirm the committed by grounding them in the historic moorings of the faith. Another affirmation of this modus operandi is that according to their definitions, if one is to call an Emerging Christian a

---

[36] Corcoran, 'The Emerging Church', p. 11.
[37] Corcoran, 'The Emerging Church', p. 20.
[38] Jason Clark, 'Consumer Liturgies and Their Corrosive Effects on Christian Identity', in McKnight *et al.*, *Church in the Present Tense*, pp. 44, See also Carson, *Becoming Conversant with the Emerging Church*, pp. 158-60.
[39] Clark, 'Consumer Liturgies', p. 46.
[40] Kimball, *The Emerging Church*, p. 187.

Christian in deed they would have to do so on the basis of their conduct rather than their propositions.[41]

While I recognize that being called Christian within their circles is not an important notion, what I am really intimating is that the anti-structural nature of this movement is ultimately self-defeating. Without definable characteristics, anyone can claim to be an adherent of your sect. And likewise, anyone can refute that claim solely on personal whim and idiosyncratic notions. Becoming a 'follower of Jesus' or a 'Christian' is ultimately a change of identity. Therefore, there must be something with which to identify in order to gauge that change.

The second theological commitment that the so-called Emerging Church has made to its own detriment is the commitment to the individual over and against the church. The basic proposition seems to be that Christians can be Christian without the church. The so-called Emerging Church is afraid that identification with the church as a requisite for Christian identity removes from the hands of the individual the power to choose his or her identity. This mentality gains momentum from the postmodern rejection of the metanarrative that the so-called Emerging Church has embraced. The ahistorical blinders that this church enjoys wearing causes it to see itself as connected to the first-century or Patristic church, but not to the church that developed throughout the subsequent centuries. This certainly means that they do not see themselves as connected to the holiness sensibilities of Wesleyanism, which developed as the church developed.

It is a strange notion. They often appeal to the early church (for which they provide little documentation) or to sacred scripture for their interpretation of how the church should gather and receive Christians today.[42] They claim an affinity to the historic church of the first century but push back on the historic church of the 20th century as if the two are not connected in any way. Though some of their adherents claim a legitimate cause for such action in the similitude of Luther and the Reformation, I disagree on the basis that Luther's reformation had serious challenges with the Roman Catho-

---

[41] John Sims, 'Exploring Pentecostal Ethics: Reclaiming Our Heritage', in Cross and Powery (eds.), *The Spirit and the Mind*, p. 218.

[42] Dan Kimball, *Emerging Worship* (Grand Rapids, MI: Zondervan Publishing, 2005), pp. 4-10.

lic Church's reading of and interpretation of Scripture as the basis of his concern.[43] The chief concern of the Emerging Church as expressed in its literature seems to be its cultural adaptability and postmodern spirituality.[44] And, with these concerns there is room for dialogue and mutual edification, not isolation.

Conclusion

There are positive aspects to the contemporary values that these movements espouse that can be beneficial to the church. Their commitment to contextualization of the gospel is laudable and necessary in order to reach generations with the message of the gospel. They share the Wesleyan sensitivity to experience as authoritative and helpful for contextualization.[45] They also have boldness for innovation and creativity that if appropriately stewarded could revitalize the church. In these aspects, 21st-century values and Wesleyan holiness sensibilities are congruent.

A commitment to holiness as germane to Pentecostal and 21st-century spirituality will benefit the Pentecostal church and its subsequent iterations by reconnecting it to its Wesleyan roots. That reconnection will catalyze a process of discovering and identifying fresh expressions of holiness for contemporary Pentecostal living, some of which is already being experimented with by younger generations. It is my hopes that by having an intramural conversation with those who are called to do something new, the church can enunciate a more clearly articulated theology of holiness for the 21st-century Pentecostal community. Practices can be unearthed, experiences can be fostered, and bridges can be built that encourage and inculcate holiness virtues in Pentecostal churches and in other Christian traditions for this generation and beyond.

---

[43] See the footnotes in Carson, *Becoming Conversant with the Emerging Church*, pp. 42-43.

[44] Kimball, *The Emerging Church*, pp. 35-36.

[45] R. Larry Shelton, 'A Wesleyan/Holiness Agenda for the Twenty-First Century', *Wesleyan Theological Journal* 33.2 (Fall 1998), pp. 67-100.

13

HOLINESS, THE CHURCH, AND PARTY POLITICS: TOWARD A CONTEMPORARY PRACTICAL THEOLOGY OF HOLINESS

ANTIPAS L. HARRIS[*]

Introduction

Theologian Conrad Wethmar points out, 'Whenever the Church is confronted by a substantial change in cultural context the question regarding the identity of Christianity becomes urgent'.[1] At the turn of the century, the question of Christian identity and the relationship between the Church and society has become a significant query for Pentecostals/Charismatic Christians. Within several historical, cultural contexts, Western Christianity has endured the mingling of belief systems encoded in society's cultural shifting. Reflecting on these changes, prominent twentieth-century theologian Jürgen Moltmann refers to this trend as 'identity-involvement dilemma'.[2] In 'My Theological Career', he explains, 'the more theology tries to be relevant to the social crises of its society, the more deeply it is itself drawn into the crisis of its own Christian identity'[3]. Stated differently, the ideology encoded into any culture presents a dilemma for how Christians understand God. It also raises questions about

---

[*] Antipas L. Harris (DMin, Boston University) is Assistant Professor at Regent University School of Divinity and Director of Regent's Youth & Urban Renewal Center.

[1] Conrad Wethmar, 'Confessionality and Identity of the Church – A Reformed Perspective', *Christian Identity: International Reformed Theological Institute International Conference* (6th: 2005: Seoul, Korea) (Leiden: Boston: Brill, 2008), p. 135.

[2] Jürgen Moltmann, *The Crucified God* (London: SCM, 1974), pp. 12-33. Also, see Moltmann, 'My Theological Career', in *History and the Triune God: Contributions to Trinitarian Theology* (New York: Crossroad, 1992), p. 182.

[3] Moltmann, 'My Theological Career', p. 182.

God's expectations for our relationship with the culture in which we find ourselves. Therefore, it is not surprising that the Church, amidst a plethora of cultural trends, has encountered an identity crisis.

In the last fifty years or so, the dilemma of the Evangelical and Pentecostal/Charismatic Church rests in the churches' close alignment with political parties. In essence, many churches have struggled to maintain identity independently of systems of society. This chapter argues that (a) the Church needs to rediscover Her identity in Christ's holiness; (b) American politics are the product of liberal philosophy and not a commentary on scripture; (c) Christian peculiarity is defined by liberation in Christ that is impermeable to liberal democracy; and (d) holiness as love and grace provides a platform for a unified Church that provides a witness for Christ in a society that cannot know Him.

From Kingdom Takeover to Influential Holiness

Over the past fifty years or more, American Evangelical and later Pentecostal/Charismatic Christians have been attracted to Dominion theology's 'possess the land' approach to Christianity. The two main strands of Dominion theology are Rousas John Rushdoony's and Gary North's Christian Reconstructionism theology[4] and Kingdom Now theology. Rooted in a Reformed perspective, Christian Reconstructionism imagines a world made Christian through an emphasis on the 'New Covenant'. Basing his theology on Gal. 6.16, Rushdoony explains that Christians are the New Israel of God;[5] thus, we have a duty to 'occupy the whole world' just as Israel of the 'Old Covenant' was called to possess the land.[6] Rushdoony's theonomic approach to Christian Reconstructionism has considerably influenced the Evangelical way of engaging the world, both ide-

---

[4] Cf. Rousas John Rushdoony, *The Institutes of Biblical Law* (Nutley, NJ: The Craig Press, 1973).

[5] Rushdoony, *The Institutes of Biblical Law* (Nutley, NJ: The Craig Press, 1973). Also, see Jcr4runner, 'Second American Revolution: Rousas John Rushdoony (1 of 9)'. http://www.youtube.com/watch?v=jkQ6DlTQ114.

[6] Rushdoony, *The Institutes of Biblical Law*. Also, see Jcr4runner, 'Second American Revolution: Rousas John Rushdoony'.

ologically and theologically. For example, this is especially evident in his call for Christian political involvement.[7]

In the late 1980s, Pentecostals/Charismatic Christians became attracted to dominion theological ideals through what became known as Kingdom Now theology. With Christian Reconstructionism as its antecedent, Kingdom Now theology also interprets Christianity as the 'New Israel' sent to possess the land. An emphasis on gifts of the Spirit in the Church and the five-fold ministry gifts (Eph. 4.11) distinguishes Kingdom Now theology from Christian Reconstructionism. Kingdom Now theology asserts that God assigns roles and responsibilities to local church leaders for the purpose of leading the Church in a charge to possess the nations.[8] It suggests that Christians are God's gift to America. The country is 'ours and not theirs'. In this view, the Christian's chief role is to defend the country against its own people, those who do not share certain theological and ideological ideals. It breeds arrogance, hostility, and bigotry, all of which are antithetical to the essence of the gospel. A serious read of Scripture juxtaposed against American history must conclude that Jesus did not leave the promise of a country – a sweet land of liberty. Rather, He left the Church to influence the world by virtue of a Christian presence. Christian presence is summarized in one word, holiness.

The 2012 Election and the Church

The influence of Dominion theology continues to threaten the identity of the Church as Christians grapple with the relationship between the Church and society. Like never in history, the country, including churches, was divided over the Obama versus Romney election. Prominent preachers endorsed the Mormon leader Mitt Romney for president, primarily on the basis of protecting marriage between male and female, certain pro-Israel ideals, economic reasons, and confessional statements as pertaining to pro-life.

---

[7] Cf. William Martin's *With God on Our Side: The Rise of the Religious Right in America* (New York: Broadway Books, 1996).

[8] Cf. William A. Griffin, 'Kingdom Now: New Hope or New Heresy', *Eastern Journal of Practical Theology* 2 (Spring 1988), pp. 6-36; and Gordon Anderson, 'Kingdom Now Theology: A Look at Its Roots And Branches', *Paraclete* 24.3 (Summer 1990), pp. 1-12.

Other prominent preachers[9] either endorsed or continued to support Barack Obama for a second term. Some of Obama's supporters believed that his Health Care Act comes as an answer to many prayers and even voices that cry from the graveyard. There are those who believe that his plans for economic recovery had promising advantages, particularly for the poor and middle class Americans. Others believe that Obama's presidency is the best vehicle for moving the country forward despite (or in addition to) his endorsement of same-sex marriage and far-left advocacy for women's rights. Still others were convinced that a 'nominal' Christian is a better fit for leading America than Romney, a Mormon cult leader.

These and other theological and ideological contentions contributed to the uproar in many of our churches – within churches and between churches. There were competing prayer vigils, praying that either Romney would win the election or that Obama would win. There were few prayers that were truly open to whomever God chose. People's minds were already made up before praying. On Election Day, very few people went to the ballot box, closed their eyes and said, 'Lord, take control of my hands and touch whichever name on the ballot You choose'. The fact is that we often want God to do what we have already decided to be the right thing to do. Usually, such judgment is grounded in systems of thought and in worldviews coded within corrupted systems more than authentic communion with God.

Just after the 2012 election, I had breakfast with a group of pastors. One of the pastors commented, 'I have come to the conclusion that [party] politics are America's religion'. Rather than continuing God's reign as Dominion theology claims, politics have co-opted American Evangelical, Pentecostal/Charismatic theology to purport certain political agendas. In this way, American politics have hijacked American Christian thinking.

---

[9] Most of the pastors who endorsed or supported Barack Obama were not from American Evangelical or Pentecostal denominations. They were African American pastors from mainline African American churches. Although not Pentecostal, they do value the role of the Spirit and affirm the presence of the gifts of the Spirit in the church. In general, African American Pentecostal preachers have tended to stay away from public political endorsements except for a few who follow the trends of European American Pentecostal preachers who align themselves with the Republican party – GOP's agenda.

Christians and the Church: In the World but not of It

There is a parallel between Barth's analysis of 'systems' and 'theology' and the current discussion of 'politics' and 'theology'. Barth draws the following line between systems and theology:

> A 'system' is an edifice of thought, constructed on certain fundamental conceptions, which are selected in accordance with a certain philosophy by a method, which corresponds to these conceptions. Theology cannot be carried on in confinement or under the pressure of such a construction. The subject of theology is the history of the communion of God with man and of man with God.[10]

The biblical Church is a theological organism and not a 'party' political organization – American or otherwise. As an organism, She must discern the Lord's way of existing in the world, independently of society's norms. Hebrews 14.12b states, 'Pursue ... Holiness without which no one will see the Lord'.[11] The inability to 'see the Lord' suggests that unholiness proves impermeable in regards to insights on divine matters. While there are some basic moral teachings such as love and peace, which are both biblical and normative in a civilized society, philosophical and political systems wherein scripture is not foundational will eventually reveal that they are impervious to holiness.

The Church, moreover, must subscribe to what Barth calls, 'theology ... [that is] based on and determined by kingly freedom of the Word of God'.[12] Holiness defines God's freedom and not national systems. Such freedom contains enduring truth that first frees the person to love God but also brings existential freedom defined on God's terms. American freedom emerges from philosophical ideals influenced primarily by European philosophy. It follows that at times, the liberation of American democracy corresponds with biblical freedom. At other times, American freedom lends itself to a type of liberation that often appears impervious to the freedom of holiness. The president of the United States is charged, moreover,

---

[10] Karl Barth, *Dogmatics in Outline* (New York: Harper and Row, 1959), p. 5.

[11] All scripture quotations are from the English Standard Version (ESV) except where otherwise noted.

[12] Barth, *Dogmatics in Outline*, p. 5.

to lead a Free Society as defined by the founding documents and not necessarily the freedom that Christians find in Christ.

During summer 2012 of President Obama's first term, he announced his support for same-sex marriage. Having previously favored same-sex unions but not same-sex marriages, President Obama admitted that his position 'had been evolving because of the powerful traditions and religious beliefs attached to the word marriage'.[13] He explained his 'evolved position' to be according to the adjudication of American freedom as granted by the founding documents of the United States. This announcement stirred a heated debate among pastors as well as ordinary Christians. The salient question relates to the presidential allegiance to traditional Christian beliefs or according to the precepts of the country's founding documents. The challenge at hand is that God expects pastors to lead churches according to the holiness of Christ. But, the origins of this country demands that the president govern according to legislation with commitment, not to scripture but to the founding documents.

Who is America?

Moreover, America purports freedom from a philosophical outlook of democracy. The Declaration of Independence extends equal rights for all citizens:

> We hold these truths to be self-evident, that all men are created equal, that they are endowed by their Creator with certain unalienable Rights, that among these are Life, Liberty and the pursuit of Happiness.

'All' means 'all', including people from a wide-range of ethnic heritages, diverse religious traditions, education backgrounds, varying economic statuses, both genders, and other categories of people.

The Pursuit of Democracy – not Holiness

The ideas and teachings in the Declaration of Independence are not a commentary on scripture. They are precepts determined by the

---

[13] Phil Gast, 'Obama announces he supports same-sex marriage', in *CNN Politics* (May 9, 2012), http://www.cnn.com/2012/05/09/politics/obama-same-sex-marriage/index.html.

Committee of Five[14] as they wrestled to assemble a commentary on freedom as expressed by influential liberal philosophy. However, God's freedom exists within the framework of holiness. Holiness satisfies the soul and helps us pursue the human's deep-seated desire to please God. However, the Declaration of Independence speaks of freedom from the standpoint of opportunity for every human being to pursue life, liberty, and happiness. Such pursuits may be achieved on human terms. It is within this later framework that the president of the United States must govern the country.

While one could argue that, at the level of culture, the United States has been deeply impacted by Christianity, the United States Constitution does not ensure that the country abides by God's command to be holy (Cf. Lev. 44.11). The president of the country has responsibility as leader of a free world; thus, his stance on issues might well be in keeping with the American claim on equality for all. The following might be a salient theological question worthy of further investigation: what is the role of a Christian leader in a free world?

---

[14] Forming the famous 'Committee of Five', Thomas Jefferson (the leader), Benjamin Franklin, John Adams, Roger Sherman, and Robert Livingston drafted the Declaration of Independence. Thomas Paine's popular pamphlet *Common Sense* somewhat influenced John Adams and Thomas Jefferson's philosophy of Independence from Great Britain. It should be noted that Adams disagreed with some of his methods and even criticized the strong anti-Christian ideals in Paine's *Age of Reasoning*. Yet, Paine's general sentiment of human freedom as expressed in his *Common Sense,* although radical, laid somewhat of an intellectual foundation for persuasion against colonization and for the Declaration of Independence. See, Michael Foot and Isaac Kramnick (eds.), *The Thomas Paine Reader* (New York: Penguin Classics, 1987), p. 65. Adams once commented on the indelible impression of Paine's work on the propagation of American Independence from Great Britain saying, 'Without the pen of Paine, the sword of Washington would have been wielded in vain'. Paine's influence continues to echo in American philosophy and politics today. 'The Thomas Paine Library', http://libertyonline.hyper mall.com/Paine/ Default.htm (accessed January 1, 2013). Additionally, although hotly debated, Benjamin Franklin's own admiration for John Locke's work, coupled with the comparable language of the document to Locke's work, suggests that the Declaration of Independence includes elements of an experiment in Locke's liberal democratic philosophy. Locke's idea of government includes the emancipation from British despotic rule in pursuit of human liberty. See John Locke, *Two Treatises of Government,* (ed. Thomas Hollis; London: A. Millar *et al.,* 1764).

Who Is the Church?

The Church is called to be the community of believers who faithfully pursue God through the life of the Spirit. Part of that pursuit is through reverencing God. Yet, another part of that pursuit is through an attitude, lifestyle, and disposition that reflect God's will for God's people. An ecclesial stance that calls for God's people to live like Christ sets Christians at odds with the rest of society. Spurgeon said, 'The Church is not formed to be a social club to produce society for itself! [She] is not to be a political association to be a power in politics! Nor is [She] a religious confederacy promoting [Her] own opinions! [She] is a body created of the Lord to answer His own ends and purposes'.[15] Holiness sums up the peculiarity that defines God's agenda in the Church. It is, moreover, increasingly prudent within a world of religious and ideological plurality that the Church come to terms with the call to holiness.

Scripture declares that holiness is the essence of God obtained by Christians through the power of the Holy Spirit (Lev. 11.26 and 44; 1 Pet. 1.16). The Church is God's gift to the world to escape the polluted ideologies. Further, the Church is to exist as a community of believers, empowered by the Holy Spirit to live out God's holiness in the world. Therefore, a more poignant discussion strikes at the heart of identity – a discussion that draws attention to potential weaknesses within divided, religious institutions that call themselves 'the Church'.

What has happened to the Church's Identity?

Spurgeon draws attention to Christ's words: '[You] are not of the world, even as I am not of the world'.[16] Addressing a Church that is called out of the world (mainstream society) – a peculiar people who bear witness to the 'out of this world' identity of Christ. To be 'called out of the world' certainly speaks to the divine invitation to public profession of faith in Christ. But it also speaks to God's call to us to remove ourselves from ideological and philosophical alignment with systems that are antithetical to that of the ways and thinking of Christ.

---

[15] Charles Haddon Spurgeon, 'The Lord's Own View of His Church and People', a Sermon Delivered at the Metropolitan Tabernacle, Newington in 1887; Sermon # 1957, p. 6, http://www.spurgeongems.org/vols31-33/chs1957.pdf.

[16] Spurgeon, 'The Lord's Own View of His Church and People'.

Peter addresses the Christian indifference in the world. He says, 'As you come to him (Jesus), a living stone rejected by people but in the sight of God chosen and precious, you yourselves like living stones are being built up as a spiritual house (the Church), to be a holy priesthood, to offer spiritual sacrifices acceptable to God through Jesus Christ' (1 Pet. 2.4-5). New Testament scholar Karen Jobes points out that this section of 1 Peter describes the nature of the community into which believers have been born (again). Here, notes Jobes, 'Peter emphasizes the community of believers … in terms of that community's relationship to God, to redemptive history, and to those outside the community'.[17] In Peter's view, the Church is not called to 'take-over' the world but rather to be at odds with the world's systems of beliefs. In other words, there is a Church and there is a world, and they are diametrically opposed to each other in ideology and philosophy. The world's systems of thought are adversative to the spiritual and holy priesthood to which believers are called.

The Church and Spiritual Freedom

There are some advantages of Christians being part of a free society. Namely, unlike religious life in communist countries, America is designed such that Christians, as well as people from other religious traditions, are free to express their religious beliefs. Distancing the founding of the United States from the State Church of England, Thomas Jefferson and James Madison, the framers of the United States Constitution, marked the separation of Church and State. As a gift to the United States citizens, the 'separation of Church and State' affords the Church the right to consist of law-abiding citizens but within a religious colony (the Church), standing at odds with decisions within the broader society, which are contrary to divine holiness. Historically, the institutions called the Church in the United States became free from the state's doctrinal governance, and Christians and people from diverse religious backgrounds were granted freedom to live and believe according to their faith traditions.

Furthermore, freedom to live and believe as one chooses is not a definitively 'Christian' position. The holiness into which we, as be-

---

[17] Karen H. Jobes, *1 Peter: Baker Exegetical Commentary on the New Testament* (Grand Rapids: Baker Academic, 2005), p. 142.

lievers, are called is not a 'free religion' or 'free spirituality' as defined by personal choice. John 8.36 has become the Christian anthem of true freedom: 'So if the Son sets you free, you will be free indeed'. Thus, Christian freedom should not be confused with human free will or even with American freedom. Human free will has to do with the divine self-constraint to permit human beings to choose to accept God's gift in Christ or not. American freedom coincides with human free will in that it offers freedom of religion. Yet, human free will as a gift from God does not imply God's ideal choice or as scripture puts it, ὄντως ἐλεύθεροι ἔσεσθε – 'you will be free indeed'.

Luke Timothy Johnson posits, 'Jesus is speaking less to his opponents than to the Christian readers of the Fourth Gospel'.[18] Johnson explains that the principle of freedom in this passage speaks against an illusion of freedom when we are slaves to sin. Only the truth can make one free (Jn 8.31-32). That is to say, only the free Son (Jesus) can liberate us from our sins (Jn 8.36).[19] Pentecostals define that freedom in pneumatological categories: 'Now the Lord is the Spirit, and where the Spirit of the Lord is, there is freedom' (2 Cor. 3.17). True liberation in Christ is freedom to live holy and not to live according to fleshly passions.

The Church that God intends is called to be holy amidst a world that is not. Paul states in Rom. 12.1-2:

> I appeal to you therefore, brothers, by the mercies of God, to present your bodies as a living sacrifice, holy and acceptable to God, which is your spiritual worship. Do not be conformed to this world, but be transformed by the renewal of your mind, that by testing you may discern what is the will of God, what is good and acceptable and perfect.

Paul explains that the only acceptable life in God's eyes is a life lived counter-culturally – not conforming to logic and principles established by the larger society. As indicated in the quote from Paul above, this life is the holy one that God accepts. It is this lifestyle with which the Church of Jesus Christ must identify. In his

[18] Luke Timothy Johnson, *The Writings of the New Testament: An interpretation* (Minneapolis: Fortress Press, 1999), p. 546.
[19] Johnson, *The Writings of the New Testament*, p. 546.

sermon 'The Lord's Own View of His Church and People', Charles Haddon Spurgeon comments:

> The church is a separate and distinct thing from the world. I suppose there is such a thing as 'the Christian world'; but I do not know what it is, or where it can be found. It must be a singular mixture. I know what is meant by a worldly Christian; and I suppose the Christian world must be an aggregate of worldly Christians. But the church of Christ is not of the world. 'You are not of the world', says Christ, 'even as I am not of the world'.[20]

The Church, as 'otherworldly', is in the world, engaged with the world, but distinct from the world. Spurgeon is correct to suggest that Christ never expected that this world would be entirely Christian. But, Christ does expect for the Church to be Christian. This means that the Church is not of this world. Christ empowers the Church by the power of the Holy Spirit to influence the world by simply being and doing the work of Christ in the world. Part of the Church's witness is Her counter-cultural approach in moments when culture resists the teachings of Christ.

The Church, the Community of Holiness

From the start of the Church in Acts 2, the Church has always consisted of a counter-cultural community of believers who live out their faith in Christ at odds with the rest of society. Although the earliest Christians were primarily Jewish, their worldview and behavior set them at odds with the other Jews. Then, as the gospel went west and became more and more ethnically diverse, the distinctive nature of the Church carved out its identity in whatever society in which it found itself. This otherworldly nature of the Church, that mirrored the peculiar life of Christ, merited them the label of 'little Christs' or 'Christians' (Cf. Acts 11.26). Although the term 'Christian' may have been a label of mockery for believers, the validity of the term was marked by an intentional lifestyle, which embodied the life, teachings, and message of Jesus Christ in a world that was indifferent to it. In other words, the early Christians aimed to transform society by being a counter-cultural reality before a watching world. That difference was recognizable because it reflected the thought process and lifestyle of Christ. Margaret Dewey as-

---

[20] Spurgeon, 'The Lord's Own View of His Church and People', p. 5

serts, 'Christ in the life of the world means to know differently. It also means to live differently'.[21]

The line of distinction between the Church and the world must be accented through lifestyle and behavior. When the Church or the faithful impose itself upon society to force laws that are indeed biblical but antithetical to trends and behaviors of the world, the Church loses its witness. Peter explains, 'You (the called out ones – the Church) are a chosen race, a royal priesthood, a holy nation, a people for God's own possession ...' (1 Pet. 2.9). The Church is chosen to bear witness of God's holiness amidst a world that is contrary to it.

Paul's theology of holiness is consistent with that of Peter. Romans 8.7 states, 'For the mind that is set on the flesh is hostile to God, for it does not submit to God's law; indeed, it cannot'. Hence, God provides free will. According to divine order, people are allowed to behave as she or he pleases. Those who are not part of Christ's Church, born again, and filled with the Holy Spirit, have no power to submit to God's will.

A local church, therefore, that pits itself against society in hostility and indignant practices, such as advocating hate towards homosexuals, burning Qur'ans, and posting hate signs towards people in society whose ideas and behaviors are not according to biblical teachings weaken their own witness. We must speak strongly to those who are within the churches, subscribing to ideas, practices, and lifestyles that are contrary to biblical teachings. A Christian should disassociate with a brother in Christ who insists on walking contrary to godly principles (see 2 Thess. 3.6). However, lashing out at mainstream media and the people who choose to live differently than a biblical position – people who are not in the church – fosters a mean religion. As a result, the loving nature of holiness is compromised.

The Church as Different from the World
If the Church is not the first to admit it, society is certainly willing to denounce holiness for fleshly passions. Churches must not become too closely aligned with political, philosophical, and theological agendas that are rooted in non-biblical ideologies and purported

---

[21] Margaret Dewey, 'The Quest for Wholeness', *Thinking Mission* (London: The United Society for the Proclamation of the Gospel, 1984), p. 44.

by mainstream society. In doing so, society sets the agenda for the church – drawing attention to certain matters and leaving others untouched. The grip of political polarities appears strong in the American consciousness. In an effort to correct what has gone wrong in America's finances and redress social inequalities, American politics have taken center stage. American people are too obsessed with political parties. They depend too heavily on the next politician in leadership as if a human being has the answers to remedy American political, economic, and social debauchery.

Many Christians subscribe to triumphalism. By triumphalism I am referring to Christian movements that historically have not only held piquantly to their own beliefs but also championed certain propositions as superior to others. These Christians interpret Christ's call to bear witness in the world to be a charge to impose their beliefs on people. They often believe that their duty is to advance particular biblical worldviews through avenues like media, education, and party politics, to name a few. For example, several presidential candidates over the past forty years have run for office with a religious agenda to sanctify what is 'wrong' in America. There are varying assumptions – depending on political interests and religious formations – that Christian identity is encoded into one political party or the other.

A Republican, a Democrat, or a Christian?

Aligning Christian identity with American political parties is unhelpful for the identity to which the Church is called. Unity in Christ must be based on an 'other worldly' system of beliefs and practices rather than any national politics. Stated plainly, whether one is 'pro-life' or 'pro-choice' – language encoded with political definition – is confusing. The usage of the terms is rooted in political interests and not biblical love. Just like political parties, political terms are polarizing and ultimately neither protects children nor their mothers. Thus, they are irrelevant to Christian identity. A more edifying conversation for the Christian should pertain to sanctification and holiness – how these terms define the Church in the world.

Within a political context, Samuel Rodriguez, president of the National Hispanic Leadership Conference, offers an alternative perspective. He professes, 'I'm not committed to the donkey or the elephant. I'm committed to the agenda of the Lamb'.[22] I agree with Rodriquez's sentiment, however, it should be clear that the agenda of the Lamb does not fit alongside existing party politics. The agenda of the Lamb is not of this world. It is God's agenda incribed upon the Church of Jesus Christ. Revelation 5.12 asserts that the Lamb is worthy (holy). So then, everyone who names the name of the Lamb must forsake the world and live holy unto the Lamb. The lifestyle of holiness is one defined on the Lamb's terms. Pertaining to politics and other matters, there is a need for the Church to engage in alternative discussion that is initiated and grounded within a biblical worldview. John Yoder calls attention to the fact that the Church has Her own body politics (broadly speaking)[23] – a separate way of being and doing in the world.

However, there are churches that spend their time lashing out at mainstream society with hostility and condemnation because the rest of the world has chosen to live as they please. Both sides present a travesty against the Church that God intends. The holiness of God is both *separate from* the world and *loving towards* the world. To this end, it is essential to the vitality of the Church that the Church purifies Herself.

Oberlin University professor Henry Cowles issued a warning pertaining to the trajectory of a depressed standard of holiness among the churches and the need for repentance. Reflecting on this, A.M. Hills observes:

> Plainly, there is no remedy but for the Church to come back to the very elements of piety. She must return to God and Holy Communion. The standard of piety must be raised. What can the Church do for the conversion of the world, for her own existence even, without personal holiness – much deep pure, personal holiness? No wonder that a conviction of this truth should have fastened upon discerning minds and painful strength. The standard of piety throughout the American Church is extremely and deplorably low. It is low compared with that of the primitive Church, compared with the provisions of the gospel, with the

---

[22] Catherine Newhouse, 'Voice of the Hispanic Christian Vote', *Urban Faith* (October 21, 2011), http://www.urbanfaith.com/2011/10/voice-of-the-hispanic-christian-vote.html/.

[23] See John Howard Yoder, *Body Politics: Five Practices of the Church Community Before the Watching World* (Scottsdale, PA: Harold Press, 1992), pp. vi-xi.

obligations of redeemed sinners, or with the requisite qualifications for the work to be done. The spirit of the world has deeply
pervaded and exceedingly engrossed the heart of the Church ...
The responsibilities and privileges of Christians in this life must
be clearly exhibited, and urged upon the conscience of the
Church.[24]

Hills' thesis is relevant today. The pursuit of power and control
in the world's systems and the loss of emphasis on personal piety
have negatively affected the Church's distinctiveness and collective
witness in the world. In the words of Jesus to John the evangelist
concerning the church at Ephesus, 'But I have this against you, that
you have abandoned the love you had at first' (Rev. 2.4).

Believers should live every day as informed by Scripture and as
empowered by a life in the Spirit. The study of Scripture cannot be
realized in the life of the believer without the powerful insight of
the Holy Spirit. Scripture teaches that the Holy Spirit is the guide.
Jesus promises in Jn 16.13a: 'When the Spirit of truth comes, [the
Holy Spirit] will guide you into all the truth'. The Holy Spirit is the
helper. Jesus also promises in Jn 15.26: 'But when the Helper
comes, whom I will send to you from the Father, the Spirit of truth,
who proceeds from the Father, [the Spirit of truth] will bear witness
about me'.[25] Paul adds that the Holy Spirit is also a protector. 2
Timothy 1.14 states, 'By the Holy Spirit who dwells within us, guard
the good deposit entrusted to you'. When the Church emphasizes
the life of the Spirit more than the emotion of the Spirit, the Spirit
captures the people's hearts and governs their lives.

Holiness as Practical Theology

The light of holiness is not merely conceptual or theological, but
practical and institutional. Raising a standard of holiness includes
building parochial schools, Christian universities, hospitals, crisis
pregnancy centers, adoption agencies, Christian homeless shelters,
and other ministries that extend Christ's love to the communities of

---

[24] A.M. Hills, *Holiness and Power for the Church and the Ministry* (New York: Gar-
land Publishing, 1984), p. 19.

[25] Also, see Jn 14.26: 'But the Helper, the Holy Spirit, whom the Father will
send in my name, he will teach you all things and bring to your remembrance all
that I have said to you'.

the world. These institutions are under-supported. As a result, many of them are struggling to remain open and others are closing down. Christians should fully support these institutional arms of the Church. They represent the practical witness of God's love in a world that desperately needs it. God calls the Christian to lead in expressions of help in the world, but not as followers of ideological trends and standards of living that are defined by the world.

At times the Church endures pressures from society to compromise Her beliefs. Looking to the Early Church for guidance, the Church must resist society's pressures even if it brings persecution upon the Church. When the situation pressures the Church to act indifferent of Her identity in Christ, the Church must not compromise Her standards.

God is not pleased when God's people compromise holiness – regardless of the source of pressure. In Exodus 32, Moses descends from a forty-day retreat with the Lord in Mount Horeb. God gave him the Word for the people of Israel. God chose them to be a peculiar people. But when Moses came off of the mountain, Israel was engaged in fleshly lusts. They were running wild, doing as they pleased – characteristic of a societal worldview that was antithetical to God's worldview. Having just experienced a retreat with God, Moses was terrified at the people's behavior. He threw the tablets of stone with the commandments of God on them, and they crumbled into pieces. Moses forcefully declared among the people, 'Who is on the Lord's side? Come to me' (Exod. 32.26). It is impossible for people to be holy according to God's commandments when they have not made an important choice to follow God with sincerity. Following God with sincerity requires an intentional demarcation in the sand with a decision to stand on the Lord's side.

While there are many expressions of ecclesiastical and theological traditions within the Church, it is imperative that the Church stakes a claim towards God's worldview of holiness. From that worldview, Christians must live according to biblical standards. One example that has been an object of discussion in this chapter has been the issue of marriage. A significant question is, 'How does God understand marriage as explained in scripture?' This query addresses many issues pertaining to marriage beyond the issue of same-sex marriage. The Church must not take positions based on what is popular. The Church must lift up a standard on marriage that also addresses heterosexual marriage, abuse in marriage, adultery, infidelity, and so forth. God's standard does not approve some wrongs while condemning other wrongs. The standard of holiness asks, 'Who is on the Lord's side?'

Columnist and blogger at the Washington Post Rahiel Tesfamariam responds to the firestorm among (particularly African American) pastors and bishops pertaining to Obama's support for same-sex marriage in America:

> As marriage equality has elicited such a polarizing effect in black religious communities, some black religious leaders believe that the church has entered the fight of its life. What both clergy and congregants seem to be vigorously debating is love – love for neighbor (loving your neighbor as you love yourself) and, of course, love for God (loving nothing over and above your maker) ... I am reminded here of Christ's own warning to his followers against mixing governance with God. Rather than give in to this tendency, I hope that the black church will be able to 'give back to [Obama] what is [Obama's] and to God what is God's'.[26]

Agreeing with Tesfamariam, the Church's standards shape the identity of the Church, but the government's standards exist within a society of ideological freedom. Even if a society assumes the Constantinian model, wherein the ruler decrees Christianity as the official religion of the nation, no national ruler, has divine authority to decree norms for the Church. The Church must submit to Christ. Moreover, the Christians must live out their identity amidst a world of ideological plurality.

A quote on the issue of the holy Church from early twentieth-century German Catholic priest and commentator Constantine Kempf seems appropriate here:

> Be the times as morally degenerate as they may, the Church knows no other chastity than that which gave to martyr-heroes [and heroines] their supernatural strength and she yields not her position, although it has often been her sorrowful experience

---

[26] Rahiel Tesfamariam, 'Is gay marriage a crisis for the black church'? in the *Washington Post* – May 18, 2012, http://www.washingtonpost.com/blogs/guest-voices/post/is-gay-marriage-a-crisis-for-the-black-church/2012/05/18/gIQAP3 gHZU_blog.html?wprss=rss_guest-voices.

that it was the very severity of her moral demands which estranged so many from her or deterred them from acceptance of her doctrine.[27]

In the twenty-first century, I hope that civility prevails over hostility. Yet, as martyrdom has been part of Church history, it is not beyond the scope of modern faith in America that some will endure severe persecution when the believer holds high a standard of holiness – even in a free society.

Holiness as Living with Peculiarity

Moreover, there are two points about God's standard of holiness. The first is that God's standard of holiness defines Christian as different from the world. The second is that God's standard of holiness, while condemning sin, is inviting to the sinner, inasmuch as it is rooted and grounded in a divinely compelling love.

The Church seeks to maintain its counter-cultural reality with Christ's love in a world that increasingly defines itself in contrast to the Church's identity. To this end, it must be clear that America is best described as a free society and not a Christian society. Efforts to bear witness to Christ through condemning society when it pursues decisions contrary to biblical teachings ironically reduces the Christian witness from a loving and holy one to an angry and mean one. Hostility is in stark contradiction to the attitude, lifestyle, and disposition of Christ's love and compassion to which the Christian is called.

Christ does not call the Church to fight and force society to respect biblical teachings or Christ. We are called to fight for people in society to come to Jesus through our lived witness and loving invitation to join Christ's holy Church. To state it succinctly, a life lived as public witness to Christ's transformation is a much stronger testimony that subverts others into faith in Christ rather than mean and hostile statements to coerce others into faith. In this sense, the Church is called to model attitudes, lifestyle, and disposition as God intends before a watching world. Christian theological ethicist John Yoder's remark pertaining to the life of the Church before a watching world is helpful here. He says, 'The people of God are called to

---

[27] Constantine Kempf, *The Holiness of the Church in the Nineteenth Century* (New York: Benziger Brothers, 1916), p. 15.

be today what the world is called to be ultimately'.[28] Yet, the world must join the Church to be holy. Other than through Christ's Body, there is no other holiness for the world. So the life of the Church must be distinct, reflecting divine holiness in everyway. Love and grace are part of the Christian witness of holiness.

Holiness as Love and Grace

Holiness as love and grace establishes a platform for a unified Church that provides a witness for Christ in a society that cannot understand the Lord. God's love is more powerful than hate, fleshly passion, and ideological differences. This love draws others to God in a subversive (not coercive) manner. The Old Testament prophet Jeremiah sheds light onto the power of God's love in a world of indifference. The prophet suggests that, 'The Lord appear[s] [to us] from afar, saying, "I have loved you with an everlasting love; therefore I have drawn you with loving-kindness"' (Jer. 31.3 NASB).

When the Church embodies God's love, love becomes the only appropriate Christian response to society's decisions, even when they are contrary to a biblical worldview. People from around the world envy the freedom and opportunities in America. American Christians have found a home in such society – a certain type of escape from hostility that many Christians endure in countries like North Korea, China, Afghanistan, and Saudi Arabia. One might even conclude that Christian history has misconstrued the divine calling for Christians to be a light in the world. American history shows that Christians have tried to lay strong hold on governance in society, assuming its mission to transform the world (itself) for Christ. This philosophical approach to ministry has been the motor behind much of world missions and western colonization in many areas of the world. In the name of God, there has been blood on the hands of many Christian colonizers. However, contemporary mission critics have pointed out that the 'Christian globalization' approach to missions has also stirred an unintended message of hostility towards people who resist them. Such hostility has advanced western imperialism more than an authentic advancement of love of Jesus Christ.

---

[28] Yoder, *Body Politics*, p. ix.

Pertaining to missions around the world and in America, the foundational Christian tenet called love is easily lost through efforts to strong-arm people and societies into certain beliefs. Hostility and coercion seem contrary to a gospel that is so inviting, so full of love and grace. God's love in Christ is compelling but not coercive. Notably, in Scripture, Christ only scorns corrupted people who were part of the household of God – in the Temple.[29] He whips them out of the Temple because they claimed the name of God but were making God's house a place of self-aggrandizement and selfish material gain. Moreover, in Peter's words, 'For it is time for judgment to begin at the household of God' (1 Pet. 4.17).

Conclusion

Barack Obama's presidency marks a critical moment in history on many levels. Not only is he the first African American president but also his leadership and policies bring national attention to the ideological realities that exist between the American society and Christian theology – what it means to be an American citizen versus what it means to be a Christian. While party politics have its place in society, there is no such thing as a Christian political party.

In summary, the Church needs to rediscover Her identity in Christ's holiness. First, the Church does have a role of influence and inspiration within society; yet, the notion of a Christian society is an inappropriate designation. Secondly, American politics are the product of liberal philosophy and not a commentary on scripture. Thus, Christian peculiarity is defined by liberation in Christ, which is impermeable to liberal democracy. Thirdly, Christ's freedom is a holy liberation that impacts both the Christian and the world around them. It unifies the Church as a beacon amidst a dark world. Fourthly, enshrined with love and grace, holy liberation fosters a witness for Christ in a society that otherwise cannot know Him. By the same token, it is imperative that the Church distance Herself from divisive allegiances to party politics in pursuit of a life that fosters unity and wholeness in Christ.[*]

---

[29] Cf. Mt. 21.12 and Jn 2.14-15.

[*] Parts of this chapter appear in Antipas Harris, *Let the Church Cry, 'Holy'* (Eugene, OR: Wipf and Stock, 2013), Chapter 7, entitled 'Let the Church Go Back to Holiness: The 4 Rs'. Used by permission of Wipf and Stock Publishers. www.wipfandstock.com.

14

HOLINESS AND UNDOCUMENTED IMMIGRATION: A DRAMATIC CHALLENGE TO MY CHURCH

WILFREDO ESTRADA ADORNO[*]

Introduction

The theme I am addressing in this essay is one that has attracted my attention intensely over the past three years. In January 7, 2011 my wife, Carmen, and I moved from Puerto Rico to Orlando, Florida. During the five years prior to that date, we had been planting our fourth church. This new church was growing and we had no intention lo leave our Puerto Rican homeland. But towards the end of year 2010 I was invited by Dr Ángel Marcial, Administrative Bishop of the USA Southeastern Spanish Region, to come to his Region and help him prepare a ministerial formation program. After consulting with my wife and family and after prayerful consideration, we decided what had seemed impossible to us – to return back to the United States as missionaries.

We spent one year in Orlando putting together the ministerial formation program, both secular and theological, for inadequately educated ministers. We traveled throughout Florida and the southern part of Georgia training Hispanic ministerial candidates and pastors. It was a joyful challenge! On my trips over this area of the United States I became acquainted with hundreds of people living on the margins and sitting in the shadows of this prosperous nation.

[*] Wilfredo Estrada Adorno (DMin, Emory University) is Director of the Center for Latino Studies and Professor of Practical Theology and Latino Studies at the Pentecostal Theological Seminary in Cleveland, TN, USA.

They were afraid to come out to some of the activities of the church because they were undocumented immigrants and feared being caught by the immigration officials. About 65% of our members in that region were undocumented immigrants. In some churches that percentage was even higher; and still in some others, all the members, including the pastor, were undocumented. The shocking thing for me about these people was that they were the most faithful with their tithes and offering in their local churches. They were really grateful to their God and expressed their gratefulness in supporting their local churches with their finances. If we project the undocumented immigrants' financial support to the Regional Hispanic Offices and the International General Offices of our church, it is safe to say that 65% of all income at both levels of our church comes from the undocumented members of the church. These people are totally committed to our church's ministries, both local and abroad. It is my position that our church should be more committed to this group of our church's membership. Generally speaking, our church does not speak on their behalf and when it does, it speaks with a weak and wavering voice. It is painful to say that our church has really been quite timid in speaking on behalf the undocumented immigrants in the public arena.

These last four years have not been easy ones for the undocumented immigrants. The annual number of deportations has been increasing: 390,000 in Fiscal Year 2009, 393,000 in FY 2010, 397,000 in FY 2011, and 409,849 in FY 2012.[1] Moreover, professor Tanya Golash-Boza, an associate professor of sociology at University of California-Merced, found that interior immigration enforcement has expanded rapidly as border crossings have slowed down, leading to more families being separated by deportation[2]. In a situation like this, one would have expected a more aggressive stand of our church on behalf of the great number of undocumented Hispanic members of our church in the United States, but unfortunately that has not been the case.

---

[1] Gabriel Learner, 'How Many People Have Really Been Deported Under Obama?', *Latino Politics*, April 2. 2013. http://www.huffingtonpost.com/2012/03/01/deportation-numbers-obama_n_1314916.html
[2] Elise Foley, 'Obama Deportation Toll Could Pass 2 Million At Current Rates', *Politics*, April 2, 2013. http://www.huffingtonpost.com/2013/01/31/obama-deportation_n_2594012.html

In this essay I address the issue of holiness and undocumented immigration and the challenge that both realities present to our church. I speak first as a Puerto Rican, Caribbean, Latino and second (by virtue of a US military invasion in 1898 and a law passed by Congress in 1917) as a citizen of the United States. I also address this issue as a minister of the Church of God, a church I love and for which I am grateful, because it has given me a place to minister all through these years. So, I address these issues not as an outsider casting stones but as a legitimate son of my church. From both perspectives, I feel somewhat awkward. On the one hand, as a Puerto Rican, I am a citizen of this nation, but at the same time, the white majority of this country treats me as any immigrant coming from any country in Latin America. For any white person who sees me in the drugstore or in any department stores of any city in the United States, I could very well be an undocumented Hispanic immigrant. I have experienced this misidentification many times! The white majority in this country does not make any difference between Mexicans, Puerto Ricans, Colombians, Guatemalans, Peruvians, etc.; for them all of us are alike – Hispanics. On the other hand, dealing with this sensitive subject from my present location in Cleveland, TN (headquarters of the Church of God) could be a very risky task. Nevertheless, I address it with a joyful heart, inviting everyone who feels compelled to talk about it, to do so openly above the table, remaining humble enough to learn from one another. If you are willing to be shaken and somewhat uncomfortable, you are invited to continue reading the following pages.

The Concept of Holiness

A brief look at the history of the Pentecostal movement shows that we Pentecostals take our holiness (sanctification/Christian perfection) stance from the Wesleyan, revivalist, and holiness movements of the eighteen and nineteen centuries. On the one hand, those Pentecostal denominations that sprang out of holiness groups emphasized sanctification as a second work of grace. That is, as a second crisis experience leading to a third crisis experience called the baptism with the Holy Spirit with the initial evidence of speaking in other tongues. The baptism with the Holy Spirit is for these denominations an experience subsequent to sanctification. On the other hand, those believers who came to Pentecostalism out of the Reformed tradition claimed William Durham's *finished work* interpretation of their new faith. This interpretation emphasized that the Christian experience was composed of conversion and baptism with the Holy Spirit. That is to say, that the saving work of Christ wrought at Calvary was sufficient for believers' justification, regeneration, and sanctification. After that conversion experience believers were free from the *guilt* of sin and the *power* of sin.

In the Latin world this last interpretation of Pentecostalism has prevailed. There are several reasons for this reality as I see it. First, the Assemblies of God, attached to the finished work interpretation, is the first Pentecostal church that did missionary work in Latin America and the Spanish Caribbean. The first missionaries to Latin American came from the Assemblies God fold and the revival in India. Secondly, most of the missionaries of the Wesleyan Pentecostal tradition were not well trained in their tradition, so they could not make much difference between the finished work Pentecostal interpretation and Wesleyan Pentecostal interpretation. This was a discussion that divided Pentecostalism in its origin and it remains an ongoing discussion.

In Latin America and the Spanish Caribbean the four-fold gospel (*Cristo salva, Cristo sana, Cristo bautiza y Cristo viene*) prevailed over the five-fold gospel (*Cristo salva, Cristo santifica, Cristo sana, Cristo bautiza y Cristo viene*). Even today, it is quite difficult for Latino ministers in the Church of God to identify accurately persons sanctified and report them in the minister's monthly report. What I have heard from some of them is that they count as sanctified those who have been baptized with the Holy Spirit. The logic behind it is clear; since we believe that the baptism with the Holy Spirit is subsequent to sanctification then if a person is baptized with the Holy Spirit he or she must has been sanctified prior to the Holy Spirit's baptism experience.

Students of American Pentecostalism have maintained for some time now that Pentecostalism represents a form of spirituality. As such is not just a religious movement but also a lifestyle experience; that is, 'a way of being and participating in the world'.[3] If that is the case, then holiness 'is a "take on life" that presses through some of

---

[3] Daniel Castelo, *Revisioning Pentecostal Ethics – The Epicletic Community* (Cleveland, TN: CPT Press, 2013), p. 129.

the most prevalent assumptions of Christianity within the Western intellectual climate'.[4] This holiness 'take on life' is a serious judgment on some of the things taken for granted in our culture and it moves contra culture.

At the same time, the concept of holiness that envisioned a consecrated life that springs out of a deep altar encounter requires more than a personal experience related to that spiritual altar encounter; the profound spirituality brought about at the altar encounter must be redirected also to reach *others*, whomever those *others* might be. I believe that holiness and spirituality should help us Pentecostals face the reality of life with a sense of communal identification. That is to say, holiness includes a willingness to understand and take into our experience the suffering, invisibility, and vulnerability of those least privileged in their community. This capacity to identify ourselves with the outcasts in society will enable us to be compassioned and emphatic with the *other* and in turn it will help us to understand our own misfortunes in our spiritual journey.

Holiness as a Lifestyle

Holiness for us Pentecostals has always been more a personal and daily close walk with God than a responsible and responsive relationship with our neighbor. We do not necessarily stress the need to bring our holiness to relate meaningfully with our neighbor in our daily living. We see holiness more in its vertical dimension, as we try to please God as individuals in private relationship with him, as if we were not related to our neighbor in our service of pleasing God with our life. Thus holiness becomes a private experience between God and the believer. Of course, there is a vertical dimension of holiness that incarnates a committed life to God. But this component of holiness cannot be separated from its horizontal dimension, that is, its expression in the life of the community, not only our faith community, but also, and maybe more importantly, in the wider community as well. In other words, real holiness is a call to live in community where the love for God for the *other*, for the one whom I see as different from me, occurs naturally. But traditionally we Pentecostals have believed that the main point of holiness is to place emphasis on our personal spirituality rather than on the

---

[4] Castelo, *Revisioning Pentecostal Ethics*, pp. 129-30.

communal aspect of our spirituality that calls us to love the *other*. That *other* could be different to me in many ways. I can identify him or her as sinner, as a member of minority group, a foreigner, a social outcast, etc. By overlooking these persons it is easy for us to keep our holiness private, untainted, and unshakable. Then one can affirm: holiness is a private business between God, and me and I do not have to worry about my neighbor.

Nevertheless, the central message of the Gospel of Jesus Christ is: 'Love the Lord your God with all your heart and with all your soul and with all your strength and with all your mind; and, love your neighbor as yourself' (Lk. 10.27).[5] If holiness is not lived and understood from the perspective of the *other* in community, we are leaving out the second key element of the nature of holiness. The clear teaching of the New Testament is that we have a responsibility for the *other* notwithstanding who this *other* may be. In Matthew 25 the Gospel's narrative says:

> Then the King will say to those on his right, 'Come, you who are blessed by my Father; take your inheritance, the kingdom prepared for you since the creation of the world. For I was hungry and you gave me something to eat, I was thirsty and you gave me something to drink, I was a stranger and you invited me in, I needed clothes and you clothed me, I was sick and you looked after me, I was in prison and you came to visit me' (Mt. 25.34-36).

This dialogue in the above quote begins as follows: 'When the Son of Man comes in his glory … All the nations will be gathered before him, and he will separate the people one from another as a shepherd separates the sheep from the goats. He will put the sheep on his right and the goats on his left' (Mt. 25.31-32). In other words, according to this narrative, holiness is intrinsically related to our service and commitment to our neighbor. In order to be completely holy we must be responsible with and responsive to our neighbor's needs, willing to participate in his or her struggles, pains, misfortunes, joys, victories, and celebrations. To do otherwise, is to miss the point of what holiness is all about. According to this narrative when the righteous asked the Lord: 'When did we see you hun-

---

[5] All Scripture quotations are from the New International Version unless noted otherwise.

gry and feed you, or thirsty and give you something to drink? When did we see you a stranger and invite you in, or needing clothes and clothe you? When did we see you sick or in prison and go to visit you?' (Mt. 25.37-39). The answer they received from the Lord was simply this: 'I tell you the truth, whatever you did for one of the least of these brothers of mine, you did for me' (Mt. 25.40). This declaration clearly states that holiness is not something one has privately with God, but it is a lifestyle one lives in community with God and one's neighbor. Our solidarity with our neighbor is always included as part of our commitment to a holy life. So our call to be holy goes beyond the vertical dimension of holiness. In other words, it goes beyond an individualistic spirituality. Holiness, then, must demonstrate a consistent way of life that takes into consideration the service, commitment, and care for the *other*. This holy lifestyle includes 'bearing with one another's weaknesses, not ceasing to love our neighbor or friend because of those faults in him, which perhaps offend or displease us'.[6] That is to say, a holy lifestyle has communal implications; it is more than having an individualistic spirituality. But these communal implications of holiness involve a true and authentic relationship with God and neighbor. One cannot be authentic without the other. The call always will be to sort out the tensions between the vertical and horizontal dimensions of holiness and live up to its ultimate holistic lifestyle integration. What this Bible narrative is affirming is that the least of these brothers constitute, in their powerlessness and vulnerability, the sacramental presence of Christ. 'The vulnerable human beings become, in a mysterious way, the sacramental presence of Christ in our midst'.[7]

Our church claims to be Wesleyan-Pentecostal in its understanding of its faith, love, and practice. This requires it to view its beliefs, affections, and actions in a broader scope. In the Wesleyan tradition love for our neighbor is never separated from our love for God. When God's grace reaches a person, through the Holy Spirit, one's love for God and neighbor cannot be divorced one from the other. That is to say, our lifestyle, the way we incarnate our faith and affections in a given community, must continue to grow in finding ex-

---

[6] Ernest Best, *A Critical and Exegetical Commentary on the Book of Ephesians* (Edinburgh: Bloomsbury T&T Clark, 2004), p. 106.

[7] Luis Rivera-Pagán, 'Xenophilia or Xenophobia: Towards a Theology of Migration', *The Ecumenical Review* 64.4 (December 2012), p. 587.

pression in loving and selfless actions toward our neighbor. Henry H. Knight III puts it this way: 'To know and love this God over time is to acquire deeply rooted holy affections such that love increasingly governs our desires and motivations'.[8] In this way we are able to transcend, through the work of the Holy Spirit in our hearts, our limited understanding of God's given grace and the culture's demands. God's given grace frees us to go beyond to our own culture's world constructs to accept the demands of the kingdom of God. Knight remarks further, 'what seems good and right to us may in fact be the contrary to the will of God. Wrong desires and limited understanding conspire to hold us in a captivity in which we are free to do almost anything except love as God loves'.[9]

To incarnate our love and commitment to our *different other* we need to learn to be part of his/her environment, hopes, achievements, joys, fears, misfortune, and suffering. At this juncture it is necessary for me to quote some beautiful lines from the German theologian, Dietrich Bonhöffer, from his works, *Letters and Papers from Prison,* where he says: 'We have for once learnt to see the great events of world history from below, from the perspective of the outcast, the suspects, the maltreated, the powerless, the oppressed, the reviled – in short, from the perspective of those who suffer.'[10] If we want to feel more comfortable, let us listen to the Bible narrative that states the following: 'The Word became flesh and made his dwelling among us. We have seen his glory, the glory of the one and only Son, who came from the Father, full of grace and truth' (Jn 1.14).

The Issue of Immigration

It is not an easy task to speak about and analyze the issue of Hispanic undocumented immigration to the United States seriously. Nevertheless, it cannot be overlooked as if it were not a reality. I

---

[8] Henry H. Knight III, *Is There a Future for God's Love? An Evangelical Theology* (Nashville: Abingdon Press, 2012), p. 163. When Knight speaks of *this* God, he differentiates him from the cultural god that many Christians in the United States and in many other countries identify as the God of the Bible. *This* God – the God of Abraham, Isaac, Jacob and Jesus Christ – is not manipulated by what seems to be natural and acceptable in any given culture. *This* God's requirements many times go against what is the normal practice of the culture.

[9] Knight III, *Is There a Future for God's Love?*, p. 162.

[10] Quoted by Rivera-Pagán, '*Xenophilia or Xenophobia*', p. 589.

will briefly address this issue in this essay with the understanding that soon I will come back to the subject to address it at a greater length.

The Hispanic undocumented immigration to the United States is directly related to two main factors. One has to do with local conditions in mother countries; the lack of economic opportunities people suffer in their own countries forces them to look to the north for better futures for their lives. Many of the Latin American countries have been ripped off by the rich and governing classes, leaving the immense majority of their people with their hands tied economically and with no immediate future. What is deeply painful is that most of these governing classes of these countries have had the political and military support of the governments of the United States. The second factor that forces people to leave their Latin American countries is related to the 'American dream'; they feel that it is worthwhile to take the risk of the deadly journey to the north, for they believe if they succeed in the process, they will find a place to work to pursue their happiness. The fact is that there is a need for cheap foreign labor in agriculture, construction, and service industries in the United States. So, on the one hand, people from Latin America come to this country because they believe they could work out better lives for themselves and their families. On the other hand, on this side of the border there are the American entrepreneurs who profit from hiring cheap foreign labor with no fringe benefits at all to these newcomers. This is the perfect combination created by the economic forces of *supply* and *demand* in a capitalist system. In recent times we call this globalization. As Luis Rivera-Pagán has rightly said,

> Migration is a salient dimension of modern globalization. Globalization implies not only the transfer of financial resources, products, and trade, but also the worldwide relocation of peoples, a transnationalization of labour migration, of human beings who take the difficult and frequently painful decision to leave their kith and kin searching for a better future.[11]

Unauthorized immigrants make up 25% of farm workers according to 2008 data in a Pew Hispanic Center report that also includes

---

[11] Rivera-Pagán, '*Xenophilia or Xenophobia*', p. 587.

estimates of unauthorized immigrant shares of other occupations and industries.[12] The Center estimates that the rapid growth of un-authorized immigrant workers also has halted. This report found that there were 8.3 million undocumented immigrants in the US labor force in March 2008. Based on March 2008 data collected by the Census Bureau, the Center estimates that unauthorized immi-grants are 4% of the nation's population and 5.4% of its work-force.[13] According to the Pew Hispanic Center, estimates based on data from the US Census Bureau, there were a total of 40 million immigrants living in the US in March 2011. Of those, 11.1 million were unauthorized immigrants.[14] More than eight-in-ten (81%) of the nation's estimated 11.1 million unauthorized immigrants are of Hispanic origin, according to Pew Hispanic Center estimates.[15] The shocking figures about the unauthorized Hispanic immigrants in 2010 were that nearly two thirds had lived in the US for at least a decade, and nearly half were parents of minor children.[16] This is re-ally due to the fact that unauthorized immigrants are young and in their childbearing years. The median age of unauthorized immigrant adults is 36.2 years old, which is about a decade younger than the median age of authorized immigrant adults (46.1) and US native adults (46.5).[17]

In recent years, the debate over undocumented immigration has often been posed as a choice between two competing priorities – increasing border security and enforcement or providing a path to citizenship to immigrants who are in the country undocumented.[18]

The Cultural Response to the Issue of Immigration
Different groups' competing interests fuel the current immigration discussion: ethnic backgrounds, religious consciousness and human-

---

[12] http://www.pewhispanic.org/2013/01/29/a-nation-of-immigrants/

[13] See http://www.pewhispanic.org/2009/04/14/a-portrait-of-unauthorized-immigrants-in-the-united-states/

[14] http://www.pewhispanic.org/2012/04/23/net-migration-from-mexico-fall s-to-zero-an d-perhaps-less/

[15] http://www.pewhispanic.org/2011/02/01/unauthorized-immigrant-popul ation-brnational-a

[16] http://www.pewhispanic.org/2011/12/01/unauthorized-immigrants-lengt h-of-residency-patterns-of-parenthood/

[17] http://www.pewhispanic.org/2011/12/01/unauthorized-immigrants-lengt h-of-residency-patterns-of-parenthood/

[18] http://www.pewhispanic.org/2011/12/28/as-deportations-rise-to-record-l evels-most-latinos-oppose-obamas-policy/

itarian aspects, civil and ethical concerns. There is no doubt that the discussion of the topic of immigration has to address a wide variety of religious, ethical, humanitarian, and economic issues. As I mentioned before, this discussion involves two opposing perspectives. On the one hand, the immigrants claim the right to reunite their families, their right to find rest from political persecution, and their hope to provide themselves a better standard of living. On the other hand, the receiving country claims its right to determine who lives, works, and benefits from its public services and other national considerations. There is no easy answer to this dilemma, but I am pretty sure that pretending that it is not an issue to the church is the worst response to this reality.

There are conflicting positions regarding the economic benefits of the immigrants for the US, with some economists affirming that immigration is a net benefit to the US economy. 'Immigrants fill jobs that US citizens often reject, help the US economy maintain competitiveness in the global economy, and stimulate job creation in depressed neighborhoods'.[19] But others argue that what is a benefit to immigrants can represent 'serious losses for vulnerable sectors of the US population'.[20] Once again, this is quite a difficult situation to call because there are many forces involved in the free market economy. The variables are so many that one by-product could not be attached just to one variable. For example, some corporations may pit workers against each other by threatening to move and sometimes moving production to lower-wage locations if their employees make demands.[21]

Nevertheless, there are reports that say that Latino immigrants are creating companies that expand the tax base, create jobs, and breathe new life into depressed commercial districts. At a time when the United States needs new consumer markets to drive economic growth, Latino immigrant-owned businesses will be indispensible for capturing growing Latino markets at home and abroad.[22] Hispanic-owned firms in particular have served as a cor-

---

[19] http://www.theodora.com/debate.html

[20] http://www.theodora.com/debate.html

[21] http://www.theodora.com/debate.html

[22] Alexandra Starr, *Latino Immigrant Entrepreneurs,* Renewing America: Working Paper, July 2012. (i.cfr.org/content/publications/.../CFR_WorkingPaper13_Starr .pdf)

nerstone for economic development and US prosperity. According to 2007 figures from the US Census Bureau, these firms generated $351 billion in economic output towards the US economy, along with creating 1.9 million jobs. The United States Hispanic Chamber of Commerce (USHCC), according to a report published in 2013, says that Hispanic entrepreneurs have more than 3 million Hispanic-owned businesses across the United States that contribute in excess of $465 billion to the American economy each year.[23]

Then on the basis of what has been said in the above paragraphs, understanding issues of Latino undocumented and documented immigration is critical to understanding the future of the United States. The future of this nation is directly related to the way it deals with the Latino documented and undocumented immigration. The US Census is projecting that for the year 2050 the Latino population will be about 30 percent of the US population. Even if immigration is limited, Hispanics' share of the population will increase because they have higher birth rates than the overall population. That is largely due because Hispanic immigrants are younger than the nation's aging baby boom population.[24] It is also a fact that foreign-born women tend to have more children on average than US-born women. Most growth in the Hispanic population from 2000 to 2010 was due to births, not immigration, a change from the long-time pattern. But most births to Hispanic women are to those born outside the US.[25] Immigrants and their US-born descendants are expected to provide most of the US population gains in the decades ahead. The present birth rate for the whole population in the US is 1.87. The present Hispanic birth rate is around 2.7, which is close to 3 births for every 1000 people. If the US birth rate falls close to 1, it will face serious labor shortages and erode tax bases as it fails to reproduce enough to take care of its aging population. From this perspective the Hispanic population in this nation will be an asset to keep a healthy balance in the labor force of this country.

---

[23] http://globenewswire.com/news-release/2013/04/10/537361/10028046/en/The-United-States-Hispanic-Chamber-of-Commerce-Applauds-Wells-Fargo-on-Its-Pledge-to-Lend-55-Billion-to-Women-Owned-Businesses.html

[24] http://usatoday30.usatoday.com/news/nation/2008-02-11-population-study_N.htm

[25] http://www.pewsocialtrends.org/2012/05/17/explaining-why-minority-births-now-outnumber-white-births/

On the basis of the statistics presented above, this nation cannot overlook the reality of the Latino presence in the continental US. Therefore, educating the young Latinos and training Latino entrepreneurs should be a priority for this nation. The future of this nation is inevitably connected, both secularly and religiously, to the qualitative attention it gives to this sector of the population that within a generation will be close to one third of the total population of the country. Certainly, Latinos are not *a national economic crisis*, nor *a threat to the national security*.[26] They really represent a presence and future promise to this land. But still some people argue that non-White immigrants pose a threat to the nation, which they clearly define as White, Anglo-Saxon, and Protestant.

As a Wesleyan Pentecostal church, we do not want this kind of thought to be enthroned in our community of faith. We need to be conscious of this reality in order to keep it away from our daily life as a community of faith that is called to love its neighbors. For all of us it is always a continued challenge to conduct ourselves beyond the limits imposed by our cultures. Prejudices are so close to all of us that sometimes we do not even notice we are behaving unlovingly toward *the other* who is not like us. In the process of working towards a better understanding of all the parts in our commitment to a life of reconciliation in Christ Jesus, we need to communicate to each other effectively, carefully assessing our own positions and prejudices. This includes helping each other correcting misconceptions and resentments that sometimes we exploit for our own benefits as a way of excusing our shortcomings for not doing what God's love demands from us.

The Biblical Response to the Issue of Immigration

The discussion of the issue of Latin American undocumented immigration to the United States on this essay is not viewed only from the sociological, political, cultural, and economic perspectives. Side by side with these, I want to pay attention to the Christian perspective of our faith. Generally speaking, the people coming from Latin America to the continental US are mainly Christians; two thirds are Catholics and one third Protestants: mainline church members, evangelicals, and Pentecostals – in a sense, these are religious people. Pentecostals, who are part of the dominant majority in this

---

[26] http://www.theodora.com/debate.html

country, should understand clearly that these people worship the same God they worship and read the same Bible they read. So it is their responsibility to look beyond the cultural filters of this country to the biblical stories to fine tune their vision of immigration. M. Daniel Carroll Rodas says it this way: 'If believers want to deal with the issues posed by Hispanic immigration and contribute to possible solutions, then they should do it consciously as Christians and more expressively as Christian biblically informed'.[27] So as people of the Bible we should look to the Scriptures as our rule of faith in dealing with the issue of immigration.

As I mentioned above, the issue of immigration goes beyond cultural, political, racial, socioeconomic, and political considerations. For committed Christians, the issue has biblical and theological implications. There are specific considerations both in the Old and New Testament as to how immigrants (the foreigners, refugees) should be treated. When we deal with an immigrant, we really are dealing with a human being with dignity who was made in the image of God. The immigrant is not just someone different from me; he or she is someone who was made in the image of God. More than anything else he or she resembles the dignity and image of God. When we see them through God's lens, that *insignificant other* immediately becomes a *significant other* in whom we see God's love and mercy for all.

The truth in the Bible's narratives is that the God of Israel always demonstrated love and mercy to those who suffered and were less privileged in the communities where they lived. The poor, marginalized, foreigners, widows, and orphans have always been special to God. For this reason, he demands from his people a special care for these outcasts as a genuine response to his love for those within the community of faith. Any behavior less than a true commitment to the undocumented is 'only a resounding gong or a clanging cymbal' (1 Cor. 13.1). A true Christian response to those who come to what we consider our land involves accepting the reality that these people are also contributing to the nation with their work, ideas, faith, and projects.

---

[27] M. Daniel Carroll Rodas, *Cristianos en la frontera: La inmigración, la iglesia y la Biblia* (Mary Lake, FL: Casa Creación, 2009), p. 51. (Translation is mine.)

On the one hand, the Old Testament's narratives present a continued movement of the people of the covenant from one place to another. Abraham, Isaac, Jacob, Naomi, David, and the people of God in general went from one geographic area to another, moved by different situations like persecution, famine, wars, progress, etc. The life of these people was characterized by a nomadic existence. Even when they settled in the Promised Land they felt it was not their land. When the author of Hebrews talks about them he says:

> All these people were still living by faith … They did not receive the things promised; they only saw them and welcomed them from a distance, admitting that they were foreigners and strangers on earth. People who say such things show that they are looking for a country of their own. If they had been thinking of the country they had left, they would have had opportunity to return. Instead, they were longing for a better country – a heavenly one (Heb. 11.13-16).

On the other hand, the New Testament also presents Jesus and his parents as immigrants in Egypt. Even the members of the Primitive church went about from one geographic place to another looking for a place to have a decent and progressive life. We must affirm then that the immigrant's reality was not strange to the God of Israel and the New Testament's God. In fact, the Apostle Paul warns the Gentile believers in the Primitive Church of their condition as sojourners strangers in their new community of faith. He says to them:

> remember that … you were separate from Christ, excluded from citizenship in Israel and foreigners to the covenants of the promise, without hope and without God in the world. But now in Christ Jesus you who once were far away have been brought near by the blood of Christ … Consequently, you are no longer foreigners and strangers, but fellow citizens with God's people and also members of his household (Eph. 2.12-13, 19).

The language that Paul uses here to describe theologically the political, cultural, religious, economically, and socially conditions of an outcast in his society is fascinating. The expression 'foreigners and strangers' was well understood by his audience. It was not a foreign concept to the people to whom the letter was addressed. Having been 'foreigners and strangers', now they should understand what it means to an authentic member of their community of faith. This new spiritual condition should make them think and act differently about those considered 'foreigners and strangers'. This should be true today in our present situation. Our spiritual status, not our cultural construes, should govern the way we treat the foreigners and strangers, the immigrants.

The Church of God and the Issue of undocumented Immigration

The Church of God faces an enormous challenge with the issue of the Latino undocumented immigration today. It is my opinion that for our church to live up to the requirements of this challenge it must raise itself beyond what is culturally *normal* and *acceptable* in this nation. As a way of explaining what I mean when I say that our church needs to live up to its calling, let me say that that has been the reality of the church in every epoch of its history. The church, as the people called by God, is always challenged to confront the cultural, political, economic, and social conditions of the nation where it incarnates itself in the light of the content of the Gospel of Jesus Christ. The content of the Gospel has to do with the morality and ethics of the kingdom of God. This morality and ethics always go against what is *normal* or *acceptable* in our secular society. A faithful church is always challenged to go against the grain of what is considered to be the *normal behavior* of the society at large. The characteristics of the kingdom of God pull us away from the stories of our own countries 'to participate in the spiritual practices of a community that is shaped and governed by the story of God in Christ'.[28] What is at stake here is the Church's fidelity – it is torn between the love of God and the love of this world. To try to be faithful to both at the same time (our own cultures' stories and God's story in Jesus Christ) is to try to live with a divided heart. In the sermon on the mount Jesus is very clear about this issue when he says: 'No one can serve two masters. Either you will hate the one and love the other, or you will be devoted to the one and despise the other. You cannot serve both God and money' (Mt. 6.24). Living out God's love, mercy, and grace in our communities will always call into question the lifestyle and principles of our cultures. 'It is

---

[28] Knight III, *Is There a Future for God's Love?*, p. 147.

this participation that helps us remain focused and open to the grace of God in our lives.'[29]

According to what has been said above, the real challenge for us, as God's people, is to be obedient to the leading of the Holy Spirit in our lives. This leading will always separate what belongs to the realm of the *permanent kingdom* (the kingdom of God) from what belongs to the realm of the *temporal kingdom* (cultural kingdoms). Talking about the *permanent* and *temporal* kingdoms the author of the Letter to the Hebrews says that the heroes of chapter 11 were 'longing for a better country – a heavenly one [the *permanent* kingdom]. Therefore God is not ashamed to be called their God, for he has prepared a city [the *permanent* kingdom] for them' (Heb. 11.16). He continues this line of thought and says, specifically, that

> by faith Moses, when he had grown up, refused to be known as the son of Pharaoh's daughter [the *temporal* kingdom]. He chose to be mistreated along with the people of God [the *permanent* kingdom] rather than to enjoy the fleeting pleasures of sin [*temporal* kingdom]. He regarded disgrace for the sake of Christ as of greater value [*permanent* kingdom] than the treasures of Egypt [*temporal* kingdom], because he was looking ahead to his reward [*permanent* kingdom] (Heb. 11.24-25).

This kind of judgment, to help us separate the *permanent* kingdom from the *temporal* ones, is what the Holy Spirit provides for us if we are open to his guidance. Jesus himself says 'this Holy Spirit will teach us all things and will remind you of everything I have said to you' (Jn 14.26). And then he adds: 'That is why I said the Spirit will receive from me what he will make known to you' (Jn 14.15).

Consequently, the leading and teaching of the Holy Spirit will inevitably help us to harmonize, in our own lives, the service to God and to our neighbor. Those who want to be citizens of the *permanent* kingdom must look for a close relation not only with God but also with their neighbor. It is impossible to love God without loving one's neighbor. In the Letters of John in the New Testament this thought comes out very clear: 'Whoever claims to love God yet hates a brother or sister is a liar. For whoever does not love their brother and sister, whom they have seen, cannot love God, whom

---

[29] Knight III, *Is There a Future for God's Love?*, p. 147.

they have not seen' (1 Jn 4.20). In other words, *works of mercy* must be complementary to *works of piety*. These two concepts are cardinal in Wesleyan theology. Nevertheless, sometimes we tend to overlook the *works of mercy* because of our lukewarm commitment to the *works of piety*. In fact, it is through the *works of mercy* that the *works of piety* come to the forefront of our spiritual journey. Yes, the *works of piety* prepare our hearts to grow in our Christian affections, but these affections are void if they do not help us to see our neighbor from the perspective of God's love. In this direction Knight affirms that 'the works of mercy are at one and the same time expressions of our love for our neighbor and means of grace that the Spirit uses to further our growth in love'.[30]

As people of God we need to develop sympathy for the immigrants from the perspective of the Gospel. This is only possible as we get close to them and begin to feel and learn from their suffering. I believe that John Wesley's evaluation of his society applies very well to us in the 21st century in dealing with the immigrants. Talking about the rich of his time he says the following: 'one part of the world [the rich] does not know what the other suffers. Many of them do not know, because they do not care to know; they keep out of the way of knowing it; and they plead their voluntary ignorance as an excuse for their hardness of heart.'[31] I do believe that my church should discover the undocumented immigrants. Pleading ignorance of what is going on with them in this country is not an authentic Christian response; it is just an excuse for the hardness of our hearts.

In producing a valuable authentic Christian response to the issue of undocumented and documented immigration our church must tear down the wall of division between the majority population of this nation and the immigrants. A heart transformed by God's love must feel and see differently. We cannot follow the leading of our secular culture that divides us into groups and keeps us apart from one another. We must follow the leading of our new creation in Christ Jesus that goes counterculture. The Apostle Paul says it this way to the Ephesians:

---

[30] Knight III, *Is There a Future for God's Love?*, p. 149.
[31] John Wesley, 'On visiting the Sick' in *Wesley's Works*, III, pp. 387-88, quoted by Knight III, *Is There a Future for God's Love?*, p. 153.

For he himself is our peace, who has made the two groups one and has destroyed the barrier, the dividing wall of hostility, by setting aside in his flesh the law with its commands and regulations. His purpose was to create in himself one new humanity out of the two, thus making peace, and in one body to reconcile both of them to God through the cross, by which he put to death their hostility (Eph. 2.14-16).

This is our real challenge as Christians when we face the issue of undocumented immigration: are we going to react as citizens of one nation or as a new humanity created by God in Christ Jesus through the pouring out of his Spirit in our hearts? That is to say, as Knight puts it:

if what God is about in salvation is the transformation of hearts and lives so that we love God and our neighbor as we have been loved by God in Christ, then the problem of separation is a serious threat to our living and our salvation. We simply must find ways to break out of cultural captivity so that we see the world more as God sees it.[32]

The Challenge of Holiness and the Issue of Undocumented Immigration

Migrations have been a constant in the history of humanity. As has already been said, there are various reasons for this phenomenon. The fact is that people move from one place to another for various reasons, among them, political persecution, family reunion, looking for better conditions for pursuing their happiness, etc. The Latino migration to United States is part of that painful reality. It is not easy to leave family members back home, come to an inhospitable situation in a foreign country, and face constant discrimination because of one's race, color, religion, and language. Of course, many Latinos did not migrate to the United States. Instead, the borders of this nation were extended over their Latino territories. Having said that, one has to admit a large numbers of immigrants have come to the USA, if only for a time, while others have come and made this nation their home country. Many of their children have no other country but this nation. They were born here, and this is the only

---

[32] Knight III, *Is There a Future for God's Love?*, p. 155.

land they know as their nation. Nevertheless, they are considered immigrants and are constantly being discriminated against.

The plain reality is that these undocumented immigrants are more than anything else our brothers and sisters. They are persons bearing the image of God just like we are and many of them share our faith and worship the same God we worship. But their lives in their adopted country are full of surprises. In their journey to this 'Promised Land' they discovered how painful and difficult their lives in this nation can be.

Somehow the people of God must learn to practice hospitality toward the immigrants. God offered his total hospitality to us in Christ Jesus. As Jesus says, 'Come to me, all you who are weary and burdened, and I will give you rest. Take my yoke upon you and learn from me, for I am gentle and humble in heart, and you will find rest for your souls' (Mt. 11.28-29). No doubt these words express God's desire to give peace and rest to those people burdened by conflicts in their lives. If we want to imitate God's love for those weary and tired, we need to be hospitable like God is. 'Being hospitable is imitating God.'[33] This is the big challenge posed to those of us who consider ourselves people of the Bible. It is important that we gain knowledge as to how people in the Bible acted toward immigrants under the guidance of the Holy Spirit. Revisiting these Bible passages will help us to see ourselves through the lens of divine narratives and will position us to see the immigrants as persons created in God's image and saved by his redemptive work in Christ.

The above reflection brings me to consider seriously the Resolution on Immigration approved by the Church of God during its General Assembly. The text of the resolution, passed August 3, 2012, reads as follows:

THEREFORE BE IT RESOLVED THAT, the Church of God reaffirms its commitment to the following principles of a just process for immigration: 'that immigrants be treated with respect and mercy by churches; that governments develop structures that safeguard and monitor national borders with efficiency and respect for human dignity; that governments establish more functional legal mechanisms for the annual entry of a reasonable number of immigrant workers and families; that governments

---

[33] Carroll Rodas, *Cristianos en la frontera*, p. 84.

recognize the central importance of the family in society by re-
considering the number and categories of visas available for family reunification; that governments establish a sound, equitable
process toward earned legal status for currently undocumented
immigrants; that governments legislate fair labor and civil laws
for all; and that immigration enforcement be conducted in ways
that recognize the importance of due process of law'.[34]

I want to look in detail at this Resolution on the basis of the
human, sociological, Christian, biblical, and theological views that
inform it. It is also important to me to do this analysis consistent
with what has been my take on doing theology in the public arena.
A recent article addresses my concern related to my church's position on undocumented immigration. I would lift up the following
quotation: 'There is a growing acknowledgment that the Christian
church needs to rededicate itself to expressing itself publicly regarding issues of communal importance for the greater good of society'.[35] We really need to be conscious of the fact that our Christian
commitment should take us beyond vain rhetoric and enable us to
become aware of how injustices within our church and society at
large, including our national and local governments, can take structural and systemic forms. Obviously, it is easy 'to go with the flow'
and to accept the government's explanation of its purposes and actions. To do that, the church does not need to be prophetic.[36] What
is difficult and painful is to challenge the beliefs of the culture and
the positions of the government. On the one hand, being prophetic
is a challenge to the church because the first line of opposition to its
prophetic message comes from within the church itself. A large
number of our brothers and sisters in the Church of God follow
uncritically what is accepted as good in our culture. If the leaders of

---

[34] http://www.churchofgod.org/index.php/resolution-new/resolution/immi
gration_2012

[35] Sang-Ehil Han, Paul Louis, Terry C. Muck, 'Christian Hospitality and Pastoral Practices from an Evangelical Perspective', *Theological Education* 47.1 (2012),
p. 20.

[36] When I talk about the prophetic ministry of the church, I have in mind the
commitment of the church's leaders to denounce openly, from the content of
God's love revealed in the Scriptures, the injustices perpetrated against any person in society, but especially against minority groups, the poor and the disinherited of our lands who most of the time do not have people to defend them from
the enslaving structures of church, government, and society at large.

the church go against what is generally accepted by the church's constituency their path to make a difference is not easy – but surely that is the role of leaders. When one is positioned to lead, one should lead rather than maintain the status quo.

On the other hand, the church is not called to please the government in everything it does. In fact, our Christian commitment should go far beyond the government's commitments. In the public arena the church should face the government based on its commitment to the saving grace of God in Christ Jesus. Without a compassionate heart and a commitment to act, the church will not make any meaningful contribution in the public arena. It is quite surprising that in a recent report of the Pew Research Center, March 23, 2013,[37] the opinion of the church in general on how to deal with undocumented immigration was less sympathetic to the immigrants than the secular society as a whole. Among secular society, 71% said that there should be a way for undocumented immigrants to become documented in the nation. One would have expected a better answer from the church's people, but only 69% of white Protestants as a whole indicated that undocumented immigrants should become documented. When the study separates the white mainline churches from the white Evangelicals, only 62% of the white Evangelicals (which includes white Pentecostals) and 65% of white mainline churches said that undocumented immigrants should become documented. It would be interesting to see how white Pentecostals would score if they were separated from white Evangelicals. These statistics speak loudly about the conservatism of the church on 'issues of communal importance for the greater good of society'.[38] The Church should lead society rather than follow it. That is to say, the Church should understand that what seems only natural in this *temporal* kingdom may not be so natural in the *permanent* kingdom. It is my contention that out of the love of God for this world the church should challenge any of the world's constructs that do not harmonize with God's vision for the world.

Correspondingly, when the Church of God says, 'that immigrants be treated with respect and mercy by churches', it falls short of the specific mandate of the Scriptures. This statement is too

---

[37] http://www.people-press.org/2013/03/28/most-say-illegal-immigrants-should-be-allowed-to-stay-but-citizenship-is-more-divisive/
[38] Han, Louis, and Muck, 'Christian Hospitality and Pastoral Practices', p. 20.

vague for a community of faith that knows itself as object of God's love. The church has a more profound responsibility to undocumented immigrants. We share in common with the undocumented immigrants a God who has acted in love in the person of Christ Jesus to redeem us. In Christ's life, death, and resurrection, every person finds the promise of a new life and future. As a result of this conviction, the church should overcome the cultural separation from immigrants that most of the time leads it into ineffectual actions with them.

The other parts of the Church of God resolution passively leave everything in the hands of the government. No commitment is made to push the government in the public arena to do what the church feels should be done. In a sense, the church does not want to make the government uncomfortable. The church should make it clear that our God cannot be domesticated by our cultural beliefs. So, at least sometimes the public witness of the church must make the political and socio-cultural powers uncomfortable. It is difficult to accept, but sometimes, 'most of us who say we follow Christ have divided hearts, in part faithfully responding to the God revealed in Christ, but in part recreating God into a more amenable divinity'.[39] Our challenge is to make the God of Israel and the God of Christ Jesus the God leading our church. This God does not conform to any cultural pattern but changes everything and creates new creatures according to his love for this world.

Final Remarks

It is time that our church accepts its pastoral responsibility for those brothers and sisters who struggle to maintain their families united in this country as they face the fears of being unmercifully deported. It is shocking to me that we remain publicly silent about this issue while other churches express themselves openly in the public arena. In December 2011, a group of 33 American Catholic Bishops of Latino origins exhorted the undocumented immigrants to keep their faith.

We the undersigned Hispanic/Latino Bishops of the United States wish to let those of you who lack proper authorization to

---

[39] Knight III, *Is There a Future for God's Love?*, p. 162.

live and work in our country know that you are not alone, or forgotten. We recognize that every human being, authorized or not, is an image of God and therefore possesses infinite value and dignity. We open our arms and hearts to you, and we receive you as members of our Catholic family. As pastors, we direct these words to you from the depths of our heart.

In a very special way we want to thank you for the Christian values you manifest to us with your lives – your sacrifice for the well-being of your families, your determination and perseverance, your joy of life, your profound faith and fidelity despite your insecurity and many difficulties. You contribute much to the welfare of our nation in the economic, cultural and spiritual arenas.[40]

I do believe that we need to recognize that in this age of globalization 'borders have become bridges, rather than barriers'.[41] In an age where globalization prevails, there are social issues, migration being one of them, whose transnational complexities call for a more rational and intelligent dialogue and debate. Pope Benedict XVI rightly reminded the global community in his 2009 encyclical *Caritas in veritate* that: 'Every migrant is a human person who, as such, possesses fundamental, inalienable rights that must be respected by everyone and in every circumstance'.[42]

Recently I heard the Cuban-American theologian, Justo L. González, say the following:

In the society at large, the American citizens may claim that this country belongs to them and that the rest of us are strangers and immigrants, whose right to be here is dependent on them the citizens. But in the church all – from all of our prominent bishops or pastors to the recently arriving person – all of us are strangers and guests. Here in the church not even the chief sinner nor the most consecrated saint could claim any right at all. Maybe some pay the bills of the church and others who are less fortunate may receive the church's services. But all, beginning with the richest

---

[40] http://usccbmedia.blogspot.com/2011/12/estas-son-las-mananitasof-hispanic_12.html

[41] Rivera-Pagán, 'Xenophilia or Xenophobia', p.12.

[42] Rivera-Pagán, 'Xenophilia or Xenophobia', p.12.

who pay for the church building to the poorest who receive second hand clothing, all of us are sojourners and strangers.[43]

It is my firm belief that our church must bring our undocumented brothers and sisters out of the shadows of invisibility and seat them with us at the big banquet table. We should not keep silent any longer while passively looking at the great injustices being performed against undocumented people. For those who silently and passively look upon the misfortune of the undocumented immigrants, it is important that they be reminded of these words given to Edom by the prophet Obadiah:

> You should not gloat over your brother in the day of his misfortune, nor rejoice over the people of Judah in the day of their destruction, nor boast so much in the day of their trouble. You should not march through the gates of my people in the day of their disaster, nor gloat over them in their calamity in the day of their disaster, nor seize their wealth in the day of their disaster. You should not wait at the crossroads to cut down their fugitives, nor hand over their survivors in the day of their trouble. The day of the Lord is near for all nations. As you have done, it will be done to you; your deeds will return upon your own head (Obad. 1.12-15).

I know our task is not an easy one; but prophetic ministry in the public arena is never comfortable and popular. But for such a time as this, God has called us. Let us stand up and be counted!

---

[43] Justo L. González, 'Hacia el desarrollo de una teología responsiva a la situación del y la inmigrante latino/a', (Summit on Hispanic Theological Education; Orlando, FL; March 10, 2012). (translation is mine).

15

THE PRACTICE OF HOLINESS: IMPLICATIONS FOR A PENTECOSTAL MORAL THEOLOGY

TERRY JOHNS[*]

Introduction

As a Wesleyan-Pentecostal, I belong to a movement that identifies with a doctrinal commitment to holiness. My holiness commitment is derived from a distinctive tradition, Wesleyan-Pentecostal, and expressed in a particular context, North America. It is certainly not the only expression because Wesleyan-Pentecostalism represents both similarities and dissimilarities within the larger family of Pentecostals and Charismatics. The purpose here is not to critique these distinctions, but rather to identify a common expression of holiness within the developmental years of the movement that has essentially been lost in recent history. This is not a call to return to an earlier time or expression, but rather it is a careful critique of doctrinal positions that were paramount to the practice of holiness as foundational to the construction of a contemporary moral theology.

Critique

With regard to historical antecedents that led to twentieth-century Pentecostalism, the consensus is that the Pentecostal movement 'emerged from the nineteenth-century Holiness movement'.[1] The

---

[*] Terry Johns (DMin, Columbia Theological Seminary) is Associate Professor of Social Ethics & Holistic Mission at the Pentecostal Theological Seminary, Cleveland, TN, USA.
[1] Robert Mapes Anderson, *Vision of the Disinherited: The Making of American Pentecostalism* (New York: Cambridge University Press, 1979), p. xiii. While I do agree with Anderson's view on the origin of the North American Pentecostal

emergence resulted from a process of development that led from John Wesley's Methodism to the nineteenth-century Holiness movement culminating in the Pentecostal revival of the twentieth century.[2] The theology of John Wesley served as the *foundational* 'theological root'[3] that led to both the Holiness and Pentecostal revivals. Emil Bruner articulates Wesley's significance to the development:

> Methodism is the most important of the modern traditions for the student of Pentecostal origins to understand, for eighteenth-century Methodism is the mother of the nineteenth-century American holiness movement which, in turn, bore twentieth-century Pentecostalism. Pentecostalism is primarily Methodism's extended incarnation.[4]

---

movement, I am not in agreement with his 'social deprivation' theory. Cf. D. William Faupel, *The Everlasting Gospel: The Significance of Eschatology in the Development of Pentecostal Thought* (JPTSup 10; Sheffield: Sheffield Academic Press, 1996), p. 45; Walter Hollenweger, *The Pentecostals* (Peabody: Hendrickson Press, 1972), pp. 21-26; and Vinson Synan, *The Holiness Pentecostal Movement in the United States* (Grand Rapids: Eerdmans Publishing, 1971), pp. 115-16.

[2] The nineteenth-century Reformed Evangelical influence is not denied. As Faupel recognizes, 'the American Holiness movement emerged as a synthesis of Reformed and Wesleyan theology' (Faupel, *Everlasting Gospel*, p. 54). But as Donald Dayton, *Theological Roots of Pentecostalism* (Grand Rapids: Zondervan, 1987), p. 64, explains: 'Methodism set the tone for many other groups ... and permeated many other denominations, especially in the Reformed camp ... Thus Timothy L. Smith can describe the dominant religious force in the United States on the eve of the Civil War as a coalition of "revivalistic Calvinism" and "Evangelical Arminianism" – a coalition dominated by Methodist-like ideas, including the doctrine of Christian perfection'. Therefore, the focus of this essay is Wesleyan-Pentecostalism with primary roots in the Wesleyan-Holiness revival.

[3] This term references Dayton, *Theological Roots*. He identifies the nineteenth-century Holiness movement as the immediate antecedent to Pentecostalism, but traces the starting point to John Wesley. 'We shall begin our story with Methodism. This is in part because it is clear that here we can pick up the story in such a way as to demonstrate actual historical links and developments that will climax in Pentecostalism' (p. 38).

[4] Emil Bruner, *A Theology of the Holy Spirit: The Pentecostal Experience and the New Testament Witness* (London: Hodder & Stoughton, 1970), p. 37; Henry Knight, 'From Aldersgate to Azusa: Wesley and the Renewal of Pentecostal Spirituality', *Journal of Pentecostal Theology* 8 (1996), pp. 82-98 (82), adds: '... both wings [*Wesleyan and Baptistic*] of the Holiness and Pentecostal movements are rooted in and indebted to the Wesleyan awakening of the eighteenth century'. Steven J. Land, *Pentecostal Spirituality: A Passion for the Kingdom* (JPTSup 1; Sheffield: Sheffield Academic Press, 1993), p. 24, n. 1, considers this work by Bruner as one of the two most 'able assaults on the Pentecostal doctrine' (the second is J.D.G. Dunn's *Baptism in the Holy Spirit*, which is also acknowledged as the 'most inviting, under-

In particular, Wesley and the Holiness movement are significant to the development of Pentecostal theology and practice in relation to the doctrine of holiness. Therefore, remaining true to my confessed tradition, the current essay is focused on the centrality of holiness (sanctification) teaching to the core ethical belief system of the Pentecostal movement (holiness of life).[5] The primary purpose is to critique common expressions of faith and practice that identified these early believers as 'holiness people'.

For early Pentecostals, holiness of life was demonstrated through an ethical lifestyle (holiness of life) that juxtaposed biblical morality against an evil world. The basic formulaic expression was a life of holiness where 'desire for sin [is] crucified, deeds of the flesh mortified and sinful stains and tendencies cleansed'.[6] Enablement to live out the commandments of Christ, 'not as burdensome or grievous' but as 'unspeakable joy and full of glory'[7] where 'love reigns supreme'[8] was understood as the expected outcome of a holy life.

Personal commitment to 'holiness of life' also included an identifiable social concern. According to Mel Roebeck, social concern was evidenced by:

> battles waged on issues of civil rights and social justice by means such as ... preaching of non-violence and engagement in selected areas of civil disobedience ... Women were recognized as legitimate heirs to the call of God into full-time ministry. Social

---

standing and helpful'.) Even though Bruner is a critic of Pentecostalism, he does accurately discern its sources.

[5] Additionally, the Holiness movement provided the necessary paradigm shift in theological understanding in two primary areas: (1) an understanding of sanctification as Spirit baptism which involved a move to the language of *power*; and (2) the understanding of sanctification as more crisis than process experience. These two important shifts in theological thinking served as catalyst for the birth of the Pentecostal movement. For more discussion cf. Dayton, *Theological Roots*, pp. 68-108; Faupel, *Everlasting Gospel*, pp. 77-114. Faupel adds that this paradigm shift 'was accompanied by a transformation of world-view. A premillennial eschatology replaced the postmillennial view that was held by the movement during the first half of the nineteenth century' (p. 114). Faupel's thesis is that this shift in eschatology is the key to understanding American Pentecostalism (p. 18).

[6] Land, *Pentecostal Spirituality*, p. 89. Sanctification for Wesleyan-Pentecostals, historically, was a salvific work of God that addressed sinful nature so that 'the desire to sin' was crucified.

[7] Land, *Pentecostal Spirituality*, p. 89.

[8] Philemon Roberts, *God's Will for God's People: A Treatise on Sanctification* (Cleveland, TN: Pathway Press, 1958), p. 37.

programs were developed to aid the poor. Laws were enacted to mediate the power of the powerful.[9]

'Preaching of non-violence' is an interesting component of early social concern. Commitment to a peace witness set Pentecostals in opposition to all forms of violence, including acts of war, and distinguished them from the world in a very identifiable way. Veli-Matti Kärkkäinen observes that:

the first Pentecostals were born with the idea of pacifism. A literalist reading of the Bible and an enthusiasm caused by the wonder of God's Spirit uniting people of different origins, worshiping in the same community, caused Pentecostals to regard war as belonging to the 'old age'.[10]

Early leaders such as Charles Fox Parham,[11] Frank Bartleman,[12] and A.J. Tomlinson[13] stood against Christian participation in war and

---

[9] Cecil M. Robeck, 'Pentecostals & Social Ethics', *Pneuma* 9.2 (1987), pp. 103-107 (103).

[10] Veli-Matti Kärkkäinen, 'Are Pentecostals Oblivious to Social Justice? Theological and Ecumenical Considerations', *Missiology* 29.4 (Oct. 2001), pp. 417-31 (420).

[11] For example, Charles Fox Parham, *The Everlasting Gospel* (Baxter Springs, KS: Apostolic Faith Bible College, 1911), cited in Jay Beaman, *Pentecostal Pacifism: The Origin, Development, and Rejection of Pacific Belief among the Pentecostals* (Hillsboro, KS: Center for Mennonite Brethren Studies, 1989), pp. 53-54, says: 'We hang our heads in shame to see Christian nations of the Moloch-God, Patriotism, whose principal doctrine was honor, there to have consumed in that death struggle the feeling of philanthropy and humanity; spending millions to build the fires for the consummation of these virtues, while the cause of Christ languishes, heaven loses, hell opens her jaws, and so-called Christian nations feed (by war) to satisfy her gluttonous appetite'.

[12] 'The Church has no place to flaunt flags of national preference. God's grace and gospel are international. Christ died for all men. Antichrist means to run the church by government edict. Then we will have state and Church. The State will dictate to the Church. The flags represent fallen nations, with fallen nationalistic, sectional prides, ambitions, etc., that breed strife, enmity, jealousy, and war, for they are without Christ. We do not belong to them' (Frank Bartleman, 'Christian Citizenship' [Los Angeles: tract, 1922], pp. 1-2 in Micael Grenholm, 'Pentecostal Pacifism', *Holy Spirit Activism: Signs, Wonders, Peace & Justice* (n.d.), <http://holyspiritactivism.wordpress.com/pentecostal-pacifism>).

[13] Most likely, Tomlinson's pacifist stance was directly related to his background as a Quaker. He made numerous statements in opposition to war, including: 'I could not take a gun and fire it at my fellow men even at the command of a military officer. I could submit to the penalty inflicted upon me for refusing, but I cannot kill. I doubt if I could take the obligation to become a soldier in the first

violence by calling for commitment to pacifism. As the 20th Century moved forward, men like Stanley Frodsham and Donald Gee added their voices to the pacifist position.[14]

Such commitment to pacifism indicates a way of being in the world that is essentially 'eccentric'[15] in nature and diametrically opposed to the spirit of the 'evil world' that Pentecostals were so adamantly avoiding and critiquing through a distinctive holiness lifestyle. Lisa Cahill observes that:

> Christian pacifism is essentially a commitment to embody communally and historically the kingdom of God so fully that mercy, forgiveness, and compassion preclude the very contemplation of causing physical harm to another person.[16]

A commitment to 'living at peace with all'[17] without 'causing physical harm' is indicative of a radical salvific transformation by the Holy Spirit as well as a theological position that takes seriously the teaching of Scripture. It is, in particular, a proleptic expectation of the coming eschatological kingdom of God (which will implement peaceful coexistence for all of creation). As thus, it stands as a definitive sign of the presence of the kingdom of God in the midst of a fallen world.

---

place' (A.J. Tomlinson, 'Days of Perplexity', *Church of God Evangel* 26 [Jan. 1918], p. 1).

[14] Unfortunately, many of these early commitments have begun to fade in North American Pentecostalism. Solidarity with the poor and disenfranchised has too often been replaced by secular success models and the prosperity gospel (which seems to be a devaluing of the word *gospel*). Women have been disallowed to participate in the higher levels of decision-making through denial of the highest level of ordination for ministry and exclusion from top leadership positions. If care is not taken, commitment to biblical truth may become contaminated by our newly found fascination with the dominant culture. Sadly, a central aspect of Pentecostal spirituality – commitment to peace and justice – has fallen by the wayside for too many. Our hope for maintaining the heart of the Pentecostal ethos may rest with our brothers and sisters in the majority world. For a provocative discussion along these lines see Cheryl Bridges Johns, 'Presidential Address: The Adolescence of Pentecostalism: In Search of a Legitimate Sectarian Identity', *Pneuma* 17.1 (1995), pp. 3-17.

[15] This term is borrowed from Daniel Castelo's use in *Revisioning Pentecostal Ethics: The Epicletic Community* (Cleveland, TN: CPT Press, 2012), p. 16.

[16] Lisa Cahill, *Love Your Enemies* (Minneapolis: Fortress Press, 1994), p. 2, as quoted in Castelo, *Revisioning Pentecostal Ethics*, p. 17.

[17] Cf. Rom. 12.14-21.

As the twentieth century unfolded, the focus on *personal* expressions of holiness began to overshadow the companion concern of *social* expressions. During the early transition to the more personal focus, a sense of corporate responsibility was maintained by the understanding that holiness as a standard of living was embraced and practiced by a larger group of people of like mind (which was essentially a corporate agreement to avoid certain personal sins). The transition from personal commitment with corporate ethos continued to morph into a more individualistic understanding of salvation. Reasons for the transition include 'reaction to liberal tendencies in theology', which became identified in North America in particular as opposition to post liberalism, accommodation to *social establishment*[18] (trends), and adoption of the Evangelical emphasis on personal salvation, simplistically defined and narrowly focused, as forgiveness of sins in order to go to heaven.[19] Thus, an understanding of the necessity of relationship with God was intensified while relationship with others (in the sense of social responsibility) was deemphasized.

The focus on personal salvation may also be directly related to a theological shift in eschatology that emphasized the 'imminent return of Christ' coming for a spotless Bride (therefore, we must prepare ourselves for his soon return). A primary catalyst for this theological shift was related to the rise of dispensational apocalyptic eschatology that became attractive to Pentecostals. Focus on the need to be ready for the imminent return of Christ along with the missionary call to warn sinners of the impending judgment added urgency to the existing evangelistic fervor. The need for personal relationship with God became the foremost priority, and for some, the only priority. Emphasis on evangelism as personal witness and corporate revival meetings to call sinners to repentance ensued as a

---

[18] John Howard Yoder in his Foreword to Beaman, *Pentecostal Pacifism*, pp. iii-iv, offers a scathing critique: 'Pentecostalism's changes have become a classical specimen of the "sect cycle," making within barely two generations some fundamental accommodations to establishment like those which took early Christianity centuries. The *prima facie* Biblicism did not mature into a solid ethical hermeneutic'. Yoder continues by accusing Pentecostals of allowing 'the prophetic discernment of the evils of social stratification *to yield* with astonishing ease to personal prosperity and institutional respectability'.

[19] Pentecostals continued to emphasize sanctification and Spirit baptism, but they also suffered from the reductionist understanding. As the twentieth century progressed, emphasis on sanctification began to decline.

natural progression of theological shift.[20] With the reductionist evangelistic fervor, social concern gave way to 'soul' concern that resulted in de-emphasizing commitment to social action as integral to the Pentecostal ethos.[21] Also represented within the de-emphasis on social action is loss of 'peace witness' as living expression of the eschatological Kingdom of Peace. The end result theologically is that sanctification is reduced to *personal* commitment to God to live a holy life – interpreted as avoiding personal vices (being separate from the 'world').[22]

Reducing personal holiness to abstinence from personal vices alone (or to simplistic belief systems) is not only wrongheaded, but is theologically problematic. In his critique of John Wesley's theology of sanctification, José Míquez Bonino correctly observes that such a position reduces sanctification to mystical union with Christ without any practical application. Bonino poses the question:

> [Is the course of human history] a merely human action, a sort of meaningless pantomime, while beyond and outside, another Actor writes and performs his own script until the day he finally sweeps clean the scene of history and inaugurates a new, totally different drama?[23]

Bonino continues:

> Our sanctification must not be measured by some idealistically conceived norm of perfection, or by some equally unreal purity of motivation, but by the concrete demand of the present *kairos*. There is an action, a project, an achievement that is required of

---

[20] The place of evangelism and revival was key to the development of Pentecostalism. The critique is not to deny their importance to the movement, but to emphasize the shift in outcome. Early Pentecostals were driven 'out' to the world in all the ways indicated previously. Evangelism and revival were keys to social concern and engagement. The shift indicated is one toward more personal and 'mystical' outcomes while moving away from social concern.

[21] I agree with Castelo, *Revisioning Pentecostal Ethics*, p. 19, that this shift to more personal concerns, in part, resulted from 'the movement becoming more culturally mainstream, and with such a move, early American Pentecostalism strove to become more like its Evangelical counterparts'.

[22] In the twenty-first century this concern with personal vices has also been identified with an irrational commitment to various political ideologies, nationalism, and the exclusiveness of fundamentalist theologies.

[23] José Míguez Bonino, 'Wesley's Doctrine of Sanctification from a Liberationist Perspective', in Theodore Runyon (ed.), *Sanctification & Liberation* (Nashville: Abingdon, 1981), pp. 49-63 (61-62).

us now; there is an action that embodies the service of love to-day.[24]

If Pentecostals are indeed an 'eschatological community' led by the Spirit whose theology results from a distinct spirituality that includes 'discerning reflection upon lived reality',[25] it follows that faithful commitment to being the 'holy people of God' requires serious reflection on the social implications of holiness. The challenge is to engage in theological synthesis that is consistent with the foundational understandings of the movement while carefully submitting the process to theological critique. Fossilization is as dangerous, maybe more so, as uncritical revision. What is needed is construction faithful to the hermeneutical process that is attuned to the voice of the Holy Spirit, processed within the community of faith, and consistent with the biblical text. The following synthesis must be dependent upon this integrative process.

Synthesis

At the heart of the current discussion is the issue of identity. The probing question is concerned with how we, as the people of God, are to be in the world. That is, there is a 'way of being in the world' that is consistent with our identity with God as His peculiar people and faithful to the call to 'be holy as God is holy'. Daniel Castelo articulates this way of being in the world as 'embodiment'. That is 'a person's spiritual integrity that is instantiated by the power of God upon a person's life and sustained through the practice of spiritual disciplines in an ongoing and constant way'.[26] Embodied life gives evidence, in a practical way, of true transformation by the Spirit, consistency with God's call to righteousness, and is expressive of true holiness. It is the work of the Triune God as we move from self-interest, confessing our sins, to total surrender, to the transforming presence of the Spirit working in us. With this, we become partakers of divine life. The corporate implication, for the community of faith, is a coinherence of doxology: 'a response to the experience of salvation that anticipates the kingdom of glory. [That is],

---

[24] Bonino, 'Wesley's Doctrine of Sanctification', p. 63.
[25] Land, *Pentecostal Spirituality*, p. 34.
[26] Castelo, *Revisioning Pentecostal Ethics*, p. 9.

in the eschatological sense, the Triune God is a mystery which is only manifested to us in the experience of salvation'.[27]

Jürgen Moltmann describes the experience as 'a new *divine presence* … where … in the Spirit God dwells in [humans] himself.[28] Through the sending of the Spirit there is an opening of the Trinity: a movement into which all people are drawn to partake of the "inner Trinitarian life" of God'.[29] The God who opens Himself, makes room and continues to make room for the other, is not a disinterested, wholly other God who is unapproachable. He is not only immanent but also imminent. This is a God who is engaged, who is near, who is passionate about those He created. Moreover, Christ suffered for us and with us, therefore, spirituality is a *real* encounter that cuts to the very core of our being, transforming our affections, so that we are truly participants in the divine life as well as the life of the community of faith.[30] It is systemic or ontological change within the community of faith (every person) by the agency of the Holy Spirit, is a creative process that begins the work of conforming us to the image of God (Rom. 8.29) and establishes for us a unique or particular way of being in the world.

A new way of being in the world results directly from the transformation of the Spirit who effects the change within us and through whom we participate in the life of God. Participation in the life of God, in turn, implies focus on the affections as the identifying characteristics of the believer and as 'the heart of Pentecostal spirituality'.[31] These affections are 'deep emotions *that* are the fruit of the Holy Spirit and are formed in those who believe the gospel of Jesus Christ and construes the world accordingly'.[32] The result is that 'righteousness, holiness, and power of God are correlated with distinctive dispositional affections which are the integrating core of

---

[27] Jürgen Moltmann, *The Trinity and the Kingdom of God* (Minneapolis: Fortress Press, 1993), p. 161.

[28] Moltmann, *The Trinity and the Kingdom of God*, p. 104. Scripture reference is 1 Cor 6.19. Moltmann sees this as consistent with the Pauline injunction that 'your body is a temple of the Holy Spirit'.

[29] Moltmann, *The Trinity and the Kingdom of God*, p. 127.

[30] Terry Johns, 'Dancing With the Spirit: Story, Theology, and Ethics', in S.J. Land, R.D. Moore, & J.C. Thomas (eds.), *Passover, Pentecost & Parousia: Studies in Celebration of the Life and Ministry of R. Hollis Gause* (JPTSup 35, Blandford Forum: Deo Publishing, 2010), pp. 191-208 (205).

[31] Johns, 'Dancing With the Spirit', p. 44

[32] Land, *Pentecostal Spirituality*, p. 134.

Pentecostal spirituality'.[33] Therefore, true Pentecostal spirituality is only seen when 'the affections in Christ and the power of the Spirit are all fused in a call to Christian character and vocation'.[34] This in turn requires social expression by humans that is consistent with the inner life of the Triune God.

Transformed affections are the core of our new identity. Real change is represented – genuine transformation that is ontological in nature. With the transformation of the affections a change of *being* takes place. We do not simply identify with God, but are transformed to the very presence of God, and participate, through the Holy Spirit, in the life of God. Every relationship is affected and our way of being in the world is repositioned. That is, our transformed nature results in a new expression of life and values.

Additionally, with John Wesley and others, transformation of the affections represents a restoration of the *imago Dei* to the believer. This is consistent with the previous argument that 'salvation is participation in the divine life'. The restoration of the *imago Dei* makes us more like God (*theosis*) and is a progressive sanctification of the affections unto the perfection of the *eschaton*. Consistent with Wesley, the penultimate expression of the 'affections as integrating core' and the *image of God* in us is love (pure and simple love for God and neighbor [the other]). It is the identifying mark of 'participation in the divine life'. Wesley referred to this transformation as full or entire sanctification where there is 'no mixture of any contrary affections'.[35]

Spirituality as restoration of *imago Dei* implies a life that reflects or mirrors in our social relationships the actual relational life of God in Trinity. Trinitarian relationality is 'perichoretic interrelatedness' where each person of the trinity fully participates in the life of the others.[36] *Perichoresis* is 'being-in-one-another, permeation without confusion'. Individuality is not compromised, but a unique relational existence that is the nature of Trinity is predominant: 'To be a divine person is *by nature* in relation to other persons. It is only [in] the communion of love [that] each person comes to be what he/she

---

[33] Land, *Pentecostal Spirituality*, p. 23

[34] Land, *Pentecostal Spirituality*, p. 129

[35] Harold Lindstrom, *Wesley & Sanctification: A Study in the Doctrine of Salvation* (Grand Rapids: Zondervan, 1980), p. 142.

[36] Land, *Pentecostal Spirituality*, p. 197.

is, entirely with reference to the other.'[37] This is consistent with the witness of Scripture that reveals God as self-communicating love. Love is the ultimate expression of social Trinity (in perichoretic relationship). Self-communication is not due to necessity or duty (which would place limitations on an eternal and limitless God). Rather, it is the result of the very nature and character of God. It is who God is – his very being. God is love (1 Jn 4.8). Because love is the self-expression of God's very character and is not due to necessity or duty, God loves the world with the same love that defines his very being and existence.[38]

It is important to note that self-giving love is expressed within social community. The persons of the social trinity are in loving relationship with one another: each fully giving of themselves to the other. Loving social relationship implies an identity of *person* that is also socially defined. That is, person is more than self-awareness and is only identifiable within a community of mutual relationships and responsibility. The perichoretic relationship of the immanent Trinity suggests that person is defined as 'from one another, for one another'.[39] It is ultimately about intimate relationship with the other. Creation in God's 'image and likeness' (*imago Dei*) implies that human existence is to reflect the true living reality of God. As human subjects, the only possibility of reflecting the image of God, corresponding to God, participating in the divine life, is in a 'communion of persons'.[40] It is by communal life that person exists as subject and where meaning for person is found through mutual giving and receiving. It is only in the face of the other that our existence has meaning.[41] It is extremely important to note that simply being together is at best minimal expression of 'reflecting the divine image'. 'The maximum consists in perfect "being toward others," in the love in which giving self to one another affirms the other and

---

[37] Catherine Mowry LaCugna, *God for Us: The Trinity & Christian Life* (San Francisco: Harper San Francisco, 1991), p. 271.

[38] For further development of this idea see: Moltmann, *The Trinity & the Kingdom*, pp. 51-54.

[39] Stanley J. Grenz, *The Social God and the Relational Self: A Trinitarian Theology of the* Imago Dei (Louisville: Westminster John Knox Press, 2001), p. 55.

[40] Miroslav Volf, *After Our Likeness: The Church as the Image of the Trinity* (Grand Rapids: Eerdmans, 1998), p. 207.

[41] Volf, *After Our Likeness*, p. 206.

thereby affirms self'.[42] Through love, life is given – not taken. This
represents a reflection through us of God's unconditional love
(ἀγάπη). It cannot be manufactured from necessity or duty, but
must flow from the core of our being in 'newness of life' that is indicative of transformation by the Holy Spirit (ontologically, a new
way of being in the world).

This is the ultimate contextualization! But, care must be taken
not to assume that participation in the Divine life is simply the result of *individual* participation with God. It is rather 'the indwelling
of the Spirit in common to everyone that makes the church into a
communion corresponding to the Trinity, a communion in which
personhood and sociality are equiprimal'.[43] This peculiar orientation
represents the true proleptic effect of transformation through the
work of the eschatological Spirit in the people of God. If these
propositions are true, then it is not possible to correspond truthfully
and faithfully – in any other fashion – to others. Again, there are
significant implications for the social orientation of holiness life.

The eschatological implications of the discussion are paramount
for an understanding of the faithful expression of holiness. Implied
is an understanding of eschatology that is more balanced than the
dispensational version critiqued earlier.

Peter Althouse proposes such an eschatology:

> The kingdom is both present but breaking into history under the
> divine providence of God. Revising Pentecostal eschatology as
> 'proleptic anticipation,' which demands our present, active par-
> ticipation for the kingdom, but also anticipates that the kingdom
> will break into the world as a sovereign act, offers a more biblical
> and theologically credible view of Pentecostal eschatology.[44]

Eschatology with 'proleptic anticipation' makes room for a more
holistic understanding of holiness as both personal commitment
and social responsibility. The consistent in-breaking of the kingdom
into the here and now (through the Holy Spirit and all of the gifts)
is an anticipation of greater things to come. Emphasized is our re-

---

[42] Volf, *After Our Likeness*, p. 207.
[43] Volf, *After Our Likeness*, p. 213.
[44] Peter Althouse, '"Left Behind" – Fact or Fiction: Ecumenical Dilemmas
of the Fundamentalist Millenarian Tensions within Pentecostalism', *Journal of Pentecostal Theology* 13.2 (2005), pp. 187-207 (201-202).

sponsibility to continue to pray 'thy kingdom come' while living out the kingdom that is to come as 'thy will be done in earth as in heaven'. Such an eschatological vision calls for responsible behavior both personally and socially.

Reconstructing Pentecostal eschatology offers an interesting and challenging focal point for continuing work in moral theology. The focus on salvation as eschatological challenges static views of salvation and pushes the discussion to consider more integrative and holistic purposes. If salvation is essentially eschatological (and I believe it is) then the concern for integration of personal and social ethics is especially pertinent. An eschatological focus also opens the dialogue for additional discussion concerning the presence of the kingdom due to the advent of the Spirit. A primary question is: 'What are the ethical implications for people of the kingdom – the peaceable kingdom of God – who must negotiate the tension of living between the peaceable kingdom and a violent world'? Continued attention to formulating an eschatology that is consistent with our commitment to experience with the eschatological Spirit is paramount to recapturing our ethical base.[45]

The discussion has emphasized the place of 'peace witness' as an early expression of holiness of life within Pentecostalism and the growing lack of concern for such a witness. The argument developed to this point has called for a particular 'way of being' in the world that is consistent with the ethos of Pentecostalism, a theology of 'identity' (being) that is reflective of our creation as *imago Dei*, and an eschatological vision that is proleptic in nature while anticipating the coming peaceable kingdom of God. By following the current argument, it is consistent to propose that a primary expression of holiness is commitment to a life of peacemaking.

Our eschatological trajectory is from God, who created us in His image, to God who encompasses the entirety of creation. This same God is actively participating in human history through the advent,

---

Thankfully, Pentecostals are continuing to take a fresh look at eschatology. This is especially represented by the creative work by Pentecostals on the Apocalypse. Cf. John Christopher Thomas, *The Apocalypse: A Literary and Theological Commentary* (Cleveland, TN: CPT Press, 2012); Robby Waddell, *The Spirit of the Book of Revelation* (JPTSup 30, Blandford Forum: Deo Publishing, 2006). The work of Peter Althouse, *The Spirit of the Last Days: Pentecostal Eschatology in Conversation with Jürgen Moltmann* (JPTSup 25, London: T&T Clark, 2003) is also significant.

life and death of Christ, by the active presence of the Holy Spirit, and at the same time is establishing the Kingdom that is to come. The implications are myriad, but for the sake of the current thesis, an important implication demands consideration. Creation of humans in the image of God immediately resulted in 'walking with God' (face to face) as the bearers of His image in an environment of true *shalom*. The garden is a vision of what a life of perfect holiness is intended to be. It is in the garden that the vision of 'the lion laying down with the lamb' is first actualized and later prophetically announced as kingdom anticipation. It is sin that allowed violence to capture human imagination (and this the result of turning to self-interest). God's response to the problem was to send one to restore Shalom – the Prince of Peace. Through the sacrifice of Christ (the Prince of Peace) the eschatological journey back to Shalom is established: the coming of the Peaceable Kingdom.[46]

The full eschatological trajectory from God to God offers evidence for a commitment to peaceful existence that early Pentecostals identified as paramount to the life of holiness. The extended implication is that holiness requires commitment to preservation of life as expression of an eschatological kingdom ethic. Stanley Hauerwas articulates this position well:

> Our concern to protect and enhance life is a sign of our confidence that in fact we live in a new age in which it is possible to see the other as God's creation. We do not value life as an end in itself – there is much worth dying for; rather, all life is valued, even the lives of our enemies, because God has valued them.[47]

The new age in which we live was established through the advent of Christ – his life, suffering, death, and resurrection. It is in Christ that we have the first sign of the 'kingdom that is to come'. It is through His sending of the Holy Spirit that the people of God are enabled to live the 'kingdom ethic'. As the kingdom continues to be established, those who are named with Christ must be committed to every aspect of the kingdom that represents the reign of God

---

[46] According to John Howard Yoder 'the message that Christ died for his enemies is our reason for ultimately being responsible for the neighbor's – and especially the enemy's – life'. John Howard Yoder, *The Original Revolution: Essays on Christian Pacifism* (Scottdale, PA: Herald Press, 1971), p. 42.

[47] Stanley Hauerwas, *The Peaceable Kingdom: A Primer on Christian Ethics* (Notre Dame: University of Notre Dame Press, 1983), p. 88.

over all things. By doing this, the people of God offer a serious critique against world systems that are 'anti-Christ' and embody a spiritual integrity that is consistent with the coming kingdom. This is true proleptic anticipation.

It may not have been clearly articulated or formally developed, but there is evidence that early pioneers of the Pentecostal movement integrated an eschatological understanding in their expression of holiness belief and practice. Though it did not endure for long, commitment to a definitive peace witness was central to the early holiness expression. Based on the short critique and construction in this essay, the importance of peace witness to the practice of holiness is worthy of further investigation. It is also a concern of theological fidelity. A logical place to begin is to reevaluate our eschatology. We have been overwhelmed with sensationalist ideas of the end times and have lost our fervor for a robust theological understanding. The stakes are too large for accommodation to imprison us. I am in agreement with Heinz-Dietrich Wendland:

> Eschatology is the root and ground of all Christian criticism of society as it is. Eschatology produces that uneasiness which refuses to admit that Christians or Churches can ever anywhere be quite satisfied with the social structure as it has so far developed or as it now exists.[48]

It is believed that the moral theology envisioned here, or one similar to it, may very well be the needed catalyst to develop the concern for social expressions of holiness that reflects God's heart for the world. *Shalom.*

---

[48] Heinz-Dietrich Wendland, 'The Relevance of Eschatology for Social Ethics', *Ecumenical Review* 5.4 (1953), pp. 364-68 (365).

16

HOLINESS AS PLAY: A DEVELOPMENTAL PERSPECTIVE ON CHRISTIAN FORMATION*

STEPHEN PARKER**

Pentecostals have not always seen the value of psychological theory, especially developmental theory, for reflecting upon spiritual formation. This omission can create various problems. For instance, it can leave the impression that holiness arrives 'full grown' in the life of the believer (e.g. is holiness an accomplished vs. on-going work). Similarly, the role of human participation is debated (e.g. is righteousness infused vs. imputed; is holiness entirely God's doing or is there human cooperation in some way). This essay explores the value of using developmental theory to reflect upon the life of holiness. It seeks to show how a psychological lens might complement theological perspectives on spiritual development.

Since developmental theory takes in a broad spectrum it is necessary to specify one's approach. For instance, some of the more substantive developmental theories include those of Piaget on cognitive development, Kohlberg on moral reasoning, Erikson on psychosocial development, and Bowlby's pioneering work on attachment.[1] Various Christian authors have offered applications of these

* An earlier version of this chapter was presented at the 42nd Annual Meeting of the Society for Pentecostal Studies, Seattle, WA. I wish to thank Robert Drovdahl for comments on an earlier version of this paper.
** Stephen Parker (PhD, Emory University) is Professor in the School of Psychology and Counseling, Regent University, Virginia Beach, VA.
[1] See for instance Jean Piaget, 'Piaget's theory', in P. Mussen (ed.), *Charmichel's Manual of Child Psychology* (New York: John Wiley and Sons, 3rd edn, 1970), I, pp. 703-32; Lawrence Kohlberg, 'Moral Stages and Moralization', in T. Lickona (ed.), *Moral Development and Behavior* (New York: Holt, Rinehart and Winston, 1976), pp.

developmental theories to spiritual formation.[2] In this essay I work with the developmental theory of D.W. Winnicott, the British paediatrician and psychoanalyst whose work is associated with object relations psychology, a developmental theory that explores how early relational interactions and patterns shape one's personality.[3]

Winnicott's theory provides a basis for examining how one's views and expressions of holiness tend to change with one's development and growth in the quality of one's relationships.[4] For Winnicott, the journey toward healthy relating is grounded in the growing ability to differentiate self and other. Unfinished work in this journey is characterized either by an on-going sense of merger with the other or by an emotional/psychological splitting within the self or within perceptions of the other that leads to exclusion or withdrawal in relationships. This essay explores how the various relational options of merger, splitting/exclusion, and differentiation play out in spiritual formation and the life of holiness. For instance, how do the variant patterns of growth or stagnation that Winnicott outlines manifest in one's relationship with God? The essay also extracts from Winnicott's developmental theory a vision of health that draws upon the tension between creativity and destruction that is present when people engage in what Winnicott called 'play', a quality of relating characterized by an ability to enter into a 'transitional', life-giving state often present in childhood but sometimes

---

31-53; Erik Erikson, *Childhood and Society* (New York: W.W. Norton, 1950); John Bowlby, *Attachment* (New York: Basic Books, 2nd edn, 1983).

[2] See for instance Tim Clinton and Joshua Straub, *God Attachment: Why You Believe, Act, and Feel the Way You Do about God* (New York: Howard Books, 2010); James Wilhoit and John Dettoni, *Nurture That Is Christian: Developmental Perspectives on Christian Education* (Grand Rapids: Baker Books, 1995).

[3] See for instance D.W. Winnicott, 'Transitional Objects and Transitional Phenomena', in *Collected Papers: Through Paediatrics to Psycho-analysis* (New York: Basic Books, 1958), pp. 229-42; *idem*, 'Ego Distortions in Terms of True and False Self', in *The Maturational Processes and the Facilitating Environment* (Madison, CT: International Universities Press, 1965), pp. 140-52.

[4] See for instance Stephen Parker, 'Hearing God's Spirit: Impacts of Developmental History on Adult Religious Experience', *Journal of Psychology and Christianity* 18 (1999), pp. 154-64; *idem*, 'Winnicott and the Spiritual Self', in P. Hegy (ed.), *What Do We Imagine God to Be? The Function of 'God Images' in Our Lives* (Lewiston, NY: Edwin Mellen Press, 2007), pp. 221-32; *idem*, 'Winnicott's Object Relations Theory and the Work of the Holy Spirit', *Journal of Psychology and Theology* 36 (2008), pp. 285-93; Stephen Parker and Edward Davis, 'The False Self in Christian Contexts: A Winnicottian Perspective' *Journal of Psychology and Christianity* 28 (2009), pp. 315-25.

lost to adults.[5] This ability to play is a hallmark of healthy relating for Winnicott; it makes life feel real and worth living. The paper concludes by exploring how Winnicott's vision of play provides a lens for thinking about the holy life.

Winnicott's Developmental Theory

As an object relations theorist Winnicott outlined human development in three broad stages. Development begins with an infant unable to distinguish itself from its caregiver and eventuates with a child able to distinguish self from its environment.[6] Of prime interest to Winnicott is the middle territory between these two developmental points.[7] This section outlines the broad contours of Winnicott's developmental theory, especially his focus on this intermediate area. It then looks at a specific dimension of healthy development associated with this intermediate area: the capacity to play.

Three stages of development; three ways of relating

For Winnicott the infant begins life in a state of merger, a state in which the infant is not able to distinguish itself from its environment. Winnicott formulated this theory from observing the interactions between thousands of infants and mothers (Winnicott saw approximately 60,000 paediatric cases over the course of his career; however, one also recognizes the speculative quality of these observations. The infant is not developed enough to say what he or she is actually thinking or experiencing.). From these observations Winnicott noted that just before and just after the birth of her child a mother is hyper-attuned to her infant and its needs so that she seems to anticipate the need almost before it is expressed.[8] During a period in which the infant is absolutely dependent upon its environment, this period of 'primary maternal preoccupation' establishes an atmosphere in which the infant begins to experience itself (at

---

[5] D.W. Winnicott, 'Playing: A Theoretical Statement', in *Playing and Reality* (New York: Routledge, 1971), pp. 38-52, and *idem*, 'Playing: Creative Activity and the Search for the Self', in *Playing and Reality* (New York: Routledge, 1971), pp. 53-64.

[6] See for instance, D.W. Winnicott, 'Use of an Object and Relating through Identifications', in *Playing and Reality* (New York: Routledge, 1971), pp. 86-94. See also Parker, 'Hearing God's Spirit'.

[7] See Winnicott, 'Transitional Objects'.

[8] D.W. Winnicott, 'Primary Maternal Preoccupation', in *Collected Papers: Through Paediatrics to Psycho-analysis* (New York: Basic Books, 1958), pp. 300-305.

least temporarily) as the omnipotent master and creator of its world. That is, it does not experience itself and the world (including the mother as an object in that world) as separate entities. When it is hungry, the mother with breast or bottle appears as though by magic; that is, as a creation that the infant seems to control. Relationships at this point in life are very one-sided; the 'other' is perceived as part of the self.

According to Winnicott, it is fortuitous for the infant that the mother's heightened sensitivity to its needs provides this temporary, though necessary illusion of omnipotence. Without it, the infant is condemned forever to seek after (albeit unconsciously) that which it was denied. However, it is even more fortuitous that having allowed this brief illusion the mother disillusions the infant through her inevitable failures to maintain this anticipatory sensitivity. For without these failures the infant cannot begin to perceive its environment as other than self and may persist in the illusion of its godlikeness (perhaps you have suffered at the hands of someone who seems not to have gotten over this stage of development!).

However, healthy development lies along a trajectory of learning to distinguish self from other. The maturing person is able to recognize the separate existence and needs of the other. The person comes to see that others are more than his or her projections and fantasies about them (what married person has not discovered this rude truth about the one we loved). With this growing ability to differentiate, relationships take on a different quality. Not only can one recognize self as a subject (a self-aware consciousness) in the world, one can recognize other self-aware 'subjects' (or 'objects' to use the technical language of object relations) who can stand both with and/or over against one at times. In Winnicott's language one's projections are 'destroyed'. With the destruction of these mentally constructed 'objects' with which one was interacting, one can now relate to the actual person. This is a higher level of development and a more mature way of relating for Winnicott.[9]

But between these two developmental points there is a rich territory of growth. Winnicott was especially interested in explorations and explanations of this middle area. He dubbed this area variously

---

[9] Winnicott, 'Use of an Object', pp. 86-94.

'transitional space', 'the intermediate area', and 'potential space'.[10] He is best known for his concept of the infant's use of this intermediate space via the special qualities attributed to objects used within this space. Winnicott called these 'transitional objects', a reference to things the infant uses to soothe and comfort itself during times of transition from the mother's presence to her absence, especially at bed time. Teddy bears and security blankets are the most commonly recognized. What parent does not know of the infant and small child's investment of these objects with a special quality that makes them alive to the infant in ways they are never alive to the caregiver. Winnicott describes this special quality as one that is in between reality and subjectivity, between the demands of the outer world and the projections/hallucinations of the inner world. Thus, these objects participate in both worlds while belonging to neither entirely. Although a transitional object might have been externally given, its life comes from the infant's psychic investment in the object. Furthermore, Winnicott points out that it is essential to this space that this area is never overtly challenged. That is, the caregiver does not ask of the child: did you create this teddy bear or did grandmother give it to you. The infant has given it qualities that could never be conferred from outside (by mothers or grandmothers). Thus, it is proper to say the infant has 'created' this object. This blending of the inner and outer gives these objects an illusory quality but by illusory Winnicott does not mean delusional or hallucinatory; rather he points to their creative potential.

Thus, it is this intermediate area that is the key to understanding creativity and aliveness for Winnicott. It was to what happened in this area that Winnicott returned again and again, ever expanding his ideas about what was going on there.[11] It is this area and what transpires there that is the basis for culture for Winnicott. It is the breeding ground for art, religion, even the creative dimensions of science. Thus, a certain type of relationship may emerge from shared intermediate qualities as long as there is no required adoption of particular stances. All human beings return to this area throughout life as a place of rest from the exigencies of the outer

---

[10] Winnicott, 'Transitional Objects', pp. 229-42; *idem*, 'Playing: A Theoretical Statement', pp. 38-52; and *idem*, 'Playing: Creative Activity', pp. 53-64.

[11] Winnicott, 'Playing: A Theoretical Statement', pp. 38-52; and *idem*, 'Playing: Creative Activity', pp. 53-64.

world and the terrors of the inner world.[12] This intermediate area is critical to understanding Winnicott's ideas concerning play.[13]

Winnicott's Theory of Play

Because play has been so variously described[14] it is important to remember that this essay focuses on Winnicott's conceptualization. For instance, play is often compared with amusement or contrasted with productivity; conversely play is analysed as a functional activity (i.e. play as its own kind of productivity). These comparisons and contrasts are not Winnicott's focus, nor are they the focus for the implications to be drawn from his theory.

However, it would be a mistake to think Winnicott was unaware that play was often treated as the child's 'work'. Early in his career he had written an essay, 'Why Children Play', focused on the functional aspects of play: it helps express aggression, master anxiety, gain experience, make social contacts, communicate with others, and promotes integration of the personality. It does this latter by helping to join together the child's growing awareness of both the inner and outer worlds and their differences.[15] However, apart from this functional analysis of play, Winnicott acknowledges that sometimes children play simply because they like doing so. It was to this latter point that Winnicott returned near the end of his life in an attempt to develop a 'theory of play' that moved beyond this functional analysis.[16]

In his theory of play Winnicott makes a distinction between play and playing. The distinction is that between a functional understanding of 'play' (i.e. its purpose, what it accomplishes, etc.) and play as a state of being. This latter he calls 'playing' and points to a more substantive approach to play – play as something in and of

---

[12] Winnicott, 'Transitional Objects', pp. 229-42; *idem*, 'Playing: A Theoretical Statement', pp. 38-52; and *idem*, 'Playing: Creative Activity', pp. 53-64.

[13] D.W. Winnicott, 'Place Where We Live', in *Playing and Reality* (New York: Routledge, 1971), pp. 104-10.

[14] See James Evans, *Playing: Christian Explorations of Daily Living* (Minneapolis: Fortress Press, 2010) for a survey of the various ways play has been characterized by anthropologists, sociologists, theologians, philosophers, psychologists, and entrepreneurs.

[15] D.W. Winnicott, 'Why Children Play', in *The Child and the Outside World* (London: Tavistock, 1957), pp. 149-52. See Jean-Jacque Rousseau, *Emile, or on Education* (trans. A. Bloom; New York: Basic Books, 1979), for the notion of the child's play as its work.

[16] Winnicott, 'Playing: A Theoretical Statement', pp. 38-52.

itself, not needing to satisfy a function. Although Winnicott does not always adhere to his distinction in his own use of these terms, sometimes using the word play to speak of the state of being rather than a function, with this distinction Winnicott also points out that it is not the content of play with which he is concerned.

As a state of being rather than a function, playing is characterized by several qualities. First, one would say that playing involves a sense of aliveness and freedom for Winnicott. This sense of aliveness includes the ability to be surprised and opens up an area of creative living. There is a quality of freedom and relaxation in play because it is spontaneous and not restricted to compliance with the demands of the external world.[17] As a state of being play is connected to the search for the true self. 'It is in playing and only in playing that the individual child or adult is able to be creative and to use the whole personality, and it is only in being creative that the individual discovers the self'.[18] Thus, this ability to enter into the creative aspects of play makes playing a measure of healthiness. The inability to play bodes ill for the person, whereas the ability to play allows for the toleration of a few symptoms, for play points to hopefulness and an ability to develop a whole personality.[19] The ability to play also points to the development of other capacities such as the ability to use symbols.[20]

Playing as a state of being occurs in the intermediate area. 'This area of playing is not inner psychic reality. It is outside the individual, but it is not the external world'.[21] For Winnicott there is a direct connection between playing and transitional phenomena. Playing is a way of joining together inner and outer reality. This movement has several implications for Winnicott.

Because playing occurs in the intermediate area, it has qualities that draw from the inner world though it cannot be reduced to in-

---

[17] In addition to Winnicott, 'Playing: A Theoretical Statement', pp. 38-52; and *idem*, 'Playing: Creative Activity', see Stephen Parker, *Winnicott and Religion* (Lanham, MD: Jason Aronson, 2012), and Steven Tuber, *Attachment, Play, and Authenticity* (Lanham, MD: Jason Aronson, 2008).

[18] Winnicott, 'Playing: Creative Activity', p. 54.

[19] D.W. Winnicott, 'What Do We Mean by a Normal Child', in *The Child and the Family* (London: Tavistock, 1957), pp. 100-106.

[20] Winnicott, 'Transitional Objects', pp. 229-42; *idem*, 'Playing: A Theoretical Statement', pp. 38-52; and *idem*, 'Playing: Creative Activity', pp. 53-64.

[21] Winnicott, 'Playing: A Theoretical Statement', p. 51.

ner psychic reality. In play the child manipulates external reality in the service of an inner reality. (This is not to be confused with hallucination.) An observer might see this aspect of playing by noting the intense 'preoccupation' that often characterizes the young child at play. In playing, there is a 'near withdrawal state' (similar to concentration in an older child) in which 'the playing child inhabits an area that cannot be easily left, nor can it easily admit intrusions'.[22]

However, playing also draws upon the reality of the outer world. Playing is a means for joining these two worlds in the child's experience. The child is able to link his or her inner reality with the world around him or her in ways that others can begin to interact with. Winnicott speaks of how the mother introduces her play into the baby's playing (infants have varying ability to respond to this intrusion). He also argues that there is a line of development from transitional phenomena to play and from play to shared playing (i.e. grouping together) and from this shared playing to participation in culture, including religion.

Because play is on the border between inner and outer reality it also has a precarious quality. It is characterized by anxiety as well as delight. Playing can be frightening according to Winnicott because it participates in this intermediate area. 'The precariousness of play belongs to the fact that it is always on the theoretical line between the subjective and that which is objectively perceived'.[23] What Winnicott means by this is that play can feel dangerous because the child is apt to get lost in either its subjectivity, or play may be lost (become laborious) if too much demand is placed on the child from the outside world.

There is another way in which playing might become frightening to the child. Playing can be frightening because it can be an arena for the expression of aggression; playing can become dangerous and violent. Because its excitement can feel overwhelming at times, the child may fear its potential for destructiveness and restrict its spontaneous excitement. Similarly, the outside world may demand a compliance that quashes the child's spontaneity and creativity. With compliance, play ceases.

---

[22] Winnicott, 'Playing: A Theoretical Statement', p. 51.
[23] Winnicott, 'Playing: A Theoretical Statement', p. 50.

Before leaving this summary of Winnicott's theory of play, one must note a problem in Winnicott's descriptions. In speaking exuberantly about the positive qualities of play, at times Winnicott seems to imply that to dwell permanently in the intermediate state is desirable. After all, he describes this as the place 'where we most of the time are when we are experiencing life'.[24] However, he also is aware that we do not always feel alive (perhaps from compliance with demands of the external world). At other times he speaks of the intermediate area as one to which adults return periodically as a respite from the pressures of either or both the inner and outer worlds and he recognizes that at some point maturity requires that we differentiate between the two worlds.[25] It seems best to interpret Winnicott at this point as promoting play as a state in which one tries to dwell as much as possible, but not a place in which one can permanently dwell, though he is not entirely clear on this point.

Implications of Winnicott's Developmental Theory For Understanding the Life of Holiness

This section looks at some broad implications of Winnicott's developmental theory for understanding the life of holiness. It then turns its attention to the specific implications of thinking about the life of holiness as a life characterized by play.

Holiness and the Stages of Development and Relating

This section looks at the implications of the stages of development, which in turn shape stages of relating and how these might work their way out in the life of holiness. That is to say, it explores how one's developmental history might carry over into one's view of the spiritual life and into the way one relates to God. It begins by recalling the two boundary points of development: merger and differentiation of self and other. How might the developmental patterns that emerge from these boundary points effect the life of holiness?

Early merger stage.

Because this stage carries the greatest potential for problems in relational and emotional development, the potential carryover of these deficits into one's relationship with God is greater. Recall that dur-

[24] Winnicott, 'Place', p. 104.
[25] Winnicott, 'Transitional Objects', pp. 229-42.

ing the early stage when the infant is unable to distinguish self from other, Winnicott outlined two tasks for the mother: to provide an illusory experience of omnipotence for the infant and to then disillusion the infant through her inevitable failures to anticipate perfectly and meet the infant's needs.[26] The way the infant comes to grips with failure to experience these moments of illusion and disillusion carries over not only into the way the infant faces life in general, but has specific implications for how he or she might relate to others including God. Let us begin with a failure to experience the moment of illusion (i.e. the infant has to adapt prematurely to environmental demands).

For the infant denied the momentary experience of an illusion of omnipotence, God (as symbol of the ultimate environment) is a withholding God; an unreliable God who can be threatening, demanding, and/or engulfing. How is the infant (and later adult) to relate to such a God? Given that its experience is not well differentiated, the infant tends to respond with a cluster of undifferentiated negative emotions. One might be fearful of a threatening, engulfing God; one might be angry with a withholding God or perhaps sad because God is so unreliable. Alternately, the infant might simply disengage emotionally. These emotional responses can motivate various behavioral responses.

One might seek to placate such a God as a way to manage the negative emotions. If one can please God enough God might bestow what was never had. Holiness might then become a life devoted to self-denial and sacrifice; perhaps to a hyper-obedience to rules and regulations as a way to earn God's favor. The point here is not that holiness does not involve sacrifice or obedience, but to note the negative emotions that motivate such acts. The life of holiness is one lived in fear (or anger or sadness).

A second possible response is that of withdrawal. One does not want to be close (either spatially or emotionally) to such a threatening, potentially engulfing God. Here again, the withdrawal might take on various forms. One might simply withdraw from God through denial (e.g. there is no God), or one might consider oneself in relationship with God, but the nature of the relationship is one of distance. For instance, Winnicott describes one form of withdrawal

---

[26] Winnicott, 'Transitional Objects', pp. 229-42.

as a hiding of the 'true self' and substituting a compliant 'false self' that interacts with others, including God.[27] One's withdrawal might even be projected onto God; that is, God is perceived as the one who has withdrawn. Interestingly enough the relational distance might be maintained by the substitution of obedience to rules and regulations. That is, the keeping of the rules, often with great strictness, becomes a substitute for true relationship. For such a person, holiness is not relationship but mastery.

A third possible response to the negative emotions that characterize the interactions with a withholding, threatening God involves 'splits' in one's sense of self or others. Such splitting might take several forms. Hiding the true self and substituting a compliant false self is a type of splitting.[28] In this response, only part of the self participates in the quest for holiness. One's true self does not interact with God, only the false self of compliance. Splitting might also take the form of splitting self or others into categories of 'all good' or 'all bad'. God might be thought the all good one while the self is the repository of the all bad. Or the converse might be assumed: I am the all good one; God is all bad for withholding or being unreliable. An interesting possibility arises here: those who think themselves to be so sinful that God cannot forgive them. Apart from the hidden grandiosity in such a position is an opposite impetus: if I am the all bad one, then God can remain good somehow; this is preferable to facing the disappointment of an unreliable God.

When such splitting is carried over into thoughts about holiness it often manifests in a kind of either/or thinking. Holiness is either all there or all absent. If one sins a little, one might as well sin a lot! No distinction is made between degrees of sin or kinds of sin; sin is an all or nothing category. One is either saint or sinner. One cannot appreciate Luther's comment about being simultaneously saint and sinner;[29] rather one alternates in these identities. This type of splitting might also manifest as the pursuit of the idealized self. This is a version of the all good self and is not to be confused with the true

---

[27] Winnicott, 'Ego Distortions', pp. 140-52. See also Parker and Davis, 'The False Self', pp. 140-52.

[28] Winnicott, 'Ego Distortions', pp. 140-52.

[29] Martin Luther, *The Freedom of a Christian* (American Edition of Luther's Works, vol. 31; trans W.A. Lambert; Philadelphia: Muhlenberg Press, 1957), pp. 277-86.

self; the idealized self is a projection, not a reality. In pursuit of the idealized self, one cannot acknowledge one's less desirable traits. The person feels holy when doing everything right or when he or she senses no impure motive within. Conversely, when one is sinful, there is nothing within that is felt worth redeeming.

In addition to the qualities of self that might emerge from a failure to experience the momentary illusion of omnipotence, there are complementary qualities that might emerge if, having experienced this illusory moment, the infant is not disillusioned. After all, the world is not one's oyster and it has demands, some of which can be harsh. A too perfect mother who has never disappointed one's needs also ill prepares one for subsequent human interactions. Without this experience of disillusion, one continues to think of others and the world as simply extensions of the self. In its extreme form, this is the psychotic, but most people meet this attitude in less extreme forms.

The person who has not sufficiently experienced the moment of disillusion continues to struggle with the differentiation of self from other. One's own desires and needs are confused with those of God and vice versa. Because the self is not distinguished from God, holiness might then be experienced as a sense of merger or union with God. However, this is not the healthy merger of selves first differentiated and then joined (as one might have in a mature adult love relationship or the kind of union/merger the mystics spoke of),[30] but a merger born of never having sufficiently experienced differentiation. One practical way this lack of differentiation might manifest is as overfamiliarity with God. Or it might manifest in exploitation of others and God. God and others are there to meet one's needs. One cannot envision God as ever taking a position over against what he or she would desire. Nor does one see such use of others as sinful. Holiness for such a person is the pursuit of his or her own desires masked as the pursuit of God. Because one is not clearly distinguishing self from other, one cannot grasp the possibility or depth of one's capacity for self-deception (i.e. an appreciation of self-deception requires one be able to stand outside oneself). One thinks he or she is pursuing a higher vision of God when all one is

---

[30] See for instance, St. John of the Cross, *Dark Night of the Soul* (trans. E.A. Peers; New York: Doubleday, 1959).

pursuing is a more sophisticated projection. Holiness is a journey of self-affirmation, but not of the true self or the self God intends. It is rather a pursuit of the idealized self of one's fantasy. (In Jung's terms, such a person cannot appreciate that God would love his or her shadow more than the *persona* of the false self.)[31]

An important point to grasp from these implications is that all these ways of interacting with God (and others) are driven by early relational deficits that brought forth these patterns of hiding, placating, splitting, or exploiting as a way to cope with one's environment. Being rooted in such early interactions, such ways of relating are mostly unconscious. Furthermore, it is important to remember that we are speaking of one's mental constructions of God. Winnicott helps us appreciate that these mentally constructed images of God need to be "destroyed" if one is to relate to God as something other than one's projections.[32]

Toward differentiation (and integration) stage.

When we move to the other boundary point in Winnicott's developmental model, health and maturity are defined as being able to differentiate self and other with the concomitant ability to integrate varying experiences of self and other. On the positive side, when one has achieved the stage of differentiation (and integration), one can think of holiness in both/and categories. Holiness is both demand and embrace; one thinks of God as both transcendent and immanent; the holy is a mystery both *tremendum* and *fascinans* to use Otto's categories.[33] Furthermore, when one relates to others (including God) in a mature, differentiated way, one sees them as related to but not identical to oneself. In addition, at this stage of development one can entertain the possibility of one's own self-

---

[31] Carl Jung, 'Two Essays on Analytical Psychology', in *The Collected Works of C.G. Jung* (Princeton: Princeton University Press, 1966), VII, pp. 1-349.

[32] Winnicott, 'Use of an Object'. I might mention in passing that the various responses outlined above draw directly from Winnicott's categories but that some of these ways of interacting have correspondences with the responses associated with the various styles of insecure attachment that Ainsworth has identified. For instance, withdrawal from relationship is symptomatic of anxious-avoidant attachment and anger is associated with anxious-resistant attachment. See Mary Ainsworth, *Infancy in Uganda: Infant Care and the Growth of Love* (Baltimore: Johns Hopkins University Press, 1967). I wish to thank Robert Drovdahl for pointing out this connection.

[33] Rudolf Otto, *The Idea of the Holy* (London: Oxford University Press, 1923).

deception. On the negative side, arrival at the stage of differentiation holds the possibility that the exigencies of the external world can become stifling, making one feel dead.[34] Attention to the demands of the external world can press for too quick a resolution of life's paradoxes according to Winnicott. Thus, for him one never outgrows the need for the intermediate state.[35]

The intermediate area.

As noted earlier, the centerpoint of Winncott's contribution to developmental theory is the notion of the intermediate area. Everyone needs occasional respites from the demands of both the external world and the internal world. This takes place in the intermediate area. This intermediate space is essential to healthy living; it is the area where one feels alive; it is the area in which one is creative. There is an excitement to participation in this area, but also anxiety. Like the two boundary points of development, this area has implications for how one might think of the life of holiness. When one recalls that playing is a participation in this intermediate area, might one think of holiness as play? What are the implications of this idea for one's relationship with God and the life of holiness?

Holiness as Play

There are several ideas that emerge when one reflects on holiness using Winnicott's concept of play and playing. I organize these implications around three main ideas. First, since play and playing participate in the intermediate area, to think of holiness as play pushes one to transcend the simple either/or categories that characterize much of the thought regarding holiness. Secondly, to think of holiness as play is to recognize a creative dimension to the life of holiness. This aspect of the life of holiness has special implications for how Pentecostals think about the role of the imagination in the holy life. Finally, to think of holiness as play in a Winnicottian sense is to recognize anxiety producing elements that attend the holy life.

Holiness as Play Transcends Simple Either/Or Categories.

Because play participates in the intermediate area it bridges inner and outer worlds for Winnicott. This paradox of the intermediate area where the realities of external and internal worlds meet and

---

[34] Winnicott, 'Ego Distortions', pp. 140-52.
[35] Winnicott, 'Transitional Objects', pp. 229-42.

mingle without imposition from either side opens up ways of thinking about some of the dichotomous questions that have plagued
reflections on holiness. For instance, is holiness an infused reality
(one is actually holy) or an imputed reality (one is only declared holy)? Do humans make any contribution to the life of holiness or is it
all of God? To think of holiness as participating in the intermediate
area opens up a new of way of thinking about these questions. Recall that the 'realness' of the transitional object (e.g. the teddy bear)
is not because grandmother bought an object that others can see;
however, neither is its realness only in the child's mind, for there is
an object in the external world (and pity the parent who has forgotten it at a motel fifty miles back). Thus, to think of holiness as play
is to recognize a paradoxical border where what belongs to God's
work vs. human dynamics cannot be separated – the question is
inappropriate to the situation (i.e. one cannot ask the infant whether
grandmother gave the teddy bear or the infant created it, for the
answer is both and neither).

One might see the question of whether holiness is best conceived as a life disengaged from (or above) the world or as a life
engaged in transformation of the world in a similar way. Recall, that
although there is a solitary dimension to play, play opens up the
possibility of entering into relationships with others. Shared play is a
basis for grouping (including religious groupings). Thus, to think of
holiness as play means that while it might have quietist dimensions,
to be only a quietist is akin to the child who remains so engaged in
concentration as to be withdrawn from the reality of the external
world. Conversely, if one only attends to the reality of the external
world (e.g. transforming the world), one loses the ability to play (i.e.
loses the creativity that belongs to the intermediate area) and the life
of holiness might become a dull or deadening compliance with the
demands of the external world. Holiness as play provides opportunities for recognizing both the creative energy derived from personal encounter with God, but also for having that experience tem-
pered by others who might share part but not the whole of such
realities. Similarly, one can recall that being able to enter into shared
playing moves one along the trajectory of differentiation. In entering into a relationship with another, one can begin to see the other
as different from one's projections about them; it also means one
can begin to surrender the need to be omnipotent.

Holiness as Play Is Characterized by Creativity.

The second implication of thinking of holiness as play is to think of creativity as a defining characteristic of the life of holiness. Recall that for Winnicott it is in play and perhaps only in play that one is being creative. Play makes one feel alive and real. Thus, to think of holiness as play is to think of it as creative and imaginative. To be holy is to feel alive and truly oneself; that is, the self that God intends.

Contrast this with an experience of the holy life as one of constraint and life-draining demands. Holiness is often thought of as a purposive ascent up 'Jacob's ladder'. Even if not thought of as a life devoted to striving after a list of commands and prohibitions, many Pentecostals tend to think of the life of holiness in functional ways. That is, one's thoughts and efforts focus on what is gained by the life of holiness (what does it help one do). Rather than engaging in spiritual disciplines because there is a sense of delight, they are pursued primarily for certain ends. In Winnicott's terms, holiness has become a functional pursuit rather than, like playing, a state of being. But again, in Winnicottian language, we would understand holiness to involve both play and playing (i.e. it is both functional and substantive), although Pentecostals have tended to neglect the substantive side.

Nevertheless, there are elements in Pentecostalism that offer possibilities for thinking of holiness in other than functional ways. Both Baer and Manning point to playful, creative dimensions of Pentecostal worship that go beyond its functional dimensions.[36] Baer speaks of the liminal aspects of Pentecostal worship that allow a temporary suspension of the rational mind; Manning likewise speaks of Pentecostal worship as transcending empirical understandings. I have noted previously how such descriptions are reminiscent of Winnicott's portrayal of the intermediate area.[37]

---

[36] Richard Baer, 'Quaker Silence, Catholic Liturgy, and Pentecostal Glossolalia: Some Functional Similarities', in R.P. Spittler (ed.), *Perspectives on the New Pentecostalism* (Grand Rapids: Baker Book House, 1976), pp. 150-64; F.E. Manning, 'The Rediscovery of Religious Play: A Pentecostal Case', in D.F. Lancy and B.A. Tindall (eds.), *The Anthropological Study of Play: Problems and Prospects* (Cornwall: Leisure, 1976; as cited in Evans, *Playing*.

[37] Stephen Parker, *Led by the Spirit: Toward a Practical Theology of Pentecostal Discernment and Decision Making* (JPTSup 7; Sheffield: Sheffield Academic Press, 1996). See also, *idem*, 'Winnicott's Object Relations Theory', pp. 285-93.

To think of creativity as a chief characteristic of holiness raises another question for Pentecostals (and Christians in general): what is the role of imagination in the holy life? This question is connected to a larger discussion sometimes framed as the role of aesthetics vs. ethics in the religious life.[38] It is beyond the scope of this study to engage this larger issue in any depth but if creativity is a defining characteristic of play, to think of holiness as play means one must entertain the idea that use of the imagination and creativity are manifestations of the holy. Such a position has traditionally been problematic for Protestants who have usually looked on the imagination with suspicion.[39] Winnicott's work provides impetus to engage this topic afresh. Because Pentecostals have been less suspicious of the imagination[40] perhaps Pentecostals can uniquely contribute to arguments regarding the role of aesthetics in the holy life. As one example, I might point out that there is a dimension of the aesthetic that is especially applicable to Pentecostals in terms of how they discern the leading of the Spirit. I have made a case that Pentecostals discern the presence of the holy through an epistemological criterion of things 'feeling right' (an aesthetic of harmony).[41]

Related to the general Protestant suspicion of the imagination is a similar suspicion of play. In his treatise on the 'theology of play' Moltmann points out that Protestants tend to interpret the statement of the Shorter Catechism of the Westminster Confession that the chief end of humans is to glorify God and enjoy him forever with a focus on the former. Furthermore, glorifying God is defined in terms of things one does. This leads to a focus on productivity as the mark of the mature Christian; that is, work is the way one glori-

---

[38] See for instance, Rubem Alves, 'From Liberation Theologian to Poet: A Plea That the Church Move from Ethics to Aesthetics, from Doing to Beauty', *Church & Society* 83 (1993), pp. 20-24; Roland Delattre, 'Aesthetics and Ethics: Jonathan Edwards and the Recovery of Aesthetics for Religious Ethics, *Journal of Religious Ethics* 31 (2003), pp. 277-97.

[39] See for instance, William Dyrness, *Reformed Theology and Visual Culture: The Protestant Imagination from Calvin to Edwards* (Cambridge: Cambridge University Press, 2004); Evans, *Playing*; Jürgen Moltmann, *Theology of Play* (New York: Harper and Row Publishers, 1972).

[40] See James K.A. Smith, 'Is There Room for Surprise in the Natural World? Naturalism, the Supernatural, and Pentecostal Spirituality', in James K.A. Smith and Amos Yong (eds.), *Science and the Spirit: A Pentecostal Engagement with the Sciences* (Bloomington: Indiana University Press, 2010), pp. 34-49.

[41] Parker, *Led by the Spirit*, p. 111.

fies God. Things not associated with work or productivity (e.g. amusement or frivolity) tend to be seen as detractions. Christianity is a serious business without room for play. Moltmann mirrors this tradition when he argues that despite some 'play' in God's creative activity, the crucifixion lies outside any concept of play no matter how broadly conceived. How can one be joyful or playful while suffering continues for so many, he asks.[42] Lost in the traditional Protestant focus is recognition of elements in one's relationship with God that are done for enjoyment rather than for their productivity. Again, the playful, creative elements of Pentecostals' worship suggest some corrective possibilities here.[43]

Finally, as Pentecostals, I would point out that to think of holiness as play means one could think of the intermediate area (transitional space) as a place where the Holy Spirit is especially at work.[44] In this intermediate area, the Spirit both affirms and challenges us, in much the same way the mother both creates space for illusion and then disillusions the child. Similarly, the mother adds her play to the child's play so that the child can turn its play from simply being a private enterprise into something recognizable in the outside world. One can think of the Holy Spirit as engaged in similar creative, life-giving work.

Holiness as Play Has Aspects of Anxiety.

In addition to the creative dimensions of play, Winnicott pointed out that play could become dangerous, not simply because it allowed for expression of aggression, but precisely because it participated in the intermediate area where inner and outer worlds mingle; too much insistence from one side or the other and play ceases. If the inner world alone prevails, one can become psychotic whereas if the external world alone prevails one can feel dead, a hollow shell of a self.

That play can become dangerous reminds one of the insight by Otto that the holy is both a *mysterium trememdum et fascinans*.[45] It is both terrifying and inspiring. Because it is on the border between the inner and the outer worlds, holiness occurs on the border be-

---

42 Moltmann, *Theology of Play*, p. 77.
43 Baer, 'Quaker Silence'; Manning, 'The Rediscovery of Religious Play', pp. 140-44.
44 Parker, 'Winnicott's Object Relations Theory', pp. 285-93.
45 Otto, *The Idea of the Holy*, pp. 181-84.

tween the terrifying and exhilarating. To lose either of these dimensions is to risk turning the life of holiness into something akin to a private psychosis or a deadening, life-draining drudgery.

The precarious nature of play also reminds one of Winnicott's problematic suggestions that one try to dwell in this state as much as possible. For Winnicott, this is because it is only in this state that one feels truly alive. What does this mean for the life of holiness? On the one hand, if play is a state not easily left and not easily intruded upon, then holiness might be thought of as an intense concentration upon God that is not easy to leave and when intruded upon by others leaves things feeling interrupted and unfinished. And yet, the child cannot stay in that state without the risk of psychotic break with the outer world. On the other hand, it might suggest that the life of holiness as a state of play is not easily maintained; we are prone to fall into false self behavior (e.g. compliance with a list of rules). Winnicott's lack of clarity on whether one can remain in a state of play[46] makes some connections tenuous at this point, but what we may say is that holiness, as a state of being, is not achieved by a supposed merger with God that removes us from the external world and its realities and temptations (something many Pentecostals long for), nor by a constant striving that becomes ever more deadening. Rather, holiness belongs to those (perhaps increasing) moments of participation in this elusive intermediate state that makes us feel alive, creative, and our most true self, the one God has desired. In Winnicott's words we continue to return to the border between the inner and outer worlds because it is there that we know most acutely that we are (still) alive and not alone.

Finally, in speaking of the anxiety that attends to play, one further aspect of holiness as play comes to mind. Winnicott speaks of the infant's ability to tolerate the mother's momentary absences through the use of transitional objects. Similarly, infants who have had enough experience of the mother's reliability can know that she will be there when the infant 'returns' from its concentration (play). To think of holiness as play (i.e. participating in the intermediate

---

[46] Winnicott, 'Transitional Objects', pp. 229-42; and *idem*, 'Playing: Creative Activity', pp. 53-64.

state) means that the life of holiness creates a space in which one can begin to tolerate times of God's absence.[47]

Concluding Thoughts

In arguing for play as a category for thinking about the holy, it is important to note that I am not suggesting play as a kind of opiate or distraction (a kind of Marxist analysis of religion). Rather than play as a distraction, the argument is closer to the notion that play belongs to our highest expression of the human spirit in the image of God.

Neither is this essay an exhaustive review of what it might mean to think of holiness as play, not even from the discipline of developmental psychology. The insights from Winnicott need supplemented with other perspectives, especially theological ones. The affinity of Winnicott's concept of playing with certain theological ideas regarding play is especially promising. For instance, theologian James Evans's definition of play as 'a set of activities or practices that occurs in the interstices between freedom and structure, between the subject(ive) and object(ive), between creation and imitation'[48] mirrors Winnicott's understanding both in its recognition of an intermediate 'in between' quality to play as well as in its characterization of what play bridges. In the spirit of Winnicott, this paper is a playful attempt to look at the connections between Winnicott's notion of play and the life of holiness. In writing this essay I have been playing with ideas (one of the ways adults play) and have found Winnicott's theory providing some creative (playful) ways to think about how developmental psychology can illuminate the life of holiness.

The paper has demonstrated that Winnicott's developmental theory provides a useful lens for exploring the life of holiness. It shows connections between growth in one's earthly relationships and relationship with God; it shows how changes in the way one thinks about holiness and the way one relates to God are connected to developmental shifts. In particular, Winnicott's notion of play

---

[47] One might also recall that the infant's ability to tolerate the mother's absence in Ainsworth's attachment styles would have correspondences in the ability to tolerate God's absence. Note also that absence means a felt state, not that God is truly absent. See Ainsworth, *Infancy in Uganda*.

[48] Evans, *Playing*, p. 11.

(and the intermediate area) provides a useful category for thinking about holiness. This study adds psychological perspectives on spiritual formation to various theological ones and is written in the hope that understanding how one's developmental history influences one's spiritual growth can facilitate steps toward relating to God in ways less driven by the unconscious dimensions of these forces.[49]

---

[49] See for instance, Parker, 'Hearing God's Spirit', pp. 154-64; and *idem*, 'Winnicott and the Spiritual Self', pp. 221-332.

17

FROM FEAR-BASED TO HOLINESS-BASED: THOUGHTS ABOUT THE WORK OF THE HOLY SPIRIT IN YOUTH MINISTRY

Joshua Ziefle[*]

> *"The wind bloweth where it listeth, and thou hearest the sound thereof,*
> *but canst not tell whence it cometh, and whither it goeth: so is*
> *every one that is born of the Spirit." – John 3.8*

Youth ministry, at least in its contemporary state, has existed for but a small fraction of the history of the Christian faith. The form it has usually adopted is one heavily bounded by American conceptions of what such work should look like. Conditioned by factors more explicitly related to economics, culture, and race than theology, a broad sampling of the average youth ministry efforts in the United States would likely reveal numerous similarities across denominational and theological borders. The pervasiveness of popular adolescent culture combined with the ready availability and widespread nature of standard literature in the field of youth ministry has only contributed to this trend. Beyond this, a parallel and shadow force constantly at work in ministry with and for adolescents has long been more reactionary: the tendency towards fear. Just as published youth ministry curricula, popular adolescent trends, and models of youth work in the local church can have a certain homogeneity and ubiquity to them, so too has fear existed as a persistent and common motivating factor in church work with adolescents.

---

[*] Joshua R. Ziefle (PhD, Princeton Theological Seminary) is Associate Professor of Youth Ministries at Northwest University, Kirkland, WA.

Because the future always remains in some sense contingent, previous generations have regularly looked to those that follow with some measure of trepidation. Within an American Christianity that has for nearly half of a century embraced focused work with adolescents as an important part of its mission, this tilt towards fear-based youth ministry is as unfortunate as it can be pronounced. In light of these realities, I would suggest that a biblical and theological look at some of the constituent elements of American Pentecostalism, with its emphasis on a transformed and empowered life in the Holy Spirit, will provide a helpful entrée into a new vision and practice of youth ministry based not on fear but Spirit-empowered holiness.[1] While Pentecostalism is not immune to fearful approaches to youth ministry, it nevertheless carries within it the possibility for a complete revisioning of this kind of thinking. Holiness – when rightly lived under the aegis and at the impulse of the Holy Spirit – means not a fearful separation from the world but a passionate cleaving unto the things of God. True holiness is not reactionary but relational and, in relation to the triune God, pneumatological. Because of Pentecostals' historic understanding of holiness as the work of the Holy Spirit, they are uniquely placed to address the vital issues emerging and persisting in ministry work with adolescents. It is to this exploratory discussion that I now turn my attention.

It almost goes without saying that any actions or programmatic decisions made out of fear ought generally to be suspect; when it comes to youth ministry this legitimate concern should be even more pronounced. Few segments of American Christianity are exempt from anxiety, and a reactionary basis for ministry with young people – however masked or coded – has a historical basis that persists powerfully. Pentecostalism and related branches of Christianity are therefore just as susceptible to the effects of such deep-seated fear as others.

No latecomers to youth ministry, Pentecostals from their first decades were aware of the needs of younger believers in their midst. From the 1920s onward the Assemblies of God published the

---

[1] A special thanks here to Michael D. Langford, who helped inspire some of my thoughts with his paper 'Spirit-Driven Youth Ministry: Responding to Moralistic Therapeutic Deism with Robust Pneumatology' (paper presented at the annual meeting for the Association of Youth Ministry Educators, Seattle, Washington, October 2011).

Christ's Ambassador's Herald (CA Herald), a regular newsletter whose expressed purpose was to provide guidance for the younger generation within the movement. Not simply for those in their teenage years, the focus of the *CA Herald* was seemingly broad enough to encompass the needs of all those imagined to be in the rising generation. While it is encouraging that the Assemblies of God was paying such attention to its junior members during its own denominational infancy, there are clear indications that the forces of fear were not absent from its motivations. In a 1935 issue of the *CA Herald*, the newsletter reprinted a sermon entitled 'Youth in the Light of the Holy Scriptures', which among other things intimated the fears of the adult world concerning wayward youth and made an emotional appeal to avoid the ways of dissolution. Within, preacher James Savell spoke evocatively of a young man 'that died from sins of dissipation' and a young woman's misspent life – 'a girl that didn't know how to say "No" to sin and to the devil'.[2] Near the conclusion he enthusiastically supported the church's efforts for young people, 'as long as you can keep youth consecrated and sanctified, and keep Christ before our youth'.[3] This is, of course just a small sign of what has continually been a theme of such work in many Christian traditions: fear for the future motivating action in the present.

As old as the Fall, this tendency persists even today in the work of someone like sociologist Christian Smith, whose work in the recent National Study of Youth and Religion has revealed some glaring deficiencies in the state of young people's faith in the United States.[4] Over the past few years this has been rather intensely reflected upon American Christianity even as it has been the occasion – intentionally or not – for a not insignificant amount of fearful handwringing. Smith's own language here is illustrative, as he himself rather descriptively sounds the emotive alarm that today's 'Christianity is either degenerating into a pathetic version of itself

---

[2] James O. Savell, 'Youth in Light of the Holy Scriptures', *Christ's Ambassadors Herald* (October 1935), p. 3.

[3] Savell, 'Youth in Light of the Holy Scriptures', p. 4.

[4] Christian Smith, *Soul Searching: The Religious and Spiritual Lives of American Teenagers* (New York: Oxford University Press, 2005).

or, more significantly, Christianity is being actively colonized and displaced by a quite different religious faith'.[5]

While in some instances fear can cause paralysis, in most cases related to American Christianity and especially youth ministry, it has instead served as a call to respond. Quite literally a re-action to bad news, separation has often been the classic response to fear-filled gazing at the future within conservative traditions such as the Holiness and Pentecostal movements. Holiness ideology, broadly and theologically conceived, has taken its cue from 'holy', the term from which it derives its name. Referring to the idea of being 'set apart' for the things of God, Holiness teaching could and often did take the form of retreat from the world, with a kind of retrenchment in a 'holy' lifestyle and set of behaviors marking off its coreligionists as separate from a world that was fearfully headed towards destruction. At their most reactionary, scions of the Holiness movement could enter into legalism and elitism as they sought to purify or better themselves in the midst of a world that sought to pollute them. Contemporary inheritors of the Holiness tradition would take exception to this approach, but the legacy is obvious: 'Holiness groups in their early conception were much more legalistic than they are now. There was a vast list of don'ts having to do with clothing, actions, and attitudes. Christians could not watch movies, dance, smoke, drink, or go to places that served alcohol'.[6] As Pentecostalism emerged in part out of the same movement,[7] similar traits persisted. Though Pentecostalism was in some ways markedly different from the Holiness Movement and had a deep missionary impulse that kept it from retreating completely from the world, it too had its list of prohibitions that represented an antagonistic and perhaps fearful look at a world from which it sought to separate itself:

---

[5] Smith, *Soul Searching*, p. 171.

[6] Shannon New-Spangler and Brett A. Spangler, 'Contemporary Holiness Living', in John H. Aukerman (ed.), *Discipleship That Transforms* (Anderson, IN: Francis Asbury Press, 2011), p. 349.

[7] C.E. Jones, 'Holiness Movement', in *The New International Dictionary of Pentecostal and Charismatic Movements, Revised and Expanded.* (Grand Rapids, MI: Zondervan, 2002), p. 726: 'The issues that gave rise to both Holiness independence and to pentecostalism can be attributed to the aims of the original promoters of the 19th-century revival, who traced the church's malady to a lack of the marks of sanctification'.

... the standard evangelical sins of smoking, drinking, dancing, and gambling were too obviously heinous to require much denunciation. For the latter rain folk, like the most radical of their radical evangelical parents, the hammer fell on seemingly inconsequential acts. The list was extensive. At one time or another saints forbade or strongly discouraged (in alphabetical order) bands, baseball, boating, bowling, circuses, fireworks, football, loitering, parades, skating, valentines, and zoos. They also denounced amusement parks, beach parties, big dinners, chatting on the telephone, Christmas trees, crossword puzzles, home movies, ice cream socials, kissing bees, scenic railroad trips and visiting relatives and going on automobile joyrides on Sundays. These were not idle threats either.[8]

A 'Questions and Answers' section in a 1920 issue of *The Pentecostal Evangel* details these tendencies in response to the question of whether a tobacco user could be a 'real Bible deacon'. The answer read 'I do not see how a man who has heard the full gospel preached can have a "pure conscience" and live as his fleshly appetite dictates'.[9] In these early days of the movement one can also read about the dangers of the world, 'our first enemy, this great evil system which has long existed and which has been growing in force and power as the years have come and gone ... a political, commercial and religious federation'.[10] On a less global scale, *The Pentecostal Evangel* also devoted space to matters of clothing, affirming that 'a Christian should dress neatly, but in moderation, be clean and tidy, not slovenly or showy'.[11] All of this pursuant, at least in some sense, to the achievement of holiness-as-separation.

Particular Pentecostal prohibitions and fears such as these were not limited to the 1920s, but persisted into mid-century as questions emerged about whether the Church as 'Bride of Christ' was pure

---

[8] Grant Wacker, *Heaven Below* (Cambridge, MA: Harvard University Press, 2001), p. 128.

[9] E.N. Bell, 'Questions and Answers', *The Pentecostal Evangel* 324-325 (24 January 1920), p. 5.

[10] A.G. Ward, 'Overcoming the World, the Flesh, and the Devil', *The Pentecostal Evangel* 330-331 (6 March 1920), p. 1.

[11] E.N. Bell, 'Questions and Answers', *The Pentecostal Evangel* 334-335 (3 April 1920), p. 5.

enough.[12] With relation to youth movements, the 1960s and 1970s provided numerous examples of Pentecostal concerns related to cultural change. Fears over 'young people who give their bodies over to beat music and mind-distorting drugs'[13] were articulated in *The Pentecostal Evangel*, as were fears over television, which in 1977 was called a 'seducer'.[14] Passionate concerns about the dangers of 'rock music' that apparently encouraged 'the disintegration of the family ... along with incest, murder, and suicide' continued into the 1980s, helping show just how deep-seated the religious response might be.[15]

I do not share these stories of Pentecostal and Holiness fears to create a 'straw man' or imply that their anxieties were illegitimate, but simply to illustrate that their concerns were well within the orbit of what we might classify as fear. Moreover, if the idea of holiness as represented in this religious milieu has historically been defined as 'separation from', then that which motivated their separation must be detailed. In light of some Pentecostal approaches to the Scriptures, their understanding of faith, and the accompanying developments in popular American culture, it is entirely understandable that their responses would be in such a direction. Though I would reject the idea of separation as best in a list of various choices, or that youth ministry should primarily be in response to persistent fears, it is true that these are understandable options in the face of such concerns.

As I mentioned at the outset of this essay, it is not only historically that we have to consider the so-called 'holiness' tendencies of Pentecostalism and related movements, but in our own time as well. We ought to be aware that the tendency towards reactionary Christianity, while perhaps more pronounced in conservative movements, is not limited to them. When it comes to young people and the future, Christians from many different traditions feel trepida-

[12] Estellen N. Crisp, 'Has the Bride Made Herself Ready?', *The Pentecostal Evangel* 2141 (22 May 1955), p. 2: 'It is a frightening and awful truth that in these days the Church is increasingly unfaithful to her Lord'.

[13] G.B. Robeson, 'Beat Music, LSD, and Antichrist', *The Pentecostal Evangel* 2800 (7 January 1968), p. 11.

[14] Roger Kerr, 'Television: The Seducer', *The Pentecostal Evangel* 3280 (20 March 1977), pp. 22-23.

[15] Charles D. Meppelink, 'Rock Music – An Epidemic is Brewing!', *The Pentecostal Evangel* 3742 (26 January 1986), p. 7.

tion. I have already mentioned the National Study on Youth and Religion from the middle of the last decade, but it bears repeating once again that the data it uncovered has shaken the field of youth ministry to its core. The idea that teenage Christianity is taking the form of so-called 'Moralistic Therapeutic Deism'[16] is shocking, and almost begs a reactionary response. United Methodist practical theologian Kenda Dean calls this current epidemic of watered-down faith amongst American adolescents one of 'benign whatever-ism', and as she does so she implicitly asks for a response: 'if we fail to bear God's life-altering, world-changing, fear-shattering good news (which, after all, is the reason the church exists in the first place) ... then young people unable to find consequential Christianity in the church absolutely *should* default to something safer'.[17] Such words and the authentic concerns they represent are not inherently fear-based, nor will they automatically lead to reactionary measures. Yet left unchecked they can do so rather easily. The line between appropriate response awareness to cultural trends versus fearful reaction can be difficult to discern.

From the evangelical side, Mark Yaconelli has rightly identified a fear-based approach to youth ministry as being dangerously damaging and well below the level of faithfulness and excellence that should characterize ministry to adolescents. In a way that was illustrative for my thinking in this essay, he rightly identified a fear of what is known (and unknown) about teenagers as that which maintains most youth ministries and contributes heavily to the pressures placed upon those tasked with working with adolescents. Anxiety is the name of the game here.

> Look behind most youth ministry programs and you'll find pastors and church boards nervous about declining memberships, parents afraid their kids lack morals, congregations worried the Christian faith has become irrelevant to younger generations, and the persistent frustration among adults that something ('anything!') needs to be done with 'those kids!'[18]

---

[16] Smith, *Soul Searching*, pp. 162-71.

[17] Kenda Creasy Dean, *Almost Christian* (New York: Oxford University Press, 2010), p. 24.

[18] Mark Yaconelli, *Contemplative Youth Ministry* (Grand Rapids; Zondervan, 2006), p. 36.

Familiar refrains in the Assemblies of God's own work have encouraged a deep call to the youth of the movement (or 'this generation' as speakers love to opine) to make great sacrifices and changes
in order to move away from ubiquitous dangers that many fear.
From a certain point of view these are vital calls to living in the best
traditions of the Scripture, yet if any part of these desires are fearfully motivated in reaction rather than based upon the best of
God's plan as mediated through the Scripture, I fear we begin at the
wrong place.

Some of the current attempts at practical theological reflection
on youth ministry can be seen as a reaction to the fear-based responses engendered by the anxieties of our current age. To call
them 'reaction' is not to say, however, that they are inappropriate,
but rather that in some sense they derive their motivation and approach in response to traditional youth ministry patterns. What
many of these new ideas share is a rejection, I think, of the anxious
approach in favor of a more 'presence-centered' strategy. Rather
than play the game of 'fixing', these methods could almost verge on
the quiescent. For someone like Mark Yaconelli, a thoroughgoing
rejection of fear-based youth ministry means that the methods utilized must be very different, deriving not from fear but the historic
contemplative tradition. His is an inspiring approach and one worthy of reflection. Yet in his desire to let go of more directed ministry efforts, Yaconelli may be reacting more to the way things have
been done in the past rather than operating out of an organic theological base. This emphasis may also be on display in the work of
Andrew Root as he writes about youth ministry as place-sharing: 'to
walk knee deep in to the messiness of her life not for the purposes
of a quick rescue mission to free her from the muck, but rather to
journey with her within the messiness' and the suffering that might
entail.[19] Though no one ought for a second to accuse Root of being
anything but deeply rigorous when it comes the use and development of practical theology, it is rather clear that his own rejection of
'agenda' driven ministry is a kind of fear all its own. Further, though
place-sharing can itself be deeply anxiety-producing amongst those
who operate a youth ministry based out of the traditional fears out-

---

[19] Andrew Root, *Relationships Unfiltered* (Grand Rapids: Zondervan, 2009), p.
54.

lined above, I agree with those who wonder if simple 'place-sharing' is incomplete. Perhaps it is merely the first step in a direction that finds its fulfillment in both journey and destination. In any case, the kind of 'not-driven ministry' that Mark Oestreicher describes in his brief essay *Youth Ministry 3.0* and the call towards less agenda in ministry seems a common refrain: 'present to the word of God in our lives and in the world … present to the moment … present to one another … present to life in the way of Jesus'.[20]

Each of the three authors' reflections has their own unique starting point: Root with a theology of the Atonement, Yaconelli with the broad contemplative tradition, and Oestreicher with a historical and sociological view. Even so, each share a distaste for what they would consider to be the 'knee-jerk' approach they see in youth ministries that are fear-driven or organized for the production of discernible results to relieve adult anxieties. In considering their response to such realities I wonder, however, if they are incomplete, a bit quiescent, or missing a particular theological and biblical emphasis (such as the active and directive work of God's presence) that would help to form an even more vital foundation for youth ministry. One reason for this may be simple, of course: their traditions are not as familiar with the living and immediate work of the Holy Spirit as are those within Pentecostalism, and may therefore be less than prepared to reflect upon the Spirit's role in such matters.

Considering the direction of a growing portion of practical theological reflection on youth ministry and the desire of many camps to rethink the sometimes fear-based approaches of the past, Pentecostalism has a unique opportunity to consider the role of the Holy Spirit within this matrix. Far from being a mere spiritual 'add-on' or peculiar segment of American Christianity, when it comes to their openness to the presence and action of God's Spirit for believers, Pentecostals have much to offer. Yet even here there is a need to reconsider and reframe the way this emphasis ought to work itself out.

It almost goes without saying that the Holy Spirit is foundational and central within Pentecostalism. Historically, theologically, spiritually, and persistently, Pentecostals have affirmed and defended the

---

[20] Mark Oestreicher, *Youth Ministry 3.0* (Grand Rapids: Youth Specialties, 2008), p. 77.

role of God's abiding presence in the personal lives of the faithful. Many times, however, this active presence of the Spirit has been more about extravagant experiences and gifts than it has been about more subtle and transformative effects. One need only turn to the nearest Christian television station to see such Pentecostal purveyors as the controversial supernaturalist Pat Roberson, the suspect Benny Hinn, or others of their ilk to understand that the supernatural and outwardly miraculous tend to be the facets of the Spirit that garner the most attention. Historically, developments such as the hyper-Pentecostal 'New Order of the Latter Rain',[21] in the middle of the twentieth century, bear witness to this, as does the Assemblies of God's continued emphasis upon outward giftings or the initial physical evidence of baptism in the Holy Spirit. In ministry to adolescents, these tendencies are manifest no more prominently than during summer camps, where the more extravagant experiences of the Holy Spirit are both sought and expected by pastors, speakers, and students alike.

Though the moments and experiences described above can be transformative in the lives of believers, Pentecostal and otherwise, it is not simply these times that draw my attention. Rather, it is the seed of what motivates them: a belief that God's Spirit is active and powerful for Christian believers in the present. Though as a Pentecostal I truly believe that this action on the part of the Divine may indeed take the form of spectacular displays, I just as readily admit that the real importance lies more in the transformative and personal work of God in our lives. That such a Christian movement remains so open to the place and role of God's Spirit is as encouraging as it is promising for the field of youth ministry.

Emerging as a restorationist movement in the early years of the last century, Pentecostalism surprisingly has not derived much of its own self-identity from the life of the early Church as described in Acts as well as the biblical epistles written during the first decades of the Church's life. The motivating and transformative power of the Holy Spirit and the growth of the earliest Christians from Acts 2 onward – together with the book's not insignificant reports of the

---

[21] R.M. Riss, 'Latter Rain Movement', in Stanley M. Burgess and Eduard M. van der Mass (eds.), *The New International Dictionary of Pentecostal and Charismatic Movements* (Grand Rapids, MI: Zondervan, Rev. and Expanded edn, 2002), pp. 830-33.

miraculous – comprise a gestalt that Pentecostals have adopted as constituent of their own religious worldview. Their openness to the role of the Holy Spirit in their lives also provides an interest and focus upon related teaching elsewhere in the New Testament. It is here that the link between holiness and the Spirit begins to form. In the writings of Paul – especially Romans – the apostle affirms the Spirit's important role in setting believers apart for the things of God. This process of making Christians holy, or sanctifying them, is one of the foundational tasks of the Spirit. In Rom. 15.16 Paul refers directly to the process in question, noting his work so that 'Gentiles might become an offering acceptable to God, sanctified by the Holy Spirit'.[22] Romans 12.2, though without direct reference to the Spirit, evokes well the path of this life in the process of sanctification in being 'transformed by the renewing of your mind'. Romans 8.4 helps characterize what our new state of holiness through God's Spirit looks like, reminding us that we 'do not live according to the flesh but according to the Spirit'.

The place of the Spirit in transformed living for God is further developed in the writings of 1 John, where the idea of love is raised up as axiomatic for the life of the believer. 1 John 4 connects the presence of God's Spirit with the reality of love for the Christian life, and in 4.12-13 powerfully asserts that God's love must needs be at work in all believers: 'if we love one another, God lives in us and his love is made complete in us. This is how we know that we live in him and he in us: He has given us of his Spirit'. Important for our discussion here is the continuation of John's thought in 4.18 as he affirms that 'perfect love drives out fear'. This necessarily and effectively calls into question any ministry practice – or Christian living – derived from fear rather than love.

If Pentecostals and Charismatics can be said to be some of the most focused of all believers on the work of the Holy Spirit, then far more than the miraculous or supernatural await them in the life of sanctification. The testimony of power and action (Acts), God's deep call to sanctification and holiness (Paul), and the overwhelming and fear-erasing reality of love (John) form an evocative trinity of realities that have definite implications for ministry. Holding

---

[22] From this point forward, all citations of Scripture will come from the New International Version unless noted otherwise.

these three ideas together under the aegis of the Holy Spirit affords us the opportunity to bring together the evangelical, Pentecostal, and Wesleyan-Holiness strands of faith in a way that will be helpful for work with students. Though many Pentecostals have played down sanctification proper in light of the more visible and surprising gifts of the Spirit, the time has come for a full embrace of all the work of God in adolescent Christian lives. A Spirit that simultaneously sanctifies (i.e. makes us like God), drives out fear, and replaces fear with love is exactly what is needed for the Church as it ministers to and with adolescents.

Irrespective of one's position on the place of the Pentecostal doctrine of Spirit baptism, highlighting the role given to the intimacy and work of the Holy Spirit in the Pentecostal-Charismatic tradition is helpful. This is even truer when one probes beyond the phenomenological issues of *glossolalia* and the like. For instance, though often eclipsed by the miraculous, the idea that love is central to believers' experience of God's Holy Spirit has not been absent from the movement. We might turn here, for instance, to the early years of Pentecostalism and the British publication *Confidence*. Within, both Pandita Ramabai and one Dr. Yoakum stated that 'we have not found in our experience, that the Seal of "Tongues", when from God, lessened the LOVE', and 'alike emphasize Love as being the great result of "Pentecost"'.[23] Pentecostal pioneer William Seymour stated in a 1908 edition of *The Apostolic Faith* that the 'real evidence' of baptism in the Holy Spirit was 'divine love, which is charity … this is the real Bible evidence in their daily walk and conversation'.[24]

Mid-twentieth century Pentecostal/Charismatic ecumenist David du Plessis spoke powerfully of the work of the Holy Spirit in ways miraculous, but was also quick to claim that Pentecostals could not be satisfied with simple experience but must seek transformation and accompanying fruit as well – all the work of one Spirit: 'the fruit of the Spirit is most important, and yet frequently in Pentecostal circles – the Pentecostal people have forgotten and overlooked'.[25] Even in the midst of the transdenominational Charismatic

---

[23] 'After "Pentecost" – Love', *Confidence* 1 (April 1908), p. 16.

[24] 'Questions Answered', *The Apostolic Faith* 1.11 (October-January 1908), p. 2.

[25] David J. du Plessis, 'Ecumenical Institute Lectures', TMs (lectures delivered at Ecumenical Institute in Bossey, Switzerland, 16 November-4 December 1959),

Movement of the 1960s and 1970s, there was a sense that the Spirit had a role beyond simple personal experience. A word of prophecy given at the 1977 Kansas City Conference on Charismatic Renewal in the Christian Churches is illustrative: 'The light is dim. My people are scattered. The Body of My Son is Broken! Turn from the sins of your fathers. Walk in the ways of my Son. Return to the plan of your Father; return to the plan of your God ...'[26]

Considering matters biblically, theologically, and historically, it is encouraging to note that Pentecostalism carries within its DNA great possibilities for a vibrant Christian life. Though its coreligionists can often become distracted by a simple focus upon emotion and experience to the exclusion of much else, those very traits when lived in the power of the Holy Spirit are transformative. The Holy Spirit is, after all, God's own Spirit – one that is full of power, love, and a call to holiness that communes deeply with our spirit even as, according to John 3.8, it 'blows where it wills' (KJV). Following God's Spirit and remaining ready to respond to the direction of the same as we are led in righteousness and grow in a love that drives out all fear is the task of responsible Pentecostal ministry, especially when that ministry is amongst adolescents.

A youth ministry with a pneumatological focus upon holiness as its foundation will operate deeply in the things of the Holy Spirit and exhibit a number of vital characteristics. In contradistinction to traditional youth ministry, our motivation will not be fear, but rather the presence and direction of the Holy Spirit who shares our place. This place-sharing will not be an end unto itself but merely the beginning of a path that will lead us to a new place in God's own time. A youth ministry with this starting point will affirm that sanctification is not so much a separation from the world as it is a Holy Spirit empowered move towards God. Though the effect on one's life decisions may look outwardly the same, the change in emphasis (fearfully running from the world versus lovingly running towards God) makes all the difference. Young people alive in the Spirit will therefore look to God not for mere protection or a set of rules by which to live, but rather a new way of living. Young people

---

David du Plessis Center for Christian Spirituality, Fuller Theological Seminary, Pasadena, CA.

[26] David Manuel, *Like a Mighty River: A Personal Account of the Conference of 1977* (Orleans, MA: Rock Harbor Press, 1977), p. 195.

seeking after God's own Spirit will by extension be seeking power and love – power for love that is, in some sense, exactly what the idea of sanctification or holiness is all about.

Considering that a truly Pentecostal youth ministry must be about providing space for our spirits to hear from the Holy Spirit, ministering to adolescents in this way necessitates allowing students time to explore God through prayer, lament, and questioning. Though the work of the Holy Spirit is not all about emotion and experience, both are deeply spiritual exercises and should be considered accordingly. Ministry in such a mode must always be reminded that discipleship is ultimately not about what one knows or does but whose we are. A truly Pentecostal approach to youth ministry therefore agrees with many today who reject a fear-based approach even as it goes beyond mere place-sharing towards the richer enterprise of Spirit-indwelling.

Practically speaking, a Spirit-empowered and holiness-based youth ministry might move in a number of different directions. Foundational in all of this will be regular times of prayer and reflection with the expectation that there is an active and personal God to whom we are praying. This submission to the power of God's Spirit and awareness that God does indeed 'show up' will provide a helpful reframing for many, especially when paired with the historic yet vital practice of testimony-sharing. Further, by stepping away from a more fear-based style of ministry with its partial emphasis on behavior modification and/or control, youth pastors ought to let students encounter the story of the Scripture on its own terms while seeking God's guidance and leading as they do so. Believing that the Spirit is indeed meant to be poured out, as Acts 2.17 says, 'upon all flesh' (KJV), youth ministries should welcome hearing about and creating space for such unexpected and transformative Holy Spirit moments in their meeting times and the lives of those that are a part of their ministries. The teaching in such ministries should involve both the traditional content needed for those growing in their knowledge and understanding of the faith, but also – and most importantly – be centered not as much on content acquisition and the concomitant 'safety' that comes with that, but on transformative and prayerful questioning and response that lifts up students as fellow believers alongside adults. Such a 'dangerous' approach is about as far from fear-based as one can get, yet because it is God's Spirit that motivates such efforts they need not be looked at with trepidation.

By means of conclusion, I will begin by saying this: a youth ministry based upon the best traditions of the Pentecostal openness to the Holy Spirit will help our work with adolescents move from fear to love. Put another way, such efforts will encourage us to reorient ourselves from the idea of holiness as separation from the world towards holiness as union with God. This essay is, admittedly, only the most exploratory effort on this theme, but one that I believe can bear much fruit. In light of the biblical testimony regarding the Holy Spirit and sanctification, it makes sense that reliance upon the continually enlivening work of the Holy Spirit is essential. Though previous spiritual reflections both within and without Pentecostalism have been pious, they also carried with them a fear that affected the practice of youth ministry in unfortunate ways. Anxiety and subsequent reactions based upon such feeling must never be the core of the youth ministry enterprise; so too must we be careful not to retreat wholly into simple notions of 'presence', when the biblical testimony seems more involved. Only a youth ministry that is alive in the Spirit can resist the urges for fear or quiescence. Though clearly this is a challenge to some aspects of the *status quo*, I feel that an overtly Pentecostal approach has great possibilities. While the movement, with its potential for interiority, the miraculous, and deep conservatism carries within it the seeds of what could solidify into a sectarian world-rejecting effort, so too its openness to the unexpected, linkage to the Spirit of God who is Love, and ability to move beyond fear in an embrace of God's transformative Spirit means its contains a potential much greater. Ultimately, the movement in youth ministry from fear to love begins and ends with the Holy Spirit, which is why Pentecostalism is a natural place for this new theological paradigm to begin.

18

A FUTURE FOR HOLINESS IN PENTECOSTAL PRACTICE

MARCIA CLARKE[*]

How might the perspective of a practical theologian or the discipline of practical theology contribute to a discussion about the future of holiness in Pentecostalism? Before embarking upon this brief discussion, a delineation of the approach to practical theology upon which the discussion is premised may foster clarity. Wilhelm Gräb states that 'practical theology seeks to describe and interpret Christian religious practice whilst at the same time developing its normative implications'.[1] Defined as such, practical theology is not restricted only to the application of doctrine to pastoral situations but rather the definition acknowledges 'practice and daily life as a site where [religious] knowledge accrues'.[2] Methodologically, practical theological epistemology begins with the concrete and the local, that is with practice. For example then, a study of the bible does not begin with what is written in the bible but rather with how what is written is received and appropriated in the church and in the

---

[*] Marcia Clarke is a PhD student at the University of Birmingham (UK) and is co-pastor of Restoration Christian Fellowship, a church plant in Virginia Beach, Virginia.
[1] W. Gräb, 'Practical Theology as a Religious and Cultural Hermeneutics of Christian Practice', *International Journal of Practical Theology* 16.1 (2012), pp. 79-92 (79).
[2] G. Dingemans, 'Practical Theology in the Academy: A Contemporary Overview', *Journal of Religion* 76.1 (1996), pp. 82-96 (83); Bonnie Miller-McLemore, 'Introduction: The Contributions of Practical Theology', in B. Miller-McLemore (ed.), *The Wiley-Blackwell Companion to Practical Theology*, pp. 1-20 (2).

world'.[3] It is in everyday practice, in the banal and the mundane that faith is expressed in its various modalities.[4] The starting point for a practical theological study is practice which leads to theory which leads back to practice.[5] A result of such a study is the description of and the reflection on the 'self understanding of a particular religious tradition'.[6]

Conversely, it is in the everyday practice that faith breaks down and hence where individuals struggle.[7] At this segue of breakdown and struggle, theological deliberation should take place because this is where real life predicaments and dilemmas demand practical reasoning. Hence we see the objective of practical theology, that is, to have relevance for everyday life and faith, to respond to questions that arise in practice. If this is not the case, practical theology has little meaning at all.[8] Practical theology can and should offer insight to faith's problems and incongruities, but as Part 1 of *The Wiley-Blackwell Companion to Practical Theology* ('Way of Life: Shaping Faith among believers in Home in Society') demonstrates, practical theology can explicate religious meaning from the day to day activities of eating, playing, and loving, activities that are often understood as being theologically meaningless.[9]

It is important that the above is clearly stated to avoid the confusion that may arise because practical theology is a broad nomenclature encompassing four distinct enterprises. First, it is an activity in which believers engage in as they seek to live out their faith. Second, as stated above, it is a methodology used by academics and church leaders who do practical theology whenever they engage systematically with any Christian practice. Third, 'it is a theological curriculum … educat[ing] for faith and ministry as well as in the classroom, congregations, and community'. Fourth, it is the academic discipline '[with]in which practical theologians and those scholars

---

[3] Paul Ballard 'The Use of Scripture', in Miller-McLemore (ed.), *The Wiley-Blackwell Companion to Practical Theology*, pp. 163-72 (170); Dingemans, 'Practical Theology in the Academy', p. 83.

[4] Miller-McLemore, 'Introduction', p. 7.

[5] Dingemans, 'Practical Theology in the Academy', p. 83; Ballard, 'The Use of Scripture', p. 170.

[6] Dingemans, 'Practical Theology in the Academy', p. 83.

[7] Miller-McLemore, 'Introduction', p. 7.

[8] Miller-McLemore, 'Introduction', p.7; Gräb, 'Practical Theology', p. 79.

[9] B. Miller-McLemore (ed.), *The Wiley-Blackwell Companion to Practical Theology* (Malden: Blackwell Publishing, 2012), pp. 21-80.

that engage in and with practical theology organize themselves into 'societies to define the criteria by which the work of practical theology will be evaluated'.[10]

So how might practical theology inform our discussion on holiness? For many Pentecostals holiness and its future can be said to fall into the categories of both the mundane and the ordinary and the category of problem. In the mundane – whether a Pentecostal subscribes to a progressive view of sanctification or that of a crisis experience – what remains is a desire among Pentecostals to maintain a radical sense of holiness. However, as a problem, a number of Pentecostal scholars (some of whom are ordained in classical Pentecostal churches) agree that holiness as it is lived by believers is facing challenges. David Daniels goes so far as to state that 'holiness has lost its currency among saints ... [it has] been dismissed as suffocating. To be honest, there is no guarantee that holiness will even be of interest to the next generation; it might not even be a topic to discuss'.

In line with practical theology's methodology then, how is holiness practiced? The remainder of this essay is an attempt to describe aspects of holiness as it is formed in holiness codes and appropriated by two classical Pentecostal denominations, Church of God (England and Wales), a denomination affiliated with Church of God (Cleveland, TN), Church of God in Christ and Pentecostal churches in Latin America studied by sociologist Bernice Martin.

The concepts of holiness and sanctification are popular maxims of Pentecostalism. The noun 'sanctification' is used and understood by Pentecostals in two ways. First, it is used in relation to believers who at salvation are said to be sanctified (set a part, made holy) – righteousness being imputed to them by God.[11] This act results in their being declared by God as being his people with the consequent privileges and responsibilities of that position.[12] The second use of the term relates to a life of ongoing discipleship, demonstrat-

---

[10] Miller-McLemore, 'Introduction'; Bonnie Miller-McLemore, 'Toward Greater Understanding of Practical Theology', *International Journal Of Practical Theology* [serial online]; 16.1 (August 2012), pp. 104-23. Available from: Academic Search Complete, Ipswich, MA. Accessed February 27, 2013.

[11] Keith Warrington, *Pentecostal Theology: A Theology of Encounter* (London: T&T Clarke, 2008), p. 206.

[12] Warrington, *Pentecostal Theology*, p. 206.

ed by commitment to a transformed lifestyle.[13] For direction in the realization of a transformed lifestyle, particularly as it relates to personal and corporate moral conduct, many Pentecostals look to the Bible.[14] Biblical guidelines have increasingly been contextualized in order that they may 'retain the underlying principle [whilst fitting] the modern and cultural contexts of believers'.[15] In addition to the Bible, a other guides for conduct are the received practices and teachings of the denominations or churches; their respective holiness codes.[16] For Pentecostals, the indicators of holiness are framed in holiness codes.[17] These codes serve to set and maintain boundaries by delineating who is inside and who is outside. By keeping outsiders in their place, those inside are guarded against what Daniels calls 'corrosive elements'.[18] Further, appropriation of the codes define appropriate behavior, help shape the senses, cultivate tastes, attuning hearing and trained vision towards holiness.[19]

Classical Pentecostal churches developed their holiness codes from nineteenth-century holiness teaching as affirmed by the Methodist movement.[20] William Kay comments that one of the reasons for the spread of holiness teaching in that era was its diversity of emphases. Holiness teaching of that time emphasized 'inner experience': 'spiritual experience ... the heart and ... conversion'. However, it also emphasized just as strongly 'outward expression': Christian lifestyle, disciplined living, and upright behavior. Kay determines that the 'correlation between the inner experience of God's love or cleansing power and particular forms of behavior allowed the subsequent development of holiness teaching in nineteenth-century America to stress one or more of these emphases without holding them in balance'.[21] The consequence of which has been

---

[13] Warrington, *Pentecostal Theology*, p. 206.
[14] Warrington, *Pentecostal Theology*, p. 208.
[15] Warrington, *Pentecostal Theology*, p. 208.
[16] Warrington, *Pentecostal Theology*, p. 208.
[17] David Daniels, 'Forging a Theological Future for COGIC: Metaphors of Holiness and Models of Doctrine, Part II', *Advocate: COGIC Scholars Fellowship* 9.4 (2011), pp. 1-8 (1).
[18] Daniels 'Forging a Theological Future', p. 1.
[19] Daniels 'Forging a Theological Future', p. 1.
[20] Donald Dayton, *Roots of Pentecostalism* (Peabody, MA: Hendrickson, 1987), p. 65.
[21] W.K. Kay, *Pentecostals in Britain* (Milton Keynes, UK: Authentic Media, 2002), p. 165.

Pentecostal churches at times emphasizing practical commitments and outward expression over doctrinal formulae, thereby producing a host of prohibitions.

Grant Wacker categorizes the prohibitions as taboos of the mouth, eyes, ears, body, and genitals.[22] Taboos of the mouths included forbidden foods, these included meat in general and shell fish and pork products in particular, 'drink products, soft drinks in general and coca cola in particular'. The prohibitions extended to tea, coffee, ice, chewing gum, and medicinal drugs.[23] Some went further by not eating at all, fasting for days, some even dying in the process.[24] Wacker comments that such deprivation was prudential for some but for others it was a yearning for direct contact with God. Further taboos of the mouth included certain utterances including 'idle talk, foolish talk, jesting with friends and telling tall tales'.[25] The taboos of the eyes and ears included the reading of novels, newspapers, and comic books. The codes further prohibited members from listening to worldly music. Alluring clothing was a continual problem; neckties and abbreviated sports attire was occasionally rebuked, as was women's clothing (or lack of it) when it attracted men's attention.[26]

Prohibitions such as these served a further purpose. Since many of the proponents of the holiness codes were often 'economically dislocated' and did not have 'material goods' or the means to acquire the paraphernalia which the codes outlawed, the codes provided a defense for their lowly social status and their lack of economic and material means. Conversely the material prohibitions implied 'an attack on those who did have more to flaunt'.[27]

The Appropriation of holiness code as Prohibition and Boundary in Practice

Though many of the codes have been relaxed in recent years, the practical theologian is interested in how these codes are received

---

[22] G. Wacker, *Heaven Below: Early Pentecostals and American Culture* (Cambridge MA: Harvard University Press, 2001), p. 122.

[23] Wacker, *Heaven Below*, p. 122.

[24] Wacker, *Heaven Below*, p. 123.

[25] Wacker, *Heaven Below*, pp. 123-24.

[26] Wacker, *Heaven Below*, p. 125.

[27] W.K. Kay and A.E. Dyer, *Pentecostal and Charismatic Studies: A Reader* (London: SCM Press, 2004), p. 128.

and appropriated by the ordinary Pentecostal, and the following provides some insight into this.[28]

In October of 2011, I conducted an empirical study utilizing focus group methodology to listen to and record the ordinary theology of Black British Pentecostal women. These women were émigrés of Jamaican origin who now lived in the United Kingdom. Some of the participants shared that they were raised in the Pentecostal church and were aware of the distinction of being in the church and not. In the church you were not allowed to have boyfriends or go to parties; you were 'sheltered' from the world outside. A number of the participants related in various ways how they had to leave the church to 'explore the world'. One woman stated that as part of the church in Jamaica her behavior was managed; and when she migrated to the England, those that managed her behavior (the church mothers) were no longer there, and she could do what she liked. Another participant shared her testimony that having left the church, one evening she was out with friends who were drinking and smoking having fun. Upon self-reflection she asked the question, 'what was she doing with her life'? This sense of conviction was a precursor to the participant returning to the church. Another realized that the church was her foundation, and she had to come back to it.

Bernice Martin, in her chapter entitled 'The Pentecostal Gender Paradox: A Cautionary Tale for the Sociology of Religion', a work principally discussing gender power relations in the Pentecostal Church, refers to a number of holiness codes.[29] She identifies the strict regulations controlling dress and bodily adornment, especially for women.[30] She further observes that in those Latin American societies which are characterized by a tradition of male dominance, Pentecostalism in general, but Pentecostal women in particular,

---

[28] Ordinary theology is a phrase used by Jeff Astley, *Exploring God-Talk: Using Language in Religion* (London: Darton Longman and Todd, 2004), p. 5, 'for the theology and theologizing of Christians who have received little or no theological education of a scholarly, academic or systematic kind'.

[29] B. Martin, 'The Pentecostal Gender Paradox: A Cautionary Tale for the Sociology of Religion', in Richard K. Fenn (ed.), *The Blackwell Companion to Sociology of Religion* (Blackwell Publishing, 2001), p. 52-66. http://0-www.blackwellreference.com.library.regent.edu/subscriber/tocnode?id=g9780631212416_chunk_g97806312124166.

[30] Martin, 'The Pentecostal Gender Paradox', p. 5.

have been enabled to institute a family discipline, one that is sanctioned and effectively policed by the church community. Such discipline puts the collective needs of the household unit above the freedom and pleasures of males and as such has halted the long-tolerated double standard of sexual morality.[31]

Within the Pentecostal movement, Latino males acquire the dignity of an authority based on the model of Jesus himself; this model requires males to consult with those on whose behalf they exercise responsibility, namely their wives and family.[32] In exchange for this new dignity, poor males – and poor Latino males have very little hope of dignity or authority in the secular economic or political sphere – put themselves under novel restraint.[33] Much of what the church expects of them – giving up alcohol, drugs, gambling, sexual adventures, and the opportunity to sire children in many households, putting the family and fellow believers before themselves – would stigmatize them as unmanly among their unconverted peers.[34] The autonomy which men must give up after conversion is a real sacrifice, even when, as is so often the case, the fruit of that unfettered autonomy has been the corrosion of individual integrity and family stability. Any derogation of the principles of male dominance which prevail in the world beyond the boundaries of the movement will tend to be experienced as a trial and a loss. Even being seen by workmates while drinking a nonalcoholic soda with lunch – 'a young girl's drink' – can be a daily torment to the recent convert.[35]

Among CoGIC women, Anthea Butler observed that as a result of salvation individuals are set apart to God and as such part of the body of Christ.[36] However becoming a part of the collective body of the saints was a different matter; one became part through lifestyle which included disciplined dress, sexual fidelity, and worship.[37] Women who tried from conversion to follow the codes and who embraced the spiritual practices of fasting, prayer, scripture study

---

[31] Martin, 'The Pentecostal Gender Paradox', p. 54

[32] Martin, 'The Pentecostal Gender Paradox', p. 55.

[33] Martin, 'The Pentecostal Gender Paradox', p. 55.

[34] Martin, 'The Pentecostal Gender Paradox', p. 55.

[35] Martin, 'The Pentecostal Gender Paradox', p. 55.

[36] Anthea Butler, *Women in the Church of God in Christ: Making a Sanctified World* (Chapel Hill: University of North Carolina Press, 2007), p. 75.

[37] Butler, *Women in the Church of God in Christ*, p. 75.

and other disciplines, would eventually find themselves on the bottom rung of the church hierarchy, from where if they kept within the boundaries they could climb. Additionally, women had the opportunity to acquire moral and spiritual authority and the possibility of achieving un-ordained status in a position of prominence within the church and as such acquire the social capital which accompanied it.[38] The church mothers were the enforcers of holy living. In the CoGIC, those who questioned the mothers' authority and or the purpose of holiness codes were labeled troublemakers or unrepentant of a past sin. Women, particularly the church mothers, became the vanguards of the codes, having the authority over women and men, including even the leaders.[39]

Conclusion

We see then that adhering to the codes was stifling and restrictive for new converts and the young, a major sacrifice for Latino males but uplifting for women in the CoGIC for whom it was not just *a* standard but *the* standard. The older saints in particular would not stray from the standard for fear they would lose their status within the congregation.[40] Together with the attaining the sanctification experience, adherence to the holiness codes exemplified the ideal Christian life and a status that was an exemplar to others.

Holiness Codes as boundaries
Holiness codes set and maintain boundaries that differentiate those who by confession (but also by conduct) are inside from those who are outside – the We and the Other. Lawrence Wills in his book, *Not God's People: Insiders and Outsiders in the Biblical World*, uses a number of biblical and extra-biblical texts to analyze the construction of the Other.[41] Neither the biblical texts nor Wills's thesis has been part of this discussion, but he does, to my mind, provide a useful model and comment for analysis of insiders versus outsiders, the demarcation that holiness codes provide. Wills identifies a sharp distinction between Us and Them, in this case the saint and the sin-

---

[38] Butler, *Women of the Church of God in Christ*, p. 76.
[39] Butler, *Women of the Church of God in Christ*, p. 76.
[40] Butler, *Women of the Church of God in Christ*, p. 76.
[41] L. Wills, *Not God's People: Insiders and Outsiders in the Biblical World* (Lanham, MD: Rowman and Littlefield Publishers, 2008).

ner, the sanctified and the unrepentant. The insiders are deemed the 'ideal community of God' – at least they are in the process of becoming so.[42] This imagery has parallels in Scripture, in which the Israelites were the community of God, the Insiders, who conceived of the nations who lived in the land before them – the Canaanites and others – as the Other, the Outsiders. As Insiders their role was to do what God expected of them; outsiders did not have to live up to the same ideal. Daniels argues that holiness codes as markers of holiness, in fact holiness per se with its smacking legalism, has lost its currency among the saints. The removal of economic hardship for many Western Pentecostals, the influences of culturally aware or affluent Christians, as well as the internet and social media have affected the lifestyles of many Western Pentecostal Christians.[43] So now, it is unclear who is Inside and who is Outside. Wills suggests that the notion of Insider/Outsider, the We and the Other [to use his term] is more complex and that like race and gender is a construct that is not fully formed from the outset.[44] Indeed, central to its formation and evolution is a constantly changing construction of Insider and Outsider. Pentecostals were 'social outcasts … [who were] believed to be insanely fanatical, self righteous, doctrinally mistaken and emotionally unstable', but they are now 'fully accepted' by wider society.[45] Identities change and yet participants are often unaware of the change, assuming all the time that they are unchanging.[46] What does such a notion mean for Holiness in Pentecostalism?

Another aspect for consideration in the future of holiness in Pentecostalism is Wills's Theorem of the Internal Other. The External other is readily identifiable, the External other is the 'antagonist on the horizon', who is perceived as the opposite of everything we are.[47] The Internal Other, to use Wills's term, lives among us, often as the Instrumental Other or the Invisible Other. Examples would be people of the Other gender, of the Other class or of the

---

[42] Wills, *Not God's People*, p. 1; Daniels 'Forging a Theological Future', p. 1.

[43] Daniels, 'Forging a Theological Future', p. 1; Warrington, *Pentecostal Theology*, p. 212.

[44] Wills, *Not God's People*, p. 1.

[45] Vinson Synan, *The Holiness Pentecostal Tradition: Charismatic Movements in the Twentieth Century* (Grand Rapids, MI: Eerdmans, 1997), p. 188.

[46] Wills, *Not God's People*, p. vii

[47] Wills, *Not God's People*, p. 13

Other race. Wills comments on the irony of the Internal Other living in close contact even intimately with the Insider. He further suggests that the Internal Other is kept in check by a 'domesticated social order', but if that order fails for even a moment the Internal Other will become the External Other because they are linked.[48]

I as a woman am an example of an Internal Other – I am Pentecostal and fully identify with the movement; however, I also identify with some feminist and womanist viewpoints, howbeit to a lesser extent perhaps in their critique of patriarchal authority and interpretation of Scripture as it pertains to the role of women in the church. My understanding of Scripture and the wider Pentecostal statement of faith keeps me in check. My belief is that one day, if I remain unthreatening, if I put together a sound argument, someone at the center of power may do something to change the status of women within the denomination. However, this order can fail by there being a complete change of the domesticated social order. For example, a new executive board not open to discussion could make me into an External Other, or I could choose to join with them as I could no longer collude with the domesticated social order.

Condemnation of the External Other serves to control the Internal Other. Are Pentecostals ready to accept the Internal Other as an integral part the construct? Are Internal Others ready to function in their role which will tend to be on the margins? These are crucial questions that remain to be answered.

---

[48] Wills, *Not God's People,* p. 13

A CONCLUDING PARABLE

THE FIRE AND THE FENCE

RICKIE D. MOORE[*]

A long time ago there was a group of God-seekers who found themselves camping in a remote area in the country. They had not come to camp in this remote area entirely of their own accord. They had been driven here by others who lived in comfortable wooden buildings and who did not want these God-seekers bringing disturbance into their buildings any longer with their loud cries. So it was that these God-seekers came together, set up their tents, and began to cry out all the louder to their God.

Suddenly, finally, it happened! A blinding ball of fire from heaven fell squarely into their midst. There was joy, of course, but the strongest feeling they felt was fear – yes, fear, a fear that left them utterly weak, but strangely clean, cleaner than they had ever felt before. There they stood, close to the fire and close to one another, never again to be the same.

After awhile the flame suddenly vanished from their eyes, but it continued to burn in their hearts. In the light and the heat of this inward fire, these God-seekers pulled up stakes like there was no tomorrow and went streaming out in all directions, telling every one every where every thing they had seen.

Days passed and these God-seekers were drawn again to go to the place where the fire had first fallen. They remembered the place well, and so again they came together and they cried aloud to God and the fire fell once more. And again they went forth in all directions with hearts burning as one. More days passed and again and

---

* Rickie D. Moore (PhD, Vanderbilt University) is Chair of the Department of Theology at Lee University in Cleveland, TN, USA.

again they came and they went forth, ever held together by the holy fire.

Years passed and these God-seekers grew in number and they had many children. Thus more and more there would be those among them who had not yet seen the fire and did not know the way to the place. So some said, 'Let us set up boundary markers to help those coming to know they are getting near and to help those going to know they are getting far from where the fire falls, for without the fire we will not stay together'. And so the markers were set up.

More years passed and one generation followed another, and the people grew larger and the time grew longer and the world beyond the markers seemed to grow bigger and bigger. And there arose a fear among some of those who had long ago been driven from the wooden buildings. They looked upon their children who had not yet seen the fire and they said to one another, 'Let us build a fence between the markers to keep those who have not yet seen the fire from straying and to keep those who dwell in wooden buildings from taking them from us, for without the fence we will not stay together'. And so they built a fence.

Time passed and those who built the fence worked hard on the fence to keep it in good repair. And they became good builders. Working on the fence took more and more time as the children grew and learned how to climb upon it. And they became good climbers. And everyone stayed together near the fence, some building and some climbing.

And the climbers grew until they could look over the fence, but they could not see anything bad over the fence and they could not see any good in the fence. Those who kept the fence saw this and posted guards and built wooden sheds. Then those who looked over the fence and those who looked *after* the fence began to burn inside against each other. And those who looked over the fence began to break it down in many places, and before long the fence was gone, and gone too were the boundary markers. But the wooden sheds continued to stand and other wooden buildings were built nearby. And many who had crossed the fence became good builders too.

So, out beyond where the markers had stood (that is, where some say they stood), at diverse places round about, other buildings were built, and some were brick. In all of the buildings they built comfortable nurseries to keep their children, just in case their children cried. They took good care of their buildings, for they all knew that without these buildings they would not stay together.

Index of Biblical References

Genesis
2.3   17
3.2-3   186
13.12   105
16.7-14   30
16.7   31
28.10-22   38
32.1-2   30, 39

Exodus
2.3   23, 55, 67
2-3   13
2.11-15   26
3   13, 14, 15,
           18, 35
3.1-12   39
3.1-6   37, 39
3.1   13
3.2   18, 32
3.5   16, 17, 19,
           35, 36, 37, 44
3.7-10   26
3.8   16
4.17   32
6.6-7   65
11.8   26
13.17-18   18
14.19   32
15.3   42
17.9   33
19-40   18
19   99
19.6   97, 98, 99,
           100
19.10-13   19
19.18   18
20   34
20.18-19   19
20.1   19
29.42-46   20
32   267
32.15-20   26

32.26   267
33.11   43
33.15   46
34.27-28   26

Leviticus
10.10   97
11.26   259
11.44-45   97
11.44   259
18.3   102
18.20-21   21
19   117
19.18   188
19.19   117
21.7   98
26   118
44.11   258

Numbers
13.16   28
14.6-9   32
16.23-24   102
20   26
20.1-13   26
20.12   26
20.16   32
21.6   49
22.23   32, 39
22.31   28
26.11   65
26.12   65
27.12   25
27.12-18   27
27.18   32
35   21, 203
35.19   204

Deuteronomy
1.29-30   29
1.30   29
4.19   30

5-8   33
5.14   184
6.5   187
8.15   12
10.1-9   21
12.11-12   21
14.27-29   21
18.1-8   21
26.11-12   21
32.8-9   30
32.44   28

Joshua
1.1-9   36
1.5   42
1.9   37, 38, 42
1.16-17   42
2.8   42
3-4   41
3.5   27
3.9   42
4.19-24   41
5-6   41
5   28, 31, 44
5.1-9   42
5.1-3   41
5.2-12   28
5.2   33
5.9   28
5.10-12   42
5.10   41
5.13-15   24, 34, 35,
           37, 41, 42
5.13   29, 35, 35
5.14   35, 37
5.15   25, 35, 36, 37
6   41
6.1-7   42
6.16   43, 44
7   41
22.26-27   41
24.26-27   41

Judges
6.11-24   30
6.11   32
6.12, 14   31
13.2-23   30
13.22   31, 32

2 Samuel
7   92
24.16-17   32

1 Kings
2.22   98
2.35   98

2 Kings
6.15-17   38
6.17   30
19.35   32

1 Chronicles
21.16-17   44
21.16   29, 39

2 Chronicles
26   48
29.21   98

Ezra
7.13   98

Nehemiah
12.22   98

Job
12.10   183
34.14-15   183

Psalms
2   69. 92
2.7   67, 93
2.9   92, 93
8   62
17.24   93
46.7   42
46.11   42
51   120, 121

51.9-10   76
51.10-12   121
51.11   120
51.13   120
84.1   49
88   91
88.25   61
88.27   91, 92
88.38   91
96.6   49
110   69, 77
110.1   67
110.4   67
113.4   48
119.71   71

Proverbs
3   77, 78, 79, 81
3.2   77
3.5   78
3.8   78
3.11-12   71, 77
3.11   77
3.12   78
3.13-18   78
3.16-18   78
3.22-33   78
3.22   78
3.27-32   78
6.23   79
14.5   91
14.25   91
16.22   79

Isaiah
1.4   51
1.15   52
2.19   49
6   34, 47
6.1-8   55
6.9-13   52, 55
6.13   55
21.9   103
40.22   48
43.14   51
43.18-21   65
44. 2-3   120

45.11   51
47.8   103
47.9   103
48.20   102
52.11   102
57.15   49
61.3   55
63   120, 121
63.9-14   121
63.10-11   120

Jeremiah
27.8   102
28.9   103
31.3   270
31.33   65
49.5   91
50.29   103
51.9   103
51.45   103, 104

Ezekiel
1   34
27.28   106
37.21-22   106
37.27   65, 105
37.28   106
40-43   101

Daniel
12.1   31

Hosea
11.1   94

Obadiah
1.12-15   296

Micah
4.13   93

Habakkuk
2.4   72

Zechariah
2.1-5   102
2.10-11   102

Zechariah, cont'd

2.14-15	105
2.14	106
2.15	106
8.8	65

Matthew

2.15	94
6.11	196
6.24	287
6.26	183
11.28-29	291
15.19	83
17.1-13	34
19.19	188
21.12	271
22.37	187
25.14-30	182
25.31-46	182, 189, 199
25.31-32	277
25.34-36	277
25.34	199
25.37-39	278
25.40	278
26.37-38	75
26.39	68
26.27	79
27.46	75

Mark

7.21	21
8.1-10	194
9.2-13	34
12.30	187

Luke

1.26-38	34
2.52	66
9.28-36	34
10.27	187, 277
11.3	196
12.24-28	183
22.44	75

John

2.14-15	271
3.8	333, 345

8.31-32	261
11.24	189
13	43
14.2	203
14.6	143, 189
14.15	288
14.26	266, 288
15.26	266
16.13	266
17	212
17.22-23	212

Acts

2	231, 262
2.17	346
4.32-33	202
2.34-35	202
2.42	196
2.43-47	195
2.45	195
2.46	196
3.1-16	193
4.30	193
4.34	195
7.55-56	193
9.5	193
9.10	193
11.26	262
13.39	193
15.21	99
17.7	193
17.25	183
17.28	186
18.10	193
19.15	193
25.19	193

Romans

2.29	100
5-6	34
6-8	117
6.19	194
7	115
7.13-25	117
8	117
8.7	263
8.29	81

8.34	66
12.1-2	261
12.2	343
13.13	83
14	143
15.16	343

1 Corinthians

1.30	190
3.16-17	118
4.3-5	142
5.11	83
5.18	201
6.9	83
6.19	36, 118
8	143
8.29	305
9.27	81
10.17	198
10.31	36
11.24-25	196
11.26-28	199
11.27-34	197
12.4-31	118
13.1	285
15.26	190

2 Corinthians

3.17	261
3.18	81
6.14-7.1	117
6.14-18	118
6.14	117
6.16	118
7.1	1
11.2	118
12.20	83

Galatians

2.20	144
5.19	83

Ephesians

1.10	190
1.21	185
2.8-10	34
2.12-13	286

Ephesians, cont'd
2.14-16   290
2.19   286
4.1-16   34
4.11   254
4.32   83
5.3   83

Philippians
1.6   74
1.16   115
1.30   84
2   214, 215, 219
2.6-11   214
2.8-9   63
2.12-18   115
3.12-15   115
3.14-15   80

Colossians
1.15   188
1.18   92
3.5   83
3.8   83

1 Thessalonians
4.3-8   194
4.3   1
4.7   1
5.23   194

2 Thessalonians
1.4   84
3.6   263

1 Timothy
1.9   83
2.5   66

2 Timothy
1.4   266
3.2   83

Titus
3.3   83

Hebrews
1   61, 62, 65
1.1-4.13   59
1.1-2.8   61
1.3   63
1.4   61
1.5   67
1.6   65
1.13   67
2   77, 80
2.1-4   59, 61, 62
2.4-10   63
2.5-8   62
2.7-8   64
2.9-18   59, 62, 63
2.9   63, 64
2.10-18   63
2.10-11   64
2.10   64, 66, 67, 74, 75
2.11-18   64
2.11-13   64
2.11   64
2.12   64
2.13   64, 66
2.14-15   64
2.14   64, 80
2.15   64
2.16-17   64
2.17   64, 66, 70, 84
2.18   64, 65, 69
3   80
3.1   80, 84
3.2   84
3.6   84
3.7-19   59, 61
3.8   65, 83
3.13   83
3.15   83
3.16   65
4   59
4.4-7.28   59
4.7   83
4.11-16   60
4.11   83
4.14   67, 82
4.15   65, 69

4.16   69, 82
5   59
5.2   65
5.5   67
5.6   67
5.7   66
5.8-9   66
5.8   67
5.9   67, 70, 74
5.11-6.3   59
5.15   67
6.1   83
6.4-20   59
6.4-6   61
6.4-5   80
6.11   85
6.12   59, 81, 83
6.19-25   59
6.20   59, 67, 74
7   59
7.16   69
7.17   67
7.21   67
7.24   67
7.25   67, 69
7.26   68
7.27   68, 70
7.28   66, 67
8.1-10.18   59
8.9-12   65
8.16-17   85
9   59
9.11   70
9.13-14   194
9.14-15   70
9.14   68, 70
9.15   65, 70, 73
9.23   70
9.26   70
9.28   66, 70, 74
10-13   59
10-12   70, 71
10   71, 72
10.1   70
10.4   73
10.5   70
10.10   66

Hebrews, cont'd

10.12   70
10.14   66, 68, 70
10.19-13.25   59
10.19-13.17   70
10.19-39   59, 61
10.19-25   60
10.20   74
10.22   83
10.23   83, 84
10.24   83
10.25   83
10.26-31   59
10.26   70
10.29   79
10.32-12.1   70
10.32-39   70
10.32-34   70
10.34   72
10.35   72
10.36   72
10.37-39   79
10.39   72, 80
11   61, 70, 72, 79, 80, 82
11.2-7   72
11.2   85
11.7   80
11.13-16   286
11.13   80
11.16   288
11.24-25   288
11.26   65
11.28   65
11.29   65
11.32   60
12   70, 72, 73, 76, 77
12.1-13.25   59
12.1-3   73
12.1   72, 78, 83
12.2-3   66, 74
12.2   65, 73, 79
12.3   66, 78
12.3-5   76
12.4-11   76
12.5-11   70

12.5-6   77
12.5   77, 78, 83
12.6   78
12.7-8   77
12.7   78
12.9   77, 78, 79, 80
12.10-11   77, 79
12.10   78, 80
12.11   77, 78, 81
12.13   78
12.14-29   59
12.14-15   78
12.14   1, 78, 82, 144, 199
12.17-18   81
12.22   65
12.25   61
12.27-33   81
12.28   65, 83, 85
13   70, 73
13.1-17   84
13.3   65
13.10   70
13.12-17   70
13.12   66
13.13   82, 83
14.12   256

James
3.15   83

1 Peter
1.1   75
1.2   190
1.14-16   1, 102
1.16   86, 259
2.1   83
2.4-5   260
2.9   263
4.3   83
4.15   83
4.17   271

2 Peter
1.3-8   81
1.4   187, 190, 195

1 John
3.18-20   142
4   343
4.8   307
4.12-13   343
4.18   343
4.20   190, 288

Jude
1   83

Revelation
1   99
1.3   86
1.5   91, 92, 101
1.6   98, 100
1.8   74
2.4   266
2.9   100
2.26-28   93
2.27   92, 93
3.9   100
3.17   97
5.9   100, 101
5.10   98
5.12   265
9.21   83
11.1-2   101, 102
11.1   101
11.2   101
14.8   95
16.19   95
17.5   95
18.2   95, 103
18   102
18.4-8   102
18.4   103, 104
18.5   103
18.6   103
18.7   103
18.8   103
18.10   95
18.21   95
19.10   31
21.1   65
21.3   105
21.6-7   74

Revelation, cont'd

21.6   74
21.8   83
21.27   106

22.7   86
22.9   31
22.10   86
22.1   86

22.13-14   74
22.13   74
22.15   83
22.18-19   86

Index of Authors

Abraham, W.J. 133, 242
Adewuya, J.A. 2, 116-20, 247, 248
Ainsworth, M. 324, 331
Alexander, K.E. 169
Alexander, D.L. 108, 119
Alexandra, S. 282
Allen, G.
Alter, R. 14
Althouse, P. 308, 309
Alves, R. 328
Anderson, G. 254
Anderson, R.M. 297
Astley, J. 354
Auld, A.G. 30, 46
Augustine, D.C. 197
Aune, D.E. 60, 86, 101, 103
Avram, W.D. 136, 140
Baer, R. 327, 329
Baker, A. 141
Ballard, P. 349
Bar-Efrat, S. 11
Barna, G. 247
Barth, K. 256
Bartholomew, C.G. 11, 99
Bartholomew I, H.A.H. 175, 178,
    185, 187, 188, 191
Bartleman, F. 300
Basil the Great, St. 190
Bauckham, R. 102
Beale, G.K. 77, 86, 95, 99
Beaman, J. 300, 302
Beck, J.A. 11, 12
Bell, E.N. 164, 337
Berdyaev, N. 176, 177
Best, E. 278
Blanchard, K.D. 172
Blevins, D.G. 168
Blount, B.K. 195
Boda, M.J. 93, 94, 97, 102
Boling, R.G. 30, 44
Bonaventure, St. 155

Bonhoeffer, D. 136, 137, 138, 139,
    140
Bonino, J.M. 303, 304
Bowdle, D. 242
Bowlby, J. 313
Browning, E.B. 46
Bruce, F.F. 72, 73, 74, 75
Brueggemann, W. 10, 11, 17, 49, 54,
    159, 161
Bruner, E. 298, 299
Bundy, D. 154
Burgess, S.M. 108, 153
Butler, A. 354, 355
Butler, T.C. 32, 33, 35, 43, 45
Buttrick, G. 120
Byrne, R. 156, 154
Cahill, L. 301
Callen, B. 239
Carlson, G.W. 127
Carroll Rodas, M.D. 285, 291
Carson, D.A. 77, 238, 242, 243, 249,
    251
Castelo, D. 3, 168, 233, 275, 276,
    301, 303, 304
Cavanaugh, W.T. 198, 201, 202
Chan, S. 4, 5, 146, 149, 151, 159,
    162, 163, 165
Charles, R.H. 95
Chase, S. 163
Chavalas, M.W. 40, 43, 44
Childs, B. 49, 50
Clark, J. 249
Clinton, T. 313
Coats, G. 20
Cole, R.A. 14
Collins, A.Y. 95, 100
Collins, K. 130, 132, 248
Connolly, W.E. 173
Coote, R.B. 31, 32, 39, 40, 43, 45
Conrad, C.W. 70
Corcoran, K. 248, 249
Coulter, D.M. 3, 147-49

Creach, J.F.D.   30, 32, 34, 35, 36, 37, 38, 41, 42

Crisp, E.N.   338

Crites, S.   158

Crossan, J.D.   179, 183, 184

Crouch, A.   178

Croy, N.C.   58, 73, 76, 77, 78, 79

Daniels, D.   351, 356

Davies, O.   17

Dayton, D.W.   1, 148, 227, 238, 298, 299, 351

Dean, K.C.   339

Deasley, A.R.G.   113

Delattre, R.   328

Del Colle, R.   114

Delitzsch, F.J.   63, 74, 75, 76

deSilva, D.A.   60, 63, 64, 75, 76, 78, 79, 82, 87, 96, 97

Dettoni, J.   313

Dewey, M.   263

Dieter, M.   110, 111, 112, 113, 115, 239

Dingemans, G.   348, 349

du Plessis, D.J.   344

Dulk, M. den   101, 102

Durham, J.I.   13, 14, 100

Durham, W.H.   146

Dyer, A.E.   352

Dyrness, W.   328

Elwell, W.A.   28, 41

Enns, P.   65

Erickson, M.J.   246

Erikson, E.   313

Evans, J.   317, 327, 328, 331

Fagerberg, D.   182

Fairclough, N.   99

Faupel, D.W.   148, 298, 299

Fee, G.D.   92, 101, 111

Fekkes, J.   87, 96, 101, 102, 104

Fisher, F.L.   99

Fisher, W.R.   158

Flemming, D.   87, 97, 99

Floyd, M.H.   93, 102

Foley, E.   273

Foot, M.   258

Foster, R.   128

Fowler, J.W.   154, 158

France, R.T.   94

Franke, J.R.   33, 38

Fretheim, T.E.   16, 20, 88

Friberg, B.   74, 75, 78

Friberg, T.   74, 75, 78

Friesen, S.J.   97

Frodsham, S.   164

Gast, P.   257

Gause, R.H.   3

Gaventa, B.   193

Gee, D.   164

Gehrz, C.   127

Gelpi, D.L.   150

Goldingay, J.   50

González, J.L.   295

Goroncy, J.   129

Gräb, W.   348, 249

Granvold, D.K.   154

Grenholm, M.   300

Green, C.   136, 139

Gregory of Nazianzus, St.   194

Grenz, S.J.   245, 307

Griffin, W.A.   254

Groody, D.G.   175

Gros, J.   147

Gundry, S.N.   108, 111, 239

Guthrie, G.H.   61

Halterman, R.   196

Hammond, J.M.   155

Han, S.-E.   292, 293

Harrington, H.   118

Hauerwas, S.   310

Hengel, M.   193

Herms, R.   101

Hess, R.S.   33, 34, 36, 39, 40

Hill, L.   172

Hills, A.M.   266

Himmelfarb, M.   99

Hocken, P.   157

Holladay, W.L.   103

Hollenweger, W.J.   148, 158, 298

Holmgren, F.C.   15

Holst, E.   127

Horton, S.M.   111, 115

Houston, W.J.   97

Hughes III, R.D.   155, 156, 157, 163

Hyde, M.J.   142

Irenaeus   95, 204
Irwin, W.   88, 90
Janzen, J.G.   15
Jauhiainen, M.   92, 102
Jobes, K.H.   96, 260
John of the Cross, St.   323
Johns, C. Bridges   159, 166, 167, 301
Johns, J.D.   22
Johns, T.   305
Johnson, L.T.   84, 194, 195, 261
Jones, C.E.   336
Jung, C.G.   324
Kaiser, W.   29, 36, 89, 99
Kant, I.   188
Kärkkäinen, V.-M.   58, 147, 154, 169,
     300
Kay, W.K.   351, 352
Kempf, C.   269
Kerr, R.   338
Kimball, D.   242, 243, 249, 250, 251
Kistemaker, S.J.   59, 63, 74, 78
Knibb, M.A.   86
Kohlberg, L.   312
Köhler, L.   103
Koltun-Fromm, N.   102
Kramnick, I.   258
Kraybill, J.N.   96
Kristeva, J.   89
Jyoung-Shik, K.   93
LaCugna, C.M.   155, 156, 307
Lancy, D.F.   327
Land, S.J.   1, 2, 3, 4, 145, 146, 148,
     151-53, 157, 159, 161, 163, 169,
     238, 240, 298, 299, 304, 305, 306
Lane, B.   10, 18, 19, 22, 23
Larkin, E.E.   155
Learner, G.   273
Levenson, J.D.   9
Levinas, E.   203
Lightfoot, N.R.   73
Lindbeck,   145, 147, 166
Lindstrom, H.   306
Locke, J.   258
Loder, J.   221
Long, T.G.   59
Lossky, V.   186, 189, 190, 194, 215
Louis, P.   292, 293

Lovin, R.W.   133
Lowery, K.T.   130
Luther, M.   129, 137, 139, 250, 322
Luxemburg, R.   202
Macchia, F.D.   4, 82, 147-154, 156,
     159, 162, 163, 165, 169
MacIntyre, A.   158
Maddox, R.L.   239, 248
Madvig, D.   31, 38, 39, 42
Mahoney, M.J.   154
Malherbe, A.J.   60
Mallen, P.   91
Manning, F.E.   327, 329
Mannoia, K.W.   238, 239
Manuel, D.   345
Martin, B.   353, 354
Martin, L.R.   5
Martin, W.   254
Mathewson, D.   106
Matthews, V.H.   40, 43, 44
Mauser, U.   18
Maximus the Confessor, St.   183
Mayo, P.L.   100
McAdams, D.P.   160
McChesney, R.W.   174
McCormack, B.   69
McGonigle, T.D.   146, 154, 155
McDonnell, K.   150
McDougal, J.   205
McFague, S.   176, 200, 204
McKenzie, C.S.   20
Meeks, M.D.   172, 175, 197, 243, 245
Menzies, R.P.   165
Menzies, W.W.   164
Meppelink, C.D.   338
Metz, D.S.   113
Meyers, C.   17
Michaels, J.R.   87
Middleton, J.R.   246
Miller-McLemore, B.   348, 349, 350
Miller, N.F.   74, 75, 78
Milligan, G.   62, 69
Mittelstadt, M.W.   58
Moffatt, J.A.   75
Moltmann, J.   152, 156, 205-19, 221,
     223, 252, 305, 307, 328, 329
Montague, G.T.   150

Mounce, R.H.   65, 87, 99, 101
Moyise, S.   88, 89, 93, 101, 106
Muck, T.C.   292, 293
Murove, M.F.   173
Mussen, P.   312
Neumann, P.D.   149
Newhouse, C.   265
New-Spangler, S.   336
Niebuhr, H.R.   178
Oden, P.   222
Oden, T.   130, 132
Oestreicher, M.   341
Olsen, R.E.   127, 128
Osborne, G.R.   99
Otto, R.   324, 329
Outler, A.   135, 229
Paine, T.   258
Pannenberg, W.   213, 214, 220, 221,
   222, 223
Parham, C.F.   300
Parker, S.   313, 314, 318, 322, 327,
   328, 329, 332
Pattemore, S.   100
Paulien, J.   94
Perdue, L.G.   60
Peters, R.T.   171, 173, 174
Peterson, D.   68, 108, 109, 111
Peterson, E.H.   9, 10
Pfeil, M.R.   182, 196
Piaget, J.   312
Pitkanen, P.A.   28
Polkinghorne, D.E.   159, 160
Poloma, M.   238
Porter, S.E.   90, 91
Radner, E.   143
Ratzinger, J.C.   129
Redditt, P.L.   88
Rendtorff, R.   100
Ricoeur, P.   160, 161
Riggs, M.Y.   202
Ring, S.H.   202
Riss, R.M.   342
Rivera-Pagán, L.   278, 279, 280, 295
Robeck, C.M.   300
Roberts, P.   299
Robeson, G.B.   338
Robinson, B.P.   18

Root, A.   340
Root, M.   158
Rousseau, J.-J.   317
Rushdoony, R.J.   253
Rybarczyk, E.J.   154
Sanders, J.   76
Savell, J.O.   335
Scarry, E.   47, 53, 54, 55
Schmemann, A.   180, 187, 193, 198,
   200
Schramm, B.   101
Sensing, T.R.   60
Seow, C.L.   98
Shaeffer, F.A.   44, 45
Sheldrake, P.   11
Shelton, R.L.   251
Sims, J.   250
Simone, C.   104
Slater, T.B.   96
Smith, A.   172
Smith, C.   335, 336, 339
Smith, I.   96, 97
Smith, J.K.A.   22, 158, 204, 240, 246,
   328
Smith, T.L.   298
Snyder, H.A.   244
So, Tae Young,   22
Soggin, J.A.   31, 45
Spangler, B.A.   336
Spicq, C.   72, 73
Spittler, R.P.   119, 327
Spurgeon, C.H.   259, 262
Staniloae, D.   179, 180, 181, 183
Stavropoulos, C.   189, 190, 194
Story, J.L.   114, 115, 116, 119
Straub, J.   313
Strauss, M.L.   92, 95
Strong, D.M.   136
Stronstad, R.   165, 167, 191
Sweet, L.   246
Swete, H.B.   86, 87, 99
Synan, V.   238, 241, 298, 356
Taves, A.   135
Tenner, K.   178
Tesfamariam, R.   268
Thomas, J.C.   97, 104, 169, 305, 309
Thompson, J.W.   64, 73, 78, 79

Thorsen, D.   238, 239, 241, 242, 243
Tindall, B.A.   327
Tomlinson, A.J.   300
Tonstad, S.   86
Uhlig, T.   49
Van Wolde, E.   89
Victorin-Vangerud, N.M.   13
Viola, F.   247
Volf, M.   156, 195, 307, 308
Vondey, W.   166
Vos, G.   67, 68, 69
Wacker, G.   337, 352,
Waddell, R.   86, 102, 309
Wall, L.   16
Wall, R.W.   87
Wallace, D.B.   75, 80, 81
Walsh, B.J.   246
Walton, J.H.   40, 43, 44
Ward, A.G.   337
Ware, K.   155
Warrington, K.   350, 351, 356
Watson, D.F.   87
Weima, J.A.D.   97
Wendland, H.-D.   311
Wenk, M.   193

Wells, J.B.   16, 18
Wesley, J.   110, 115, 130, 131, 133,
   134, 135, 136, 141, 289, 298
Westfall, C.L.   60
Wethmar, C.   252
Wiersbe, W.W.   36, 42, 46
Wilhoit, J.   313
Wills, L.   355, 356, 357
Winn, C.T.C.   127
Winnicott, D.W.   313-22, 324, 325,
   327, 329, 330, 332
Witherington, B.   99
Wong, K.M.   220
Woods, R.   154
Wyatt, N.   15, 16, 20
Wynkoop, M.B.   141, 248
Wyschogrod, E.   200
Yaconelli, M.   339
Yamauchi, E.   14
Yoder, J.H.   84, 265, 269, 270, 302,
   310
Yong, A.   4, 58, 146, 149, 150, 151,
   153, 162, 163, 166, 328
Young, E.J.   16

www.ingramcontent.com/pod-product-compliance
Lightning Source LLC
Chambersburg PA
CBHW070327090426
42733CB00012B/2389